Selected Letters of

VIRGIL THOMSON

Edited by
Tim Page and
Vanessa Weeks Page

Summit Books
New York   London   Toronto   Sydney   Tokyo

Copyright © 1988 by Virgil Thomson
All rights reserved
including the right of reproduction
in whole or in part in any form.
Published by SUMMIT BOOKS
A Division of Simon & Schuster Inc.
Simon & Schuster Building
Rockefeller Center
1230 Avenue of the Americas
New York, NY 10020
SUMMIT BOOKS and colophon are trademarks of Simon & Schuster Inc.

Designed by Levavi & Levavi
Manufactured in the United States of America

1   3   5   7   9   10   8   6   4   2
Library of Congress Cataloging in Publication Data
Thomson, Virgil.
Selected letters of Virgil Thomson.

Includes index.
1. Thomson, Virgil, 1896-   —Correspondence.
2. Composers—United States—Correspondence.   I. Page,
Tim.   II. Page, Vanessa Weeks.   III. Title.
ML410.T452A4   1988   780'.92'4 [B]   88-2220
ISBN 0-671-62117-3

In memory of Maurice Grosser
and to William Dean Page,
whose lives intersected during the
preparation of this book.

Acknowledgments

Above all, we are indebted to Virgil Thomson for the honor of editing his letters, for his cooperation, tireless energy, and meticulous care. His assistants, Lou Rispoli and Allan Stinson, were invaluable in locating letters and identifying obscure references. We are grateful to our associate editors, Nancy Chapple, Charles Passy, and Suzanne C. Taylor, for many hours of research and manuscript preparation, and to Jeffrey Herman, Jerry Miller, and Leslie Olsen for services great and small. Our editor at Summit, Ileene Smith, must be thanked for her patience and many suggestions; thanks also to her assistant, Alane Mason, for after-hours help with the manuscript. Patrick Dillon's copyediting was sure and penetrating. Mr. Thomson's agent, Robert Cornfield, contributed his expertise, and our representative, Geri Thoma of the Elaine Markson Agency, provided unwavering support. We are grateful to Harold Samuel of the Yale School of Music Library for access to the Thomson collection (and for his hospitality in New Haven); to SUNY-Buffalo for permission to reprint the letter to James Joyce; to Charles Eubanks of the New York Public Library; to the American Music Center, June Carlson, Philip Claflin, Aaron Copland, George Cornish, Sidney Cowell, Anna Lou Kapell Dehavenon, Jane Gottlieb, Stephen Holden, James Holmes, Allen Hughes, Richard Hundley, Mary Schuster Jaffe, Richard Kluger, Allan Kozinn, William Mackay, Vivian Perlis, Eva Resnikova, Alan Rich, John Rockwell, Ned Rorem, Ira Rosenblum, William Schuman, and Elie Siegmeister, who graciously answered our questions.

Tim Page
Vanessa Weeks Page
New York City
July 14, 1987

Table of Contents

Introduction

As composer, critic, and memorialist, Virgil Thomson has been a crucial figure in American cultural life for more than half a century —an elegant and improbable synthesis of *boulevardier* sophistication, churchy consonance, and Midwestern plain speaking. The roster of artists with whom he collaborated includes Gertrude Stein, Marianne Moore, Truman Capote, Frederick Ashton, John Houseman, Lincoln Kirstein, Robert Flaherty, John Cage, Florine Stettheimer, and many others. If we were to enumerate the people with whom Thomson came into contact over the course of his long career, this introduction would quickly devolve into a laundry list of the century's most glittering and brilliant personalities.

Many of these will, as it happens, make an appearance or two in this collection of letters, culled from some twenty-five thousand documents spanning the years from World War I through the mid-1980s. From the very first letter, addressed from boot camp to the folks back home in Kansas City, it is obvious that Thomson knew that he was somebody very special. Despite his lack of formal experience, he is already an eloquent writer, and the clipped, exacting, and unsentimental tone he assumes in 1917 will not greatly change in the next seventy years.

The letters reveal Thomson as a diligent artist; a shrewd businessman; a staunch, confident critic (of music, books, landscapes, and people, by turn); a sympathetic and sensitive friend; a skillful reporter; a resolute champion of modernism in all its guises; a bon vivant and man of the world who never forgot his Kansas City roots.

As we began to sift through the 154 cartons that line the shelves of Thomson's apartment in Manhattan's Hotel Chelsea, we realized that there was much more material than could possibly fit into a single book. And so some difficult choices had to be made. Those readers particularly intrigued by Paris in the 1920s may question some of our exclusions, as may those with a special interest in the genesis of an artistic collaboration or in the musical politics of New York in the 1950s. Still, we hope that what remains will present a portrait of Thomson and his many times, and that we have retained something to satisfy every reader.

Thomson's circle of acquaintance encompassed the great and the humble, the famous and the forgotten, people born in the 1830s and in the 1970s. We decided to succinctly identify as many characters in the book as we could, at the risk of cluttering the manuscript with dates and footnotes. Some references were beyond recall or impossible to track down and, in a few cases, addressees modestly refused to reveal their ages. Although we have not identified everybody mentioned in passing, virtually all of the people to whom a letter was addressed or about whom a letter was written have been accorded biographies.

We've tried to keep these biographies short, particularly those of well-known people. Indeed, the identification of Vladimir Horowitz as a "Russian-American pianist" may seem unnecessary to some, and there is certainly more to be said on the subject. But those who want detailed information on Horowitz can easily find it, and this tiny phrase might clarify a point for a reader at some later time.

Despite its sheer bulk, there are some unfortunate gaps in the correspondence. Because of James Joyce's eyesight, he and Thomson rarely communicated by letter, and their acquaintance is represented by only one brief note. The historic film collaborations with Robert Flaherty and Pare Lorentz are, in the main, presented in retrospect through Thomson's responses to inquiring scholars many years after the fact. And intimate letters are few: "When you see somebody every day, you don't write letters," Thomson explained.

Still, there is much to inspire, fascinate, and amuse. The contents fall naturally into several sections: the long, descriptive letters to his family from the army, New York, and Harvard; his initial encounter with Europe and his immersion in the celebrated artistic and literary milieu of Paris, culminating in his association with Gertrude Stein and its musical manifestations; his years as Music Critic for the *New York Herald Tribune;* and, finally, the concentrated notes from Thomson's many years as one of America's "grand old men" of music.

A disproportionate number of letters date from Thomson's tenure with the *Tribune.* As a working critic, with his opinions spread before the public every day, he received more mail (both curious and furious) than at any other point in his life. Thomson answered his readers courteously, with quick acknowledgments, refutations, and elaborations. We believe this section of the book to be an ideal exegesis of daily music criticism—a virtual primer, couched in epigrams, that details the manner in which a master accomplishes a difficult job.

The last letters reflect a sound, productive, and remarkably self-confident mind, serene and secure. Thomson obliges autograph collectors, most happily when a postpaid envelope is sent; he is generous to friends and the needy but appropriately wary in daily fiscal matters; and, as throughout this volume, he is often very, very funny.

Dates have been standardized—21 avril is April 21—and we have not always included signatures. Through connective passages and occasional footnotes, we have provided a skeletal biography. But for that, we have remained on the sidelines (applying some judicious pruning now and then). Although he has allowed us maximum latitude, this is, ultimately, Virgil's book, and we have tried to make our presence as unobtrusive as possible. We believe Thomson will be remembered not only for his music and his criticism but for his correspondence, which, with wit, vivacity, and penetration, chronicles the most remarkable century in human history. Now in his nineties, Thomson continues to live at the Hotel Chelsea, to compose, lecture—and write letters.

Tim Page
Vanessa Weeks Page
New York City
December 27, 1987

Part One

YOUTH

(1917–1925)

*V*irgil Garnett Thomson was born in Kansas City, Missouri, on November 25, 1896, the only son of Quincy Alfred Thomson (1862–1943), a farmer and post-office employee, and his wife, Clara May Gaines Thomson (1865–1957).

"To anyone brought up there, as I was, 'Kansas City' always meant the Missouri one," he recalled in his autobiography, entitled simply *Virgil Thomson* and published in 1966. "When you needed to speak of the other you used its full title, Kansas-City-Kansas; and you did not speak of it often, either, or go there unless you had business." Thomson remained fiercely proud of his midwestern roots; despite the fact that he divided most of his career between New York and Paris, the hymn tunes of the nineteenth century have rarely been far from the surface in his music.

Thomson's cousin Lela Garnett (1884–1960) gave him his first piano lessons at the age of five. But even before that he had improvised "with flat hands and the full arm, always with the pedal down and always loud, bathing in musical sound at its most intense, naming my creations after the Chicago fire and similar events."

After he got into a fight on his second day of elementary school, Thomson realized that he was "going to have to find other ways toward gaining respect than head-on physical encounter." "My choice was simply not to compete," he continued. "This choice kept me mostly out of fights and always free from broken bones. It also left me time for music and reading. And if it often brought me the taunt of 'sissy,' it caused me to grow strong in other ways of defense and attack, psychological ways, and in the development of independence."

17

Thomson proved himself a top student in all subjects throughout his schooling. A voracious reader, he had completed *The Golden Bough* and all the works of Nietzsche by his late teens, and served as a page in the local library. But he devoted most of his energies to music, and by the time he was eleven he was intently pursuing the study of music.

It was Robert Leigh Murray, a tenor soloist at the Calvary Baptist Church and an employee in a local piano store, who was the most important influence on the young man: Thomson later referred to him as "the mentor of my musical progress." Murray introduced Thomson to his first proper teachers, Moses Boguslawski and Gustav Schoettle, and gave him his first regular employment by using him as an accompanist. His principal piano teachers were Rudolf King, a pupil of the legendary Theodor Leschetizky, and E. Geneve Lichtenwalter, a woman of refinement and, as Thomson later observed, "a pianist-pedagogue of the highest aims." In addition, he studied organ with Clarence D. Sears of Grace Episcopal Church, where he would occasionally substitute for his teacher during services.

By his sixteenth year, Thomson's circle of adult acquaintances included both Murray and Lichtenwalter, his sister's painting teacher, Mrs. Hannah Cuthbertson (affectionately called "Cuffbutton"), and Mrs. Cuthbertson's friend James Gable, an English writer. Encouraged by his mother, Thomson would regularly invite these acquaintances, as well as friends his own age, for Sunday suppers at his house. He hoped, he later said, "to create and to sustain a symposium of the arts," thus readying himself for the salons he would attend—and often preside over—during his years in Paris and New York.

While living at home, he studied at the Kansas City Polytechnic Institute and Junior College, where he founded a literary club and published his own magazine; he was also nearly expelled for reading aloud from Edgar Lee Masters's *Spoon River Anthology*, which was considered a shocking book.

He survived this minor scandal, but the country's increasing involvement in what was then called "the Great War" posed an immediate threat to his educational continuum, and by 1916, American intervention in the European conflict seemed more and more likely. Thomson, inspired in part by his emulation of Nietzsche, was determined to join in. "All those millions being killed, the sinkings at sea, the filth and vermin of trench life, the pictures of bayonetted guts and burst Belgian babies, everything about it made it seem, to a boy just going on twenty, a lovely war," he recalled. "You wanted to be a part of what so many were experiencing, to try yourself out, prove your endurance. You certainly did not want the war to end without *your having been through something. You wanted it to go on till you could get there."*

So Thomson enlisted. He served as a member of the National Guard and made a futile attempt at joining the European-bound Ambulance Corps. And during a brief trip to New York he considered joining the navy, with the hope of conducting a naval band. But he finally turned back to Kansas City, where he signed up with the medical detachment of the 129th Field Artillery, stationed at Camp Doniphan in Oklahoma.

It is at this point that we begin our collection of Thomson's letters. Between 1917 and 1925, he will grow from an impressionable but supremely self-assured novice into an established composer and gentleman of cosmopolitan sophistication.

The first letter was written to Thomson's sister, Ruby Richerson Thomson (Mrs. Roy Gleason, 1885–1979). Eleven years his senior and his only surviving sibling—another sister, Hazel, had died at the age of two—Ruby was one of Thomson's closest confidantes, and the two corresponded regularly for more than sixty years. She was a gifted painter, particularly of china and enamel; Thomson treasured a vase she sent him at Harvard (described in the letter of December 19, 1919) for the rest of his life.

To Ruby Gleason

Camp Doniphan
September 30, 1917

My dear sister:

Today was supposed to be Sunday, but there was so much to be done that none of us had any holiday. That doesn't mean that I actually worked all day, but simply that I was around waiting to work. In fact, I read about an hour or so this morning and slept two this afternoon and loafed some in between.

A wooden hospital is being built for us, and we are putting up temporarily some big tents to use till that is done. We have not put up our living tents yet. We are living in a small mess hall that is all screened in, and I don't know just how soon we will be moved. We are messing with the headquarters company. The food is very good, the meats especially. Today for breakfast we had ham and fried potatoes and stewed peaches and bread and coffee. At noon there was roast beef and mashed potatoes and beans and bread and coffee. For supper, steak and potatoes fried with onions and tea and bread and cookies. It is quite satisfactory and well cooked. The water is poor. It tastes bad and I think is slightly constipating. At least, many have complained of that. When you send my box, I would like some raisins and some figs. The box I took went the first day. However, I don't intend to supply the whole detachment. One of the boys received a big chocolate cake yesterday that was awfully good.

You mustn't believe anything you read in the newspapers about Camp Doniphan; it is all faked. Such stories and rumors we call here "latrine wireless." For example, the account of our arrival here was all a lie. Nobody came to meet us but the quartermaster trucks for our supplies. We quite calmly marched over to our encampment and ate supper. The one battery already here fed us all, and the men were quartered for the night in the mess halls, some with and some without cots. The second section came in during the night and was quartered likewise. The third section arrived next morning and marched into camp without fuss. We didn't know they were here till we saw them march into their company streets. None of the incidents related happened on the way down. Nobody got off to talk to cotton pickers, and the band never played the "Marseillaise."

The country is beautiful and admirably adapted for artillery practice. The mountains to the west are beautiful, just freckled with trees, and the rest of the reservation is perfectly bare, that is, bare of trees. It is covered with short grass and several varieties of pretty flowering weeds. It rolls in great sweeps of round, wide, low hills, or rather, not hills, just big round inclines. The atmospheric effects at morning and evening are extremely delicate and beautiful. The first morning was misty, and to the north I could see only two long white streaks far away, and just above, three mountain tops, low and pointed and dark, like a Japanese print. We get up at 5:45 every morning and we can see the sunrise. Last night McKelly and I walked over to the aviation field which is not much more than a mile from us. The men fly around over us all day.

I am really having a nice time. I am feeling fine. And I am perfectly content. Don't worry. If anything goes wrong I will write home about it. I am awfully glad I am here.

Please have Papa send my box by express so that it will be delivered without my having to fool with going after it or paying for its delivery. I think it would be something of a nuisance otherwise. I should like a small pocketbook for change, preferably one that doesn't snap. You know how they look. I also want some shoe strings, a shoe brush and dauber, a box of red shoe polish, and some more shoe rags. Mine has torn in two already. I need some dish towels, as I suggested. I think a few pieces of cheese cloth a yard square will be good. Also a fresh bottle of mentholatum.

I asked you to send me these trinkets not because I am too stingy to buy them, but because Lawton is four miles away, and it costs 80 cents by jitney to go and come back. Besides, I don't know when I can go in.

I have written this letter during a service at the Y.M.C.A. and I expect it is a little confused. I will write again soon.

With love,
Virgil

P.S. George* says to send his trunk, prepaid like mine. If Papa could fit up one of those old flashlights with batteries, it would be awfully handy.

To Clara May Gaines Thomson

Camp Doniphan
October 10, 1917

My dear mother:

We are still enjoying the food you sent. The whole wheat and jelly was eaten up by four of us at one sitting. By the way, the small glass of jelly was so tough and stringy that it wasn't as good as it ought to have been, but the other glass was nice. I think the pears and raisins will last several days yet, because I don't deal them out wholesale. Everybody liked the liver paste but didn't eat much of it. I still have a can left. I think it would be nice if you could send me a little box of something, say a little candy or a few cookies or a glass of preserves and some bread, maybe a few sandwiches, every week or two. Just a taste sent often is a nice reminder and isn't as much of a nuisance to you as an occasional big box.

I went to Lawton last night and took a hot bath in a tub. That was a luxurious feeling. There isn't anything of interest in town.

Sunday night there was a genuine dust storm. I was over on a far side of the camp and, with another fellow, made my way home through the pitch dark, lost sometimes, nearly blown over by the wind, choked and blinded by sand and dirt. It was cold, too. But that walk was the most fun I have had since I came. We floored our tent the other day and bought a lamp. So we are living in something

---

*George Phillips, a high-school friend, served with Thomson in the medical detachment of his artillery regiment; he was later a successful journalist.

like luxury. Tomorrow we are going to take a long hike over into the mountains.

It has been pretty cold this week. After the dust storm, it rained. The ground was so hard that there hasn't been any mud, and the dust was quiet all day Monday. The air was so clear that we could see a great distance clearly. Neither the dust nor the wind has been bad since; and although it was very hot this afternoon, the nights and mornings have been very cold, and it is pretty cool now. I like it much better than warm weather, for I have plenty of clothes for both day and night. We were issued beautiful gray riding gloves a few days ago. They are heavy and soft with a strap about the wrist, perfect beauties.

Everything you sent in the box was satisfactory, and I was glad to get them. George's trunk has never arrived. I wish Papa would inquire about it.

I must quit. I think I will write on Wednesday after this.

Lovingly,
Virgil

We had "sow-belly" for lunch. That is one food that I refuse to taste.

To E. Geneve Lichtenwalter

Camp Doniphan
October 16, 1917

My dear Miss Lichtenwalter:

I felt inspired to write to you Sunday morning just before dinner and started a letter, when I remembered that my washing, which was boiling over a fire outdoors, ought to be put on the line before I forgot it. So I rinsed out the clothes and hung them up to blow about in a dust storm that was going on at the time. We have these dust storms usually four days out of every week, although sometimes they come oftener. They are not like ordinary storms, for they last all day, sometimes all night, and the wind blows stiff and hard and steady. There is rarely a day without wind, and these are uncomfortable because of the heat, but on some days the dust is not as bad as on others.

We are right next to the band, and every day we hear their practice. In the morning they practice together and in the afternoon they practice separately. The morning practice is not bad, because they really play well; but the afternoon practice is fascinating. It is like an orchestra tuning up for two hours at a time. What is the attraction about this chaos of sounds? Is it the exercise of our analytic faculty that we enjoy? I don't know but this is the chief pleasure we derive from the symphonies of certain ultra-moderns. They are like an orchestra eternally tuning up. At least, I find the "concourse of sweet sounds" that the band makes in the morning not nearly so interesting as the dissonance of sweet sounds that the individual practice produces.

There isn't much exciting here to relate. One day is like another except in the violence of the wind, and the nights are all alike except when we can afford the 50-cent jitney fare to Lawton. In Lawton we buy a hot bath and some ice cream and some bakery stuff to take back to camp. There is nothing else to do there. However, pay day having been delayed some time, we haven't been to Lawton for a week or so.

As far as amusements and diversions are concerned, this place is utterly barren. But somehow, I am enjoying myself nevertheless. And I am seeing a lot in the way of human character.

I wish you would send me some reading matter, anything that appeals to you. You probably have some books that are not especially valuable in binding, but are good reading, some old things perhaps. I will return anything you send, but I shouldn't risk any of my nice volumes down here if I were you. The Y.M.C.A. buildings have books to lend, but there doesn't seem to be a book of poetry on the whole reservation.

My mother said she talked to you the other day and that my sweater was nearly done. When you send it, you might send the socks Mrs. Grey made too, for they will both be handy. Several of our fellows have these sweaters, and I know I shall find one a pleasant luxury on brisk days and nights and a necessity later on. The socks will be fine to sleep in on cold nights, for the nights are, indeed, very cold sometimes.

I am going to write you a long, long letter about the life here before long, but for the present a mad scrawl is all I can do. Not that I haven't time. I have more leisure than I have allowed myself for three years. But leisure is one thing and privacy is another; and I haven't yet reached the point of self-control where I can concentrate completely and where the proximity of other people doesn't bother. It isn't so much their noise or their interruptions as their mere presence or personality. I think I am coming to believe in auras, the kind that sticks out all around the body and interferes with other auras.

Sincerely,
Virgil

To Clara May Gaines Thomson

Tuesday night, October 23, 1917

My dear mother:

I am writing tonight because tomorrow is a holiday, and I don't know what I shall be doing. It is Liberty Bond Day, and there is to be a big affair at Lawton for the soldiers with a free picnic lunch and other events that may be diverting, if not so thrilling. I don't know whether I shall go in or not, because not a soul in our company has any money. I think I'll go, though, if I can find a partner to walk with.

I enjoy coming to the Y to write letters. In the first place, I can think better than I can with the fellows in the tent talking around me and at me and over me. And then, it is a variety, a change of scene that refreshes my mind when I haven't left the company street all day. And I can sit and watch the fellows write. The seats at the long writing tables soon fill up, and the others who want to write have to find themselves a corner. Some sit on one seat and write on the seat in front, for the long benches have no backs; some kneel on the floor, putting the paper on the seat. Sometimes they put one bench on another for a desk, while a benchful of soldiers lines up on each side of this. Some kneel around the platform. Some go back to their tents.

The attitudes they take are especially curious too. One will sprawl his elbows out on the desk and let his pencil flow swiftly, while another will cramp himself up and write by wriggling his fingers. And the left-handed ones write almost upside-down. Smoking seems to be a soldier's chief comfort, and those are few without a cigarette or pipe or occasionally a cigar he has got in a box from his girl, which he chews with self-conscious pride and poise.

The most fun is to look over their shoulders at the letters they write. A chap will begin vigorously, "My dearest darling Louise," and then stop. Pretty soon he will get a thought and go ahead. "Although we have only met once, I again must assure you that I love you dearly and that you are the only girl I write to." And so on. The next letter comes easier, because he has already thought this up, and so he writes it over again to the girl he met at some Kansas town on the way down. The man next to him may be assuring his mother that the food is good and that he is happy, and the fellow just across will be telling how hard he is worked and how unfairly treated and how bum the victuals and scarce and how vile and insufferable the weather. I suppose they are really all sincere, whether they ramble on or not; and there are grounds for any manner in which the different men are affected. But those who complain would probably complain no matter where they were.

There is scarcely a night when there isn't some extra entertainment at the Y, either a song service with exhortation, or a boxing match, or a speech from some visitor. Tonight a young lady from Kansas City, who was stopping over with her mother to see her brother, sang a few songs very well indeed, and you should have heard the applause and seen the attention she got.

I usually just sit here awhile and watch, and that is like holding court or having a reception. The different fellows who wander past either speak or stop and chat a bit, some who know me and some who don't. Some spring their jokes, and some confess their sins.

The thing I want most in camp is solitude, and that is why I go off on long errands whenever I can and why I come to the Y. The fellows in my tent are fine, every one, and improve on acquaintance; but they are too close. It is as if some active psychic influence extended from them and monopolized my mind, for I can't think properly or feel like my own self as long as any of them is around, whether he talks or not.

The little cakes were fine, a great hit. There were enough for two messes after supper. How on earth did you ever make them? Were they iced separately? The jelly was good, although we argued about the flavor.

I had a new experience yesterday as K.P. (meaning kitchen police). I did a little of everything. I peeled onions and potatoes. I washed pots. I drew water. I piled cord wood in a dust storm. I ran the coffee urn at meals. I emptied garbage. I sprinkled the floor and swept the tables. I nearly sawed wood.

Tell sister to write again. Her other letter was fine.

With love,
Virgil

Eager for a European assignment, Thomson left the 129th Artillery and transferred to aviation. In some respects, it proved to be an unfortunate choice, since shortly after he left, the 129th went on to England and France while Thomson remained stateside. He was ordered to Pilots' Ground School at the University of Texas in Austin, after which he went to Dallas for further training.

One of his closest correspondents at this time was Alice Smith (1899–1973), a great-granddaughter of Joseph Smith who founded the Mormon religion. Thomson remembers her as a girl of high intellectual powers and later described her as "a mirror, also a pupil, someone to educate and to protect a little against being blighted by a virtually indigestible religious inheritance."

To Alice Smith

Austin, Texas
March 21, 1918

My dear Alice:

Your letter was a treat. You ask why I write so superficially of army life. How else could I write? It is a superficial life. It is a life of action, of accomplishment, of efficiency; and not only is there no time or stimulus for analysis, but too much reasoning out of the whys of things is unpatriotic and disintegrating. In my spare moments, I am as wildly patriotic as any and more than most, I think; retreat with the bugle corps, the regimental parades, the wonderful old ceremony of escort to the colors, which we did last week, are thrilling; but you must realize if you think about it some more that emotional patriotism is not for soldiers.

It is both the privilege and the duty of those at home. But don't think it surprising if the doughboy who digs a trench all day long fails to get many thrills out of his work. He is doing a plenty, and very few would quit if they could.

I have been here at the Ground School for two months, just graduated last Saturday. And I am going to the camp at Dallas for a few weeks before going to a flying field. We have worked here harder and steadier than I have ever done in my life, I think. From 5:30 in the morning till 10 at night, we drill and study. The drill is our salvation; if it weren't for the two or three hours a day that we spend at that we would all go mad. The rest of the time we take rapid-fire lecture notes. At night we learn the day's notes in order to make room for the next day's in our minds. The work is entirely a matter of hearing everything and remembering it all. Consequently, two months of it becomes a little dulling. I have swallowed so much information in the last eight weeks that I feel mentally like a stuffed boa constrictor.

To give an idea of the material covered here—we study machine guns, radio operation, the organization of foreign armies, airplane theory, rigging, military law and military hygiene, army paper work, engines, types of airplanes, maps, night and cross-country flying, artillery observation, photography and camouflage, instruments, meteorology, bombs and bombing, reconnaissance and contact patrol, care of the teeth and repair of wings. Of course,

26

everybody is on his tiptoes because everybody passes a quiz in every subject every week or else busts back a week. More than one bust and a man leaves the school. I was really proud of myself to have the best grades in my class, because there are fellows here from everywhere and from many professions. There are between 1,000 and 1,500 in the school, and the discipline is strict in the extreme.

I am more than glad that you have tasted the Episcopal Church. Just now you are reacting [against it], as I do from time to time. But in a month or two, drop in at the morning services at St. Mary's in Kansas City and see if you don't get a kick out of it. St. Mary's is a small, old, very beautiful church with an extremely high ritual. They have incense, and a male choir; they sing the creed and use only Gregorian music; and they have communion mass every Sunday at 11. Now don't forget to go there sometime.

Alice, I can't help a feeling of depression when I think of your situation, condemned only to emotional patriotism.

Sincerely yours,
Virgil

After graduation from flying school, Thomson was given a choice: either to wait for an overseas assignment or to go immediately to New York to study radio telephony at Columbia University. He opted for the latter and enjoyed an exhilarating time in New York, after which he returned to Oklahoma for further training, then moved on to Louisiana. It was during this period that Thomson received the inevitable nickname "Tommie."

The following letter introduces Leland Poole, later a successful stockbroker and one of Thomson's closest friends through the 1920s.

To Ruby Gleason

New York
[May 1918]

Dear Sister:

I was too busy writing up experiments last week to write home. And there are so many things to do when the weekend liberty comes that I am afraid I am going to be neglectful. Let me see, I have two weekends to tell about now. Last week, I saw the Washington Square Players do *Salome,* had supper at the nicest little French place called La Petite Bretonne, and went out to dinner Sunday at Cuffbutton's.

Last night Poole and Cuffbutton and I had dinner in the Village and went to see Ethel Barrymore afterwards. Today he and I went to church at St. Thomas's on Fifth Avenue and a couple of charming ladies invited us to dinner. They live on 57th, just off the Avenue in a rather gorgeous old brownstone. Dinner was served beautifully. We had a fine time. They are going up to their country place this week. They have a place up the river at Newburgh, near West Point, and they invited us to spend the weekend there week after next. The husband of one of them, Mr. Braman, will drive us up Saturday and they said we would go over to West Point and to several other interesting places on Sunday. I think it will all be a quite grand adventure myself.

The restaurants of Greenwich Village are awfully funny. We ate at a saloon, Bertolotti's,* where there is sawdust on the floor and a bar where the women walk over and drink between courses. They have excellent Italian food, and the place is just as it was 25 years ago. We had dessert at the Samovar. This is a small room that you have to walk between ash cans and climb a ladder to reach. It is clean and the food is cooked by an immaculate old Negro woman, all woolly and a yard wide. They serve a fine 60-cent table d'hôte. There are a lot of awfully interesting restaurants in the Village. Cuffbutton says, though, that barns for studios are getting to be dreadfully expensive down there, so that it is no longer a cheap place to live.

I made the highest grade on last week's exam, 94. That makes me in charge of the class this week, and a sergeant at drill. I don't know how long I can keep it.

I am having a really wonderful time here, and I haven't done half the things I want to yet. I haven't been near the Metropolitan Museum yet. I am going to an orchestral concert Friday. Most musical things are over this year, but the theaters are having a lot of good things. We always go Dutch and buy cheap seats but heavens! Money doesn't last long.

Write to me about how things are going at home and Mama's foot. Did you give up exhibiting this year? I have a letter from Aunt Lonie† about my soul. She wanted me to look up some gentleman who used to teach school in Boone County [Kentucky] and went to Dallas 25 years ago. She also offered to send me some cookies.

By the way, from the train, Boone County looks awfully dilapidated. I didn't see any nice houses or good farms, only shanties. Is everything off the railroad? We came through there on the L&N.

---

*Bertolotti's would thrive on West 4th Street into the 1970s.
†Leona Thomson Field (1859–1917), Quincy Thomson's older sister

Time for bed. I would like to have sent Mama a rose or an orchid today. But telegrams cost so high, and I am really bust as usual.

Love,
Virgil

To ALICE SMITH

Columbia University
May 21, 1918

My dear Alice:

I don't remember whether I accounted for my presence here or not, and it is too long and bushy a tale to spread out just now, when I've such a lot of other things to tell. I have been here a month now and will remain two more, receive a commission as Squadron Radio Officer (probably a 2nd Lt.), fly 5 weeks at Fort Sill, and go across. I am very glad I chose this course, as the fellows I graduated from ground school with may not be sent over for two years.

During the week, we study an extremely technical and specialized branch of electrical engineering. On Saturday afternoon and Sundays, we are free to do the town; and there are so many, many wonderful things to do here that we chuck our weekends full. I saw Mrs. Fiske* in a beautiful play called *Service,* which failed, and Ethel Barrymore in a delicious nothing called *Belinda,* which is lovely. The real thriller was the Washington Square Players in Wilde's *Salome.* Mme. Yorska† did the vamp role and Louis Calvert‡ did Herod in corking Henry VIII fashion, while Jokanaan, as they call the prophet, uttered scathing and beautiful speeches and a couple of handsome young men without clothes (much) talked about the moon. I have never sat thru such a fascinating hour and a half, such intensity and tragic horror and beauty and disgust.

I went to an orchestral concert the other night and climbed stairs like an Alpine before I reached my 50-cent seat at the top of Carnegie Hall.

Alice, you would love New York in wartime. The war is much closer here, very much closer than at home; and the whole town feels it. Really systematic work is done so that no soldier or sailor in

---

*Minnie Maddern Fiske (1865–1932), celebrated American stage actress
†American-born actress of Russian-French heritage, protégée of Bernhardt; billed first as "Mme. Yorska," later as "Vahslav Yorska"
‡(1859–1923), prominent English stage actor, who first had toured America with Lillie Langtry in 1888

town, even if he is broke, need lack entertainment or comfort. And the patriotic demonstrations that are seen occasionally are superb. The Liberty Loan parade was a wonder. I believe the most impressive was 40,000 women, wives and mothers of men in service, who marched in platoons and carried service flags. Saturday was the Red Cross parade. It took from 1:30 till twenty minutes of eight for it to pass; and of course Fifth Avenue was be-flagged as only Fifth Avenue can be when it wants to turn itself out. There were nurses and nurses and nurses and ambulance units and Boy Scouts and home guards and women knitting and more nurses and such a lot of bands. There were bands playing "Onward, Christian Soldiers" and bands playing "They Go Wild, Simply Wild Over Me," and bugle bands, and a French band that limped and wore blue spiral leggings. The President, who walked at the head of the parade, was cheered wildly, of course. But the most thrilling sound was a heartbreaking man's voice that I could hear above all the rest when the French band passed me. He was crying "Vive la France!"

Last Sunday I went to the very high Episcopal church, the Church of St. Mary the Virgin. Have you ever been there? It is just like a medieval Catholic church. They have a grand procession around the aisle first, choir, crosses, a trumpeter, priests with little boys holding back their robes in front, young men with great candlesticks, boys with incense pots and the priests in the rear, the outer two holding aside the robe of the chief priest, a robe of salmon-colored satin with green bands. They have a choir and organ in the church, and a mixed choir, another organ, and an orchestra in the loft at the rear. The priest intones the epistle and gospel to a weird unintelligible chant, and the air is full of good thick stupefying incense smoke. And in the midst of all this lovely, silly folderol, there was spoken the wisest, most thoughtful, most soundly philosophic and religious sermon I have heard in many a day. I liked it. You would have liked it. My father would have liked it. And so would yours.

George [Phillips] came in to see me the other night. The 129th is at Mineola, getting ready to sail. As it was only Thursday, we couldn't lark around, but we had dinner at one of the French table d'hôtes that are so attractive to me, and I returned to study under guard at 7:15. I hope he can come again before they leave; it was a fine feeling to sit at a table with him again and to talk vaguely and with authority about life and letters thru the flavor of good cigarettes and French ice cream, just as at Fort Sill (it seems such a long time ago that I was there!).

I have become awfully fond of a fellow from California* who

---

*Leland Poole

30

goes to the theater and the restaurants with me. Saturday we are going up to the country at Newburgh on the Hudson and the people who invited us have promised to take us over to West Point and several other places I should love to go to. I think we are going to have a great time.

I shall write later, Alice, of more adventures. Please write me again one of those nice patriotic and domestic letters.

Very sincerely yours,
Tommie

P.S. It is worth noting in my new character that I am no longer called Virgil, I am Tommie! It is much more human, don't you think?

To FRANCIS POINDEXTER*

Gerstner Field, Lake Charles, Louisiana
September 11, 1918

My dear Poindexter,

Last week somebody told me about your accident, and it must have been third-hand news, because there were all sorts of lurid details about your being totally blind and half burned; but I couldn't learn where you were. It was only yesterday, when I arrived here, that I learned from a pilot who had just come from Dayton that you weren't quite as badly messed up as I had feared. I need not tell you, of course, that I am very glad to be that much relieved, but I am sorry about your luck and interested—not gruesomely but really interested—to know just what did happen and how you are coming on. I wish you would get me a line. Now and then I've heard some reports of your progress in flying; and they have been very thrilling, I assure you. I gather that as an aviator you are "some jazz." Well, I am most proud of you, Poindexter, and if you are in such a position that correspondence is convenient, don't let modesty prevent you from recounting your achievements and exploits to me, because I am honestly eager to hear of them all.

After three months of fairly hard work and mostly adventure in New York, I returned in the last of July to the sun-scorched hell-heated desert of Fort Sill and remained there, doing bunk fatigue mostly, till this week. I am here for only a short time, taking the two-week course with the radio telephones that all the radio officers

---

*a friend and sergeant from Thomson's Kansas City regiment

have to do before going overseas. That doesn't mean that I am positively going across immediately. After this is finished, G.O.K.—which is our abbreviation for "God Only Knows." I am more pleased with the radio service than I had intended to be. It is by no means a stupid or dull job, and when I am permanently enough assigned to take my training, to which I am entitled, I think it is going to be keen. As an aviator and a radiator both, I think I shall have a jump on the fellows who laughed at me for going into radio. However, I haven't been in the work long enough to have any sound opinion yet of its real merits and advantages.

Two or three letters from the regiment have contained interesting news and entertaining tales, but I don't think they are actually on the line yet. I am anxious for them to get into the big mess and show off some. Some of the fellows I saw at Fort Sill told me that Norris* is still at Fort Worth, not quite finished yet. He seems to have had a streak of hard luck, boils and things that have delayed him every time until the course was lengthened a few more weeks. Everywhere I go I've run across fellows I've known somewhere and each has his particular woes and a different story. The military air is certainly different from what it was in the nation a year ago, isn't it? And New York! There never was such a spirit! Our people are *growing!* Well, Poindexter, pardon this rather formal letter of condolence. I don't know how to say what I want to, but dammit I pretty near envy you, after all. Write me something if you can.

Very sincerely yours,

To ALICE SMITH

Lake Charles, Louisiana
October 25, 1918

Dear Alice:

You can't guess what I have been doing. I have had the "flu." Isn't that disgusting? Well, it wasn't entirely, after all, because it got me out of some disagreeable work and gave me a week's mild adventure in the hospital, where I was starved and sweated and doped and rubbed and examined and bathed in bed by a nurse. The treatment was far more weakening than the disease, and one day when I tried to walk, I fainted. That, too, was interesting, because I had never fainted before. I am glad it happened. I have been out now for nearly ten days, and I think I am entirely convalesced. But I lost so much

---

*Norris Ryder, a friend from Central High School

32

weight in the hospital that I came back with an appetite like a starved poet, and I still eat like a draft horse, a good moderate-sized one. The camp is quarantined, so that life is pretty stupid around here. I mostly play bridge and eat candy. That, with tinkering at the piano and reading a little and writing a few letters, is the way in which I am spending the days of my golden youth. But you just wait. You haven't heard the real news. I received notice some time ago that I am to be ordered *overseas!* Twenty of us are going together. I don't know when I shall get away from here, as the final orders haven't come yet. But I don't think it can be very long, as it was ten days ago the advance notification arrived. I get all worked up when I think about it and I am especially keen to be getting on East. I shall probably have a week or ten days in New York before reporting at Hoboken, and I am counting on a great lark, looking up my friends and going to the theaters and concerts and buying equipment and encountering all the strange and exciting adventures that come to one in New York—as George says, almost the only place in America (he ought to except Cheyenne) where any real wickedness is preserved in these moral and decadent times.

Alice, I have just finished a charming and stimulating novel about a boy. It is called *Youth's Encounter,* by Compton Mackenzie,* and I know you would be pleased and fascinated by it. It tells of his boyhood, and, still more interesting, his youth up to the time he goes to Oxford. The story from there is another book, *Sinister Street,* which I am going to get. When he goes up to matriculate, an old lady, lovable and worldly-wise, gives him this advice: "In your first year, establish your sanity; in your second establish your charm; and in your third year you can do absolutely anything you like."

Outside of this, the only book of genuine distinction that I have read in a long time is a French novel about Constantinople, *The Man Who Killed* by Claude Farrère.† It is sharp and keen and brilliant and very French, very Latin, and to the last degree *distingué.* It is about quite different things and in a quite different manner from Mackenzie's English novel, but even more worth reading, although I fancy it is hard to get, and I sent my copy to Mr. Murray.

Our party at Geneve's was a huge success, and it turned out at the last minute that I shared the honors with Miss St. Clair, a lovely girl who had just received overseas orders from the Red Cross. She is to be a "supervisor of domestic relations" and write letters home for fellows in the hospital or something like that. Doesn't it sound excit-

---

*(1883–1972), English novelist, founder and first editor of *The Gramophone,* a monthly recordings magazine
†(1876–1957), French novelist

ing? A truly wonderful experience, I think. She writes from New York of all sorts of events, too, especially the [Conservatoire Orchestra], that make me more than ever eager to be getting on there.

The Polytechnic seems dreadfully dull to me. I suppose it always was. I know you must be longing to get away. You are somewhat in Eugene's* situation. Ready, ever ready, for excitements and thrills and experiences and stimuli that the surroundings don't offer. Your mother's plan to take you to Columbia is immense, and I am looking forward to high times for you.

I am going somewhere myself when the war is over, if there is enough left of me to perambulate; it may be abroad or East, I don't know which. But I know it will be somewhere, and Eugene is planning to come along. It would be great if you could be in New York at the same time!

Please give my regards to your father and my compliments to your mother. Tell her I did have my mug shot at Miss White's, and that although I haven't seen the prints, I am told they are rather decent. And thank her for a most pleasant evening.

Write to me.

Very sincerely,
Tommie

To Ruby Gleason

New York
November 6 [1918]

Dear Sister:

Thanks for the money. I have already bought the fold I want. And I shall think of you whenever I spend a dollar from it. Came back last night from Newburgh. Lovely time, beautiful country, and especially beautiful to me after Louisiana to see the fall. We walked and drove and played music and boated and had country cream thick like molasses. Tonight I am going to sit in their box at Carnegie Hall at a patriotic meeting at which the Lord Bishop of Oxford, said to be the cleverest man in England, is to speak. There is to be a rather interesting party with us, Admiral Usher of the Navy, Commander Belt of the British Army (an ex-lion hunter) and Mrs. Belt, who has been with the Queen of Roumania for three years doing Red Cross nursing. Mr. Braman is taking me to the Stock Exchange today, and several days ago he sent me a guest membership card to his club (the

---

*Eugene McCown, a painter friend from Missouri, later in Paris with Thomson

New York Yacht Club), a fascinating place with models of all the great yachts and a room with all the famous cups and the best chef in New York. I got the two overseas letters and the comforter with the things in it. I heard the orchestra from the Conservatoire de Paris, saw Wilde's comedy *An Ideal Husband,* [and] went to a bohemian studio party in the Village. In fact, I am too gay and too plutocratic for words. I wish I had time to write more.

Love,
Virgil

The "Great War" ended on November 11, 1918; Thomson had missed his opportunity for overseas adventure by a matter of days.

He returned to Kansas City, where he spent the next few months sharpening his musical skills, resuming classes at the Kansas City Polytechnic Institute, and planning his future. He ultimately decided to move east and matriculate at Harvard; a loan from the Mormon Church, acquired with the help of Alice Smith's father, made this possible, and he arrived in Cambridge in the autumn of 1919.

"Harvard had been chosen for my especial needs, which were three—good keyboard lessons, available in Boston; training in harmony, counterpoint, and composition, said to be excellent at this university; and full access to its arts and letters," Thomson recalled. "My ultimate aim at this time was to become an organist and choir-director in some well-paying city church and from there to pursue a composer's career."

To Ruby Gleason

Cambridge
October 8 [1919]

Dear Sister:

I am about settled into a decent routine now and I really have a whole evening to myself. My courses are well underway. I have stopped my piano lessons, I begin the organ next week. I am practicing now, and I played a trial at two churches Sunday. I haven't heard from them yet. I have four courses and a half in college: German, Medieval History, Modern Philosophy, Harmony, and a course in modern French composers (Debussy, Ravel, Fauré, etc.).

I am quite comfortable and am even getting to know a few people, though that is a slow process at Harvard, because nobody ever speaks to anybody else without some authority for it. I am boarding at a house, not at the University dining halls. The food is better and the price the same—$8 [a week]. However, that is getting a bit tiresome and I may go back to the restaurants for a week or so. I sing in the University Choir and the Glee Club. Both will go on the road during the winter. The choir is wonderful. We sing medieval things in Latin without accompaniment and sing them beautifully. Thank you for having the picture framed. Mother sent cookies and a hat, both of which arrived safely and both of which furnished wood for my fireplace.

I am glad you joined the country club. It will be a lot of fun and do you good, because now that you've paid money and belong, you'll have to get out and use it.

The letters from home are great with all the news of weddings, sicknesses of neighbors, public scandals and everything. You and Mother keep on writing. I'll try and compose a real letter also at least once a week.

Love,
Virgil

To Ruby Gleason

Cambridge
Wednesday, Oct. 14, 1919

Dear Sister:

In a grand rush as usual. I am sorry your present was slow. I was going to buy it Saturday, but the book shop was closed, also Monday, which was Columbus Day.

I have two new jobs, three in fact. I play at the Tremont Street Methodist Church. I don't know how much I get; I think it is $9. I play duets an hour a day with a freshman for $5 a week. And I have a Frenchman to whom I give piano lessons in exchange for French. This is not necessary, as I passed my oral French exam last week and am free from any French requirements. But it was such a good chance to talk, and maybe read a little, with a Frenchman of the upper class (and from Paris too) that I grabbed it. I hope to get my accent down pat before the winter is over.

What all did you get for your birthday? Did you have a party or anything? I don't gad about much these days. I haven't time. I go to the Symphony concerts every Saturday night in Boston and every other Thursday out here. Then with classes to meet, and the organ, and such tons of books to read, I don't get to gad as I'd like. I manage to get some exercise by walking or going to the gymnasium or playing tennis; but I never have time to go on the river, as I want to. Everybody sculls around here, and I am dying to do it. I will write Mother soon.

Love,
Virgil

To Ruby Gleason

Thanksgiving Day [November 27, 1919]

Dear Sister:

Thanks like everything for the money. I think I shall buy a dictionary with it. One of those small "collegiate" dictionaries will be quite good enough, and not cumbersome to have either.

I was just thinking of some things I might mention to the family for Christmas, too, but if I do, please don't send them all, because it will embarrass me to appear to have asked for so much. The birthday was almost a deluge, a huge success, however, from my point of view. I have just discovered the picture underneath my blotter, and it is so good looking, I think I should hang it up if I didn't need the blotter. I am all excited about the enamel piece. What is it? Or is that the surprise? If you and George both like it, it must be a masterpiece, because you both have good taste. I am beginning to repent my economy already in buying cheap shoes, because they hurt my feet where there is a lump in the sewing. I am going to take them back and kick. Those Liberty Bonds are certainly a nice pet to have, like the hen who laid gold eggs. I had forgot they paid interest and I am sorry I have to sell them. But I don't want to ask for any more money now, especially for such an unsaintly device of the devil as dress clothes.

My new church job is great fun. The bunch is really singing well, too. At the chapel choir here at Harvard, we are getting the Christmas carols ready. Thirty of us and thirty girls from Radcliffe will sing, and it is going to be quite a great event. We do them two evenings, Dec. 16 and 17, and everybody comes. We have some old carols, some of the great Bach chorales, and a Russian piece for eight parts that raises the roof.

We had a huge dinner at Mem Hall, where I eat, today. Tonight seven of us are having a feed in a room, broiling steak over a fire and such things. I have loafed all day. I need it every once in a while, working everyday and Sunday too. I suppose you are all in the midst of cranberry frappé and such.

The talking machine (not for talking) is a great idea. I am in favor of it. Don't get too good a one. Spend the money on records. Would you prefer it to a pianola? I think I would. Cheaper, too.

I am eagerly waiting for the enamel piece. Don't wait till Christmas, if it is done before.

Love all the time,
Virgil

You'd love the Arts and Crafts Society in Boston. They have great things.

To Ruby Gleason

Cambridge
December 19 [1919]

Dear Sister:

The vase has been sitting on my mantel for 24 hours now and every time I look at it I find it more interesting than before. It is positively the most stimulating piece of pottery I have ever seen. You should have seen me tear the box open and skim off the tissue paper. Then I took it around and showed it to the household. I refuse to exclaim at the *quantity* of work on the vase. That goes without saying and has nothing to do with its artistic value. I appreciate every hour of work on it as a special gift to me. But the vase as a thing of beauty has plenty of artistic merits without that. I was expecting something nice and elaborate, but the first sight dazzled me. And the funny thing is that it continually grows more and more interesting, instead of calming down.

The design is very witty, I think. I laugh at it all the time. Isn't it funny how a pattern of flower forms can suggest so many foods. There is a beautifully stuffed date, some blue doughnuts, noodle tarts, raspberry-colored French pastry, cookies with raisins in them, the classic fried egg, something that is between a candy lobster claw and a bean pod, slices of stuffed olives, chocolate drops, perfume balls, and a tomato that also suggests a slice of green pepper on a salad. There is something tremendously exciting about that great red figure. What a lot of material you have used on the piece! Colors! and Shapes! And those fascinating cloud lines in the background, if it has such a thing. It sits on my gray mantel under the print.

For utility, it requires rather expensive flowers. Think how sick a stupid pink carnation would look in it, or a rose. Fancy white flowers, lavender petunias, yellow narcissus or orchids (particularly green ones) would be fine, I fancy.

I must dress now and get the 3:30 train for Fall River. The Glee Club sings there tonight. Dinner, concert, dance. Return in time for a nine o'clock class Saturday. We come west in April, maybe to St. Louis.

Thanks like everything for the vase. I love you for making it for me and for other reasons as well. As Geneve told Cuffbutton once, a musician works like everything to do something good and when it is all over nobody has much of anything, but a definite and tangible thing like this vase is a thing of beauty all the time. I love it.*

Love,
Virgil

The landlady thot it a "fine imported piece" till I told her you made it. Of course, it does show lots of Chinese influence, of the very best sort. Nothing ordinary or tame about it. It has quite a few kicks of its very own, too.

By this point Thomson had become acclimated to Harvard life, enveloping himself in his studies, singing in the Glee Club, finding odd employment as a church musician, and enjoying the cultural life of Boston, while making the occasional foray into New York. His chief mentors at Harvard were the choral conductor Archibald T. Davison,† known as "Doc"; the composer Edward Burlingame Hill,‡ and the poet Samuel Foster Damon,§ who introduced Thomson to the works of many contemporary writers, including Gertrude Stein.

Thomson divided the summer of 1920 between Cambridge and New York. It is from this period that his first acknowledged compositions date: "Vernal Equinox" and "The Sunflower," for soprano and piano, set to texts by Amy Lowell and William Blake, and De Profundis, for mixed choir a cappella.

---

*Thomson still owned the vase in 1988, and kept it in a display case in his apartment.

†Davison (1883–1961) was also an organist, editor, and teacher.

‡Hill (1872–1960) was associated with Harvard for nearly four decades; his other students included Leonard Bernstein and Walter Piston.

§Damon (1893–1971) later taught at Brown University and published studies of Amy Lowell and William Blake and also of American folklore.

Cambridge
August 26, 1920

Dear Sister:

The news of the stork's visit is the most excitement I have had yet. It is exactly what I had hoped would happen for a long time, because I think a child in the family will do us all good. Of course it's difficult and expensive and dangerous, but we mustn't be afraid of things like that. A family that doesn't go through them and risk things is decayed. There is no way of protecting ourselves from life that isn't stupid, and the only way to be somebody is to do all the important things and do them with gusto. To get married without having children is rather begging the question, I think, side-stepping the main issue. I am glad the family isn't delaying, and I hope when you can afford it there will be one or two more. I hope it is a squalling lusty boy with dark red hair and freckles.*

If the others weren't pleased at the prospect, it was clumsy not to say so. But I suppose we are nothing if not frank in the family. Mother has always had the idea that there was something a bit vulgar about having a baby, as if the best people didn't do it, whereas the "best people" are exactly the ones who still have families of eight and ten, while the middle classes nowadays are getting selfish and timorous and either have no children at all or else devote themselves to one spoiled baby. I'll bet Roy is glad.

By the way, you must not let the family in. Be sure and go out every day to exercise, clear up till the confinement, and go in the motor all you can. Also please don't economize. I insist on your going to a hospital and having a nurse for the first few months. Anything else is not safe.

Please tell the family they deserve a good spanking for not wanting to tell me (which would have been outrageous) and for being selfish and stupid in their attitude.

If you are not too busy with sewing and things, I'd love the luster china. And I'd like it as soon as I can have it. I'd like some cups and plates and a tea set with a thick, squatty pot. If you have to buy any of the china, I'll pay for it. A little bowl or so would be useful if you have one around.

I just came down this morning. The boat trip yesterday afternoon was very lovely. Sunny and cool and a brilliant, Mediterranean blue,

---

*In fact, the baby was a girl: Margaret Elizabeth (Betty) Gleason, later Stouffer, born December 8, 1920.

as we came through all the islands and thoroughfares on the coast. I had a great vacation and I've gained many pounds.

Lots of love and be careful,

To Ruby Gleason

Cambridge
September 16, 1920

Dear Sister:

I wish you hadn't asked me about the china, but just painted it some color and sent it. It's so hard to decide. If the china is thin, I imagine blue would look better. If it's thick, orange. Blue on the outside and orange on the in might also be quite lovely. Please use whichever you think will look nicest. Some of the lustre things I see here are a little wishy-washy. Use the color that looks strongest. And if the blue and orange mixture I suggest sounds good and isn't any more trouble, try that. If it is trouble, make them plain, the best color. If both colors are good, and you still can't decide, make blue cups and orange tea set (or vice versa). If you can't get cups and plates, send the saucers and make the plates when you get time or, better still, send the plates and make the saucers later. They will be nice to have. Creamer isn't essential. I can use a cow can. But I'd like to have the whole outfit. Don't spend much worry about shapes or colors. I'm not fussy.

Glee Club sings in Kansas City a few days before Xmas. Electric lights are in the house now. No more smell.

Love,

To Ruby Gleason

Cambridge
Saturday, March 19, 1921

Dear Sister:

Thanks for the cuffbuttons. They are nice; I like the dark blue. And they look very good in a shirt. Thank you very much. I haven't been ill. In fact, I haven't been weller all year. But I have been awfully rushed. The river is open now, and I am rowing in an eight. The exercise is doing me good but makes me sleepy nights. How are you getting along with M.E.? I suppose all babies are a nuisance, but so is everything else. A house is, for that matter.

I am writing a novel.★ I find it the easiest way to solve the problem of my composition course, where a long theme is due every other week. Instead of thinking up something new each time, I simply write another chapter.

I think I may not be here next year. There are two new travelling fellowships in music ($1400 each) and Prof. Hill says I can probably have one if I want it. If the incumbent is very good he can keep the thing for three years. So I think that if I can get it, I shall simply stay over next fall and study in Paris. I don't know just what I shall study, probably organ playing and counterpoint. Maybe fugue and free composition later. I think it all sounds quite attractive. Don't talk about the fellowship till I get it.

I can't write more just now. I have to get a train.

Much love,
Virgil

To LELAND POOLE

Cambridge
April 20 [1921]

Dear Old Point Comfort,†

To think of you ripping off the Sinding and Chopin! Why I can hardly do it myself nowadays. But some day I shall play the piano again! I know how. I occasionally protest against people who confuse *music* with *piano-playing,* and certainly the piano has limitations of sostenuto and of contrast and particularly of voice-leading, but it is after all the greatest single instrument, because it can *almost* do so many things. When you come to Paris in two years, we will play duets together and pieces for two pianos. Because I believe concerted music is greater than any solo performance, team-work for the production of something beautiful being, if not the highest end of man, at least symbolic of nearly all that we consider good. So much for my inevitable moralizing. It is appropriate, don't you think, that the imaginative and artificial music of Debussy should get tied up in your mind with the imaginative and artificial days in New York. Surely the nearest thing to my own remembrance of those romantic, exotic weekends would be a series of Impressions in the style of Debussy. One might call the pieces something after this manner.

★Thomson began this as his weekly work for English 5, Harvard's most advanced writing course. The novel was never completed.
†Slang for "chum"

I La Cité en parade
II Au Théâtre
III Soir à la Rivière
IV Eglise
V Sonatine victorienne
    Assez vif, mais sonore
    Large et calme (Improvisations au piano)
    Très vite (Galop au train)

I should be glad of any advice about francs. I think I shall take abroad for summer-money a letter of credit. It will be simpler, and I can make some on it, as I buy it in pounds.

I am on Spring Vacation this week, trying to get some back chapters of my novel done, but I haven't done anything yet. I did sell my piano today for $750. The buyer got a bargain, but I was glad to sell, as buyers with cash are *very* scarce. I lose about $100 on my two years' use of it (pretty good, don't you think?) and when my account is paid in I shall have $300 left, just as if I had put it in the bank saved. Do write me often abroad, because we'll both enjoy it. San Francisco and Paris!! Hmm—! Not so awfully different, I fancy.

For God's sake, quit boasting about the balmy night. It doesn't *go* in New England, seeing we've had about three evenings this spring when one could go out without an overcoat.

Toujours votre, Tommie

After finishing his classes in the spring of 1921, Thomson set sail with the Glee Club for his long-awaited introduction to Europe. He stayed on after the tour was over, visiting Switzerland and England; then, as planned, he continued his musical education in Paris, with the aid of a Harvard travelling fellowship.

To Ruby Gleason

On board S.S. *La Touraine*
June 11 [1921]

Dear Sister:

I should have written before I sailed, but there were too many things to do. We were packing and sightseeing and taking exams. The visit was fine, though. I had a wonderful time, and I know the family did too. The voyage has been very pleasant indeed since the second day. I was sick at first and the weather was stormy, too, so that I didn't enjoy that part. The servants on this boat and most of the passengers speak only French, excellent practice for us, and there are some quite charming people to talk to among them, because they are very amiable and lively. The sea air is vigorous and fine. One can have plenty of exercise and the food is quite good. Everybody has an enormous appetite.

This is Saturday and we are due at Le Havre sometime during the night Monday, special boat-train to Paris Tuesday morning. I shall try to write every few days, even if it is only a little. I wish you were on the boat, you'd love it so. Fine air, lazy deck-chairs, conversation, reading, long and elaborate dinners, sometimes a little concert or a dance in the evening, sometimes a passing ship far off. Always the sea to watch, different every day with moonlight and clouds and blue sky and sunset afterglow. It really is enormous fun. You must come sometime. And when you do, be sure to bring lots of chocolates and cookies and extra fruit for the hungry hours (although we have ice cream at three and tea at four every afternoon).

Love,
Virgil

To Ruby Gleason

[London]
Sunday, August 21 [1921]

Dear Sister:

I came up to Paris from Geneva last Monday by day train and enjoyed every bit of the journey. We came thru the French Alps and the Vosges and the beautiful Burgundian country (the Côte d'Or, they call it). You can understand the French devotion to pink and blue when you see their hills and their sunsets. French sunsets are invariably Louis XV, delicate, slightly grayed, graceful in line, and always pink and blue. And their whole landscape is like French art, simple and plain, clear, and always delightful with the same delicately varied monotony.

I saw Geneve in Paris, spent a very pleasant afternoon wandering thru the Luxembourg and the Panthéon with her. There isn't anything I can do in Paris now, though I should really like to begin work. So I am taking the opportunity to see England a little. I came over yesterday afternoon alone and I intend to remain alone, as I am tired of doing things with people. Had a very pleasant day today without a guidebook or a map. Whenever I wanted to find something I just started in some direction and I always found it easily. This morning I walked all around the Abbey and the Parliament building, down the Thames to London Bridge, to St. Paul's and all thru the shopping district. Read *Tom Jones* this afternoon till tea, then went over to the Abbey to an evening service, dined at a nice little tavern and walked home again, doing much window shopping all the while. I am not so far enormously pleased with the Abbey. The exterior is not nearly so graceful as the good French cathedrals. The north portal is fine because there are statues, but the rest is a collection of empty niches repeated and repeated. The interior is better. Although I don't know what the height really is, the effect of height is immense, probably due to the fine fan vaulting. Tombs and statues, as usual, all out of style. Cloister small and delicious, somehow genuine. I might attempt the generalization that the English always do cosy bits better than large scale scenery. Even the grand palaces and avenues of Paris are dangerously near to being ineffective (tho of course they are not) on account of the quantity of decoration. Only the Italians can be magnificent on a grand scale. The great London buildings are either monotonous in decoration or else simply borrowed from classic styles. I will say, tho, that their large buildings in classic style are seldom overdecorated and often of quite fine proportions, quite massive and solid, as suits a severe climate. Smoke and rain seem to have produced a curious and charming color effect. Not real color, as in Italy, or the soft gray (too delicious to describe) that French stone takes, but a contrast of black and white. Sides of buildings become very black, and exposed cornices and capitals or other ornaments like rime or frost. Lovely effect.

The service at the Abbey very unpleasant. Routine atmosphere, smug, silly sermon (about nothing at all definite), sentimental music, bad choir. I hated it. Strange thing, this matter of the religious atmosphere of a country. I found it least annoying in Italy (next to Switzerland, I suppose, though I am not even sure of that) and most annoying here. I sensed none at all in Germany, although I was at Wiesbaden on a Sunday. In Switzerland it is perfect like everything else. Perfect country! They speak French, they can cook, they charge as little as possible for anything, they are amiable, there are no profiteers or thieves, the police are incorruptible, there is no graft in the government or smoke in the cities, they have beauty both of art and of nature and every modern improvement for efficiency and comfort, and the only pressure of public opinion is in the direction of tolerance and freedom.

In France the Roman Catholic atmosphere is a bit oppressive, at least in the churches. I can't say just what it is, but it is something like the Irish ignorance one smells in America wherever the Church appears. Unpleasant also because of the manifest insincerity of much church art. Not much spirit in any except the churches built before 1300.

None of that in Italy. Church is purely decorative there. Buildings beautiful and the service harmless. Sweet-voiced intonations and long services in monotone are at worst only a little hypnotic (they make me sleepy, like sermons) and at least rather pleasant. Music usually Gregorian, simple and dignified, never emotional. Church practically powerless in politics; Italians derive the necessary satisfaction of their need for religion out of the Church without letting the Church meddle in temporal matters. They are very civil to her but firm. The so-called backward condition of Romanized countries is an illusion so far as Italy is concerned. Italians well-educated, great linguists (always speak French, English, and German and usually Spanish), sportsmen—learned, versatile, and charming. Peasantry has every opportunity for education and they always take what they need, ambitious and capable people. A man has to speak four languages to get a waiter's job in Venice. The railways are excellent (best engineers in the world are Italians, as also the best stone-masons). Even the smallest towns are clean and pleasant. Milan the finest modern city I've ever seen. Agriculture too beautiful for words. They grow hemp and wheat and other grains in small fields, put fruit trees between the fields, and then raise grape vines on the fruit trees, all in the neatest and most symmetrical fashion. And the largest manufacturing concern in the world is at Genoa. Wonderful country!

To get back to this religious atmosphere in England. Very prosperous and unpleasant gentlemen are always shooing you out of a seat (seldom into one) or fastening a cord across something or trying to make you get out of the place (as at St. Margaret's this morning, because another service was beginning). There was a jam at the Abbey tonight and I was standing behind one of those red cords waiting to be allowed into the center of the church, the sides being full, though there were 50 or more places among those in there. Now none of these are pay seats, such as French churches have in the center, and I don't know why they were roped off. Anyway, as the person directing would discover a seat somewhere he would let somebody in. And as I stood there, 5 men of evident prosperity came up and were shown thru with great courtesy, then I was finally allowed to sit down, and the moderately shabby people were not looked at. Mostly women, they were. There was an atmosphere of fake sentiment and undertaker's grief all thru the service, not a plain formalism, but a sort of smirking sham. Both sermons I heard today were empty and windy and patronizing. The music was not florid,

46

but just mildly sentimental and trashy, no character and no feeling. The Amens were always long and sobby. Nobody in the audience looked devotional, and the priests still less. The crowd acted just about as it would coming out of a rather dull play, neither silent from emotion nor relieved from boredom, but just decently and indifferently sociable.

Beggars are another matter. I never saw any in France or Switz—, or Germany. A good many in Venice. But they just beg, that's all. Enormous number of them here but they've all got a trick. They draw pictures on the sidewalk in colored chalk, they sell booklets or something at trebled prices, and they all (to a man) have signs saying they are ex-soldiers trying to support a wife and three children. Invariably three. I hate them. I think it's a mean way to kid oneself along, or the public either, by bluffs like that. If they want to beg, all right; if they want to play an organ or draw pictures, all right. But if they try to skin you by playing war sympathy or to beg without being beggars, I won't give. Well, so much for all that. The papers are full of talk about religious personages too, bishops and deans and canons, and about meetings and collections but not with any but a snobbish air. I think what I mind most is the collection business. It came today as the climax or important crowning of the services, with much clinking of change and careful watching by the passers to see that nobody was missed, a glorious lifting up at the altar, and finally two men to carry it out in the procession behind the priest as a sort of trophy. Ugh——!!

However, London is pleasant and quite adventurous. I may go to Oxford later on and read a little, or get a bicycle and tour. Going back to Paris about the middle of September, I suppose. Got your letter and many thanks. Only don't tie yourself in with baby all the time. In spite of everything, you must go out a lot and see people and do things. All the more necessary to make the effort now that it is a temptation to stay home and do your duty all the time.

The baby-buggy story is fine. I laugh again and again. Tell me something to bring her or send her from somewhere. I am always being tempted to buy French baby-books. Maybe I'll try one of those lovely little dresses French children wear. If it's too big, she'll grow. And anyway, she'll be nearly 2 years old when I see her next. Write oftener.

Love,
Virgil

To LELAND POOLE

Oxford
[August 1921]

D.O.T.* (who never writes)

Well, old dear, I hate to admit it, but there really is such a thing, I am afraid, as the "Oxford atmosphere." Part of it is age, part of it sheer beauty, and most of it a literal trick of atmosphere, damp, heavy, hazy even in sunshine and altogether giving a diffused illumination, especially in twilight, that makes old stone almost translucent. The English countryside has it too. It is all so quiet, charmed, contemplative. I go about a good deal on my bicycle, but I am really trying to get some work done. I have read a great deal of music and *Tom Jones* (God bless him!) but I haven't been able to get at other work very vigorously. Exercise and read is all I want to do. No morale for composition, either musical or literary, tho I want to get some articles done which I promised the *Boston Transcript* and which I should have written long ago.

Do write me sometime, old stick-in-the-mud. Are you ill, or busy, or in love? I refuse to open my head again in your direction until you respond. That is, of course, unless the spirit moves me.

No. Oxford is very pleasant, and I can imagine loafing here for several years with good profit. But as for me, give me an American college every time. Our rich may be vulgar, but they are seldom idle. And really the undergrad life here is terribly childish, with all their roll-calls and chapels and bed-hours and hazings. I think a man of college age ought to be turned loose. He's old enough to be on his own in such matters. However, Oxford is an excellent institution. No denying that.

Toujours,
Tommie

My house is 400 years old and has a haunted room with a ghost. I am going to sleep there tonight. I have also learned to punt.

---

*Dear Old Thing

South Western Hotel, Southampton
Tuesday, September 14 [1921]

Dear Sister:

I have just finished the English part of my bicycle trip tired but happy and agreeing that a good time was certainly had. I have been to Stratford-on-Avon, Warwick, Worcester, Hereford, Monmouth, the Wye Valley, Tintern Abbey, Chepstow (there is a castle & a Norman church there), Gloucester (where I stayed at a hotel mentioned as excellent in *Tom Jones,* which, by the way, is a magnificent novel—do read it!), Bristol, Bath (beautiful place, I love it), Salisbury, and Winchester. I am disappointed in English cathedrals. They haven't anything of the grace of the French, there is no good glass, and they are terribly mixed-up as to styles. Winchester I do love. It is among the oldest, and the Norman transepts are beautiful, also the effect of length. The towers are all square & in the center of the churches. No good façades like Notre-Dame or Rheims. Only Salisbury has a steeple at all, and that is a poor one. Tintern Abbey (ruins) is beautiful 12th-century Gothic. Bath Abbey (16th-century) has superb fan vaulting. Bristol and Worcester have fine Norman chapter rooms there with interlaced arches. The Worcester one is round with a pillar in the center, so that the ceiling is shaped like the upper crust of a doughnut. Beautiful! Much fine scenery. Wye Valley is green hills & river. Oxford & Warwickshire are quiet and hazy meadows. South country is all downs, too lovely for anything. At Winchester today I lunched at a hotel built in 1052 by the wife of King Canute as a rest house for warriors, where anybody could be safe for a night. It rejoices in the fascinating name of "Ye Old Hostel of God Begot." I am going tomorrow or next day, whenever the boat does, to St. Malo in Brittany. I shall go to Mont-Saint-Michel and Chartres. By the way, do read the book of that title by Henry Adams, which is among my things. It is superb & you will love it.

I have enjoyed being in England and seeing it and all that. Old England is fine. It has flavor. Modern England is rather hard to sense, I think. I fancy the English people are in a state of profound change since the war, and nobody seems to know just what the national mind is like. Just now there is, as with us, enormous unemployment and a sort of truce in the labor & Irish matters—preludes to compromise, I fancy. I am still unreconciled to the English Church. I have attended a dozen services in great churches & small. Invariably the reading is insincere, the sermon routine, & the music unspeakable. Always much rattling of money. I don't think, however, that Church of England people consider their religion seriously at all, as such. I can't find any mysticism or any eagerness, any faith. And I imagine nonconformity is much the same. The English seem to be supported nowadays by animal spirits and an inspired devotion to England. God knows why they need them both, because with the Irish, the taxation, the land redistribution which is bound to come, & all the general remaking of England socially and economically that the war has made necessary, they've got a huge job on their hands.

Someday we shall go to England and Venice together.

Love,

To Ruby Gleason

Paris
February 3, 1922

Dear Sister:

It's really some time since I wrote. I've been back since the 12th of January. I gave Eugene [McCown] my room while I was away, he being about to return from the country, and when I came back I told him to stay on with me, because he was completely broke. Now he has a job. He plays jazz for dancing in a very chic "bar-dancing" and makes about 100 francs a night. So now he pays part of the room and lends me money. Et tout va bien.

I have just recently had an experience. I took the hair off my legs. Eugene told me I was ugly with such a growth on me. So to amuse myself I put some of this depilatory paste on, and now I am white and clean as a baby. I am really quite infatuated with my looks as I take my morning exercises in front of the mirror. But I am depressed at the thought of its all coming back. I am told there is an American preparation that removes hair permanently. Is there? If you know, do tell me about it, or send me some (my expense). I think it's called Zip.

Capri was heavenly. I did lots of work. Wrote four articles and six pieces. Work here goes as usual, the grind of counterpoint a continual bore, but good for me.

Do send me a picture of the baby. Is she pretty? And is the head well-shaped? When will she be old enough for French picture books? She might just as well begin to learn French early.

Much love,

Settled in a small furnished apartment on the rue de Berne, Thomson began his studies with Nadia Boulanger (1887–1979), the French pedagogue who taught counterpoint, harmony, and analysis to many American composers over the course of the next half-century; her pupils ultimately included composers as diverse as Aaron Copland, Roy Harris, David Diamond, and Philip Glass.

A history professor named Bernard Faÿ (1893–1978), who had studied at Harvard, introduced Thomson to many of the important artists, musicians, and men of letters of the time, including Jean Cocteau, Pablo Picasso, and the members of "Les Six," the influential group of French composers that consisted of Georges Auric, Louis Durey, Arthur Honegger, Darius Milhaud, Francis Poulenc, and Germaine Tailleferre. He also grew close to Faÿ's brother Emmanuel (1902?–23), a talented painter who died young.

Throughout this time, Thomson supplemented his compositional activities by submitting critical articles to the *Boston Transcript*. These marked his first publications as a writer. He had already decided that he had no gift for poetry or fiction. "I can describe things and persons, narrate facts," he said many years later. "But I do not assemble my pictures and my people into situations where they take on memorability, which is what storytellers do. Nor can I make a language change its sound or words their meaning, which is the faculty of poets. Language, to me, is merely for telling the truth about something."

To LELAND POOLE

[letter incomplete and undated; clearly from early 1922 in Paris]

... And now that I've explained to you that:

1. I don't read books.
2. I don't do things.
3. I don't see people.

I shall regale you with an account of all these very things.

Found Floyd Dell's *Moon-Calf* dull and quite empty. *The Way of All Flesh* has bad spots, but it's a book to be reckoned with. That is, we can't be as if we hadn't read it. There is a terrible vogue for it here now. It's just been translated and all the young intellectuals, at least Cocteau and his outfit, are mad about it. Butler, Whitman, and Stendhal are their gods at present. I am afraid the Cocteau school are a harvest of leaves, both in music and [in] poetry. Their main public consists of Catholics, homosexuals, and snobs. Glad you read *The*

Idiot. And now don't omit the finest of them all, *The Brothers Kara-mazov*. *The Brothers Karamazov* and *Tom Jones* are the two greatest novels in my experience. Avery Claflin★ says I should add *Le Rouge et [le] noir* of Stendhal, but I haven't read it. Don't omit to read *Three Soldiers* by John Dos Passos. It's bitter; it's one-sided; it's unfair. It's even badly written. But something of the sort wanted doing damn bad.

Do you like *La Valse?* I think it lovely. It may be ephemeral music; all Ravel may. A little over-dainty, a little à la mode. I don't know. Only I find it quite charming. Your piano-playing is a marvel to me. I am sure you play far better than I do, and I envy you the pursuit, because I love playing the piano, tho I don't often like piano-playing.

Was deeply moved by *The Trojans* of Berlioz at the Opéra. In fact, I turned out about two columns for the *Transcript* on the strength of it. *Opéra* is *very* bad here. *Comique* is better but none too good. Orchestral concerts are plentiful but, as might be expected of France, rather routine; tho they play an enormous repertory of classics and modern French stuff, no living Germans or Italians or Englishmen ever get played. German classics thru Wagner, and much Russian and French music. Nothing more. Heard *Rheingold* at Opéra. Terribly disappointed. Most of it I call just plain homely. A Russian conductor, Koussevitzky,† is giving some magnificent concerts now and playing catholic programs. Paris is full of Russian refugees, thank God. Italians have fire and a sense of beauty and the French have finesse, but thank God for the Russians with real ecstasy in their souls.

I have entry thru the Foreign Affairs to everything in Paris (the excuse being that I write articles for the *Transcript,* the fact being that I was properly introduced by Bernard Faÿ). Saw a private performance (the only one to be given) of the German film *Le Cabinet du Docteur Caligari* which was given in America last year. Found it full of ideas. The dadaists pretended to dislike it. But of course they criticize very easily.

I am studying organ, counterpoint, and composition with Mlle. Nadia Boulanger, who is half Russian. Find her an astounding combination of learning and spirit.

Oh dear, I must stop. Write me again about all the things you do. It's nice to know someone who keeps up. It keeps us sort of comple-

---

★Claflin (1898–1979), an American composer and banker, served as Thomson's financial advisor for many years.
†Serge Koussevitzky (1874–1951), who became conductor of the Boston Symphony in 1924, credited Thomson's *Transcript* articles for calling the attention of the orchestra's trustees to his work in Paris. He was a tireless champion of contemporary music.

mentary that way. God, I wish you were in Paris now. Well, another time you will be perhaps.

> Je vous serre bien cordialement la main
> Tommie

To LELAND POOLE

Writing in a restaurant
April 21, 1922

Very Dear Old Thing,

Of course you did write eventually. I have sensed your presence strongly during the last month. Wanted to write often but somehow didn't. Slept late last night. Went to the Concert Koussevitzky at the Opéra and danced till two at Le Boeuf sur le toit. Had a premonition there was some good mail for me. Got out of bed at nine and looked out the door, where I found your letter reposing on my shoes. Carried it back to bed and read it under my red comforter. Such a real letter! The essential Prim. Faithful and passionate and determined. And as usual charmingly sentimental about natural scenery. I like you that way, because I am myself, on occasion, and I have difficulty achieving that necessary naivete about it. I have so many sophisticated inhibitions of speech.

I have finished my lunch, a large one today.

> Radishes and butter
> Shirred eggs
> Sour spinach-like greens called *oseille* [sorrel]
> A banana (to be eaten with a knife and fork)

I am now waiting for my *filtre*.

How the eternal superficialities do intrude themselves upon life. Things like food & sleep & sex and baths & exercise. One is always interrupting some really poignant emotion to go to bed or to lunch. It isn't like dressing for dinner or a party, with the insides quivering. That has its dramatic value. But to have to put aside one's thoughts or whatever may be one's *vraie vie* simply because it's time to go to bed or to go lunch alone is ridiculous. And as I sit here trying to put my impetuous mind into thoughts on language that have some semblance of order—I find myself telling you what I had for lunch. And that I danced last night.

Rather a winter I've had. From my point of view at least, a trifle spectacular. Arrived from England in September. Did society madly (and Paris in general) for two months. Getting rather to work when I packed off to Capri for a month. Wrote some good music. Then came back broke and found Eugene living in my room and destitute. We lived on my last 500 francs and borrowed some more till he got a job. Then he kept me till my quarterly payday arrived. I am afloat now financially, though just barely, till summer, maybe till fall. Eugene is quite prosperous. He plays jazz on the piano nights (10 till 2) at Le Boeuf, which is the rendezvous of Jean Cocteau, Les Six, and les snobs intellectuels—a not unamusing place frequented by English upper-class bohemians, wealthy Americans, French aristocrats, lesbian novelists from Roumania, Spanish princes, fashionable pederasts, modern literary & musical figures, pale and precious young men, and distinguished diplomats towing bright-eyed youths. He plays remarkably well and is the talk as well as the toast of Paris. He paints afternoons and has recently had a sudden access of financial success. Sold some drawings, painted a couple of portraits. Received orders for four or five more. Well, I take my social life vicariously now. Thru Eugene. I almost *never* go out. I practice the organ, do counterpoint and write music. I mostly eat alone and seldom see Gene except mornings. I have written three or four choruses, a few piano pieces, half a dozen organ pieces and some stray opuses of one sort or another. I am doing now a long business in three movements for organ and orchestra. Eugene and another chap and I are halfway planning to spend the summer on the island of Majorca (Very cheap. Villas $5 a month etc.), where he will paint, John★ write a novel, and I orchestrate my symphony.

Don't know about next year. Doctor Davison, on whose account I was coming back to Harvard, has been refused a year's absence. But I, being still an undergrad, am not eligible for a renewal of my fellowship abroad till I go back and graduate. I may have to do that. I may be able to stay on here, however, by one means or another (preferably another). Don't know anything yet. What do you mean about our spending the summer together in New York? Why New York? Shall you be working there? Why not come to me over here? Of course I understand that you were not certain of your plans when you wrote. Do write, right off, tho, and tell me the results of your N.Y. trip and if you could make a trip in the European direction. I also shall let you know of any determining of my financial position. And you spoke of cabling me. I wish you had. I've never received a cable. Do send me one sometime. I'd love it. Really.

Heard some good music. Not too much, tho. Paris orchestras

★John Mosher (1892–1942), an American author described by Thomson as "vastly companionable," was later a film reviewer for *The New Yorker*.

bad. Programs good. Concerts Koussevitzky a glaring exception to the bad playing. *Horace victorieux* of Honegger is thrilling. Heard two great operas: *The Trojans* of Berlioz and *Boris Godunov*. Real musical event was *Pierrot lunaire* of Schoenberg for semi-speaking, semi-singing voice and small orchestra. Fascinating concurrence of noises.

Read a few things of value. The *Satyricon* of Petronius (done in heavenly colloquial French). Henri Lichtenberger on Nietzsche. *Ulysses* of James Joyce (forbidden in America) is out here. Suppose you read his *Portrait of the Artist as a Young Man? Ulysses* is amazing. Style and matter. *Three Soldiers* is a poor book, I suppose; but I like it.

Oh my! All that matters little. We have been not far apart all winter, haven't we? Do make another little gesture in my direction soon. I'll reply.

> A bientôt, j'espère.
> Je te serre tendrement dans les bras.
> Tommie

In the fall of 1922, unable to retain his fellowship, Thomson reluctantly returned to Harvard. There he completed his college degree, continued his work as a church musician, and served as a teaching assistant to Davison and Hill. He also joined the Liberal Club, a Harvard meeting ground for the artistic elite, where he would meet some of his dearest friends.

Most important of these was unquestionably the painter Maurice Grosser (1903–86), who would be Thomson's best friend until his death. His Harvard circle also included the poet, novelist, scholar, idiosyncratic Marxist, and eventual Time correspondent Sherry Mangan (1904–61); and Briggs Buchanan (1904–76), later a distinguished archeologist.

Following his graduation, Thomson, fortified by a grant from the Juilliard Trust, made plans to return to Paris. But he changed his mind and opted for New York, where he studied conducting with Chalmers Clifton (1889–1966) and composition with Rosario Scalero (1870–1954).

Cambridge
September 12 [1922]

Dear Lee,

I am rapidly gathering impressions of America. Naturally I like it better than I thought I should. I am tempted to say "It's a poor thing, but mine own." Only it's not really a poor thing. But its unpleasant qualities annoy me more than similar ones ever would in a foreign country, exactly because it is my own. Instead of being amused at dullness and obstreperousness and waste and disorder, at virtue which is so virtuous that it is completely tamed and at vice so vicious as to be almost inspired, I find myself annoyed and ashamed. I suppose that attitude will pass off. There was an old gentleman on the boat who was returning to America after 25 years of residence in France. I was sitting with him one evening and watching the passengers parade. Mostly young girls and schoolteachers on conducted tours, from the South and Midwest, with padded hair and hair nets, and flat chests and awful throaty or adenoidal voices and empty, discontented faces or empty, satisfied ones. They annoyed me. And I kept thinking, "My God! Are Americans like that? Am I like that? Is that what I was brought up with?" But the old gentleman chuckled and said, just a bit méchant, I thought, "You know, if you look at these people as you would at your companions in a third-class railway carriage, you'll find them thoroughly charming. It's our own snobbery that makes them seem objectionable to us." Of course he's right.

The reason why New Yorkers hate Jews and Southerners hate Negroes and Californians hate Japs is that they sense a rival in every one of them. Now I am not trying to achieve a foreigner's detachment in regard to my own country and people. But I've discovered that since, after all, I'm not competing with anybody in anything, that independence allows me to see with sympathy many aspects of American life which used to annoy me dreadfully, and which still do when I forget my philosophy.

I am sending you a necktie which I bought for you at Doucet Jeune's. I hope you like it. I do. I brought home a good deal of music and many books, including James Joyce's *Ulysses*. That will be a raisin for you to taste when you come east, if raisin is not too small a word for such a juicy fruit-cake. Je t'embrasse.

Toujours,
Tommie

*The following letter refers to the death of young Emmanuel Faÿ.
According to Thomson, Faÿ "took sleeping pills and lay down by an
open window. Found unconscious . . . he was removed to a public
hospital, where, still unconscious, he died of pneumonia."*

To Briggs Buchanan

[New York]
October 26 [1923]

Dear Briggs

There is only one thing to say of Emmanuel's death. That it was a
triumph. And for the last months as he moved eagerly toward it, he
had about him an air of achievement. He became more beautiful and
calm and lucid the last weeks. His conversation was positively lumi-
nous. (*Ceux qui atteignent un salut dans ce monde n'y restent pas long-
temps.**) He had had all the essential experiences and found them
bitter. To live longer would only be a repetition which he didn't care
to face. He was too intelligent to compromise or to forgive the uni-
verse for its essential tragedy. And he saw very well that the only
way to triumph in tragedy is to will it. The French above is from my
letter to Bernard. Please excuse it. I can't come to Cambridge. Can't
afford it. Tacking dangerously close to the wind in money. Will see
what I can do by Thanksgiving.

I await your advent here.

Love,

To Briggs Buchanan

New York
Saturday [December 1923]

Dear Briggs:

The news items are
Boston Symphony is excellent.
[e e cummings's] *Tulips and Chimneys* is worthy of the man who
wrote it. It has so many virtues that I shan't begin to enumerate
them till Christmas. I have been getting such a potent kick from it
that I haven't even been able yet to analyze it all, though it is not a
bit complicated.

---

*"Those who achieve salvation in this world don't stay here long."

The *Tertium Organum* of Ouspensky has been a comfort and a delight. I read in it.

I have commenced my new movement. Sex is a bore. As is proper, I have begun by converting myself. Sincerity on the part of the leaders gives a touching and gracious character to any religion.

The Picasso exhibition is first-rate. Best Picassos I've ever seen. One or two are quite masterpieces. All are fine.

I have a new overcoat. Quite a success. Not paid for.

I have an old man.* He is rich and eighty-nine and lets me practice at his house on the organ. No complications.

The landlady continues devoted. She is really a jewel, though a bit difficult to handle.

I shan't plan anything for Christmas. Nothing exciting in sight. Even Mozart isn't exactly a treat sung by Germans.

Do your *Ulysses*† as if for an ideal audience or publication. I can't do anything with it till it's written. Once done it can easily be adapted to any particular magazine.

I am consoled about Duse‡ by two persons of good taste. Both thought she put on a rotten show.

I am tempted to go to France after Christmas. Would if I had the money.

Love,
Tommie

To Briggs Buchanan

[Summer 1924]

My summer is most agreeable, that is, I have the illusion, so difficult for me to trap in Cambridge, of "being one being living." Not that anything I am doing is tremendously vital or vigorous, or that there is anything noticeably high or noticeably plain about either my living or my thinking. Nevertheless, I am conscious from day to day of a certain very personal and private sentience, which is subject to no *right of search* by any instructor and which involves no obligation to mountebankery for the education of my contemporaries, for indeed the dears have no need of education, being genuinely consecrated to their businesses and their wives and to the happy process of begetting upon them incomes and babies. And this private existence

---

*Elkan Naumberg (1834–1924), musical philanthropist
†possibly a review of Joyce's new book
‡Legendary Italian actress Eleonora Duse (1858–1924) had entered the final phase of her career; she died in Pittsburgh shortly thereafter.

of mine represents a small but growing deposit in a sort of intellectual savings bank, against the rainy days of the mind which December in Paris is likely to bring, or against the next "winter of my discontent" in Cambridge. To be perfectly definite, I do a little of everything except orderly work. And I find that I enjoy myself so. In fact, it is probably my enjoyment of the various agonies of "being one being living" (no less terrible, by the way, for their being savored in moments of repose, as in bathing or picking the feet) which sustains the next illusion: namely, that time passed so pleasantly is surely profitable as well.

I read Cabell's* *Chivalry* with great gusto, and tonight I have been rolling with laughter and approval at his *Beyond Life*. It is the most heavenly intellectual lollipop since Wilde's *Intentions*. Even in Harvard English, if one can imagine it, the book would be a good plate of beans. Done up in Cabell's best, it is a Virginia dinner with champagne. It is rich as plum pudding, nourishing as sirloin, and as fluffy as a piece of sponge cake. It is (God save the pun!) ambrosial. Do read it and report.

Love
Tommie

I am going to the hospital. Monday have my tonsils out. Another experience.

After a season in New York, Thomson returned to Boston, where he once again found work as a teaching assistant. He continued to compose, and regularly submitted articles to the Boston Transcript *and the bright new* Vanity Fair. *He also accepted a weekend post as a church organist in Whitinsville, a family-owned factory town near Worcester. Here he became close to the wealthy Lasell family, whose members included Hildegarde Watson† and Philip Lasell‡ as well as Mrs. Chester Whitin (Jessie) Lasell,§ Hildegarde's mother and Philip's aunt. The family provided Thomson with both financial and moral support during a period of transition. Hildegarde's husband, Sibley Watson, was a patron of* The Dial, *the influential American literary magazine of the 1920s which helped launch the careers of e e cummings and Marianne Moore.*

After leaving his job in Whitinsville, Thomson departed for Eu-

---

*James Branch Cabell (1879–1958), American novelist and critic
†(1888-1976)
‡(1905-87)
§(1863-1950)

rope once again, this time accompanied by a friend from the Harvard Liberal Club, Sherry Mangan.

To Ruby Gleason

[Cambridge]
[Autumn 1924]

Dear Sister:

I sent you a vase over a week ago, but no letter. I got the vase from the Paul Revere pottery. I am well settled in a charming little room that looks like Oxford. I have leaded panes and windows that push out. The building where I live is a sort of unit all in itself. It has lecture rooms, lounge, offices, dormitory, a library, and a chapel. Everything except a dining room. I have breakfast in my room, however. That is, I have it in another man's room, use his stove and electricity and make the mess there. It is much nicer than making it in my room. I am feeling very well indeed and working a great deal. Not overworking or hurrying or getting flustered. But I have a great many things to do. I find more every day. And I have to organize my time pretty carefully in order to keep everything going. I am writing for the *Boston Transcript*. Every week the orchestra plays at least one brand-new piece (first Boston performance) and I have to get hold somewhere of the score, decipher it, and write an advance article with some description and analysis of the piece. I enjoy the score reading, but it takes some time. I have played two Sundays, including today, at the Old Cambridge Baptist Church, for a chap whose mother died. Cambridge is very pleasant now. Wonderful blue weather. I am thinking about writing a book. Not on Cambridge weather. A sort of history of American popular music, including hymns. It would be a great deal of work and I am not decided. I am trying to work up the courage, however. At least I shall do some articles. *Children's Vogue* has asked me for an article on musical education of children. I've promised it for November 15th. I have promised also to edit a book of anthems for Dr. Davison. You see, various odd jobs turn up. Not much money in any of them. But they will help. I live quite frugally and I am contented. I wash my sox and undershirts and sometimes darn, when necessary. I even have time to write music, though not much to practice the piano. Not having a piano in my room is rather a nuisance, though there is one downstairs in the common room. The only other inconvenience I have is gravel walks. I can't get anywhere without getting dust on my shoes. I *hate* gravel walks. Especially in dry weather. I thank you for the cookies. They were delicious. They lasted almost a week. I am going to a lunch party tomorrow for eighty people. I had lunch last Sunday at Mr. Koussevitzsky's home. He is the new conductor. The party tomorrow (which Mrs. Hill* gives at a women's club) is for him and wife, though I don't see what good a party of that size can do.

Love,
Virgil

Much love Betty!†

To BRIGGS BUCHANAN

Kansas City
July 3, 1925

Dear Briggs:

I haven't written you, because I haven't wanted to. Same reason I didn't come to the country with you. I was afraid. You appreciate my difficulty, no doubt. The summer passes. I've been here a month. It's been very hot. I've been enormously bored. Most of the days I spend either in sleep or in a bored kind of reading or in an equally bored sort of meditation. If being amused counts for anything, I am afraid the summer is a total loss. If just plain production is the standard, my showing is a little better.

Here is the accounting sheet to date.

2 articles written and mailed:
One on "The Future of American Music" (contains my point about music being *the* American art and some brand-new material about Negro speech-rhythms)
One on "What the Well-Dressed Mind Will Hear" (rather piffle, I should say. Predicts an *American* season and announces the musical bankruptcy of Europe. Some of it is all right.)

2 articles planned:
One on Modernism vs. Fundamentalism in Music (I am not too enthusiastic over this)
An entire new plan for my hymn-article (this is O.K.)

3 compositions worked on:
New material for the Waltzes

---

*wife of Edward Burlingame Hill
†Thomson's niece

All material perfected for the Chorale, Tango, and Fugue* except the fugue (the most important). That remains a blank in my mind. Just tonight had the glimmer of an idea about it.

Texts chosen for three vocal settings from G. Stein and one of them practically finished. It is also a brand-new idea. Being an esthetic idea, however, it must be observed in action.

That completes the list of real work done. Of real life lived there has been very little. A few sex-adventures which don't count, because they were somehow of no importance. No new people of any consequence encountered. One esthetic experience—a Negro tent-meeting. I learned more about the rhythm of the English language in a half-hour than I had ever known before. Also African scales. You see, the sermon was intoned. And fitted into a regular rhythmic scheme. Basic rhythms (clapping, swatting Bible, jumping) very simple. Complex and syncopated rhythms to fill in the spaces. These determined by language, but sufficiently exaggerated that they are recognizable as interesting apart from the language. The extraordinary thing to me, however, was their aptness to the language. All this in a nice old African "blues" scale, with continual responses from the audience at every pause and breathing-space. Responses adjusted in length, loudness, and tonality to the character of the preacher's "lead." At exciting moments, women would scream in the dominant. Withal, as you may gather, a most interesting spectacle from almost any point of view. Curiously enough, I've not been back, though I still intend to go. Write me a note.

Love,

To Briggs Buchanan

Kansas City, Mo.
August 4, 1925

Dear Briggs

I hope to see you in New York before I sail. I calculate to set out from here about the 20th or 25th of this month. Sail around the 1st Sept.

There isn't much you can do on my journalese from a distance. Either now or later. I should like to have you handy for corrections and for midwifery, but I can't see how either can be accomplished thru the mail.

---

*The piece later became the *Sonata da Chiesa*.

My plan is to go abroad and stay awhile. I shall go to Paris, because that is where people are, especially Nadia [Boulanger]. I like to have her handy. I've no plan or intuition for the future. I shall practice my trade. If I practice it competently, I shall make money. Some, at least. That's all there is to the story. I could do the same anywhere. Except that it's too easy in America. And too uncomfortable. By *easy,* I mean there's no competition, only rivalry. By *uncomfortable,* I mean I'm a misfit. I'm not a vegetable, a salesman, or a joiner. Paris, as such, is bunk. But, my God! So is America. Besides, I want to go to Paris. And there is no reason why I shouldn't. Can't one choose one's bunk? *Ubi bene ibi patria,* says Erasmus; that's that story.

Various activities keep me mostly occupied here. The local prints have published my face and history. The Little Symphony will play the damn Tangos next season. I've rescored them for their combination. My Synthetic Waltzes have progressed to a conclusion. They would orchestrate nicely. Perhaps I shall later. The C. T. and F. [Chorale, Tango, and Fugue] unfolds slowly but surely. I fancy it is for wind instruments, perhaps four saxophones and banjo. That is vague yet. There isn't any description I can give till I see the finished piece. The Stein things also mature slowly, because they are a knotty problem. Wrote an article last night. Will do another soon. Satie died. I've lost my faith in Stravinsky. And jazz (high-brow or low-brow) is a dead art already. The world is blank and lovely like a clean blackboard. My love-sores grow less painful every day. I feel 21 again. Competent and not afraid of anybody. In such a mood, Paris is inevitable. I am writing a philosophic work. *Maxims of a Modernist.* Begun in conversation with G. Phillips about the lovely tomfoolery in Tennessee.★ It was evident that first day that [William Jennings] Bryan, though a wicked man, had a program, and the foolish defense, though right, had none. I am consequently engaged in producing a statement of *radical agnosticism*—to include work, sex, pleasure, art, war, theory of the state, ethics, and so forth. Be a nice boy and write me another letter soon. I reply to yours same day. And say when you'll be in N.Y.

Love,

★The famous "Monkey Trial"; the unnamed defense attorney was Clarence Darrow.

Part Two

MASTERY

(1926–1940)

*O*nce, when asked why he left staid, secure Boston for the economic uncertainty of France, Thomson replied "I prefer to starve
where the food is good."

He moved to Paris in September, 1925, with only a little money
(which was almost immediately exhausted) and his sole livelihood an
occasional opportunity to contribute articles to American magazines.
Still, Thomson never starved, for he made friends and cultivated
patrons. Moreover, Paris was cheap.

"It was not that America was not in the long run rewarding,"
Thomson later explained. "It was simply that our country was a
trap. Earning enough to live there was not impossible, but earning
enough *not* to live there was. Income and costs seemed always to
come out even, and the results of money spent lacked surplus value.
In France the shabbiest secondhand chair or stool could still be sold
again. And living, loving, dining would create an afterglow,
whereas at home whatever happened seemed to leave either a bad
taste or none at all. Which is what led Maurice Grosser to discover
that 'France is a rich country and America a poor one'; and indeed
that was so in the days when business figures read the other way. In
terms of just plain feeling good, France was in those days, even for
the poor, the richest life an artist ever knew.

"I was leaving a career that was beginning to enclose me," he
wrote in his autobiography. "I was leaving also an America that was
beginning to enclose us all, at least those among us who needed to
ripen unpushed. America was impatient with us, trying always to
take us in hand and make us a success, or else squeezing us dry for

67

exhibiting in an institution. America loved art but suspected distinction, stripped it off you every day for your own good. In Paris even the police were kind to artists. As Gertrude Stein was to observe, 'It was not so much what France gave you as what she did not take away.'"

Thomson made Paris his home until 1940, although he returned to the United States on several occasions. During this time, he was at the core of an ever-growing and ever-changing circle which included many of the distinguished friends he had made on his first Parisian jaunt, plus a host of others. Among the artists were the Dutch painter Kristians Tonny (b. 1906), the expatriate Russians Eugene ("Genia") Berman (1899–1972) and Pavel ("Pavlik") Tchelitcheff (1898-1957), the Frenchmen Christian ("Bébé") Bérard (1902-49), Jean Arp (1887-1966) and Marcel Duchamp (1887-1968), and the sculptor Jo Davidson (1883-1952).

His writer friends and acquaintances included Janet Flanner, Robert McAlmon, Mary Butts, James Joyce (1882-1941), Georges Hugnet (1906-74), Ezra Pound (1885-1972), and Max Jacob (1872-1944) while Thomson's musical orbit encompassed George Antheil, Theodore Chanler, Henri Sauguet, Vittorio Rieti, Igor Markevitch, Paul Bowles, and the Scottish soprano Mary Garden (1877-1967), whose musical and dramatic gifts Thomson greatly admired. Other friends included the architecture scholar Henry-Russell Hitchcock, the art collector and bookbinder Mary Reynolds, and the publisher and bookstore owner Sylvia Beach (1887-1962). It was, as a later historian would observe, "a charmed circle."

Sherry Mangan stayed on through the years, eventually becoming a foreign correspondent. In addition, Thomson was frequently visited by friends from America, including Maurice Grosser, who first came to Paris sponsored by a Harvard fellowship similar to the one Thomson had enjoyed. And he came to know a representative of a younger Harvard, Lincoln Kirstein (b. 1907), then a poet and editor, later an impresario and, with George Balanchine, a founder of the New York City Ballet.

But his most important artistic association was the one he developed with Gertrude Stein (1874–1946) who, like Thomson and many of his Parisian friends, was an American expatriate. He had been introduced to her work during his student days; after their first meeting, he would remark that they got on "like Harvard men."

Thomson's first settings of Stein poetry included Susie Asado, Preciosilla, and Capital Capitals. "My hope in putting Gertrude Stein to music had been to break, crack open and solve for all time anything still waiting to be solved, which was almost everything, about English musical declamation," Thomson said.

My theory was that if a text is set correctly for the sound of it, the meaning will take care of itself. And the Stein texts, for prosodizing in this way, were manna. With meanings already abstracted, or absent, or so multiplied that choice among them was impossible, there was no temptation toward tonal illustration, say, of birdie babbling by the brook or heavy heavy hangs my heart. You could make a setting for sound and syntax only, then add, if needed, an accompaniment equally functional. I had no sooner put to music after this recipe one short Stein text than I knew I had opened a door.

Eventually Thomson and Stein collaborated on an opera, *Four Saints in Three Acts,* completed in 1928. Despite the title, it boasted four acts and more than thirty saints. Thomson set every word that Stein gave him, stage directions and all, to strongly rhythmic, primarily diatonic music.

Six years elapsed before the opera was first performed—in 1934 at the Wadsworth Atheneum in Hartford, under the direction of a group called The Friends and Enemies of Modern Music—but the premiere was a sensation and firmly established Thomson's fame. His influence on the production, which moved to New York and Chicago after its run in Hartford, was everywhere apparent: he decreed that the entire cast should be composed of black singers; he enlisted the inexperienced John Houseman to direct; he imported a young, little-known choreographer from London, Frederick Ashton, and to design the sets and costumes he selected an obscure painter, Florine Stettheimer (1871-1944), who did the whole thing up in cellophane. *Four Saints* was an immediate *succès de scandale;* although the critical response was mixed, everybody who cared about theater, music, literature, or choreography had to see it and form an opinion.

Through 1940, Thomson worked on a variety of commissions and collaborations, including the film scores *The Plough That Broke the Plains* and *The River* (1936 and 1937, both with Pare Lorentz); the ballet *Filling Station* (1938), with a book by Lincoln Kirstein and choreography by Lew Christensen (1909–84); some chamber and symphonic works; and a series of musical portraits (inspired, in part, by Stein's literary exercises in this medium) whereby friends and acquaintances would sit for Thomson while he, with only pencil and paper, would attempt to capture their essence in music.

After a hiatus, Thomson continued his work as a critic, submitting a number of articles requested by the influential quarterly *Modern Music,* edited by Minna Lederman (b. 1898). In 1939, he published his first book, a still-amusing, still-relevant, and still-controversial examination of music as an art and as a business, aptly titled *The State of Music*. And finally, in 1940, unwilling to remain in France under the German occupation, he returned to America by way of Spain and Portugal.

Back now to the mid-1920s, when Thomson, a struggling, as yet largely unrecognized but by no means unhappy composer, had settled once again in a small Paris apartment.

Shortly after returning to Paris, Thomson became close friends with George Antheil (1900–59), then a celebrated ultramodernist composer, whose works grew increasingly conservative in his later life, whereupon his fame dwindled. Thomson also resumed his studies with Nadia Boulanger, but on a less frequent and rather less enthusiastic basis. Under her tutelage, he completed one of his finest early works, the *Sonata da Chiesa*, which received its premiere at a special concert arranged in part by Boulanger. The program included the works of six American composers, the others being Antheil, Theodore Chanler, Aaron Copland, Herbert Elwell, and Walter Piston. The event was attended by the artistic and social elite of Paris, as the following letter, written during a brief vacation, vividly relates.

To BRIGGS BUCHANAN

[May 1926]
[beginning of letter missing]

As specific account of the American concert, let us proceed in order.

1) The audience was distinguished.

French music was represented by N. Boulanger, Florent Schmitt, Louis Aubert, Albert Roussel, and others.

Society as mentioned on the program.

American music (not on the program) by George Foote, W[alter] Damrosch, E[dmund] Pendleton, Roger Sessions, Blair Fairchild.

American crit. and intell. by Pierre Loving, Gilbert Seldes, Ludwig Lewisohn.

American diplomacy by the military attaché, tone-deaf, but serious in the performance of his assignment.

James Joyce also appeared. He never goes out.

2) The performances were uniformly excellent.

3) The program was impressive, though long and tiresome. (Six first auditions are too much.) The most impressive work (by number of players engaged, novelty of form, and strangeness of noises produced) was the *Sonate d'église* [*Sonata da Chiesa*] of V. Thomson. Second in importance on the program (though, in my opinion, not inferior in quality, probably even superior) was the String Quartet of George Antheil. The other works, more modest in pretension, less well realized in style, but all genuinely musical in conception and not bad to listen to, were distinguished by the 2nd mov't of Chanler's Violin Sonata, which is a real piece.

The *Sonate d'église* contains a novel and quite successful 1st mov't, notable for its melodic material and its extraordinarily curious blended sonorities, particularly for the *logicité* of its harmonic style. In fact, it sounds like nothing else on earth.

The 2nd mov't (which isn't a real tango at all) comes off as it should. It is the popular success. It is all right.

The fugue, though most admired by the general listener, is in the author's opinion the least satisfactory. A more melodic and less symmetrical development of the 1st subject would have made a more living organization. Also the clarification of the harmony at more frequent intervals would give it a repose which it lacks. On the other hand, the instrumentation is such that the dumbest layman follows the fugal development with ease and pleasure; the attention is held. The piece is gay and lively.

In general one may say that, leaving out about two ill-advised experiments, the instrumentation is unquestionably a knockout. The chorale is a genuine new idea, the other movements decently satisfactory. The faults are a dangerous rigidity of rhythmic texture (especially in the chorale), an excessively contrapuntal style in the fugue, and an immature comprehension of the profundities of classic form. The work manifests, however, a mind of great strength and originality. The public awaits (or ought to) with eagerness Mr. Thomson's next work, a symphony in the form of variations on an American hymn tune.

[Later]
Personal items:
I moved back to Paris the 1st of April. Maurice went to Italy. I have been flat broke, but not especially discouraged. I continue my resolution to do no manner of profitable drudgery. People lend me money. A few give it. I live economically. Maurice came back 1st of May. He has taken for the summer a studio on the French Riviera; wants me to join him. I may. I shan't leave Paris before June 15th or

20th, however. I search for a patron. Some prospects, but no cash yet.

Retrospection of the winter:

Great progress in tranquillity. Consequently in expression. Great satisfaction (spite of weather, poverty, and mishaps) with Paris as a place of residence. For the present I shall remain. I do well here. Elsewhere in Europe I should feel lonely. In America I should go mad.

Personal relations:

Nadia has been excellent, though of personal rather than musical utility. She insists that I have greater possibilities than I give myself credit for, that I am a real composer. But frankly she doesn't understand me. She only recognizes, which after all is a lot.

Gertrude Stein has been impressive and unconsciously encouraging. She takes for granted so many of the same things that I do.

Maurice has been pleasant in domestic affection. Mental intimacy impossible, however.

Antheil has been the chief event. For the first time in history, another musician liked my music. For the first time since I left your society, somebody said hello. Somebody recognized what I was all about. Or recognized that I was about something worth looking at.

Imagine my gratitude.

More particularly since this support and admiration came from the finest composer of our generation (of this there isn't any doubt) and was supported by deeds. I must admit that the encouragement has been mutual, that the contact has bucked up George just as much as me, perhaps more. The point remains. Antheil is the chief event of my winter. He has admired me, he has quarreled with me about theories, he has criticized my pieces, he has consulted me about his, he has defended me to my enemies, to his enemies, to my friends, to his friends. He has forced my acceptance by people who intuitively feared me, notably Mrs. Antheil and Sylvia Beach. He has talked, wined, and drunk me by the hour. He has lodged me and fed me and given me money. At this very instant he is trying to persuade a rich lady to give money to me instead of to him, although he is perfectly poor himself.

Sherry was sweet but insistent.

Teddy Chanler lent me an apartment.

Hildegarde Watson sent me $100.

And now for you.

Your letters have a confidence that is in every way pleasing. Progress is evident. Be quiet, but make no concessions. You are marvellous. It may take a year or so. Maybe longer still. No matter. You'll find it if you keep still. Don't even let them know you are looking for anything. They can be very dangerous if they suspect. You'd have to jump the country, as I did, if they found out. It is well I am not with you. I should disturb you, compromise you, make demands.

Later, when you have found it, I shall join you. Naturally, if you should need any help—advice, refuge, even money—you will ask me for it. I have been so clumsy always about forcing myself on you that I prefer now to sit back and wait. After all, you know by this time that I am there. And what a pleasure, what an assurance, to hear from time to time that you are too!

Love always,

To HILDEGARDE WATSON

May 6, 1926

Dear Hildegarde:

You are an angel without disguise. Never was message so welcome. Never was impudence so graciously rebuked and forgiven. I am your debtor for life. My gratitude is exuberant. It wants to shout. Also sing. In fact, I am sending you some vocal noises by another post.* They may delay a few days or even a week because I have some copying to do before I can send them. I shall include explanation of how the noises are made, because they don't read like plain musical notation. However, they will arrive shortly, and you can divert yourself with them. They are really nice to sing. I enclose a program of last night's concert. It was apparently a grand success. Lots of important musical people there. I had the honor of having my piece whistled at. The program was really an impressive collection of good pieces by competent composers. By all odds the best were George Antheil's quartet and my sonata. But everything was of some real interest. (How often has one slunk away from "American music" evenings, blushing, embarrassed, and furious!) There aren't any six French youngsters in France who could turn out as good a show. If you had heard the concerts of works by Georges Auric and Francis Poulenc (11 princesses present) you would have been doubly impressed with ours and grateful.

Write to me.
Long devoted,

---

*"Five Phrases from *The Song of Solomon*" for soprano and percussion.

Paris
May 30, 1926

Dear Alice,

My Church Sonata has had rather a *succès de scandale*. Musicians, Catholics, and atheists were pleased. The unbelieving were shocked. My symphony has been postponed until next season because I have been ill. Not really ill. I never am. But unable to work. I am also invited to give a concert of sacred works next year in a church, including the Sonata and a Mass for men's voices, with a religious service to add tone. It would be a Benediction or a Salut in the evening. I am afraid to try having a real Mass, because the proper audience wouldn't come to a morning affair. I am learning just now to play a pianola. One of my friends, George Antheil, is giving a concert of his works next month, including a *Mechanical Ballet*, with xylophones, drums, electric bells, and airplane motors for the orchestra. I am to play the pianos. There are sixteen all coupled together. We are having difficulty with the coupling mechanism. If it doesn't work out right, we will use one piano with an amplifier. My job is to pump hard enough so that even when a great many notes are sounding at once, there will be enough wind to make a loud noise. Also I have to make the clumsy thing follow a conductor. Weather is lovely. Six thousand Americans arrive every day. Cherries are marvelous. When are you coming over? Finances go from bad to awful. A Jewish gentleman remarked the other day that the least a work of art could do was pay its way. Whereupon Mr. Ezra Pound, in best New York accent, "What price the psalms of David?"

Love,

In the summer of 1926, Thomson took a vacation at Thonon-les-Bains, near Evian, where he wrote music and rowed on Lake Geneva. During this trip he met Louise (Mme Jean–Paul) Langlois (1856–1939), a Frenchwoman some forty years his senior, who became, in Thomson's words, "my close companion for thirteen years (not mistress, nor pseudomother, but true woman friend ever jealous and ever rewarding) till her death at eighty-three on the eve of World War II."

To Ruby Gleason

Thonon-les-Bains
Haute Savoie
August 15 [1926]

Dear Sister,

I am delighted with the place I am at. I have mountains and lake and sunshine and cold nights. It is reputed to be (the borders of Lake Geneva, I mean) the most sedative climate in Europe. Certainly it is the most sedative place I've been to since Bar Harbor. I feel marvellous every minute. I work every day quietly and quickly and without getting excited. When I don't work I sit still in a chair and just let my mind run down. Or wind up. I'm not sure just what it is that happens. But it is the same thing that Mother does when she sits on the front porch. Around noon I always take off my clothes and have a little nap in the sun. I am utterly contented. There are some French families at the hotel whom I talk to sometimes in the evening, or make music with. Otherwise, I don't know a soul. Haven't heard the American language since I left Paris. Rather pleasant that. If you could see and hear the perfectly unbelievable Americans who come to Paris in July, you would blush. The English and the Germans are just as funny. But there aren't so many of them. And besides, they are not us. I haven't had any letter from you for a long time. I suppose you have your dress by now. I hope you can wear it. Today being Sunday, there was a celebration. The Fête des Cyclamens. With a parade of floats made out of flowers and a so-called Battle of Flowers. Meaning that everybody threw flowers about like confetti or little cotton balls. I am waiting to go down to dinner. I have a large and pleasant appetite all day and eat two six-course meals besides morning chocolate and usually pastry in the afternoon. I eat about eight usually in the evening, on a porch which looks over the lake from a high cliff. Sunset with dinner. Sit around a little or make music, and go to bed at ten. You would love it here. And Betty would have adorable children to play with.

Love,

To Gertrude Stein

December 2 [1926]

Dear Miss Stein

I've heard nothing of you since the summer. Are you in Paris? And may I come to see you sometime soon? I don't go out much lately. Have seen none of your friends for news of you.

Very sincerely,

Philip Lasell came to join Thomson in Paris in 1926, living for a time in the room next to him. It was through Lasell, whom he once described as a "playboy of wondrous charm," that Thomson came to know the writer Mary Butts (1892–1937), who became his girlfriend for some time.

To Briggs Buchanan

Paris
Monday, December 27, 1926

Dear Briggs

Such a nice Christmas! Much food and gaiety. And parties. Two great dinners, great rowdy family affairs with punch and champagne and children and movies in the dining room of Charlie Chaplin (*Easy Street* and such classics) and turkeys from Lyon as big as sheep and plum puddings from London and mince pies from a swell Negro restaurant. And an egg-nog party in the afternoon. A Xmas Eve tea with Bernard [Faÿ] and Sherwood Anderson. A Xmas Eve party at Gertrude Stein's with carols and a tree and a great Xmas cake with ribbon and candles on it. A dance Xmas night with the hard-drinking artist set. And so to bed. Alone. Excepting for the Xmas celebrations, now finished and slept off, no excitements, no emotion, no drama, no vice. No artists, no snobs, and no thrills. Not even people. My old French lady (whom I love, but who gets emotional about me) safely deposited in Africa. Philip (whom I love, but who has lived for three months now on my vitality) satisfactorily finished off by a sort of ethereal Proustian quarrel (a marvellous quarrel conducted with the greatest dignity on both sides and the nearest to an open display of affection that we have ever allowed ourselves. A sort of tearful but indignant graduating exercise, Philip

76

be hard towards the institution he was so fond of, and the best he could achieve being to offer me his ten Picassos from which he has never been separated more than three days since he bought them in 1923). Well, finished off that and Philip gone south. George Antheil still away, Budapest now, I think, relieves me of the duty of admiring publicly work I don't really approve, simply because dumbbells sneer at it for the wrong reason, and the still more difficult situation of what to say to the gushers! All life is good now. Nothing exigent. Only simple behaving and quiet working, and no thinking to speak of.

Love

Thomson and Stein conceived the idea of writing an opera together in early 1927. "Naturally the theme had to be one that interested us both," Thomson later explained. "Something from the lives of the saints was my proposal; that it should take place in Spain was hers. She then chose (and I agreed) two Spanish saints, Teresa of Avila and Ignatius Loyola. The fact that these two never knew each other did not seem to either of us an inconvenience." From these beginnings grew Four Saints in Three Acts.

To Gertrude Stein

Paris
[undated]

Dear Gertrude

I shall be delighted to come on Wednesday. Reading lately in encyclopedia about saints. Teresa & Ignatius Loyola might make a good Spanish pair. I fancy best plan would be fictitious names, using as much of real character and history as suits the needs, but avoiding the pretense of historical drama.

Love

To Briggs Buchanan

[Paris]
March 4, 1927

Dear Briggs

There isn't much news. Mardi Gras day before yesterday was fun. Especially the Bal des Tapettes at the Magic City. Men in women's clothes, women in men's clothes, women got up to look like men in women's clothes, vice versa, all possible deceptions and ambiguities about the sexes. And all very polite and gentle, even genteel. Spring weather is in the air. And tiny green beans at the restaurants. And salads of watercress. And dandelions. And baby lamb. And potatoes as big as your fingernail. Went to the opera the other day to see *Rosenkavalier*. It's a rather swell piece. Antheil is in New York. Some kind of a bang-up show for him in Carnegie Hall. There is talk of publishing some of my [musical] versions of Gertrude Stein in *transition*, a new review. Ezra [Pound]'s review has not appeared yet, due shortly. I wonder what is happening in New York. One gathers that a so-called American opera★ by somebody whose name is vaguely familiar has been well advertised. That Ernest Hemingway's last book was a best-seller.† That vice is on the rampage again. And that a number of one's good friends are too busy to write letters. Do go to the Antheil show and tell me what you thought of it and what happened there.

Greetings and all

To George Antheil

[Paris]
Monday, March 13 [1927]

Dear George

The concert was nice. I like the new pieces. In particular, the coda of the suite and the first movement of the concerto. Mr. Lazarus'‡ Scherzo was dead as a doornail. But so very loud and noisy that half the dumbbells in the audience thought it was the Antheil piece. The

---

★Possibly *The King's Henchman* by Deems Taylor (1885–1966) who was also a music critic and later a radio commentator.
†*The Sun Also Rises*
‡Daniel Lazarus (1898–1964), French composer and conductor

little Golschmann* played well. The big one conducted as usual. The audience was small but fairly select. And agreeably enthusiastic. No scandal, of course. Everything went off with a complete respectability. I doubt if more than a half a dozen people there got anything out of the suite. It fooled them. They were still expecting noise and fury from you. Never mind. It's the right thing. You are going to have some trouble from now on living down Ezra's advertising. That you might some day write quiet music was an exigency that he didn't foresee. That's all right. The new pieces are good. Rather better than the old, perhaps. And as I said, in the coda of the suite and the 1st mov't of the concerto, something really happens.

Have a good time in N.Y. Knock 'em dead, if necessary. Think of me now and then. And come home with all the money you can lay hands on.

Love Böske† and love George and love Böske and George

To Briggs Buchanan

Paris
March 15, 1927

Dear Briggs

Now wouldn't you just love to trick me into a good bang-up quarrel in the old style? Well, let that pass. Maybe it's my own instinct for such a show that makes me suspect. As you observe, it can't be done by mail. And as I reflect, thank God we are not close enough to try it in the flesh. I have a little money. Philip gave it. Again. I am going away to the country at the end of the month. For some weeks. Probably Pau, in the Pyrenees. Philip wants me to come to Vence, where he stays, near Nice and Cannes and Monte Carlo. But I don't like to see him too much. He fatigues me. Like anybody with whom one ought to make love but doesn't. He and Mary Butts have become great pals. She's a good gal. I like her myself. Of culture news there is not much precise. A good deal is vaguely stirring. The apparent future of painting lies with a Russian, Pavel Tchelitcheff, and a Frenchman, Christian Bérard. Both around 27 years old. Picasso, from lack of competition, has become a public monument. One by one, his rivals have faded to obscurity. Matisse,

*Boris Golschmann (1906–43), a pianist; younger brother of the conductor Vladimir Golschmann (1893–1972)
†Antheil's wife

Derain, Braque, Picabia. (Juan Gris, "the perfect painter," remains just that.) Music is carried on by me and George Antheil. (Stravinsky shares Picasso's fate, with Satie dead and Germany not a serious rival, even in New York.) Letters remain in the older generation, because there are still two figures to make a polarity. No youngster can do anything till something happens to either Gertrude Stein or James Joyce. And I doubt if anything will, short of either's death. They are strong because they don't do each other's stuff. Gertrude is occupied with composition; Joyce with reporting.

Bérard, Joyce, and Antheil stand for representation, depiction, emotion, the "true to life" effect. Their shapes are borrowed. Tchelitcheff and Gertrude and I represent play, construction, interest centered in the material, nonsense, magic, and automatic writing. The issue is clear. Between knowledge and wisdom. Between the tabloid newspaper and Mother Goose. Between culture and anarchy. The law and the prophets. Kant and Spinoza. Duty and pleasure. The stage and the home.

America, naturally, is active. England out of the picture. France the battleground. The rest send recruits. Save Germany, who is extremely occupied with herself, though unable to deal in international values. Cocteau is about. At his usual work of ruining young artists. Having safely finished off the Six, damaged (but temporarily) Picasso (I mean the fat lady period), he is at present doing an *Oedipus* with Stravinsky (for Ballets Russes) and preparing the premature exploitation of Christian Bérard (from whom his late exposition of pictures and such was principally stolen). Pound and Eliot remain respectively 2nd- and 3rd-rate poets and 3rd- and 2nd-rate editors. Ezra's magazine *Exile* is pretty dumb. *transition* has appeared with 1st installment of the new Joyce. It turns out to be like *Ulysses* only more so. This time a parody on the Bible. A French youngster, Henri Sauguet,* writes truly elegant music. Vittorio Rieti† writes fresh and brilliant music. An American named Roy Harris‡ writes sound and honest same. Sherry Mangan's magazine (called *larus the celestial visitor*) is the most beautiful piece of modern printing that (to my knowledge) exists. The contents are gay and unpretentious, distinctly pleasant. Though anything—the *Philadelphia Ledger,* a Boston Symphony program, the Harvard *Advocate*—would be beautiful in such a format. I repose in bed of a cold with sore throat. Don't

---

*(b. 1901), French neo-romantic composer

†(b. 1898), Italian neo-classical composer of Egyptian birth, long resident in the United States

‡(1898–1979), American composer who adopted a deliberate nationalism in his symphonies

forget to send me dope on the Antheil show in New York. And more tabloids from time to time. They please me.

Love and what the hell

To George Antheil

March 22 [1927]

Dear George

Just a word. Things sink into the mind slowly. Now, ten days after your concert, I know more than I did then. It is the little suite that remains in my mind. It is the expression of something very real in you, and consequently it is beautiful. People are dumb. They don't see it. But no matter. It is authentic. It is the beginning of something that will grow. I have every day a stronger sense of its being a real presence. You were right when you predicted I would like it.

Love

In the summer, Thomson was joined in Paris by Jessie Lasell and her teenage granddaughter; the three planned to motor through Brittany and Normandy.

However, as Thomson recalled, "it turned into a two-months' caring-for-the-sick when Mrs. Lasell came down in Rouen with an ear infection. By good luck, and through my friendship with Madame Langlois, I was able to command, in August, out-of-town and out-of-season visits from a first-class otolaryngologist. When eventually the mastoiditis had been cleared up without surgery, Mrs. Lasell was grateful, became for several years my patron."

To Briggs Buchanan

Rouen
July 17, 1927

Dear Briggs

Some time since I wrote you a gossip letter. Well, this isn't one. I am here with Philip's aunt who is ill. We started to motor Normandy and she came down with a bad ear abscess. I loaf and take granddaughter aged fourteen to see churches. I have a room with bath and the food is swell, but I'd rather be in Paris. I repose, and assume what masculine responsibilities arrive.

The Paris season ended rather brilliantly. For me at least. No, for everybody. Stravinsky's *Oedipus Rex* turned out to be the mature masterwork one expected. Sauguet's ballet *La Chatte* was simple, unpretentious, and quite genuine. No false notes. Sounds like Bizet. Damn good. My *Capital Capitals* has created considerable curiosity. Given privately at the house of the Duchesse de Clermont-Tonnerre. Great costume ball. At midnight *divertissement artistique*, namely the *Capitals*. Four men and a piano. Text by Gertrude Stein. Time twenty minutes flat. All singing antiphonal. Never sing together. Not a sacred work but sounds sort of so. Seems to remind everyone of what he heard in childhood.

Fania Marinoff*—Jewish synagogue

Miguel Covarrubias†—Mexican church

Mary Butts—Greek chants

Jean Cocteau—Catholic liturgy

Edward Ashcroft‡—Gilbert and Sullivan patter.

Since its performance there has been a stream of visitors to my door, including the above, for purposes of hearing said work and others. All French people at the duchesse's. More dukes than you could see for the ambassadors. Not the Princesse crowd. Cocteau came to see me more or less as their representative, I presume. His comment on my music was "At last a table that stands on four legs, a door that really opens and shuts." The French who know no English all exclaim "What an extraordinary sense of English prosody!" I suppose they mean that it is English that sounds like English. Opera text all done. I have begun the music. Christian Bérard (new French Picasso, discovery of Cocteau) will do the scenery. (My and Gertrude's choice, not Cocteau's.)

Sentimental life vaguely melodramatic and semi-frustrated, as always. I'm getting used to that too. I do a good deal of quarreling with Mary Butts. I won't quarrel finally, because she is a person of too great value. Because she is very dear to Philip. And because she is able to uncover certain wells of tenderness and of emotivity in general which have been closed for some years in me. There are also

---

*Actress, wife of critic and author Carl Van Vechten (1880–1964)
†Mexican painter and folklorist (1904–57)
‡English poet

some nice sweet people (real ones) whom I love as comrades or something. There is Madame Langlois, my old French lady. There is Edward Ashcroft, English and Italian by birth, French poet by calling. There is Eric de Haulleville, Belgian by birth, a real poet. There is Sauguet. There is Gertrude. There is Bébé Bérard. There is even Cocteau, a little. At home, there are you and Sherry. As I began to observe a little time ago, a new generation exists. Cocteau says it became possible about the middle of January. No one knows why, but it suddenly did. (I have a whole theory. Ask me sometime.) Mary says, "The good chaps are beginning to get together again." Anyway, six or a dozen people have suddenly begun to function. Poor Antheil (I am sorry) is not among them. Since his New York trip, he has been too sad to bear. He doesn't know what to write next or how to write it. We can only wait and see. He is undergoing the middle-twenties change of life. I feel ashamed of not having seen more of him and been nice. But I was very occupied with the *Capitals* performance and he didn't come around much and I didn't have the guts to seek out the sorrowful.

This has turned out to be something of a gossip letter. At least about me. Let me know something when you get around to it.

As you know I love you always. Not that that is any damn business of yours. But you know. "Private bell"* and such.

In any case.

Love

In the autumn of 1927, Thomson moved into a studio at 17, quai Voltaire, which would become his Paris residence for the next fifty years. "The quai Voltaire is a row of eighteenth-century houses standing between the rue des Saints-Pères and the rue du Bac and looking across the Seine to the Louvre," Thomson wrote in his autobiography.

Just above it sits the seventeenth-century Institut de France, arms open like a miniature Saint Peter's for receiving daily its college of lay cardinals, the forty "immortals" of l'Académie Française. A further short walk upstream brings the medieval world—the Conciergerie, Sainte-Chapelle, and Notre-Dame. Downstream one passes the 1900 Gare d'Orsay and the eighteenth-century Hôtel de Salm (Palais de la Légion d'Honneur) and looks across to the Tuileries Gardens before arriving at the

---

*The poet Tristan Tzara (1896–1963), a leading figure in the Dada movement, said that art was a "private bell for inexplicable needs."

Chamber of Deputies and Place de la Concorde, both dominating
from on high excellent swimming-baths that sit in the Seine with-
out using its water. The situation could not be more central or
more historical.

To Briggs Buchanan

Provins
November 2, 1927

Dear Briggs

I've wanted very badly in these last weeks to write to you, but I haven't because I wanted you too badly. There was nothing really to say except that I was miserable. A dozen reasons for it. Lost my baggage. Cold on the chest ever since I arrived. Couldn't work. Missed two articles. Paris cold and damp. Rain rain. No heat. No satisfactory dwelling. No piano. And besides, after three years of America, I had to get a certain amount of vice off my system— never a cheerful procedure. Came down here to spend a few quiet days in a warm provincial hotel. Since then I've been industrious and cheerful. Rainy weather and heated room, sore throat and weary nerves, sleep, work, and country meals are more pleasant indoors than local sightseeing out. Spite of tenth-century towers and twelfth-century churches. I have soiled great quantities of music paper, written letters, eaten food and reposed in solitude. Tomorrow I go back to Paris. My cold is some better. My house will be heated. Baggage and money are still short, but my depression is so much lifted that perhaps I shall eventually write an article or so. In any case, I rather plan to spend my last hundred dollars (if it arrives) on a trip to Vienna in December. The lost trunk contained dress clothes, suit and a half of day clothes, 2 overcoats, raincoat, shoes, manuscripts. I shall probably never see them. Steamship company's fault, however, mostly. Work under construction. The last few days have started the well to flowing again. Feel infinitely better, as always when I can work. Think I shall go away somewhere every week for a few days. Costs no more than eating in Paris. (Here a heated room is 10 francs, eight-course meals with wine, 9 francs. 1 franc = 4½ cents) Now that my crisis is over, everything is all right. Nothing matters but to sit quiet and work. And for the moment I don't want to do anything else. If I get all involved again and unhappy and everything, I may not have the sense to keep still. Any time you get a tragedy letter from me like the one I so nearly wrote last week, just send me a cable saying to shut my damn mouth and quit bellyaching. The cable will be a certain consolation (to know someone would go to the trouble), and the message should have its effect.

Write of your state and doings. Are you working? What at? How do you like it? Any time you want to visit me I'll house and feed you for the pleasure of your company. Get you a job if you want it.

Paris is pretty dull. I think it's going to be an awful season. If anything happens in America, write me of it. It's a dull winter everywhere, I presume. 1920 is finally *démodé* and there is nothing to take its place. *Surréalisme* has not been as fecund as one hoped. Everyone has gone out hunting for an idea. [André] Gide has gone to Africa, Stravinsky (at last) to Russia. I, for one, welcome a dull season. I shall probably work from ennui. Nadia and I are engaged in a search for my character. With usual clairvoyance she comes right to the point at the second interview. "In spite of the fact," she says, "that I am acquainted with you as a talented musician, a charming person, and an incredibly intelligent young man, I have the feeling of not knowing you at all inside." Imagine the effect of that on an already turbulent and unhappy mind. I came home and wrote fugues for three hours, and today I started a symphony. If I only had your clarifying presence, I should likely write an article.

Love

To Ruby Gleason

[Paris]
[undated]

Dear Sister,

I got home yesterday and found the package. I love them. The handkerchief is beautiful. I am delighted. I am skeptical, however, about what my laundress will do to the fringe. I suppose I can send them to my stiff-and-silk-shirt laundress. She will be careful, anyway. And what happens to the color? Tell me before I have them washed. My good laundress is really very nice about colors, but yellow is the most difficult of all. I had a nice Christmas party and marvellous food. Stand-up-and-walk-around supper for twelve people. There was pâté de foie gras and a green mixed salad of mâche and beets and celery and peeled walnuts and a Stilton cheese soaked for a week in port wine and the most marvellous chicken in the world and plum pudding burning in rum and good champagne to drink and Swedish bread and also tiny fluffy rolls that taste like cake.

The chicken was really two chickens, big fat white ones with sliced truffles put between the skin and the meat and the chickens cut into nice pieces and then put together again to look like one large one with four wings and surrounded by little round jellies of a chopped vegetable salad in mayonnaise and the whole thing covered with transparent brown jelly. It was too beautiful for anything and heavenly to eat. I didn't know it would be so nice. I just ordered a cold chicken because I thought the pâté might be a little short. But they sent me that and it became the principal object of the dinner. I didn't eat hardly at all because I was tired and then I sang the whole first act of the opera and then I was awful tired and then they went home and I got up next day and packed to go away and as I got on the train I had fever and I knew I was going to be sick. So I was. And I enjoyed it. And I got a swell rest, as I always do when I am sick. Then I got well and then I got too well so that mountains and English people and Switzerland were an awful bore and then I came back. And I found your package and some ties from Boston and a quart of terribly swell toilet water from my tailor. About your perfume. It is made by the Prince Youssopoff. He is a rather spectacular Russian, the man who murdered Rasputin. He started a dressmaking shop here called Irfé where he also sells hand-painted china which he makes himself and which is very beautiful and he has a special perfume of his own make, as all the grand dressmakers do, only he has only one, called Irfé like the shop. I don't know if you like heavy perfumes, but I thought you might. I remember Mary Garden [the perfume] was heavy and musky. Give Betty my love and I hope she is well again. I sent Mama some Swiss pictures and said to show them to Betty when she finished.

Love,
Virgil

I sent Betty a book about Paris.

To Gertrude Stein

[Grand Hotel, Engelberg, Switzerland]
January 1, 1928

Dear Gertrude

Busy day today. I got up and dressed. Fever suddenly disappeared under quinine. Went in 24 hours from 104 to 94 and up to proper and stopped. Throat improves apparently and I am officially convalescent though not allowed to go outdoors. That should come shortly. Anyway I shaved and put on my clothes and went down-stairs and sat in the lobby for an hour while my ankles got cold and had my first meal in the dining room in solitary state and tried to smoke a cigarette but couldn't taste it and came back to my room and went to bed as per instructions and read a whole novel [*The Glimpses of the Moon*] by Edith Wharton all about love and Modern Life and Society and everything during which I ate a respectable tea and dinner and tried to smoke two more cigarettes but couldn't taste them either so you see it was a busy day. Edith's novel was a scream. 364 pages including 1½ bright remarks and a galaxy of prize exam-ples to illustrate bad grammar, bad language, bad thinking, bad noise, and openly bad construction. Chief character was surprised and horrified twice within one week's time and fifty pages spent at learning the same piece of news. The hero is supposed to have seri-ous literary talent but is named Nick Lansing. He never decides whether to be an archeologist or to write novels about archeology although he is sure his books will never sell. However at the end he sells an article for $200 and gets an order for more and he decides to finish a novel called *The Pageant of Alexander* which may sell after all. He is full of high moral scruples and offended at the more worldly ways of heroine. Eventually they both decide that if one has a great love in one's life and the possibility of a swell writing career, one can forego the Ritz, for a few years. Heroine is then safely allowed to return an ill-gotten sapphire bracelet. Excuse my writing you at such length about the Wharton or anything else but it really aroused me and besides I haven't anybody to talk to and I fancy you won't mind because you do a good deal of reading anyway. The plot is modern classic. Difficulty not getting the opponent to begin sexual relations but to continue them. Poor but experienced society girl named Susy Branch. Ought to marry a man with a *dot*. But has acquired the habits of the pampered rich and must have an artist. Meets poor but well-bred writer. They kiss. He offers to give himself. But she says "no you will always regret it. I will marry you." So he puts all his little income in her name and she manages to get contributions from rich friends enough for simple necessities of a honeymoon villa at Como and a *bel étage* in Venice. Naturally she doesn't bother him about business details and all is sweet and lovey-dovey and one day their joy is complete when he whispers that he thinks he is going to have a novel. So they go back to Venice and he spends his mornings quietly working and she sees that he keeps up his health and good spirits. But one day he learns that her business methods are not what he thinks honorable. A very fine point here, but he is a very tender plant from any moral point of view. So he just runs away and disap-pears. Gets a job as companion to other rich friends on a yacht. She is sorry. Tries to forget at various Ritzes. Nearly marries an English lord. Announces engagement and prospective divorce. Then hubby who has nobly refused his employer's rich daughter and seriously pursued archeology (plus a bit of Roman society life) returns to arrange her divorce. He doesn't cry or anything but she sees how sorry he is and after all she hasn't been really happy herself and so she suddenly cries out "Why this must be love!" And indeed it is no other. And so there is a genteel finale and the check arrives and they both forego chinchilla and pearls for love and a career while she returns the sapphire bracelet and promises to earn their living honestly with a new sense of her sacred responsibility. There are three sideshows of sad noble and hard-working husbands who suffer silent while wives philander or divorce or import Italian princes. Alice is right. If hero and heroine had divorced, she would have been forced to offer him alimony. He of course would have been too high-principled to accept.

Good night.

Love

To Gertrude Stein

June 17 [1928]

Dear Gertrude

I am glad to know you had a nice trip and that you ate on the way. I remain *en ville* because health goes bad and music good. One week of bed and bronchitis and three days of sunstroke plus blisters have advanced Act III to what is practically the end. The weather is bitter cold. And the Deux Magots is full of my American rivals. I have a new picture by Bébé and that is something. And Act III is of course very grand (got the tenor up to high C). But on the whole life is very sad and my neck is stiff.

Love

To Hildegarde Watson

July 30, 1928

Dear Hildegarde,

The opera is finished. I mean the music is finished. I haven't made the score yet which is maybe the longest task of all certainly the dirtiest and there is a ballet and an intermezzo and an appearance in person of the Holy Ghost and a procession and a great many fine arias for everybody and in general just about one of everything and the whole show makes a composition. Then I made a portrait in music* for violin of a Spanish lady and her daughter who stay in our hotel which is also nice music and which the daughter plays handsomely and which has been recognized as a likeness so maybe I can do yours one day and that would be nicer than having Saint Hildegarde in the opera because there is already Saint Philip and Saint Michael and anyway Gertrude won't let me tamper with her text. Spain is very grand. And very much like Texas. And the Spaniards are all enclosed like Americans and very sad though not about anything in particular and they are sweet and gentle and they like you. They are really very tender. Yes, very tender in their bashful way. I think they love the bull which they kill with such a loving gesture. Don't worry about my throat. An unmarried man has to have something to fight against and a perfectly harmless household malady is the safest opponent I know. It will be nice to arrange a concert in Rochester but let's leave that till I come and see how the land lies and there is always time no use making too many preparations in fact rather better to improvise it and surprise everybody.

Toujours love

To know Gertrude Stein was to know Alice B. Toklas (1878–1967), the author's longtime companion and the subject of her deceptively titled Autobiography of Alice B. Toklas. *Although Toklas did not initially care for Thomson, the two later became close friends. Inveterate cooks and lovers of fine food, they shared many recipes over the years.*

To ALICE B. TOKLAS

[New York]
[1928]

Dear Alice

I never had the letter you mentioned. I hope there was nothing important in it. If so, please repeat. But a curious incident has arrived. I receive a program from New York where one of my works

---

*Señorita Juanita de Medina Accompanied by Her Mother, the first of Thomson's musical portraits

is being played and right next to me is a real live Mexican composer named Carlos Chávez. And I thought it was a made-up name* and maybe it was but whichever way it was terribly nice of him to come to life.

Love,

Thomson spent much of the late summer of 1928 exploring the French countryside in the company of the surrealist poet, editor, art critic, and essayist Georges Hugnet (1906–74), the composer and pianist Henri Cliquet-Pleyel (1894–1963), and the latter's wife, the singer Marthe-Marthine.

To GERTRUDE STEIN

Bagnoles-de-l'Orne
September 2, 1928

Dear Gertrude

It has been very nice here with Georges & Cliquet & Marthe and I have done a great deal of sleeping and cracked my nose wide open on the bottom of the swimming pool and made a portrait of Marthe for the fiddle and I am going back to Paris tomorrow. I also played on the piano Acts III & IV because I have worked all summer without a piano and I hadn't heard any of it and wasn't I surprised it is very swell and full of inspiration and variety and I can only hope it isn't as bad as my contentment would indicate. St. Malo was nice too and we swam and ate café Viennois. Your picture of Georges as an explosive little soldier reminds me that you must make him re-count his military career to you because it is a good story and very him. I meditate your portrait. When do you come back to Paris because I shall be awfully glad to see you again and Alice and sing opera and tell stories. Georges writes a long poem every now and then and improves steadily. My portrait trick is developing nicely and seems to be quite new. That is, for music, because the idea of it comes obviously out of you. We had chicken today for lunch, and good wine.

Love,

---

*St. Chávez is a character in *Four Saints*.

To Gertrude Stein

Paris
September [1928]

Dear Gertrude

The cake is grand and many thanks it arrived just before tea guests and was a great success and it is beautiful to look at not to speak of eat. Hugnet sent me also a round glass ball with a mirror on the lining. And my own spirits are higher, fall having nicely arrived with warmish cold fog overhead and diffused light and Paris is herself again. I continue trying Act III on everybody in sight and I don't know yet what to make of it. Hugnet reenters Sunday. The flower market has handsome dahlias. I was dragged to Folies-Bergère by visiting Americans. Tonny is sweet these days. Eugene [McCown] consorts with princesses in Marseille and sailors in Toulon. Nancy Cunard★ has bought Bill Bird's [Three Mountains] press and is about to publish something or other. A few Christians† appear.

My love remains

In December 1928, Thomson returned to America for the first time since his arrival in Paris in 1925. His visit included stops at Whitinsville, Massachusetts (where he stayed at the home of Jessie Lasell through Christmas), Boston (where he showed his recently completed Symphony on a Hymn Tune to Serge Koussevitzky), Kansas City, Santa Fe, Rochester (where he gave a lecture and visited Hildegarde and Sibley Watson), New York City (where he gave the United States premiere of Capital Capitals and stayed at the Watsons' Gramercy Park apartment), Boston again (for performances of the Sonata da Chiesa, the processional scene from Four Saints, and the world premiere of the newly commissioned Conversation for Four Clarinets), and back to New York before sailing for France.

★British heiress and patron of the arts (1896–1965)
†The sculptor Jo Davidson referred to all outsiders as "Christians."

To Gertrude Stein

[Whitinsville, Massachusetts]
December 2, 1928

Dear Gertrude

What luxe what snow what sun and blue skies what food and oh my god what a bore.

The *Capitals* are being performed on February 24 at the Little Theatre in New York. I go tomorrow to Boston to arrange what can be arranged there. This is just a note with love.

I have no impressions of America. It's just the same as before only the liquor is better.

Love,

To Gertrude Stein

[Boston]
December 29, 1928

Dear Gertrude

All goes well. Koussevitzky refused my symphony cold. I was a little surprised. I knew it was pretty good but hadn't really imagined it that good. Opera pleases everywhere. Harvard Glee Club wants to sing processional scene. I go west next week. Glad. Tired of quail and strawberries. Visit quite successful, I suppose, on the whole. America as usual.

Love,

To Alice B. Toklas

[Kansas City]
January 16 [1929]

Dear Alice

Here are some things you might try over on your kitchen piano. The salmon dish★ I recommend especially. It makes a delicate and fluffy entrée, highly digestible, and elegant to offer. Kansas City is charming and I enjoy home and mother though the weather is hope-

---

★"A sort of soufflé but turned out" is Thomson's description

less. Oceans of slush froze last week and everything is now solid ice (motors waltzing). Today it rained and froze, so that all the little bare spots are covered now with slick ice and even walking is impossible. Temperature at zero. Humidity at 100% (official reports). I write music at home and cure a cold and enjoy it all. Saturday I go to Santa Fe for a week. It will be warmer there. I am invited to lecture at Rochester with illustrations from my own works. The opera continues to excite and to please. The male-chorus arrangement of the *Saints Procession* (for Harvard Glee Club) is a wow. I shall be glad to get back to Paris where I am not a public character. I write a piece (for Boston) for four clarinets. My mending is being brought up to date. And new pyjamas are being made. The score and parts of my symphony (left to be finished in Paris) have never arrived. If they do, same will likely be played in Rochester. I make observations of Missouri speech. It is curious and interesting. In its local or provincial condition it is incredibly low. And yet it seems to lose all its horrid quality with only a very little training and to become quite beautiful when properly educated. Unlike Kansas or Illinois, which are difficult to train and almost never lose their harsh intonation. And there are marked differences between male and female speech. And as for strawberries! The town is very gay.

Love,

Thomson's musical portraiture—spontaneous sonic depictions of people who "sat" for him—was inspired by Gertrude Stein's literary experiments with this genre, though hers had always been composed in absentia. While he was in the United States in 1929, Thomson received a verbal portrait she had made of him.

To Gertrude Stein

[En route to Rochester]
February 2 [1929]

Dear Gertrude

Thanks and many. The portrait is very beautiful and serious and like me too: Yes very serious and with a quite gratuitous beauty an extra beauty *par-dessus le marché*. The train wiggles and makes it hard to write straight. I am on my way to lecture on us at Rochester. Then New York and having to find singers for *Capitals*. I wish it were all over. Two months is enough not to work, especially visiting. Though I arranged the *Saints Procession* and wrote a *Conversation for Four Clarinets*. But I bear up and am of course very well and not even a cold so far. It was nice visiting my grandfather who at ninety-seven was full of wise political comment and people comment and questions about French life and agriculture. I am glad the *Americans*★ are finished and I shall see them when I return.

Please write many and often.

Love,

To Gertrude Stein

February 20 [1929]

Dear Gertrude

Capitals swell success. N. Y. talks of nothing else these days. Audience roared with laughter during and bravos afterwards. Critics charmingly confused. Some thought it a good joke, some a bad joke, and one or so got quite angry. It is being repeated next Sunday at [a] swell theatrical party with champagne and such. All got up by Gertrude Newell† (the lady who had a brawl with a Sitwell in your house), and the Chamber Music Society of Boston (tony private concerts they have) is asking for it next month & they intend to pay not only singers but composer as well. Which is swell. I enclose assorted clippings. Don't throw them away. Met your friend McBride‡ liked him & him me & he heard some opera and liked it. Theater Guild man not useful at present because he was mad he hadn't thought of it himself and he bit his fingernails in fury all during. I neglected to mention that at the *Capitals* show the poets were all disgusted with the words and the composers thought the music too low for anything. But the audience's way of taking it proved to me the possibility of having a regular boob success with the opera, at least it might run long enough to pay its expenses and it might just might (and without surprising me at all) make a little money. I return on *Ile-de-France* March 29, arriving April 3. I shall be glad.

Love,

P.S. Ganna Walska§ gave a concert last week and sang as an encore a song entitled "If No One Ever Marries Me."

★ *The Making of Americans* excerpts translated into French
† a decorator with literary and theatrical connections
‡ Henry McBride, American art critic
§ A much-married beauty

To Gertrude Stein

Paris
May 13 [1929]

Dear Gertrude:

I am glad you are proper and so is your new house. Mine is all in disorder but hope is eternal and I have also a visitor, Maurice Grosser, who is nice and I am glad Carl [Van Vechten] says I am a lamb and I guess I mostly was with him but then that wasn't much. Bébé did me again as portrait very good and I did him but very bad because it was premature and I shouldn't have really tried to make music just yet otherwise all fine and weather balmy. I was glad seeing Picasso at your house and in the flesh and I have remembered it a good deal. So far.

Love,

Thomson spent part of the summer of 1929 in Madrid with Jessie Lasell and in the Haute-Savoie with Mme Langlois, her Russian doctor friend, Mme Catherine Henri, and Maurice Grosser.

To Gertrude Stein

Villefranche-sur-mer
[1929]

Dear Gertrude

I am glad you have come to the same conclusion about Genia [Berman] as I did. I looked him over (and the painting too) last spring after you left and arrived at ditto only I didn't say anything because I wanted to see if you wouldn't come to same on really seeing him some and of course the painting is good even very good only it isn't really what we are looking for and Bébé comes out awfully well in the comparison especially for livingness and sweet humanity. Georges writes tenderly from St. Malo and enthusiastically of the floods and Tonny writes from Paris that he has no money and can't paint because he has no more canvases but that he promenades with Bébé in the Bois de Boulogne. We are having *fête du pays* today and the square is full of young wops in shiny shoes. One day we walked to Monte Carlo and Maurice goes swimming a great deal to keep out of *Saints'* way. Weather fine, swimming fine. Score advances. Sun shines. Give my love always to Alice and

toujours fidèle,

In 1929, the Hessiches Landestheater in Darmstadt, then known for its productions of left-wing and avant-garde operas and ballets, expressed an interest in Four Saints, *to the point of finding out whether the piece would work in German translation. The project was ultimately scrapped; Thomson always suspected in this the handiwork of the troupe's music director, Karl Böhm (1894–1981), who poet and critic Edwin Denby (1903–83), at that time a dancer and assistant régisseur in the company, believed "had decided to begin tapering off on modernism by taking a firm stand against* Four Saints.*"*

To Gertrude Stein

Paris
[1929]

Dear Gertrude

There has been a long and cordial correspondence with Darmstadt and they have read the libretto and like it and want to see the score and I very nearly went and showed it to them and then we couldn't come to any agreement about the language because I said no I didn't want it translated and they said they couldn't give it except in German and there the matter rests they protesting that they can make a good translation which no doubt they can and I hesitating to explain by letter that this opera isn't like any other opera because I presume every composer thinks that of his first child. Of course it is not at all impossible that even with all the linguistic sense cut out of it the *musique* might still have some intrinsic interest and of course the dramatic value of the libretto remains and whatever of the poetic texture they can translate. What do you think? And what do Alice and Georges [Hugnet] think? [The trip with Mrs.] Lasell well over, nice, money continues. I'm glad it's all finished though. You know how exigent the rich are en voyage. Give my love to Alice and there is always for yourself a perpetual fount of same.

Toujours

In 1930, the Duchesse de Clermont-Tonnerre, at whose house Capital Capitals was first performed, commissioned Thomson to write a vocal work—perhaps to a text by his friend Georges Hugnet. Although Thomson and Hugnet were unsuccessful in this collaboration, Thomson did set Bossuet's Oraison funèbre (for Henriette-Marie of France, widow of England's Charles I).

The following letter mentions another of Thomson's Parisian companions, the architecture scholar Henry-Russell Hitchcock (1903–87). As Thomson later said of their friendship, "I'd walk all over Paris with Russell and he'd explain to me how to read the architecture. After two years, I practically knew all of it."

To Gertrude Stein

May 11, 1930

Dear Gertrude

Please excuse silence very busy with Bossuet now finished and very beautiful indeed with a great ampleur and I had a party last night and nobody can find fault with French prosody (thanks to slight aid of Mme Langlois who knows more than all of them about it) and everyone is terribly impressed. Mrs. Lasell has sent sweet letters & a check for May & no mention of stopping. Darmstadt is at a standstill with everyone sold on us but the musical director who is standing pat. Who would have thought it? Marion Davies,* who when in England was asked what she thought of British pictures replied, "I have a Reynolds in my own home." Hitchcock is here and departing daily for Germany but still here and God knows when and Maurice had a tiresome visitor from Duluth so we put them together and it has become a tender idyll for them & a great relief for us. Antheil writes tender letter (dictated) encouraging my attendance at Frankfurt premiere of his opera. I am very well. I have some red lilies. I hope your garden is doing as gardens should and that you are having nicer time.

Love,

P.S. I'm a bit chagrined that Darmstadt finds my music not *à la hauteur.*

---

*(1897–1961), American film actress, longtime mistress of publisher William Randolph Hearst

*Three events of note took place between May 1930 and the follow-
ing letter: another trip to Spain; another concert of Thomson's
works; and, most important, in late 1930, a misunderstanding with
Gertrude Stein that would separate them for the next three years.*

To Hildegarde Watson

In the country
July 30, 1931

Dear Hildegarde,

I am having a strange and, so far, not very satisfactory summer. I
have not however moved out of the quai Voltaire. At least twice a
year I announce to all my friends that I am about to move. The
moving day never arrives. I am announcing it now for early fall.
Don't be surprised if you still find me there and predicting my evac-
uation for, say, January 1st. At the moment the rent is reduced by
half (kindness of charming proprietress) but it is not sublet (dearth of
summering travellers). I am an hour or so out of Paris near the forest
of Rambouillet in a farmhouse. The house is comfortable and the
country charming. Maurice is with me. We bore each other considerably but it is better than being entirely alone. We are four or five
miles from the train and from any considerable town. There are
beautiful walks to take but that is all, having no means of locomo-
tion, not even bicycles. Coldness of the weather, which makes me
nervous, and the necessity of running in and out of Paris on small
business errands has prevented me from settling down quietly to the
work I want to get at. So as I say, the summer so far has not been
very satisfactory because satisfaction lies in having done what one
had in mind or at least something else just as pleasant. But one never
knows and maybe the latter end of the summer will be a surprise;
certainly the late fall will be a pleasure if it brings you with it. I am
meditating again an American visit. Meditating means I hope like
hell that it will arrange itself. I could use a little contact with my
motherland just now. I haven't seen Joyce (is it James you meant?)
for the last year. He has been living in London. And I practically
never see the *Hound and Horn*.* This letter sounds sort of depressed.
I hope I am not falling into the "depression." What Kristians Tonny
called years ago "le pessimisme americain" seems to be having its
epoch just now. I was amused at a cousin of Maurice's who came to
see us. She is an interior decorator in Philadelphia. She seemed most

---

*Lincoln Kirstein's quarterly magazine

98

discouraged about what she called vaguely "conditions at home" but in the midst of the lamentations she confessed naively that she was making more money than she had ever made in her life and had been to Europe twice this year, instead of the usual once. If the prosperous ones can pull as sad a face as she did, what gloomy mugs must the rest of us offer? The depression isn't about money. People have been poor before. It's this "pessimisme americain," so long denied expression, just spreading itself for once. You would have a good laugh if you could see some of the visitors from home getting themselves into the most absurd sentimental difficulties in order to have a reason for "feeling bad." Dear dear Hildegarde I hope you come over this fall. It has been so long since we took a walk together. Come and take me home with you.

Love always,

Aaron Copland (b. 1900) had already been influential in presenting some of Thomson's music in Manhattan as well as at Yaddo, the artists' colony near Saratoga Springs, New York. In the fall of 1931, he organized a concert of American music in London where Capital Capitals was a featured work; Thomson himself played the piano accompaniment.

Soon after the performance, Copland sent one of his best young pupils, Paul Bowles (b. 1910), to Paris for Thomson's guidance. Bowles, who later distinguished himself not only as a composer but as a critic and novelist, lived in Morocco for many years with his wife, the writer Jane Bowles (1917–73). They were among Thomson's closest friends.

Copland was also helpful in arranging the publication of Thomson's Stabat Mater, which marked his first generally available music. (Other compositions written during this time include the Violin Sonata, the two string quartets, and the Symphony No. 2.) Copland kept Thomson apprised of developments in American music, and their correspondence helped spur Thomson's return to music criticism, a talent he mostly had let lie dormant since his return to Paris.

Paris
November 26, 1931

Dear Aaron:

Paul Bowles was here this morning to ask advice about Nadia. He had seen her and made a date to start lessons, she refusing to name a price but insisting she was very poor, her bank having closed. He wanted to know the minimum he could pay her. I said under no circumstances more than 50 francs and I offered the additional and entirely gratuitous advice to study instead with Paul Dukas. He decommanded his rendezvous with Nadia, pleading tonsils, and asked me to write you. Naturally, he will follow your advice. Please answer by air mail because he is eager for something to start.

My story is this:

If he wants Nadia's particular and special merchandise, namely, a motherly guidance to overcome American timidity about self-expression, then he had better go and get it and take the trimmings with it. Otherwise he had better buy his trimmings where they are cheaper and better.

Nadia is not the same as when we were there. The flattery and guidance was precious to us and inspiring and the counterpoint lessons were competent enough and that's all there was.

When I went back in 1926 I discovered that the counterpoint was still fair (though expensive, because she talked all the time about things in general and seldom got through the work I had done) but that the main thing was all changed. The guidance wasn't worth a damn. On the contrary, quite troublesome. Once the habit of composition was established, she used every art of sympathy and generosity to make it grow into her own pet channels. I refused and stopped my lessons and she has never forgiven me. Long before I stopped I formed the habit of never showing her an unfinished piece. Roy Harris had the same trouble. She rooks any work in progress she can get her hands on. Rarely is her advice practical, never disinterested. Everybody must be school of Lili.* Her tastes are sentimental and *démodé*. Her lack of comprehension of everything that is vivid or simple is complete. She lives in a temple of adulation and knee-bending that is disgusting and her aged parent scents any heresy a mile off and begins putting the screws on to make you feel ashamed of eating her cakes and tea while you are secretly question-

---

*composer Lili Boulanger (1893–1918), Nadia's younger sister and the first woman to be awarded the Prix de Rome in music (1913)

ing the divine oracle. It's all very debasing and profitless, unless one must have her motherly guidance at any cost. All this could be got in six months. But then of course there's no getting away. The only ones who get away do it by going home. It took me a year and a quarrel and she has never forgotten.

All this was to explain to Bowles that he might reflect a little before he put his head into the noose. After all if he is going to live in Paris he had better make relations among the young composers than among the old ones and it's not possible to see many young ones while under Nadia's thumb. Mama scents heresy very quickly.

Bowles wondered if he mightn't start Dukas and Nadia together and then drop the one he didn't prefer. It might be done discreetly. In any case, I've told you my story and you can give him any advice you want because he believes in you and I shan't say any more about it. I've sent Nadia pupils for years and very little good has come of them, none for European purposes. This is the first time I've advised otherwise. I think it's time to change.

Love,

To Oscar Wagner*

Paris
April 25 [1932]

Dear Mr. Wagner:

Just a word of amiable protest. I have received my score [Symphony on a Hymn Tune] and thank you for its safe return. I presume it has been read, although nothing in your letters would indicate one way or the other except perhaps the twice-repeated erroneous reference to it as a "composition entitled *Symphony.*" My little protest is partly that and partly that you didn't tell me what you wanted. You merely asked the privilege of seeing this particular score. If you had told me something beforehand about what you consider "suitable in length, content, etc.," you would have saved me a dollar and a half in postage and spared me the humiliation of your unceremonious refusal. It seems to me that a solicited manuscript, transmitted at the author's expense, merits the courtesy of a reply showing that it has been read and explaining wherein the work fails to agree with the commercial or artistic policy of your house. A professional publisher

*(1893–1970), then secretary of the Society for the Publication of American Music, was associated with the Juilliard School for many years.

usually adds a perfunctory compliment by way of showing good will. Perhaps that is too much to ask of a committee of composers.

Very sincerely yours,

To Oscar Wagner

Paris
May 20 [1932]

Dear Mr. Wagner:

If you still think there was no discourtesy, allow me to remind you that I contributed a dollar and half in postage and the use of my score for six months (at your request, please remember) and that all I got out of it was an extremely cold thank-you and an unsubstantiated assurance that "judges" had inspected it, although neither the secretary's nor his secretary's repeated ignorance of the title of the piece gives much confidence to the composer.

I also remind you that "thanks for giving our judges an opportunity to see your manuscript and with continued good wishes" is a phrase of general utility equally applicable to solicited and to unsolicited manuscripts.

There isn't much point in my laboring the point, except that you so completely misunderstood the nature of my little protest that I must make clear what annoyed me. It was simply that after having (much to my surprise) asked to see my manuscript, your society returns it without any explanation (and with a certain rudeness), just as if I had submitted it voluntarily. You have put me in a position into which I should never have put myself, as if I were an aspirant for your favors, a position extremely humiliating to me considering the difference in our generations and in our musical tendencies.

There are rich musical foundations that periodically award somebody an academic honor or a cash prize. One is used to their high-and-mightiness and to their discourteous ways, although they seldom risk their prestige by openly requesting a score, drumming up trade, as it were.

But unless I greatly misjudge the Society for the Publication of American Music, it is no such foundation. It is, I take it, a private and amateur publishing society like any other (of which there are many). In correspondence it enjoys the same prestige and the same obligations as the composers whose names are printed on its letterpaper. A discourtesy, however banal, from the society is a discourtesy from one musician to another. My protest is a simple calling of this to your and to the society's attention.

Very sincerely yours,

Thomson spent his summer in the countryside and on the Côte d'Azur, then focused his energies on returning to the United States, where he hoped to stage the first production of Four Saints.

To Aaron Copland

Paris
October 17, 1932

Dear Aaron,

I am coming to America around the 1st of December (sailing S.S. *Paris* Nov. 30), for no particular reason except that I very much want to and I have a few lecture engagements that will pay something. If you know any more (which I imagine is doubtful from Mexico) for God's sake let them and me know. Also if there are to be any Copland-Sessions concerts this year and what prospects generally. I learn from Paul [Bowles] that you are having a big festival blowout and I wish you lots of success and grandeur. I did a Markevitch article for Minna Lederman, a rather mean one, which she asked for, and which she should publish in her next issue of *Modern Music* unless she thinks it is too harsh.* Paul spent 10 days with Maurice and me at the island of Porquerolles and we all enjoyed it. I don't think you need worry much about the future of his musical talent. He worries quite enough all by himself. And it runs along quite properly, develops with speed and fatality. He finds out everything he needs to know as he needs it and writes quite a lot of music and of extremely good quality. What more do you want? The truth is he really shocks everybody. He shocks Bernard and Gertrude because he refuses to lead the conventional life of a young man of talent. He prefers the life of a *poule de luxe* and he lives quite well thatway and gets his work done all the same. You are shocked because he won't follow the conventional education of a young man of talent. He is frightfully impressed by what you tell him and gets awfully worried because he can't do it. But the force of his own genius

---

*The conductor Igor Markevitch (1912–83), a Boulanger protégé, was then primarily a composer. Thomson's article, published in the November 1932 *Modern Music*, asserted that "the career is more interesting than the music."

is stronger in him than any reason or affection. So with the best will in the world to do as you say and learn the contrapuntal routines, he just can't be bothered. Of course, at bottom he's right. His musical procedure is far too contrapuntal now. What he is really interested in learning just now is how to write for all the instruments and how to compose in free form. He is learning by doing and all the lessons he needs he gets from you and me and others by showing the finished piece and saying "What's wrong here?" If he ever needs systematic instruction, he'll go get it and pay for it and absorb it quickly. I assure you there is nothing to worry about.

Best love and see you soon,

Thomson's trip to America laid the foundation for the first production of Four Saints. *Through friends and contacts in the art world— notably the architect Philip Johnson (b. 1906), the art dealer Kirk Askew (1903–74) and his wife, Constance (1895–1984), Thomson's old friend Russell Hitchcock, and A. Everett ("Chick") Austin (1900–57), the director of the Wadsworth Atheneum and art museum in Hartford—financial support was found for mounting the work. Meanwhile, Thomson started busily planning all aspects of the production itself, inviting Florine Stettheimer to do the costumes and set-design and Alexander Smallens (1889–1972) to conduct.*

As Thomson recalls, "Nobody knew yet what [the production] would cost, but I knew something of what it would look like and sound like. And I was not to be stuck with the banalities of professional stage design, the poor enunciation of professional opera singers. I was to have the ultimate in dream fulfillment, a production backed by enlightened amateurs and executed by whatever professional standards I chose to follow."

While in the States, Thomson also visited Kansas City and arranged some lecture dates to help pay for his expenses. He also arranged performances of his Stabat Mater *in New York and Philadelphia.*

In April, he returned to Paris only to encounter another detail that needed some attention, his financial arrangements with the estranged Gertrude Stein. The two had not had any contact since their quarrel in 1930, and their correspondence reflects, to some extent, the distance that had grown between them.

Paris
May 30 [1933]

Dear Gertrude

Mr. Bradley* has communicated to me a passage from one of your letters to him in which you express some reserves about the opera mounting as I described it, and he has suggested that I might correspond directly with you on that subject, which is after all a part of our artistic collaboration and outside his domain. I am eager that the production should represent your text as closely as possible and so is Miss Stettheimer. Hence my eager acceptance of Mr. Bradley's suggestion to establish, if that is agreeable to you, a direct correspondence on the subject.

Before I go on about the mounting, however, I am taking the liberty of mentioning a business matter which I have already spoken of to Mr. Bradley and which I have his permission to write to you about, he being slightly embarrassed, as both your personal agent and our joint agent, about reopening the question.

At the beginning of my conversations with him I mentioned that although the usual practice was otherwise, I preferred, in view of the closeness of our collaboration and of the importance given to the text in my score, to offer you a 50–50 division of all profits. It has since been called to my attention by the Société des Droits d'Auteurs that such an arrangement defeats its own end and that the contract commonly made in France allowing two-thirds to the composer and one to the author is designed to establish that very equality:

1) because the manual labor involved in musical composition is so much greater than that of writing words that half the proceeds is an insufficient return for the composer, considering him as a joint worker.

2) because a literary work is perfectly salable separate from the music and thus brings further profit to its author, whereas the music is rarely salable in any way separated from the text it was designed to accompany.

The 2–1 division of profits is already, it would seem, to the advantage of the author in that an inferior text is assured of paying profits as long as the music lives, and a poem of merit is in no way injured in its independent literary career by the performance of an inferior musical setting. In cases where the musical setting is noteworthy, the sale of the book has often surpassed the normal sale of that author's work, thus bringing a very considerable independent

*William Aspenwall Bradley (1878–1939), a Paris literary agent

profit to the author in which of course the composer has no share at all. I am told that this has been true recently of [Paul] Claudel's *Christophe Colombe* (music by Milhaud) and of Edna Millay's *The King's Henchman*, which was written for Deems Taylor. *Four Saints* has already, if I mistake not, been published twice, and I hope Mr. Bradley will arrange to have it printed in America (with perhaps a few minor changes to permit American copyright) so that it can be sold as a libretto at performances.

In view of these considerations would you consider it just on my part to ask that our projected contracts (and any eventual publication of the score) be based on the 2–1 rather than the 1–1 division of profits, a proportion which, as I said above, is the one used in France? The same proportion would naturally apply in sharing the expense of copyright.

About the mounting, we are all in accord that the idea of a parochial entertainment must remain. Miss Stettheimer suggested, however, that since any interior is less joyful than an outdoor scene, and since Sunday-school rooms and chapels have been done in so many religious plays (black and white), perhaps the same entertainment might take place on the steps of a church, in this case the cathedral of Avila itself, though represented in a far from literal imitation. Spring at Avila could thus be expressed doubly. Also the general atmosphere somewhat lightened. The colors and materials she suggests are merely an amplification of the fairy-tale effect ordinarily aimed at in the construction of religious images out of tin and tinsel and painted plaster and gilding and artificial flowers. Her idea seems to me more efficacious than our original one in expressing the same thing, especially in view of the enormous lightening of every effect that is necessary in order to get a dramatic idea across the barrier of footlights and music. I must admit I am rather taken by the whole proposal, having seen the extraordinary elegance which Miss Stettheimer has produced in her own rooms with exactly those colors and materials. We are all, however, open to persuasion and to suggestions, and no maquettes have been made.

The idea for the Maypole dance in Act II is even less definite than the other. That also is Miss Stettheimer's. The Negro bodies, if seen at all, would only be divined vaguely through long dresses. The movements would be sedate and prim, and the transparence is aimed primarily not at titillating the audience with the sight of a leg but at keeping the texture of the stage as light as possible. This end is important to keep in view when there are as many things and people on a stage as this opera requires and all frequently in movement. Naturally, if the transparent clothes turned out in rehearsal to be a stronger effect than we intended, petticoats would be ordered immediately for everybody. I think the idea is worth trying, however. If it can be realized inoffensively, the bodies would merely add to our spectacle the same magnificence they give to classic religious paintings and sculpture. One could not easily use this effect with white bodies, but I think one might with brown.

My Negro singers, after all, are a purely musical desideratum because of their rhythm, their style, and especially their diction. Any further use of their racial qualities must be incidental and not of a nature to distract attention from the subject matter. . . . Hence, the idea of painting their faces white. Nobody wants to put on just a nigger show. The project remains doubtful, anyway, till I find the proper soloists.

Very faithfully yours,

To FLORINE STETTHEIMER

Paris
May 31, 1933

Dear Florine

Again thanks and many thanks for the heavenly candies in the pretty box. Everybody is showing great interest about the opera and there is even question of doing all or a part of it or of asking you and me to do a ballet for the Russians* next year. Could you do such a thing? That would mean your coming abroad next spring, probably to Monte Carlo in April. Also could you possibly send me a sketch or two, any kind of hasty sketch, of Act I and maybe St. Teresa, or anything that is fairly precise in your mind about the opera. The simplest kind of sketch will do, as long as the colors were either indicated or written down. Even if the trip is impossible, I should very much like to have a sketch to show. Paris is being very agreeable just now and there are lots of pleasant things to do. I have begun scoring of the opera. Gertrude is greatly excited by the opera plans and is also most desirous of seeing a sketch. Tenderest affection to Ettie and Carrie.†

Love and kisses
Virgil

P.S. The ballet plans for next year envisage two American works, a fashionable and witty one by Cole Porter and Peter Arno and a more serious modern one. George Antheil and Alexander Calder are being considered for the second. Also you and me. Ours would certainly be less *vieux jeux* than anything that pair could do.

---

*Ballets Russes de Monte Carlo
†Florine's sisters

June 9 [1933]

Dear Gertrude

Thank you for your kind and frank letter. If the only reason, however, for holding to a 50–50 division, aside from the natural enough desire to obtain as favorable an arrangement as possible, is the commercial value of your name, I should like to protest that although your name has a very great publicity value as representing the highest quality of artistic achievement, its purely commercial value, especially in connection with a work as hermetic in style as the *Four Saints,* is somewhat less, as I have found in seeking a publisher for our joint works, although I have found a publisher for other works of mine. Moreover, it is not the value of your name or the devotion of your admirers (I except Mrs. Chadbourne,* who began very practically indeed but didn't continue very long) that is getting this opera produced, but my friends and admirers, Mr. Austin and Mr. Smallens and Florine and Maurice, who are all giving their services at considerable expense to themselves, and a dozen other friends who are contributing $100 or more each to Mr. Austin's costly & absolutely disinterested enterprise. The value of your name has never produced any gesture from these people, whereas every one of them has on other occasions manifested his interest in my work by creating commercial engagements for me and by offering me further collaborations with himself. And dear Gertrude, if you knew the resistance I have encountered in connection with that text and overcome, the amount of reading it and singing it and praising it and commenting it I have done, the articles, the lectures, the private propaganda that has been necessary in Hartford and in New York to silence the opposition that thought it wasn't having any Gertrude Stein, you wouldn't talk to me about the commercial advantages of your name. Well, they *are* having it and they are going to *like* it and it isn't your name or your lieutenants that are giving it to them. If you hadn't put your finger on a sensitive spot by mentioning this to me, I should never have done so to you. However, I've got it off my chest now and the fact remains that even were the situation reversed, a 50–50 contract would be, so far as I know, absolutely without precedent.

About joint ownership of the musical material, I accede to your reasoning and thank you for your generous gesture about hiring it out, although I think, in view of the fact that we are making a busi-

---

*Emily Chadbourne Crane, a wealthy friend of Stein's from Chicago ness agreement that may involve heirs or something, everything had better be divided properly.

The other matters can, I think, be easily arranged with Mr. Bradley. The "unreasonably withheld" phrase can be eliminated from our personal agreement if we are convinced of each other's reasonableness, and it can be kept out of the other if Mr. Austin doesn't mind. It is usual, however, in such contracts to offer some protection to the producer, who may have spent real money on a show only to find himself completely at the mercy of an author who might use his right of forbidding the performance as a weapon in some minor dispute which could normally and fairly be settled by arbitration.

I am glad you approve of the scenic plans. The second act includes just such a night scene as you have described. I don't know whether a river can be got on the stage too, but I hope so.

The *Capitals* was in a folder with the opera text which I took to the copyist. Bringing it home, it dropped out of my pocket in a taxi. I am glad it has been found and if you will instruct your concierge to give it to me, I shall call and get it. I'm terribly glad it isn't lost.

Best of greetings
Always faithfully

To Gertrude Stein

Paris
June 22 [1933]

Dear Gertrude,

Everything is arranged now, at least for the duration of our present contract, and I have signed it and Mr. Bradley is sending it to you. The copy of score is ready (or will be tomorrow). It is in the original form plus Maurice's stage directions. I suggest (since they are neither your nor my invention and though they will be used in the production are not the only ones that are possible) that I cross them out of the copyrighted work.

I find on working over the opera and orchestrating it that I should very much like to make a few simple cuts. . . . You offered me that privilege at the beginning of our collaboration and I didn't care to avail myself of it, preferring to set everything and wait for a later time to make any such cuts in view of actual performance. I find now that there is a little too much singing and not enough instrumental relief. I should like to eliminate for example a few of the stage directions as sung, especially where they are repeated frequently. I don't mean systematically to remove them, just a few repetitions now and then, in every case (or nearly) to replace them with an instrumental passage of the same length and tune. This makes a rather amusing effect and is as if an instrument were saying the words that somebody has just sung. There are also a few passages that I should like to eliminate for the purposes of this performance, substituting in one or two cases a short instrumental passage, in others nothing at all. This in view of tightening the structure musically and making a more simple and effective musical continuity. The aria in Act III about roses smell very well, for instance, comes right after another aria for tenor and rather impedes the advance of the spectacle toward the ballet. I should like to cut it out.

The cuts I propose are only for the purposes of my score for this performance. The copyright score would include everything. I mention the cuts because I don't want to avail myself of a permission offered so long ago without its being renewed. I hope you will allow me to do this. I assure you the theatrical effectiveness of the work will be enhanced.*

Many thanks for your gracious acceptance of the consent clause in our agreement. We now have, I think, a simple way of settling any differences that may arise without bitterness. As a matter of fact, we understand each other so well and our interests lie for the most part so close together that I am sure we shall always be mostly reasonable with each other anyway. Best of greetings.

Always devotedly yours,

To complete the task of orchestrating *Four Saints,* Thomson sought the solitude of the countryside. As he explained:

In those days, when you had lots of work to do, you went somewhere, for life away from Paris was a saving, and third-class train fare very cheap. My usual work place was the southern coast; but I did not care to go that far so soon, having been asked, with ticket paid, to spend a week in London with the Askews. So first I went with Grosser to Honfleur, ancient small port town on the Seine opposite Le Havre. . . . And after having scored a hundred pages there, I knew the time the whole of the job would take. I had only to average ten pages a day to be through in two months, and this would leave time for a copyist to extract the parts before I left for New York in late October.

---

*Stein acceded to Thomson's proposal.

The works referred to in the following letter are the String Quartet No. 2 and the song "Le Singe et le léopard," to a text by Jean de la Fontaine.

To Aaron Copland

Ile de Porquerolles
August 25, 1933

Dear Aaron

I did intend to send the quartet and had a copy made with parts especially for you and then the BBC in London asked for it and I thought it was a better shot than Yaddo, seeing as how you were so lukewarm anyway, and the other copy has presumably been given to the Pro Arte people★ to learn and that's why I didn't send it. No possibility of getting you the La Fontaine. It is locked up in Paris. As a matter of fact, I am glad that everything turned out as it has. I would rather not expose myself to a refusal about the quartet. You know how committees are. They always refuse anything that isn't forced on them or explained. And you would probably be very indiscreet to do either, which would amount to a declaration of war on the Schoenbergians and the Bang-Bangs and after all you do have to live with them. Even the La Fontaine would give you trouble, because it is frightfully difficult to sing, at least to make it sound like anything but the most abject nincompoopery. I got a good laugh out of your phrase about "lesser-known songs," because I suddenly realized that not one of my songs (at least the piano songs) has ever been sung in America (to my knowledge). If anybody wants to publish any, however, we won't quibble about what is and isn't known.

I am rapidly orchestrating my opera. Two acts finished. Will finish all by Sept. 15. Be in New York late October. I am using

Flute (+ Piccolo)
Oboe
2 Saxophones (1 plays clarinet)
Bassoon
Trumpet
Trombone
Accordion
  Celesta

★The Pro Arte Quartet, founded in 1912 at the Brussels Conservatory, played a great deal of contemporary music.

Glockenspiel
and lots of other battery
4 Violins
1 Viola
1 Cello
1 Double Bass

I only hope it sounds like I hope it sounds. I asked all the Amer. composers I know to send you things. Namely, Pendleton, McKee, Wald, and the Boulangerie. Braved the lionesses rue Ballu to demand the latter. Found her pawing Markevitch like a dowager with a gigolo. Foote was the only one of all, I gather, to really send anything. I shall be in N.Y. before you could send me any news of the show. Maurice sends his greetings, I embraces.

toujours

Thomson returned to New York in October, and the production of Four Saints began to take shape. The first thing needed was to find a director. Through an old acquaintance, the French-American writer Lewis Galantière (1895–1977), Thomson met John Houseman, a British- and French-trained actor eager for the directing experience, who agreed (like many of the principals behind Four Saints) to work for no fee. (Houseman would go on to a notable career in the theater, and he remained a close friend and frequent collaborator of Thomson's.)

Frederick Ashton (b. 1906), the British choreographer and dancer who would later become director of the Royal Ballet, supervised the movement, and Maurice Grosser, who worked on the scenario, also contributed to the production. Thomson held auditions for his all-black cast (he felt that black singers could better enunciate English). Meanwhile, Chick Austin and his Friends and Enemies of Modern Music raised the necessary funds.

To Gertrude Stein

[Hartford]
December 6 [1933]

Dear Gertrude

Here is a newspaper article that will amuse you from the *Hartford Times*. The cast of the opera is hired and rehearsals begun. I have a chorus of 32 & six soloists, very, very fine ones indeed. Miss Stettheimer's sets are of a beauty incredible, with trees made out of feathers and a sea-wall at Barcelona made out of shells and for the procession a baldachino of black chiffon & branches of black ostrich plumes just like a Spanish funeral. St. Teresa comes to the picnic in the 2nd act on a cart drawn by a real white donkey & brings her tent with her and sets it up & sits in the doorway of it. It is made of white gauze with gold fringe and has a most elegant shape. My singers, as I have wanted, are Negros, & you can't imagine how beautifully they sing. Frederick Ashton is arriving from London this week to make choreography for us. Not only for the dance numbers but for the whole show, so that all the movements will be regulated to the music, measure by measure, and all our complicated stage action made into a controllable spectacle. Houseman is a playwright, friend & collaborator of Lewis Galantière. He "understands" the opera too if you know what I mean by that word. Everything about the opera is shaping up so beautifully, even the raising of money (it's going to cost $10,000), that the press is chomping at the bit and the New York ladies already ordering dresses & engaging hotel rooms. Carl [Van Vechten]'s niece has taken a Hartford house for the opera week. Rumors of your arrival are floating about and everybody asks me is she really coming and I always answer that it wouldn't surprise me. Certainly, if everything goes off as fancy as it looks now, you would be very happy to be here and see your opera on the stage and I would be very happy to see it with you and your presence would be all we need to make the opera perfect in every way.* (February 7th is the opening date, I believe.) Many people, seeing my copy, have asked me where *Operas and Plays* can be bought here and those who have tried tell me it isn't to be had. Couldn't you send a consignment to several of the good bookstores? Big stores are best now. Nobody goes to little ones anymore & they've mostly gone out of business, anyway.

Always affectionately,

Four Saints in Three Acts received its premiere in Hartford on February 8, 1934. As Thomson recalls, "For six months and more the show was named at least once every week in every New York paper and in some paper somewhere in the United States every day." So successful was the production that it was decided to take the opera to Broadway, where it had a six-week run.

---

*Stein did not in fact attend the Hartford production of *Four Saints,* but heard it later, in Chicago.

April 21 [1934]

Dear Gertrude

The opera is closed now for the summer and everybody has had a lovely time about it and I must say that in every way it was very, very beautiful and of course there were some who didn't like the music and some who didn't like the words and even some who didn't like the decors or the choreography but there wasn't anybody who didn't see that the ensemble was a new kind of collaboration and that it was unique and powerful and I wish you could have seen the faces of people as they watched and listened. In the fall a tour is being planned and in the meanwhile I am meeting with various publishers. I have given *Susie Asado* to the Cos Cob Press and you will have a contract about it shortly. The usual 50–50 is all right and I will do the proofreading and work free because I happen to have an extra copy and the proofreading on it will be easy because the piece is very short. I don't think I can do that on the opera. Any fair arrangement that you think of will probably be all right with me. You see I sold the *Four Saints* to a producer and I didn't ask for any commission and I gave my services to the preparing of the production just as everybody else did and I made two trips to America to do these things at my own expense and all that was all right because I wanted the opera produced and it couldn't have been produced if I hadn't done those things. But I can't go on doing them free of course.

I should like to add that I have always considered that our not seeing each other in the last few years was a completely personal and sentimental matter and that I have never had any reason to question your fairness about anything or your good-will and I don't think you have ever had occasion for disbelieving in mine.

Always devotedly and loyally yours,

Upon his return to Paris after the Hartford and New York performances of Four Saints, *Thomson turned his thoughts again to a ballet. For Lincoln Kirstein's Ballet Caravan, Florine Stettheimer suggested the story of Pocahontas at the Court of James I, but Thomson felt that the subject lacked dramatic urgency. Kirstein proposed* Uncle Tom's Cabin *with a scenario by e e cummings; this, too, never came to fruition. And James Joyce suggested a ballet based on the children's games chapter of* Finnegans Wake, *to be produced at the*

Paris Opéra with choreography by Leonide Massine (1896–1979).
Thomson expressed interest in such a collaboration but eventually
declined, in part to avoid offending Gertrude Stein.

To Florine Stettheimer

[Paris]
July 8, 1934

Dear Florine

Beginning where your scenario stops, why not have major-domo presenting a miniature ballet of the John Smith beheading with Indian war dances and peace pipes and maybe even a wedding and then end with a pavane for King and Queen and entire court and Indians jumping and whooping (politely) at same time? This makes a place for a pas seul of Poca, and a pas de trois with Smith and Rolfe and then the debs as handmaidens to Poca. For the wedding party the pages as ushers and a finale apotheosis with the couple being blest by K and Q while the company dances the big finale.

I've done nothing. Been sick all the time. Better now but not well yet. Askews having very gay time in London. Would be there with them but I still have some X-ray treatments to go through. Everybody here demanding *Saints* for next year and much excited by photos. The most amusing spectacle of the season (as novelty) was the night races at Longchamps with marvelous lighting and supper and fireworks and everybody terribly dressed up. There is a revolution scheduled for today but so far nothing has happened. James Joyce is very desirous (rather insistent) that I do music for a ballet of his. The story is good, the subject is charming, everything is right with it, only I can't get interested. Pocahontas amuses me a great deal more. Ran into Carl V.V. by accident and the first thing he said was he wasn't intending to see me in Paris because he could see me in New York. Real reason, he was just arrived from Gertrude Stein's and didn't want to talk to me about it. Love to all of you.

Devotedly
Virgil

To James Joyce

August 24 [1934]

Dear Mr. Joyce:

Do forgive me for delay about the ballet. I was ill and then I went to London and then you were away. But I did read it all very carefully and I am certain there is a good spectacle there. If you have no objection I am going to take the text with me to New York next week and give Maurice Grosser a try at it. He is awfully good at getting a literary text on to a stage. It was Maurice, in fact, who performed so successfully the transposition of the Stein opera from a text about an opera to an actual scenario; and I am sure he will have happy solutions for many points where my own would be dull. As soon as we can get it into scenario form, I will send you the result. If, of course, you don't want me to do this, or to carry away your page proofs, please let me know and I will send them to you at once. I am sailing on the 29th of this month. *Ile-de-France.*

Very cordially yours,

Thomson spent the summer in Paris working on the incidental music for John Houseman's projected production of Euripides' Medea (never realized) and then returned to the States to prepare for the Chicago performances of Four Saints, which would be attended by Stein, Toklas, and Thomson's parents.

After the week's run, Thomson made New York his home until 1938, rooming in different apartments and only once venturing to Paris. Among his activities during this period was the organization of a series of concerts for Chick Austin at the Wadsworth Atheneum, many of which Thomson participated in as composer, conductor, or performer. The first such event was the premiere of two scenes of Avery Claflin's Hester Prynne, an opera based on Hawthorne's The Scarlet Letter.

To Chick Austin

Hotel Leonori, New York
November 2 [1934]

Dear Chick,

I'm off to Chi— tomorrow. Gertrude is going and Alice and Carl V.V. and the show is in fine shape and there is a new large flower

Valentine heart for Act I and gloves for all and new shells. I shall miss you. I've got a swell scene out of *Scarlet Letter* (A. Claflin) and Victor White is designing scenery and Avery is finding singers. No orchestra. Piano only. We might have a concert in early December. *Medea* is planned now for January. We ought to have it for F. & E. [Friends and Enemies of Modern Music] first in Hartford, an idea very pleasing for Houseman etc. Could we do maybe part of a week, like for the *Saints* only at cheaper prices and get in all the students and culture hounds?

> Toujours à toi
> Virgil

Gertrude and I have kissed, I wouldn't quite say made up, but kissed.

To Marc Blitzstein*

New York
February 26 [1936]

Dear Marc

I was ill all last week and I wrote you a letter just the same but it never got mailed so here is another.

I can't really sign that manifesto† because it doesn't make sense.

a. It accuses Pettis‡ of using the WPA for political purposes when the most he has done is to refuse to let somebody else use it for political purposes. If even that.

b. It turns out that the poem is quite normal politically anyway. Could be published or performed practically anywhere. It is the use of names and titles in an accusatory manner that makes it a case. It is less incendiary than it is libelous. Hence, although there may be small chance of Mellon or Ford making trouble, one cannot seriously object to the director of the concerts wishing to keep within the letter of the law. It may be foolish of him, but it is his right. In

---

*(1905–64), American composer best known for his stage works, many with radical political content, and for his adaptation of the Brecht-Weill *Threepenny Opera*

†Elie Siegmeister (b. 1909), the American composer and educator, recalls that the situation involved a Composers' Forum-Laboratory concert of his works. The program was to have included his satirical rounds about famous millionaires, which the WPA directors found too controversial.

‡Under the sponsorship of the Federal Music Project of the Works Progress Administration, pianist Ashley Pettis (1893–1978) founded the Composers' Forum-Laboratory (now simply the Composers' Forum), which offered the public the chance to discuss new music with its composers.

this case administrative sanctions are more probable than legal ones, but the issue remains the same. *Modern Music* has on several occasions refused to allow me the use of names in a like manner, while permitting freely the general exposition of my complaint.

c. I suspect, considering the weakness of the case, that Siegmeister may not be entirely pure in his motivation. Framing up situations to get oneself persecuted in, however entertaining it may be as a private amusement or as a source of annoyance to a personal enemy, does not justify marshalling the phalanxes of a solid professional front.

No, Marc, the case stinks. I hope you let it drop. I am sending a copy of this letter to Pettis.

Best and always,

While continuing the concert series in Hartford, Thomson was involved in a number of other projects and composed incidental music for plays directed by Houseman and Orson Welles (1915–85) under the auspices of the WPA Federal Theater. But Thomson's principal artistic association from this time was with the film director Pare Lorentz (b. 1905), for whom Thomson scored two documentaries sponsored by the U.S. Government, The Plough That Broke the Plains (1936) and The River (1937), which established Thomson's credentials as a film composer.

Before travelling to Paris, Thomson made his entry into the ballet world with Filling Station. The first successful ballet by an American on an American theme, it was given its premiere by Kirstein's Ballet Caravan at the Wadsworth Atheneum in 1938.

To Clara May Gaines Thomson

[New York]
March 24, 1936

Dear Mother,

It's been a long time since I answered any of your questions. My movie is all finished several weeks ago and is very handsome. It is called *The Plough That Broke the Plains,* was made for the Resettlement Administration in Washington, is the story of the big grass and cattle country out west and how it got to blowing away, and the dust storms and everything. The President has seen it and likes it and you will probably be able to see it before very long. The Negro Theater is also a government enterprise (WPA) and is doing beautifully. We have done 2 plays so far. The present one is a mystery-detective play and terribly nice and being successful. We are preparing a great big production of *Macbeth* which opens on April 9th. I hope to go to K.C. sometime this spring. There is possibility of making film about the Mississippi River and that would bring me very close. I am writing Ruby now to ask about floods. I hope she isn't too much inconvenienced by them.

love and kisses
Virgil

Yes I live in a flat, 12th floor, but no strike in this building. A nice flat, which I share with John Houseman, who is away all day and so I have it all to myself. Two bedrooms, big sitting room and kitchen. A German girl who cleans, lots of sun and air, no noise. The nicest flat I've had yet.

To Ruby Gleason

New York
March 24, 1936

Dear Ruby:

I'm worried about you and the floods. Please send news. I remember the floods in K.C. when I was a child and it was very romantic seeing people in boats in streets and going in McGinley's buggy to get spring water but I imagine it is all a good deal more disquieting to grown people and especially if you aren't feeling well. And how are you anyway and please write me all the news and how strong you feel and able to cope with all the troubles that arise like lights and water and such when they go off and maybe even food shortages and certainly a great deal more housework than ordinary. I wrote Mother today and told her to send you the letter all about what I've been doing.

love and kisses,
Virgil

New York
July 29, 1937

Darlings,

Yes I have been sort of out of view but the film finally got itself finished. I made 50 pages of score a day for a week and we recorded last Thursday and Friday with Alex [Smallens] and the [New York] Philharmonic and the music is fine (I like it) and the recording superb and we are now doing the final montage of music and speech and film which even with Lorentz's fantastic delays and inefficiencies can't take more than a few more days and then I shall either go away or stay vaguely near New York (probably the latter) and finish off some theater jobs I have for fall. Otherwise, news is scarce. Gershwin's death has made a great scandal about psychoanalysts, because for two years George's psycho had been telling him his headaches were due to incorrect thinking when all the time he had a perfectly real brain tumor. I am upset about Mary Butts' death and of course now regretting that I haven't communicated with her for some years. Please bring all information and documents available about her. Freddy [Ashton] and the Vic-Wells* seem to have a not so good press everywhere. What is wrong and does Freddy need a change? Maybe Lincoln should bring him over.

Please bestow my love abundantly on appropriate people.

For you and Kirk add kisses

V——

To Gertrude Stein

New York
February 1, 1938

Dear Gertrude

A Negro troupe belonging to the Federal Theater wants to produce *Four Saints* in Philadelphia for two weeks, starting rehearsal as quickly as possible. Since the admission charges are low, the author's fees are low too, but we are offered the maximum figure, which is $150 a week ($75 each). This is all right by Dramatists Guild. I consulted various persons, including Carl V.V., as to the advisability of

---

*London's Vic-Wells Ballet, later called the Sadler's Wells Ballet, became the Royal Ballet in 1956.

allowing it to be done, and the advice is to go ahead. I also am in favor of allowing it.

Since, however, your consent must be delayed by the mails, I have told the Federal Theater to go ahead with their plans, under all reserves of course regarding your wishes. No contract will be signed until I know them. Please inform me immediately.

As to the contract itself, the Federal Theater doesn't seem to be quite equal to the novelty of signing a contract with two persons, and since I should prefer not to do the signing & lending of money, I have prevailed upon Bennett Cerf* to act as both your and my agent. He was willing enough to act as yours but not too eager to act as mine, since it means nothing to him except a service to you. So if you are willing to let the opera be done, please write him authorizing him to sign the contract for you and handle the fees and requesting him to be so kind as to render a similar service to me (since that seems to be the only solution that doesn't present elaborate red-tape difficulties). He doesn't really mind doing it.

I've no idea what sort of show is planned, but it must be mostly a new one, since none of the old directors is available. It is the idea of new & different production that mostly tempts me about the whole idea. Because sooner or later that must be done. Otherwise the work is frozen. Like Satie's *Mercure,* which had such a fancy production by Massine and Picasso in 1923 that nobody has dared do it since.

I am very busy just now with a ballet. I did another movie too (*The River,* about the Mississippi) and some plays and I shall be in Paris before very long. I read your autobiography with pleasure.

I enclose my devoted affection,

Thomson returned to Paris in June 1938 and immediately took a long tour of the French countryside with Maurice Grosser. It was time for a change. "Getting back to work after America is never easy," Thomson later said, "because in Europe one's best work is spontaneous, whereas in America practically all work is done either on order or out of determination. This is a difference not to be quickly brushed aside; in Europe one must always wait till ready— otherwise there is no boldness in the product, nor any ease, nor lightness."

He began another opera, a setting of Webster's The Duchess of Malfi, but the project was soon abandoned.

---

*Co-founder of Random House and media personality, Cerf (1898–1971), as Stein's U.S. publisher, occasionally performed such favors.

TO GERTRUDE STEIN

Thonon-les-Bains
July 16, 1938

Dear G.

We know eagerness of old friends to believe the worst but your first guess was right. I don't look like the portrait. Not yet anyway. I am back at Thonon my old love and doing a *cure d'eau et de solitude* and writing things and having a lovely time. I was with Maurice in Nantua (delicious site) and the high Jura where he remains because he liked the altitude and the landscape all of which was fine by me because it gave me pretext for coming here which I've had on my mind for 12 years. So all is happy and I quite forgot to write to you about Philadelphia after being so firm indeed with Bennett Cerf that he must act as financial agent for us both because the Federal Theater couldn't think up a way of signing a contract with two authors of the same work and I didn't see any reason to do all the signing myself when you had a perfectly good publisher around and so he said he would and divide the proceeds and then there were long delays and it finally turned out that the man who was going to direct everything had administrative troubles because having got himself temporarily assigned to some radio work the radio unit found him valuable and wouldn't let him be assigned back or even lent to a theater so that is what happened to *Four Saints* in Philadelphia and it's really kind of a shame because it was Tommy Anderson* who was to run it and he was in the original company and knows everything by heart and he had a brand-new idea of making it all modern and about the Spanish war which I think might be quite fine. Regularly once or twice a year somebody has a plan to revive the *Saints* and I always say yes naturally but I don't really believe in any of them just yet. The epoch isn't right. The original production isn't forgotten enough. All of a sudden one day it will be forgotten and then *Four Saints* will be very easy to perform and it will start its natural life as a classic repertory piece which I know will be a long life. But don't forget we had 60 performances in 1934 and 60 in a year is a lot of performances for an opera and we had them because of Freddy [Ashton] & Florine & Mrs. Wayne† etc. so we can't regret our elegant production or its sixty performances but at the same time said elegant production weighs heavily on the mind of anybody who thinks of reviving the work now. All this to explain why I don't do

---

*(b. 1906), assistant stage manager of New York and Chicago productions of *Four Saints*
†Beatrice R. Wayne, later Godfrey (b. 1904), created the role of St. Teresa I.

anything myself about putting it on again. It is really all right and the score is all ready for any time anybody is serious about it.

Love toujours,

In the fall, Thomson settled into a smaller apartment at 17, quai Voltaire and began work on his first book, The State of Music, *which was published by William Morrow in 1939. In the following letter to Thayer Hobson (1897–1967), the company's president, Thomson offers not only a progress report but a premonition of World War II. The Germans had furthered their advance on Europe, and in 1940 they would conquer France.*

To Thayer Hobson

October 4, 1938

Dear Hobson

All goes well. There was a war and now it is over and I have written a book that is to say part of a book but don't be alarmed it is not about the war. I have also written one act of an opera and on the whole am not unpleased with myself except a little annoyed at the book which seems to go on in its own chaotic fashion no matter how much I try to force it into other fashions. That is all to the good eventually but it means that I am not able just now to slice it into neat chapters that I could send off for my agent to sell to magazines. I had hoped I could send some sample chapters to you at least but I don't really have them in a properly polished-up state. Because it is becoming quite a largish book and I don't think it advisable to stop the flow till I come to a natural stopping place.

It is to be a complete account of the musical world (no less) and includes esthetics economics politics and even some technical matters, the whole show in fact from pedagogy to opera and movies, including the business policies of symphony orchestras and an exposé of the pseudo-educational rackets.

Not an encyclopedia of course. Just my opinions about all these things. But still I have to do lots of explaining in order to have my opinions make sense. I've written 15 or 20 thousand words and that is practically all introduction. I haven't touched the main meat of the book which is my economico-esthetic theory. No doubt I shall do later a good deal of pruning and transposing in what I've written but at the moment there is no use. Nor am I doing any travelling around until I am nearer the end and need some flashy bits of news and scholarship for embellishment.

All goes well now and the war's over and France is settling down to a good winter's work. I presume New York is ditto. If you have any giveaway copies of new detective stories (I hear there's a Perry Mason), they would come in handy.

Cordially and very sincerely yours,

To Ruby Gleason

Paris
October 10 [1938]

Dear Ruby,

This will go off today but certainly too late to wish you a happy birthday at the proper birthday time. However, I do and I send you kisses. I do not send at this time a present (I'll mix it up with Christmas) because of my delays. I came to Paris a month ago and started to look for a flat. And there was a war. And then there wasn't a war. And then the flat I had expected to take was not available after all. And then I found another. And I presumably am taking that one. So with all the day to day uncertainty I kept thinking I would write tomorrow because there would be more definite news and now that's a month gone by and I hope you haven't worried about me too much. I am taking a flat because I want to sit quietly for some time and finish the work I've begun and it will take some time. I can't tell you what a pleasure to be back after those years in New York which were useful and all but not at all pleasant.

I don't know what is in home newspapers about Europe. But whatever it is don't worry about war. There isn't going to be any. Not this winter at any rate.

Love & kisses,
V——

To Kirk and Constance Askew

Paris
November 5, 1938

Angels,

You are very bad angels to keep me in the dark about everything. I just now learn from practically strangers that Kirk had his operation but beyond that I know nothing at all. Now Constance please sit down and scribble me a factual note. Thank you papa for a nice letter from Pennsylvania even though it avoided all reference to yourself. I've a new flat at my same quai Voltaire house. I am very happy about it. It is full of bright color. And the pleasure of being at home again after five years of trunk life is quite something. Theodate* is around, taking lessons and being charming. Also looking beautiful. D—— and L—— R—— are near neighbors of mine. I am devoted to L—— but I find D—— (who is being poor, alcoholic and in the midst of getting psychoanalysed) about as nasty a character as I have encountered in some years. I hope it may all be just a phase of the psychoanalysis. Nancy Cunard has been around and charming, temporarily out of Spain, going back shortly. She fights the Spanish war violently, as she always fought her private ones. She is handsomer now. Janet Flanner† is being seen some and she is full of her passion for Kirk Askew. I wish you a pretty birthday, Kirkywirky.

Paris is utterly charming and dirt cheap. The provinces are even cheaper and charminger. I've never seen France so happy. (Nothing to do with the war. It was that way all summer.) Blessings and kisses for both of you. Please come and see me in my yellow walls.

L & K,
V.

Marian Chase Dunham (1915–51), the wife of film journalist Harry Dunham (1910–43), was a close friend of Thomson's. In his many letters to her, Thomson related the activities of his wide circle of colleagues and acquaintances.

---

*Theodate Johnson (b. 1907), American soprano, later an editor of *Musical America*; sister of the architect Philip Johnson
†(1892–1978), American writer long resident in Paris; a regular contributor to *The New Yorker* from 1925 to 1975

To Marian Chase Dunham

February 20 [1939]

Maggie angel

You have never seen such an industrious literary man as I am. Every day I write a book from 9 to 1 and almost every day from 1:30 to 5 or 7. It is a long book and takes lots of writing but it goes on quite rapidly and is I imagine half or more done. Maurice paints vegetables and sea shells. One day it's a dozen white endives and another it's a red and purple cabbage with lace on the edges that Mary Garden's sister sent him by air mail from Scotland. Sherry made money on a big Picasso number for *Time* and is doing now a Joyce one. Plus regular reporting. His fortunes are picking up and M★ is being charming and efficient. The Breton-Hugnet war is at a standstill, Breton having won an empty victory in one small battle.† Georges retains the moral advantage and has taken away all the good surrealists. Arp & Man Ray & Eluard & Max Ernst & Marcel Duchamp & Hugnet are doing a magazine of their own, called *Plastique,* very pretty with trick typography. Breton and his little boys that remain chez Deux Magots we call Snow White and the Seven Dwarfs. Yesterday a big picnic lunch at the Cliquet-Pleyels and we giggled for hours and made music. And about once a week bridge with Mary [Reynolds] and Marcel [Duchamp] and Mme Langlois. The latter still has her shingles but she goes out all the time and is really all right except the shingles hurt. Sauguet's opera [*La Chartreuse de Parme*] has premiere the 6th of March. It is going to be a colossal success. The [Café de] Flore is a zoo and so crowded you can't get a seat. The Askews never thanked me for presents. BBC is dickering about *Four Saints,* and the Théâtre de la Monnaie in Bruxelles (which is the big state opera) about *Filling Station.* I have sent my *salamandre*‡ to the basement and I now make open wood fire which is heavenly and I am much happier, not so dried out and restless, and I don't sleep all the time as I did before. Mary Garden is coming to tea on Tuesday. I have a silver tea tray (German silver) from the flea market, a present from the Mangans, and a new chair, also from puce. Bicycling is done too and much gymnasium and much reading of books chez Sylvia Beach. He went to call on G. Stein and was prettily received but didn't care for either of the girls. Janet [Flanner] is doing a *New Yorker* job on the concentration camps

★Margareta Mangan, second wife of Sherry Mangan
†Thomson remembers this as a "surrealist squabble."
‡"a hard-coal Franklin stove" (*Virgil Thomson*)

for Spanish [refugees] and has gone to the border to do it. It would seem (according to leftists) that the camps are made as uncomfortable as possible so as to encourage refugees to go back to Spain, but until some kind of political amnesty is arranged nobody wants to go chez Franco. At the moment you can apparently get gold watches for two cigarettes. Every known kind of collection is being taken up for the refugees here and shows being given all the time. We miss you. I miss you. Will April bring you back? The springish weather just now is lovely and the sun comes in my windows. We are expecting Touche* as per schedule and please give my love to Harry. Also send news of [Maurice] Evans's *Henry IV.* Do you think Orson will dare to do it? I doubt it.

llllove and kkkkisses
V——

To Aaron Copland

Paris
March 20, 1939

Dear Aaron

I imagine you are as vague about news of me as I am about what you are up to. Besides which I have never thanked you for *The Second Hurricane* and for the book.† I now do so. And very seriously indeed. The *Hurricane* in score is as satisfactory as it was in performance. It is a very beautiful work, a very rich work, touching, exciting, gay and a real music-pleasure. Your book I read through twice and I still find it a bore. Marian writes me it sells swell and that is a good thing of course. Not that the book doesn't contain a hundred wise remarks about music. But it also contains a lot of stuff that I don't believe and that I am not at all convinced you believe. Supposing you do believe that analytic listening is advantageous for the musical layman, it is still quite possible and not at all rare to believe the contrary. It even remains to be proved that analytic listening is possible even. God knows professional musicians find it difficult enough. I suspect that persons of weak auditive memory do just as well to let themselves follow the emotional line of a piece, which they can do easily, and which they certainly can't do very well while trying to analyze a piece tonally. In any case, I find it a bit high-handed to assume the whole psychology.

---

*John Latouche (1917–56), American poet and lyricist
†*What to Listen for in Music* (1939)

I find similarly unproved assumptions in the musical form chapter. I do not believe, for instance, that the loose and varied sonata form practiced by the great Viennese has very much relation to the modern French reconstructed form that d'Indy made up for pedagogical purposes. The first kind, even in its final Mahlerian decay, retained a spontaneity, a Viennese *désinvolture,* that enabled it to be written consecutively, and most certainly it was practically always written consecutively, Beethoven's notebooks being precompositional reflections, like anybody else's notebooks. The modern French version, on the other hand, is really written as you describe, that is to say, pieced together like a picture puzzle. That there is a cardinal difference between the two is proved by the fact that the mock synthetic version has never been able to be reintroduced into Vienna successfully. The Viennese thing is dynamic, even as late as Strauss and Schoenberg. The French thing is static, like nearly all French musical conceptions. The composition procedure in the two cases is hence quite different. I don't say you should discuss such controversial matter in an elementary textbook, but I don't think you are quite justified in discussing the sonata form as if it were one thing instead of two and as if no controversy existed about it. You know privately that it is the most controversial matter in all music, has been so since Beethoven. I find it a little dull of you and a little unctuous to smooth all that over with what I consider falsehoods.

That static-dynamic business you never go into either. You describe even rhythm as if it were a static pattern. Prosodic meter *is* static mostly. But what about muscular impulsions? Dance music and the ballet are nothing but, rhythmically. The Viennese sonata form (and this is known historically, is in the books) is a superimposing of this dynamic, muscular dance rhythm on to the static French overture, the fluid Italian song-style being the combining agent.

I'm not trying to rewrite your book for you. I'm just complaining that you didn't think it up for yourself. Almost any music teacher could have written it. Maybe not quite so smooth and high-toned. Certainly not nearly so clear and authoritative as when you give your own answers to things. But that is far from always.

Enough of that.

What the hell has happened to our music-printing business? Not a word, a catalog, a copy of anything have I had. The last letter I had from Lehman★ was in September and he was about to publish my

---

★American conductor Lehman Engel (1910–82), along with Thomson, Copland, and Marc Blitzstein, had founded the Arrow Music Press, a cooperative music-publishing venture, in 1937. Thomson refers to *Scenes from the Holy Infancy According to Saint Matthew,* a set of three choral pieces.

Christmas pieces. Please write or ask him to do so about it all and if anything has been published why can't I have a catalog or even a complimentary copy. After all, my name is (or was) on the incorporation papers.

Lincoln writes *Billy the Kid* is a success and I am happy.

My book gets toward being finished. I like it better than yours. I only hope it sells as well.

Devotedly,

To Clara May Gaines Thomson

Paris
September 19 [1939]

Dear Mother,

Another little note which I am giving to a lady to mail in New York. The mail is so uncertain these days that I try to send a note every time I can by somebody who is sailing. Everything continues to be quiet here and pleasant. I shall probably leave for the U.S. in a month or so. I don't see much use in it just now, because boats are very seldom and very very expensive. Only first-class passage is to be had and that has gone up 50%. So I think I might as well wait till the crowd thins out. There is absolutely no danger here now. If there should be air raids (which is very unlikely) I have a good solid cellar. Also I can go stay with friends in the country if I want to. I like it better now in town. You wouldn't really know there was a war except for the newspapers and also that the streets are dark at night. So don't bother about me. I'll be along eventually, but I'm not hurrying.

Love,
Virgil

To Kirk and Constance Askew

September 22, 1939

Angels,

I wrote you one note but you never know what arrives at its destination these days so here is just a kiss from quiet Paris and I shall probably be seeing you around November. I am at home and I write some music. Max Ernst, Hans Bellmer (all the Germans, in fact) are in concentration camps. Sherry lives in the country and comes to town every day. He is rather weighty about the war. One might think he was running it. Gertrude is still in the country but she writes she will be coming to Paris later. The best war joke is Miss M—— who has organized at her chateau a unit to rebuild devastated France. The gov't suggested an ambulance unit or hospital but she said no, rebuilding devastated France was her specialty. So she has it all organized and lots of lady truck drivers at Blerencourt. Sauguet and the Dali sisters★ are also at Arcachon. Bébé had a month's leave (he is a machine-gunner) to take an opium cure. When that is over I fancy he will maybe get transferred to camouflage. It is not decided yet whether camouflage will be surrealist, neo-romantic or what. Certainly not cubist, like last time. I am betting it will start neo-fauve.

Love & Kisses

By now, according to Thomson, "many of France's Americans were undecided about whether to go home; and our Embassy was advising flight, even chartering ships to hasten it, since normal berths were scarce and out of price. Within the first month, most of the nervous ones had been got off, and by November nearly all were gone. Among those who had chosen not to leave were a number who had jobs in France and some with property, also a few habitués attached to living there, like Mary Reynolds and Sherry Mangan and Gertrude Stein." And Thomson himself.

To Aaron Copland

January 5, 1940

Dear Aaron,

Thanks for glowing review of my book and I'm delighted you liked it. Write me please how you found Hollywood. I mean working conditions and are you pleased and was there any serious trouble.

Paris is calm and very pleasant. The Arrow Press sends me music every now and then, some of it pretty, some of it the same old shit. Was rather pleased by a Cowell number. If I make any money from the book, as seems likely, I shall publish something. What are you publishing, if any?

★Salvador Dali and his wife, Gala

130

I don't know when I shall go to U.S., certainly not this season. Is our A.C.A.* behaving? Let me know all the gory. I have some recent sheets from them. The committee activities sound fine. I'm skeptical about the value of the composer vs. critic protest re American pieces. That there should be bad will on either side requires, I think, some proof, some fuller explanation of motives than has been offered yet. The whole dispute smacks of small time to me.

The funny thing about it is that it only comes up with regard to the subsidized orchestral concerts and the subsidized opera houses, practically never in the case of concerts that are supported by their box-office intake, like the big soloists, the string quartets, and such. Stadiums and pops don't have that trouble either. I suspect I am right in maintaining that contemporary local music is framed in the big orchestras, framed to flop. The critics may be unconscious stooges in the process, and maybe a wicked few of them are not quite so unconscious about it. But whether they are or aren't aware of their attitude makes little difference on a job that they would get fired from if they changed their attitude. (Remember Teddy Chanler's quick exit from the *Boston Herald* when he wrote of the Boston Symphony as if it were a human organization possibly capable of error, when he wrote daily-press criticism as composers would like to see it written.) I think it useless and pretty undignified to attack the little men that write the stuff, because I don't think they could get away with doing it otherwise, even if they wanted to. Please tell the A.C.A. boys this for me.

L. & K.

To Briggs Buchanan

Paris
January 13, 1940

D.B.

It was a pleasure a great pleasure to have your letter full of affection and photos (one looks like each of you) and clippings and critical comment on prose opus. In reply to your comments,

1. I do think class distinctions are necessary in professional life and the only such possible are distinctions about real ability and real ability (dependable ability) never comes from anything but training and

---

*In 1937 Thomson, Copland, and "several dozen others" had founded the American Composers Alliance, "a society for licensing the performance of 'serious' music, a need at that time not being met by existing societies" (*American Music Since 1910*).

practice. Talent merely gives people a reason for acquiring ability, and technique is what provokes the higher flights of fancy. Note that I am not speaking from the consumer's point of view; for him anything is fine that pleases him. But my business is to know in advance

a. what music will sound like in execution, and
b. whether it will hold the consumer's attention while he finds out whether he "likes" it or not and can remember it.

One only learns these things dependably by training and experience. Naturally the young are full of bright ideas, many of them lousy; the trying out of them I include under experience.

2. About the absence of controversial criticism of the book. I didn't expect any. There isn't much of that in music. Anyway this isn't the 18th century, when people used to "refute" one another. We are more likely just to swallow or to spit out. The music world seems to be swallowing *The State of Music* with considerable smacking of lips. I expected a wry face from Harvard; it's only natural. But I guess they all read it, from what I hear. The poets and painters like it too. The only anger has come from the exploiting worlds. The symphony trustees are shocked and silently thankful, for both my sake and theirs, that I didn't mention Toscanini. The ladies who run the Metropolitan Opera Guild are openly furious, as if they had been made to look a little ridiculous. The Museum of Modern Art opines the book is brilliant but fallacious. You see all that is just side issues. The book was aimed at the profession and seems to be hitting its mark surprisingly. And in spite of the continual wisecracking in it, it isn't supposed to be controversial. It's supposed to be just God's truth every word of it and time somebody said same out loud.

We hear from the newspapers that a war is going on. That means that European states are exerting economic and military pressure on one another. What it's all about is anybody's guess. Mine is that it is a doing over of the 1914–1918 war (whatever that was about) and that since it is being directed by people who remember the other very well, it is being done in every way possible as differently as possible. But the differences, as you have no doubt noticed, only bring out the essential similarities. The intention in the repetition of the other war would seem to be rather like that in replaying bridge hands. To see if by redoing everything very carefully indeed the same cards might not be made to give a better result. Everybody connected with the English government says it will be long. Paris tends to opine it will be over this year. I've liked it so far. Paris has never been sweeter and quieter and pleasanter and kinder and more sensibly reasonable about everything. The war itself, of course, is rarely mentioned. Neither are those tiresome old peacetime subjects that we worried around for 20 years, such as the surrealist quarrels and the perfidy of Salvador Dali and the bad manners of G. Stein and the death of J. Cocteau and the extreme elegance of Christian Bérard's never washing and the superhuman excellence of P. Picasso, our local and equally tiresome Toscanini.

Sherry Mangan has moved into my building. Also Leonid Berman.* Also Theodate Johnson. We spend the weeks dining with one another. I have a poetry salon on Friday evenings. I admit painters because they are fun, but we never mention painting (I've heard enough about that in the last 19 years of Paris residence); I discourage musicians from coming too. And I won't have any of those unhappy women whose husbands are at the war or anybody who knits. But the poets and their muses and their domesticated friends are fine and we have nice times. Give my love to Florence† and spank the kids for me, just to remind them that I exist.

Devotedly

To Maurice Grosser

April 13 [1940]

D.M.

Here all is much the same. I continue the portraits. There are 21 now in the new series, and they are extraordinarily varied. They are sometimes quite long. Peggy Guggenheim‡ turned out to be a whole sonatina in three movements (the 1st movement consisting of 6 canons at various intervals) all done in one sitting. I do Mary Widney§ this afternoon, Mabille‖ tomorrow, [Mary] Garden the next day and so on. I am two weeks behind in my copying. The portraits are attracting considerable attention. Picasso came to hear them (and other things) and is giving me lots of praise and advertising. I've written to two more people in U.S. for money, but no cables have come so far. I expect something or other this week. My physical culture continues also and my figure is something you haven't seen for ten years. I'm not sure if it ever has been quite like this; I even have a girdle of Apollo. The war seems to have started up again, but

---

*older brother of Eugene Berman, also an artist
†Buchanan's wife
‡Maguerite Guggenheim (1898–1979), gallery owner and artists' patron; niece of Solomon R. Guggenheim
§an American friend in Paris who later lived at the Chelsea Hotel
‖Thomson describes Mabille as "a doctor with surrealist connections."

so far nobody I know seems to have been hurt. Sherry's trip to America would seem to have been cancelled for the moment and his salary raised. Tonny is having a show soon. Mlle Philibert* is devoted, domineering, and a bit gaga; also she complains her legs don't hold her up like they ought to. I've definitely scrapped *The Duchess of Malfi* for good. At least as an opera. I should like to do music for the play, because that would help, but just music, as indicated in the text, for the Loretto scene and the madmen's ballet and maybe a noise intermezzo for offstage while she's having a baby with screams. And do the play without cuts and without scenery but with fancy clothes, regular Elizabethan production system. A smallish theater too, it needs, so everybody could hear all the words and be in the midst of it. I find that anything you do to the words in the way of singing them alleviates their effect rather than sharpens it and that too much music tends to formalize the characters, whereas their great potency in the play is their lack of formalization. So, after much fiddling around and two years trying to make it an opera, I'm off it for good, except as just what it is, a magnificent & poetic melodrama in Elizabethan verse about a Spanish family resident in the south of Italy a century previous to that. As such it would make a swell show and a vehicle for elocutionary acting. *Am* I happy to be rid of it! Arp has presented me with a sculpture made especially for my mantelpiece. Asparagus and strawberries are in. I found among my papers a song I wrote in Italy last summer, the dirge out of *The White Devil*. It is very fine. All my music is good these days. It has jumped up a step. And I've learned a new Mozart sonata.

L. & K.

V——

To Maurice Grosser

April 16 [1940]

D.M.

Your letter finally [arrived] yesterday announcing 2 sales and that very pleasant, though it only pays the voyage. I am doing portraits again and I am pleased with them because they are more direct than the old ones and easier to understand musically. I do one practically every day. My Picasso cover for *La Valse grégorienne* is quite hand-

---

*Mathilde Philibert, older sister of Louise Langlois. Thomson recalled that when Mme Langlois died in April 1939, "in the French way . . . [Mlle Philibert] set out, as surrogate, to be my friend."

some. It is just the words of the title as I gave them to him and a couple of curlycues added, no picture or anything, which is exactly what I wanted, also the signature large and impressive. Everybody is getting mobilized these days. Sauguet left today. Hugnet leaves (presumably) next week. That will leave nobody much in Paris but Max* and me and a couple of consumptives. Plus, of course, the old and the very young. Lots of very young about; the Flore is lousy with poets, and the cafés of Montmartre and the Place Cambronne running over with child whores and baby pimps. I wrote an article for *Modern Music.* I continue to practice Mozart, which I play very beautifully, and I have a new theory about the piano sonatas. They are not camp, as I had thought, or just sort of routine writing, as most musicians think; they imitate things. Sometimes they imitate symphonies, which makes them easy to understand; but then sometimes they imitate music-boxes or wind-instrument pieces and are not personally expressive at all except unconsciously, so those have to be played like music-boxes or wind-instrument pieces, and then they come out not dull at all but sharp and lovely and terrible fun and quite loud and rich. I have some new friends, mostly Jewish *femmes du monde,* the Marie-Laure de Noailles† group, though I steer as politely as possible away from that one, who is a nice enough woman but a pure figment of her own imagination (except as a professional hostess, which she is good at). Otherwise she is just Tallulah‡ or Garden or any other vedette out of water, and I find Garden is enough of that sort of thing in one's life at any one time. I don't know anybody coming over to bring Tomassin's portrait. I am disappointed in him, by the way. He let me read a lot of his poetry, and it turned out to be just god-awful cheap and silly. I said that to Philip Lasell, who replied "don't tell me about that young man, I've had him living with me in the next room for weeks and I assure you there is nothing 'pure' or disinterested about him. He's just a smooth little *artiste.*" I continue to get thin and my physical culture man does things about stomach muscles and my chin and cheeks are beginning to hang a little. If the new figure seems permanent I shall have to have all my new clothes taken in. At the moment I swim around in them and enjoy it. I seem to enjoy practically everything these days. I haven't had so much energy in years and everybody loves me. The Friday nights are crowded and everybody calls them brilliant. April has been bitter cold for two weeks but I suppose eventually warmth

---

*Max Kenna, American fashion designer

†(1902–70), Parisian hostess and patron of the arts; helped support Luis Buñuel, Salvador Dali, and Ned Rorem, among others.

‡Tallulah Bankhead (1902–68), flamboyant American actress

must arrive. My publisher wants another book and I said I would do the musical prosody one (I could do it in no time) if he wanted it at the same terms as the other. In that case I would do it this summer, or maybe start now. I should like to go to N.Y. in the fall if there is any work for me. That and if the war keeps on here. I'm still liking the war, but I doubt if shall be liking it much next year.

L. & K.
V——

Thomson published the following article in the quarterly Modern Music, *casting it in the form of a letter to the editor, Minna Lederman.*

April 18, 1940

Dear M.L.:

It's been a long cold winter and on the whole one of the nicest I've ever spent, although I am not one that cares much as a rule for snow and ice.

One of the delights of this pleasant city has always been its poverty of music. Not concert music and opera; we have more of those than New York has; but music-in-the-air, I mean, that ambience of musical noises, the sound of gramophones and radios, of vocalists at practice and of pianists at play, not to speak of junior's ineluctable assiduity on the saxophone, that makes residence in any American city predominantly an auditory experience. Italy is noisy with music like America, only the pitch is higher; and the sound of an Italian village in the evening can be pretty beautiful sometimes, especially if each of the five or six cafés has an outdoor loudspeaker to blend the bleatings of infants and of tenors into a sumptuous tutti that quite puts to shame any timidly insistent nightingale that may be needing to voice its libido in a garden at the same time.

Well, this year not only have the lights been dimmed in the Ville-Lumière (and very prettily too), but sound has been reduced to present needs. Street-singers have disappeared; buses disappear after nine o'clock at night; even in the day they are fewer. After midnight, when the cafés close, there is literally no noise anywhere except for a few taxis and private cars bringing private people home from private gatherings. One never hears a radio through a window anymore; I think that the strict application of the regulations about not letting light filter through curtains and shutters makes everybody unconsciously more careful about noise, though there are no regulations on the subject any different from those already in force. (Imposing your radio on the neighbors has for some years been frowned on by the law.)

Anyway, Paris, which has always been, compared to New York or to anything Italian, a quiet city (only London, which is lonesome, as Paris distinctly is not, can be more tomb-like at night), has become even more reposeful to the ear than it was. One almost wishes for a little roar sometimes, so pleasantly suburban have our lives become.

Of course, in peacetimes (a silly word that, because never have I passed such a peaceful time as these first eight months...), just as Paris was the one musical capital where one didn't have to hear any music one didn't want to hear, it was also the best place there was for hearing practically any music old or new that one did want to hear. The latter charm has disappeared. One does not hear any new music; there isn't any. There are a few modern concerts, of course; the Triton puts on a show occasionally; the subventioned orchestras play their minimum legal number of minutes per year of first auditions of French work. The radio tootles its way through many a trio too for wind instruments in ye moderne style. There is plenty of all that and innumerable festivals of Ravel. But still there isn't much that could be classified as musically news.

Perhaps I had better say just what there is, beginning with the radio. The British radio is occupied entirely with cheery numbers of a music-hall nature meant for soldiers and with comforting political speeches for the home-folks. The French radio does plays, modernistic chamber music, classics from discs, and political propaganda in foreign languages. Never have I heard so much German on the air. The two Paris operas and the symphony concerts are broadcast regularly also. Germany gives us, in addition to the famous and completely charming Lord Haw-Haw★ (in English), symphony concerts (largely Wagner) and excellent American jazz. The best radio jazz in Europe always did come, I don't know why, from Florence and from Berlin. Since the stations of Danzig, Warsaw, and Katowice were taken over by the Germans, they have been putting out the same massive orchestral programs as Berlin and Hamburg and the same excellent American jazz, all with added kilowatts. Prague does not seem to have been incorporated into that particular chain. Its programs, less massive and less jazzy, continue to send out the Czechish Opera and to indulge the Czechish taste for string quartets.

★William Joyce, who broadcast Nazi propaganda to England; executed for treason after the war

The Rhineland stations do quartets too and a good deal of Mozart and Haydn. Vienna is mostly waltzy now and Budapest Hungarian-dancey. Algeria and Morocco play native-style music too. Spain not; from there one gets little beyond politics and church services. And Spanish church music would seem to rest content on the Bostonian Catholic level where it has reposed for some years already. The Belgian stations have picked up a little, but on the whole their public seems to prefer light music of the Delibes sort and dance music that is definitely "sweet." Holland and Switzerland hold the fort for Sebastian Bach and for the oratorio style. Italy, in addition to the Florentine jazz I mentioned above, and to some quite decent news broadcasts in various languages, has been doing super-first-class opera. Most of the good Italian singers being at home this year, because their government is as skittish as ours is about giving out passports, the operas in both Rome and Milan have been brilliant as to execution. I heard a *Trovatore* one night that revealed a degree of expressive variety and of theatrical power I didn't know was in the old thing. The roles were sung by Maria Caniglia★ and Cloe Elmo† and [Beniamino] Gigli.‡ [Gino] Marinuzzi§ conducted, and I assure you the orchestra "talked." I also heard, superbly rendered, Pizzetti's‖ *Fedra*. It is quite a fine number. It is *Pelléas et Mélisande* keyed up (or down, as you like) to the melodramatic intensity of *Tosca*. I doubt if it will change any composer's life much, but it is certainly a fine big number. My radio doesn't get Moscow very well or Helsinki or Athlone, but when it does the programs seem to be mostly routine stuff one knows and the performances in no way extraordinary. I might close the subject of radio by mentioning that last summer, when I was in Italy, the young people used to sit around pretty sadly till eleven o'clock, when the Juan-les-Pins station began its international hour of popular music, and that even they sat quietly enough through a certain amount of Spanish tangos and French javas and the inevitable "Santa Lucia" (the hour's theme song) for the satisfaction of hearing real American music, by which they mean Duke Ellington• and Bob Crosby★★ et al. If you could see the faces light up when that comes on, you would understand why America, with immigration to it virtually stopped by both their government and ours, still represents to the youth of Italy a dream country, although

---

★(1905–79), Italian soprano
†(1910–62), Italian Mezzo-soprano
‡(1890–1957), Italian tenor
§(1882–1945), Italian conductor and composer
‖(1880–1968), Italian composer of conservative tendencies
• (1899–1974), American pianist, composer and bandleader (b.1913)
★★American bandleader (b. 1913)

instead of its being the country of Business Opportunity it once was, it has become now the land of Beautiful Music. They don't call that music jazz or swing or anything special; they call it *la musica americana*. And their hats are off to it.

To return to Paris and to what we have here. The orchestral concerts are very much what they always were (except for one orchestra less) and they all play to full houses at the same time, which is Sundays at a quarter to six. There are Polish and Finnish benefits at other times. The Polish programs seem to concentrate on Chopin, not a semiquaver of Szymanowski or of his school. The Finnish ones make a little gesture about Sibelius, a tiny little gesture, you know, nothing graver than *Finlandia* and a few songs. I fancy it is considered that the playing of a whole symphony might conceivably alienate Parisian sympathies.

Wagner has been played, and all went off fine. Three pieces were announced for the end of a regular Sunday, though later two of these were removed, as presumably the playing of the first would provoke such a demonstration that the others couldn't be got through. Demonstration there was, indeed, all for Mr. Wagner. When the conductor (it was Paul Paray)* first appeared, there was a tumult of angry protest demanding why he had cut out two of the numbers. So he made a speech that didn't make much sense, as it had evidently been prepared in view of an anti-German demonstration, about how he had been a soldier in the other war and that culture knows no frontiers. Applause and loud cheers from all and some grumbling from the Wagner aficionados, who still wanted their three pieces. They didn't get them; but the *Tannhäuser* overture they did get was cheered for a quarter of an hour. All that was two months or more ago; I haven't heard of any Wagner being played since.

The opera repertories are much as always, except for Wagner, although works that require lots of scene shifting are avoided, because the stagehands are mostly mobilized.

Alfred Bruneau's† *Le Rêve* has been revived. I haven't seen it; Garden tells me it is Bruneau's best work and that the American baritone [Arthur] Endrèze is superb in it. I did see Xavier Leroux's‡ *Le Chemineau* for the first time in nearly thirty years (the French Opera of New Orleans used to give it) and was delighted. It has a good libretto by Jean Richepin; it is admirably written for voices and sonorously orchestrated. Its musical material is honest and direct. There are tender passages and great climaxes and from beginning to

*(1885–1979), French composer and conductor
†(1857–1934), French composer and critic
‡(1863–1919), French composer

end less folderol and musical chichi than I've practically ever heard in my life. It is music that is both competent and sincere. Such music is shockingly rare in this age of our art's decline. Hearing it gave me seriously to reflect whether any effort toward sincerity, the kind of terrific and humane sincerity that makes Molière Molière, for example, has ever been systematically exerted in music. Maybe a little by Sebastian Bach and by Schumann and a very little by Brahms. Practically everybody else has had his eye on a different ball, either the sharpness of auditive effect or the force of personal projection, or the sensuality of mystic contemplation, not to speak of the celebration of traditional rites, theatrical and religious. I have no conclusions to offer on the subject; I merely note that Leroux's *Le Chemineau* provoked that bit of meditation one Sunday afternoon.

Honegger's *Jeanne d'Arc au bûcher* for orchestra, chorus, soloists, and Ida Rubinstein* (isn't the text by Claudel? I think it is) I missed last June and again of late here. Music lovers consider it a most impressive work. In Brussels recently its performance provoked a francophile demonstration, although Honegger is, I believe, technically Swiss.

The Milhaud *Medea* goes on being announced and postponed year after year. A part of it was given (successfully, I believe) last spring in Flemish at the Antwerp Opera. Flemish Antwerp has been for several years now Europe's Hartford.

There is stage music by Sauguet with Sheridan's *School for Scandal,* now playing to good houses. Haven't been. There are no new movies, French movie-production being, ever since September, at a complete standstill.

I fancy my account of these little matters doesn't make very clear why I have enjoyed my winter so much. I'm not sure I know exactly. I've tried to tell you what it's like here musically; for other matters there are plenty of reports in the weekly press. What I can't describe very well is the state of calm that permeates our whole intellectual life. Not the vegetable calm of a backwater country or the relative and quite electric calm that is supposed to exist at the center of a moving storm. Rather it is the quietude of those from whom have been lifted all the burdens and all the pressures, all the white elephants and all the fears that have sat on us like a nightmare for fifteen years. I am not referring to any imminence of German invasion or of its contrary. I am talking about that imminence of general European cultural collapse that has been hanging over us ever since the last war ended. As long as the tension was mounting everybody was unhappy. Fascism in Italy, the Jewish persecutions in

---

*(1885–1960), Russian dancer and actress

Germany, the Civil War in Spain, a hundred other scenes of the heartbreaking drama have kept us jittery and trembling. It has been imagined and hoped that possibly some of the brighter boys might stop the progress of it all by taking thought. Our opinions were demanded on every imaginable variety of incident in power politics and in class warfare, whether we had any access or not to correct information about such incidents (which we usually didn't) or any degree of political education that would make our opinions worth a damn, even if we had had access to the facts of life. For ten years now all sides have been pressing us to talk; indeed many have talked, and I should say that in consequence a great deal less real work got done in those years than was done in the preceding decade.

That's all over now. We are on the chute. And in spite of the enormous inroads on a man's time and money that being mobilized represents, and in spite of the strictness of both military and political leadership over all sorts of intellectual operations, the intellectual life has picked up distinctly. The lotus-land of whether surrealism is really gratuitous and whether such and such a picture by Picasso is really worth the price asked (for, dear Reader, it was indeed by becoming passionate over such matters that many fled the impossibility of being anything beyond merely passionate over matters like Jewry and Spain, because they knew that mere passion wouldn't get anybody anywhere and that passion was all anybody had to offer on any side, excepting maybe a little a quiet opportunism in England and in Russia), anyway, the 1930s, that stormy lotus-land of commercialized high esthetics to which New York's Museum of Modern Art will long remain a monument, have quietly passed away. It is rather surprising and infinitely agreeable to find that poets now are writing poetry again rather than rhymes about current events; that painters paint objects, not ideas; that composers write music to please themselves, there being no longer any Modern Music concert committees to please. Most surprising and agreeable of all is the fact that the young (with so many of their elders away now and with all their elders' pet ideas very definitely on the shelf) have again become visible as young. They are doing all the things they haven't been allowed to do for some time, such as talking loud in cafés and sleeping with people of their own age. Also, instead of discussing esthetics with intelligence and politics with passion, as their elders did for so long, they are discussing esthetics with passion and politics with intelligence. I find the change a happy one indeed. I also find distinctly agreeable the presence around of young poets and young painters who look us squarely in the eye and say "hooey," who don't even look at us at all if they don't feel like it, who behave towards us, their elders, exactly as we behaved toward ours some twenty-

141

five years ago and as no young people have been quite able to behave really since.

I must admit that young composers are not as visible in the cafés as poets are; they never were. Pianists, however, peep out from every corner. To a man, and at all ages, they are occupied with what seems to be the central esthetic problem in music today, the creation of an acceptable style-convention for performing Mozart. I've spent a good deal of time at that job too this winter, and I have found out some things about Mozart's piano music I will tell you another time. . . .

I've discovered music all over again. And it turns out to be just as it was when I was seventeen, the daily function of practicing a beloved instrument and of finding one's whole life filled with order and with energy as a result.

But of all that, more another time. Give my best to the fellahs.

Je t'embrasse en camarade,
Virgil

To Briggs Buchanan

Paris
May 6, 1940

Dear Briggs

Can I get some money off you? $500 is what I need, and I realize that for a married man with household and children that sum is not always floating around loose with nothing to do. However, do try to fix it up for me if you can. I will pay you back whenever I come to America and start earning money again, which I fancy to be probably beginning next October. I didn't intend to bother you with this matter, but all of a sudden I learn I am not to be paid certain money I was expecting to be paid at this time, and so that means I haven't any, except enough to last till June 1st. If you can do this, please operate it in the following way:

Deposit the money to my credit at the French-American Banking Corporation, sending me at the same time a deferred cable saying *Okay Briggs*. If you can't do it, cable *Nothing doing Briggs*.

Aside from the slight inconvenience about money, everything goes fine. I've taken to doing musical portraits again and I do one every day mostly. I've done 20 since April 1st. I've also taken to practicing the piano (you should hear me play Mozart sonatas at five times the usual speed). And then I have to learn to play my own portraits, because everybody wants to hear them, and some of them are hard as hell; and that all takes hours a day, the result being that I am two weeks behind in my musical copying, which means I have to play half of them from quite illegible and pale pencil script. And every day I pile up a new one. I am sending you a very chichi piece of private publication, got out by *L'Usage de la parole*. It is some songs of mine in reproduction of my manuscript with cover by Picasso, the whole on special paper with authors' signatures and what have you. I did Picasso's portrait to thank him for the cover. Spring is on us, after a long winter, and a pleasant thing it is. An English friend mutters quietly, if asked, "I've decided to ignore the war." The attitude is a current one, and that is pleasant too. The secret hope is that it will last long enough for us to get the epoch really changed, because certainly the last ten years have been of an insufferable silliness from every intellectual and artistic point of view everywhere. That's why I'm staying here and shall return after a short money-making (I hope) trip to U.S. in the fall. It seems to be the quietest place for getting everything ready.

Sherry is going to U.S. in about two weeks, for what I imagine to be a two-week visit. My publisher writes America is getting ready to invite herself into the war. My book is selling steadily slowly, it seems. In short, everything is going on in the best possible way, except that I haven't any money; and I am so busy with pleasant matters (I am rather pleased with myself of late) that I even forget to worry about that. You've no idea what a joy it is to play the piano properly again after 25 years of not.

Virgil

This letter is not evidence of paper shortage. It is to keep under 10 grams, which is air-mail maximum for 12 frcs. 50.

To Maurice Grosser

June 4 [1940]

Dear Maurice,

All continues great, except we had our first bombardment yesterday. Georges & Germaine Hugnet got married so he could inherit his mother's property (she's been locked up as crazy) and put it in Germaine's name and never be responsible for earlier debts. Paris looks very empty indeed but I seem to see just as many people as usual. Gertrude Newell invited me to her chateau in the Pyrenees but I said I thought I would stay on here a while. What I think now I will do is maybe not go away at all (I am sure country is crowded with Belgians and evacuees from everywhere) but leave for the U.S. around August instead of two months later. I was expecting to have to go in the fall anyway. These plans, naturally, mean God and Germans willing, because everything might easily be changed any day. M—— took me to dinner the other night and tried to rape me. It was just like a cartoon by Thurber. Lots of middle-aged women try to rape me these days. Aunt Jessie wires "Send us news what can we do." It seems to me she might have thought of what to do herself. Sherry has a car. Theo left for Bordeaux. Mary Reynolds went to Amsterdam to join Marcel [Duchamp] but is mad as hell at him for leaving town.

Love & kisses

Next day: With the new German drive on Paris, I've decided to accept Gertrude Newell's invitation and am leaving day after tomorrow for the Pyrenees. Continue writing here unless you should read Paris is taken.

TO CLARA MAY GAINES THOMSON

Paris
June 6, 1940

Dear Mother

I've changed my mind about leaving, on account of the new German drive on Paris, and I'm going day after tomorrow to the Pyrenees, where I was invited some time ago. Keep on writing here, unless you should read of Paris being taken. I'm not expecting that, but I am expecting maybe some heavy bombardment here, especially if the city is not taken. Anyway I'm getting out for the moment.

Love and Kisses,
Virgil

Part Three

% NEW YORK HERALD TRIBUNE

(1940–1954)

With the German occupation of France now complete and another world war imminent, Thomson departed for the United States, from Lisbon, on August 12, 1940.

Shortly after his arrival in New York, Thomson spent a weekend at Alexander Smallens's house in Stamford. There, he was introduced to Geoffrey Parsons (1879–1956), chief editorial writer of the *New York Herald Tribune*. Parsons, who had known Thomson's critical work from *The State of Music* and his articles in *Modern Music*, asked him if he would be interested in replacing Lawrence Gilman (1878–1939), the newspaper's music critic since 1923, who had just died. At first Thomson demurred, but after meeting with the paper's staff and lunching with Helen Reid (1882–1970), wife of publisher Ogden Reid and eventually Reid's successor in that position, he reconsidered.

He was candid about his reasons for taking the job: "The general standard of music reviewing in New York had sunk so far that almost any change might bring improvement. Also I thought perhaps my presence in a post so prominent might stimulate performance of my works."

Indeed, Thomson's presence at the *Herald Tribune* had tremendous impact on the New York musical scene, and his coverage gave music criticism a clarity, scope, wit, and erudition it had never known before. "My literary method, then as now, was to seek the precise adjective," he wrote in *Virgil Thomson:*

Nouns are names and can be libelous; the verbs, though sometimes picturesque, are few in number and tend toward alleging

147

motivations. *It is the specific adjectives that really describe and that do so neither in sorrow nor in anger. And to describe what one has heard is the whole art of reviewing. To analyze and compare are stimulating; to admit preferences and prejudices can be helpful; to lead one's reader step by step from the familiar to the surprising is the height of polemical skill. Now certainly musical polemics were my intent, not aiding careers or teaching Appreciation. And why did a daily paper tolerate my polemics for fourteen years? Simply because they were accompanied by musical descriptions more precise than those being used just then by other reviewers. The Herald Tribune believed that skill in writing backed up by a talent for judgment made for interesting and trustworthy reviews, also that the recognition of these qualities by New York's journalistic and intellectual elite justified their having engaged me.*

But Thomson's success was based on more than just brilliant descriptions. He was the first important American newspaper music critic after James Gibbons Huneker to place a strong emphasis on contemporary works; he also expanded upon the idea of "serious music" by considering a wide variety of musical styles—including jazz, gospel, and folk—rather than simply preserving the sanctity of Western art music.

Equally important were his attacks on the mighty and powerful in the musical world. Thomson recalled, for example, the "guerrilla war" he waged against the conductor Arturo Toscanini (1867–1957), "sniping constantly at his preoccupation with the 'wow-technique,' at his seeming preference for second-rate singers, at his couldn't-care-less attitude toward modern music, at the blasting sound of his brasses in Radio City's Studio 8-H, at the military-police ways of the ushers there... and at the overbearing nature of his publicity." And then there was Arthur Judson (1881–1975) who as both manager of the New York Philharmonic and president of Columbia Concerts represented both buyer and seller rather too often when it came to engaging artists for the orchestra. Thomson took Judson on and made a lifelong enemy.

As Thomson explained it, he was merely following a set of principles, first detailed in *The State of Music:* "to expose the philanthropic persons in control of our musical institutions for the amateurs they are, to reveal the manipulators of our musical distribution for the culturally retarded profit-makers that indeed they are, and to support with all the power of my praise every artist, composer, group, or impresario whose relation to music was straightforward." With such an approach, Thomson was inevitably a source of controversy. On occasion his reviews prompted harsh response from the power brokers of the musical community. Early in his tenure, the New York Philharmonic threatened to discontinue its advertising in the paper. But the Tribune management supported Thomson.

"I had established my routines very early," he later said. "During seven months of the year I wrote a Sunday article every week and averaged two reviews. During the summer months I did no reviewing; I also skipped seven or eight Sunday articles. Since these could be sent from anywhere, I toured on musical errands of my own or stayed in some country place writing music. I also wrote music in town, published books, went in and out on lectures and conducting dates. The paper liked all this activity, because it kept my name before the public. Also because I usually came back with a piece about San Francisco or Texas or Pittsburgh (after the war, Europe and Mexico and South America, too), which was good for circulation." Three collections of Herald Tribune pieces were published in book form: The Musical Scene (1945), The Art of Judging Music (1948), and Music Right and Left (1951).

He built up a distinguished music department for the Herald Tribune: John Cage, Paul Bowles, Elliott Carter, Lou Harrison, Lester Trimble, William Flanagan, Jay Harrison, Allen Hughes, and Peggy Glanville-Hicks were among the contributors. Thomson felt strongly that a thoroughly trained musician with a gift for writing (rather than a professional writer who knew something about music) made the best critic. During this time, Thomson also organized the New York Music Critics' Circle, which flourished into the 1960s.

Thomson's major compositions from this period include Three Pictures for Orchestra, concertos for cello and for harp, two books of piano etudes, Five Songs from William Blake, Four Songs to Poems of Thomas Campion, and the music for Robert Flaherty's Louisiana Story (which received the Pulitzer Prize for music in 1949, still the only film score to be so honored). But his most important musical work from his Tribune years may be his second opera with Gertrude Stein, The Mother of Us All (1947). Less abstract than Four Saints, Mother has a quality of sentiment and familiarity. Stein's text is about the women's suffrage movement in America (Susan B. Anthony is the central figure); Thomson's score evokes marches, bugle calls, parlor songs, waltzes, and hymn tunes, often subjected to complex treatments.

The Mother of Us All soon became one of the most widely performed American operas; many critics think it the greatest. "From its beginning, *The Mother of Us All* has often been produced by colleges, though it was never designed for amateurs and is difficult for young voices," Thomson said. "I have not seen all these productions by any means; but in all that I have seen some charm has come through, for there is in both text and music a nostalgia for nineteenth-century America which makes any presentation warm and touching." During this period also Thomson supervised and conducted an abridged—but much celebrated—recording of *Four Saints* and saw the work through several revivals.

After 1940, Thomson lived in the Hotel Chelsea in Manhattan, a favorite of many writers and artists (other residents have included Thomas Wolfe, Dylan Thomas, and Arthur Miller). There he hosted many parties and gatherings, peopled by New York's artistic and intellectual high society. After the war, he returned to his apartment at 17, quai Voltaire, although it was sublet much of the time, and he visited only when time and opportunity permitted him.

The letters from 1940 to 1954 contain a large number of Thomson's responses to letters from readers of his *Tribune* criticism. "From my first review they received, as also did I, reams of protest mail. Mine I answered, every piece of it, and with courtesy. 'I thank you for the warmly indignant letter,' was one of my beginnings, before going on to some point raised, such as, for instance, that of my own incompetence." These responses form the best exegesis of daily musical criticism that the editors have ever encountered.

Thomson began his tenure at the *Tribune* with a blistering review of the New York Philharmonic. He called the orchestra's playing "dull and brutal," and described the Second Symphony of Jean Sibelius as "vulgar, self-indulgent, and provincial beyond all description."

"Parsons, naturally worried on my first night, prowled about till I had finished writing, then held his breath in the composing room while I checked my proofs," Thomson recalled in his autobiography.

He suggested in these one change, the omission of a slap at the audience ("undistinguished" had been my word). At Bleeck's [a popular hangout for *Herald Tribune* writers], when the papers came down, my piece read clearly as a strong one, though it contained, I knew, any number of faults, including seventeen appearances of the first personal pronoun. I had entitled this review of the concert that opened the Philharmonic's ninety-ninth season "Age Without Honor," and I had snubbed the orchestra's conduc-

tor, John Barbirolli, by publishing with it the photograph of his concertmaster, Michel Piastro. It was unfavorable throughout—"hard-hitting," my admirers at the bar had called it—and it ended with a quote from my companion of the evening (actually Maurice Grosser), "I understand now why the Philharmonic is not part of New York's intellectual life."

To a Reader★

October 23, 1940

I am sorry that my approach to musical criticism in general and to the Sibelius symphony in particular is distasteful to you. I can only say in print what I think about music; that is what I am hired for. It may be as you suggest that I should eventually be fired for doing just that but I cannot pretend to be uplifted by a work which I find depressing, any more than I can pretend that my reaction to a work with which I am not extremely familiar is any more or less not a spontaneous reaction. The charge of vulgarity is one, of course, upon which I would be the last person in the world competent to defend myself.

I thank you for your letter. The intensity of your feelings on all these matters is proof of their sincerity and I hope that you will not take my occasional violence of expression as anything essentially different.

Very sincerely yours,

To a Reader

October 23, 1940

I am extremely grateful to you for your letter of protest.

My spontaneous reactions and my reflective judgments are my

★Throughout his tenure at the *Tribune* Thomson received a tremendous amount of unsolicited correspondence. His responses are given the generic heading "To a Reader" unless there is a specific reason for identification of the addressee.

own, of course, and I can do no other than to put them down truthfully in my column. I am sorry, however, to have been a little brutal in my style of expression and to have caused pain to any music lover. Please don't hate me for it. I am only saying what I think. You would be surprised at the number of letters I have had from people who don't like Sibelius either and who think that the Philharmonic has gone off shamefully in the last few years.

Besides, my bark is worse than my bite. I hope you will find, as many of my closest friends have, that although they found me a revolting "smarty pants" when first they encountered me, I am really not at all such a horrid little guy when one gets used to me. People who really love music don't hate each other for very long.

Very sincerely yours,

To a READER

November 6, 1940

I wish I knew how to advise you on the matter of concert ticket investments. All I can suggest is that you do very much as I do myself when going to concerts, which is to hear pieces about which I have a certain curiosity and artists or occasions that have always in the past provided me with good musical nourishment. When one is listening to a piece one doesn't know, the way it is performed doesn't make much difference; neither is it very important that one should like it or not, as long as one's curiosity is satisfied. If one likes to hear lovely renditions, past experience and gramophone records are the only guides I know of.

The radio, of course, is invaluable because in the course of a winter it usually gives you a taste of almost everything. It has the further advantage of costing nothing but the initial investment (for New York City the cheapest ones are the best) and of being very easy to turn off when you strike a lemon.

Very sincerely yours,

November 22, 1940

My Stokowski brickbat* was not mandatory. I hadn't even
known that Mr. Stokowski's musical taste had such valiant de-
fenders. The musical world that I know has mostly taken it for
granted in the last fifteen years or so that his technical mastery of the
conductor's art was more profound than his musical culture. That
other conductors, all of them, give indefensible readings of classic
works is certainly true. I do not know any in his technical class who
so regularly fall into the traps that insufficient understanding of the
procedures of musical composition and scholarship lays open for
them.

The following instance is not grave in itself, though it does indicate a certain carelessness. Mr. Stokowski orchestrated a few years
ago a motet formerly attributed to Palestrina called "Adoramus Te."
The text he used for his orchestration, as well as the attribution of
authorship, was that published by E. C. Schirmer and Company of
Boston in their edition of the Harvard Glee Club repertory. Neither
the musical text nor the attribution is correct, as any consultation of
a standard Palestrina edition would have shown him. The piece is
not included in Breitkopf and Härtel's edition of the complete
works. Even at the time of its publication in the Harvard Glee Club
series Dr. Archibald T. Davison, conductor of the Glee Club, knew
perfectly well that it was not by Palestrina and that the music contained certain revisions by him. Dr. Carleton Sprague Smith† of the
New York Public Library tells me that the piece is now considered
to be the work of Nanino.‡ Mr. Stokowski's acceptance of a modern
commercial edition as basis for his transcription, even though that
edition bore the name of a Harvard professor, was either careless of
him or naive.

No musician is perfect, of course. Everyone is more master of
certain elements than of others. Mr. Stokowski's interpretations of
classic works are occasionally superb. One often has, nevertheless,
the feeling of having been let down by him. Of having been sold
second-class goods in a first-class box.

I do not reproach him for letting me down, but I think I express
the opinion of a large number of musicians and of disinterested

---

*Leopold Stokowski (1882–1977), conductor, organist, arranger, and media pioneer. *Pace*
Thomson's qualms about Stokowski's "musical culture," the conductor was an avid
champion of new works, including several of Thomson's own.
†(b. 1905), American musicologist and music librarian
‡Giovanni Maria Nanino (1545–1607), a contemporary of Palestrina's

music lovers when I say that his chief contributions to the musical tradition are all of a technical nature. I agree with you completely, of course, that his showmanship has served nobly toward the dissemination of whatever his contributions to our musical life have been.

I thank you for your extremely interesting letter on this subject, and I hope you will read my reply not as an attempt to break your allegiance to your dearest musical memories, rather as a re-statement of my own reflected ideas about a musician whom I both admire and respect and against whom I have not the slightest personal animus.

Very sincerely yours,

To Douglas Moore*

November 29, 1940

Dear Douglas:

The following are the best I know among unperformed American operas:

The Scarlet Letter by Avery Claflin
A title I don't remember by Henry Brant†
Denmark Vesey by Paul Bowles.

The Brant and Bowles are bright and lively. The Claflin, serious, somber, and sumptuous. I am not sure that it is the best thing for either the composers or the audiences to play too many frivolous and inconsequential works, because these can be just as much of a bore in the long run as the soggy and serious. If I were you I should take a look at *The Scarlet Letter.* I think it's pretty fine. The others are excellent, too, and exactly what you would expect from Brant and from Bowles. The Bowles is a Negro subject with libretto by Charles-Henri Ford‡

Greetings and cordially yours,

---

*Moore (1893–1969), best known for his opera *The Ballad of Baby Doe* to a libretto by John Latouche, was MacDowell professor of music at Columbia University and instrumental in producing the world premiere of *The Mother of Us All* there in 1947.
†Brant (b. 1913) had helped Thomson arrange the scores of *The Plough That Broke the Plains* and *The River.* The opera in question was most likely *Miss O'Brady* (1936).
‡editor and poet (b. 1913)

December 11, 1940

I should be very sorry if any review of mine spoiled anybody's musical pleasure. The performances of the Metropolitan Opera Company vary a great deal in musical quality. I consider it my duty to state as dispassionately as possible and according to my sincerest opinion the nature and degree of that quality. I realize that a great many people have worked hard and some have made real sacrifices to help the Metropolitan meet its deficit. I am respectful of the effort, but I do not think it is my duty to mention alleviating circumstances in the course of criticizing a performance that is not quite all it should be according to professional standards.

I think you will find no critic in New York more eager to plug excellence at the Metropolitan than myself. But the Metropolitan Opera Company is a major musical enterprise and, in view of its large radio public, practically a national enterprise. It would not be fair to criticize it too kindly, as if it were a village stock company or an amateur dramatic society. As for constructive criticism, it is not my function to tell the Metropolitan Opera Company or any of its artists what to do and how to do it. I can only state, honestly, what I think of their performances.

It is a mistake to think that persons who write musical criticism regularly get embittered about music, rather the contrary. We develop an almost hypochondriacal sensitivity. A good performance and a beautiful work puts us in humor that endures for days, and a bad or unpleasant one throws us out of tune.

It is easy to write a review of something that is very beautiful. When something is disappointing we have to use all our power of self-control in order not to express our displeasure too intensely.

Very sincerely yours,

To a READER

December 18, 1940

I find that the musical world in New York is rather worried about the case of Mr. Bjoerling.* He is obviously the possessor of a beautiful voice and a man of thorough musical schooling. On account of the dearth of real bravura tenors in the world, every major opera

---

*Jussi Bjoerling (1911–60), Swedish tenor

house has trouble casting the nineteenth-century Italian repertory, particularly the Verdi operas.

I am thoroughly in agreement with you that Mr. Bjoerling is the best available; but, as most of the musical world here seems to think also, the effort to force a lyric tenor into a bravura style may quite possibly ruin Mr. Bjoerling's voice for good. His voice is lovely, his schooling impeccable, his musical and acting style of the highest distinction.

I can imagine him giving a performance of *Rigoletto* or *L'elisir d'amore* which would be more beautiful than anything anybody had heard since Bonci.* In *Un ballo in maschera* and in *Trovatore* he seems to feel himself obliged to force from time to time. Until I shall have heard him sing those operas without straining, I shall continue to think him miscast in both. If he continues to oversing roles not suited to his voice, I view with alarm what that magnificent instrument may sound like by the end of the season.

I thank you for writing me on this interesting subject. I assure you that I yield to none in my admiration for this artist, and that I am more worried about Mr. Bjoerling's future than I am about the proper casting of *Un ballo in maschera*.†

Very sincerely yours,

To a READER

December 27, 1940

You are not the only musician who was somewhat shocked at my reviewing of the first movement of Beethoven's *Eroica* as a "dud." I realize now that I should have explained more fully what I had on my mind, which was that that particular movement had always been more interesting to musicians, on account of its rich musical imagination and skillful writing, than to the listening public in general, which always seems to me to accept the movement passively and without great enthusiasm. Certainly its direct expressive quality is less precise than that of the first movements of the Fifth, Sixth, and Eighth symphonies, let us say.

The second movement, though probably the finest funeral march in the world, presents such difficulties about tempo that not one conductor in twenty ever manages to keep it from sounding inter-

---

*Alessandro Bonci (1870–1940), Italian lyric tenor noted for the grace of his style
†In fact, Bjoerling continued to sing beautifully for almost 20 years, until his early death.

minable. A beautiful work it is, yes, a very beautiful work, but far more often than not a well-known putter-to-sleep of audiences.

I meant no slur on a great work by a great composer in mentioning these facts. I am sorry that my lack of thorough explanation gave me the air of taking an underhand crack. Beethoven wrote some very great music. He also, like everybody else, wrote movements that are not up to his best.

Please accept my apologies for having made an ungracious statement which led you to think I held this work in estimation different from that of the whole body of musicians.

I sometimes differ with my musical colleagues about musical values, but I assure you that I do not hold any controversial opinions about Beethoven. I do not think, even, that there is much possible controversy about Beethoven's musical works.

Very sincerely yours,

To a READER

December 27, 1940

Are you sure that you have written to the right man? I have reviewed the Metropolitan Opera four times this season. Three of those reviews were full of the highest praise for the performances. The other one recounted as dispassionately as possible what I thought was well done and what I thought badly done in a performance that every critic in New York agreed was not up to Metropolitan standards.

You quote somebody as speaking of the scenery in "tatters." I assure you I have made no such reference. The scenery at the Metropolitan is sometimes very beautiful and sometimes, as is inevitable in any repertory company, a reflection of the taste of some previous period when the work it was built for was last revived. But I have seen no tattered scenery this winter in that house. On the contrary, I have seen a good deal of brand-new scenery, much of it very pretty indeed, and all of it in ship-shape condition. I was amused to notice, though I did not comment on it in print, that Isolde's couch still gives out clouds of dust every time she touches it.

As for my "selling" the Metropolitan to the public, that is hardly my job. The *Herald Tribune* pays me a salary to describe and appraise musical performances, not to do publicity work for any institution. It is normally considered that critics render their best services to the public by listening to musical performances disinterestedly and recounting what they hear without regard to persons or institutions.

Thank you again for your letter, though I am still convinced it was not intended for me.

Very sincerely yours,

To a READER

February 6, 1941

The broadcasters and the orchestral conductors tell me that Tchaikovsky is no longer considered by their public as "serious" repertory. Dr. Stock* informs me that Chicago will not even take much of it in the Pops Concerts. It is from similar sources that I hear the American public to be slightly less interested, or perhaps thought to be about to be less interested, in the constant rehearing of Beethoven's masterpieces than was true ten years ago. People who go to orchestral concerts do not seem to mind a good deal of repetition of the better repertory pieces, because their interest in the technique of orchestral conducting and the variety of possible interpretations of these works is very great.

Radio listeners, on the other hand, seem to have very little interest in conducting, or even in who is conducting. When the great symphonic repertory was first made available to the American population almost daily over the radio, the listeners were more interested in well-known classics than in rarities. In 1941 the American listening public seems to be approaching, with regard to the more familiar classics, if not a saturation point at least a certain familiarity which gives them a higher degree of interest in novelties, ancient and modern, than they had ten or fifteen years ago.

As to Mahler, yes, I know the Second Symphony. I do think that Mahler's work was more distorted by his life as a professional conductor than by his desire to storm Parnassus as a composer. He was an ambitious man, of course; every man of talent is. But it has always seemed to me that the facile eclecticism of his musical style was evidence of a certain easygoing quality in his character that is the opposite of Wagner's megalomania. (In applying the word megalomania to Wagner's musical method I wish to imply no low opinion of his musical achievements. I am describing a man's attitude, not his action.)

I have never found in Mahler either the ruthlessness or the tension

---

*Frederick Stock (1872–1942), conductor of the Chicago Symphony Orchestra for more than thirty years

that are characteristic of Wagner or Berlioz or Richard Strauss or of many another composer who seems to have his eye constantly on success.

Very sincerely yours,

To a READER

February 12, 1941

I fancy you may be right about Miss Elsie Houston's* breath. If it were properly controlled, I think she would do more sustained singing. I don't agree with you that her vocal placement is faulty. I find, on the contrary, that it is extremely resonant and dependable. I should like to protest just a little at your under-estimation of an experienced concert artist due to her having sung folk-song repertory in a nightclub during the last few years. Miss Houston's artistry was not formed in nightclubs, nor will it, presumably, much longer be available there. Besides, it isn't very gracious to reproach an artist who is singing, not for the first time, in Town Hall with having sung in another locale in which you have probably been yourself, and not necessarily for the last time, a patron.

Very sincerely yours,

To a READER

February 20, 1941

I thank you for your extremely indignant letter.

I am afraid I do consider Schumann to be a greater and more original composer than Brahms.

Very sincerely yours,

To a READER

February 20, 1941

I thank you for your extremely interesting letter about Mahler. I still think, however, that the contrapuntal technique employed in *Das Lied von der Erde* is essentially the modern French technique.

---

*(1902?–1943), Brazilian singer, who moved increasingly from popular music into the classical repertory before her early death

This does not mean that *Das Lied von der Erde* sounds like French music. It means that it sounds different from almost all other modern German music, on account of its contrapuntal freedom. I may be wrong in crediting this contrapuntal freedom to Mahler's acquaintance with French research into music of the fifteenth and sixteenth centuries and with the pedagogical methods based on this technique that were practiced in Paris at the Niedermeyer School way back in the 1880s and the '90s. I do not know any German source where he might have become acquainted with this matter as it is capable of affecting composition. I do know of the French source; and in view of Mahler's cosmopolitan musical experience, I am inclined to think he may have become acquainted through the modern French composers with a system of contrapuntal writing not founded on thoroughbass.

I should doubt very much if Mahler or any other single composer had worked out this modern revival of a very ancient technique all by himself.

As to the intrinsic value of the chief melodic material in *Das Lied von der Erde,* I find that enthusiastic Mahler admirers are about equally divided: some admire it enormously; others agree with me that it is not always first-class. In any case we are all agreed that *Das Lied von der Erde* is a magnificent and unique musical work. I hope that my attempt to analyze briefly its compositional procedure did not give the contrary impression.

Very sincerely yours,

To a CORRESPONDENT*

March 6, 1941

I thank you for the admiring letter about my *River* music. I cannot tell you why certain passages were more noticeable than others in the film beyond the reasons that you yourself propose—namely, that in the final mixture of music, speech, and sound-effects made by Pare Lorentz, musical high points were deliberately toned down in several places lest they attract too much attention. Mr. Lorentz is better at that sort of thing than most movie directors and loves to use music for the advantage of the whole effect whenever he can.

Let us be sure what we mean by the words "naturalistic" and

*Thomson's replies to unsolicited correspondence not related to his *Tribune* work have been given the generic heading "To a Correspondent" unless there is a specific reason for identification.

"realistic." When I say "naturalistic" I refer to style and when I say "realistic" I refer to effect. Photography is naturalistic because it reproduces nature without any voluntary stylization. The effect may be realistic, fantastic, or natural.

It is nice to know that there are a few people who reflect seriously about these important matters, especially all the necessary and possible relations between music and speech and realistic sound, as these three elements are finally combined with narrative photography in the film.

Very sincerely yours,

To Elie Siegmeister

March 6, 1941

Dear Elie,

I enjoyed reading your article and am considerably chagrined at not being able to publish it.* As an advance note on the concert about to be given it is long and a little argumentative. As an article on folklore it contains too much advance publicity about your own forthcoming concert. And so I don't see what I can do with it. I shall publish, of course, the program of your concert in advance—if it arrives at the office in time (it may be on Perkins's† desk now for all I know).

I shall also publish a news item in advance of the concert when and if space permits. I am sorry about the article because I like it very much. But there isn't anything I can do about material that falls between the categories of disinterested musical information and managerial propaganda.

Always affectionately yours,

To a Reader

March 12, 1941

I thank you for your interesting letter about Ezio Pinza.‡ I do not think people have to be intellectual stars themselves in order to be

---

*Neither Thomson nor Siegmeister remembered the article's subject in 1987.
†Francis Perkins (1897–1970), critic and music editor of the *Herald Tribune* during Thomson's tenure there
‡Italian bass (1892–1957), who after a successful operatic career conquered Broadway in *South Pacific* and *Fanny*

interesting to the "intelligence." Miss Josephine Baker★ is a case in point. I have always found Mr. Pinza's singing and acting to be well organized and clear and not without subtlety. That is what I meant by its being interesting to the "intelligence."

Mary Garden was another case like that. She learned slowly but thoroughly and penetrated rather deeper into the content of her roles than many an artist of broader musical education and more facile intellectuality.

Very sincerely yours,

To a READER

March 12, 1941

There was nothing deliberate about my omitting Milstein† from my review of the New Friends of Music Orchestra. I was chiefly interested in writing a little essay on Mozart performing style and Mr. Stiedry's‡ version of that. Milstein played all right, but I don't see that there was anything especially novel or penetrating about his manner of doing so. Consequently it seemed to me better to publish his picture and say nothing than merely to comment that he played all right. It happens that I had never heard Mr. Milstein play before and I did not wish to make a superficial judgment about his work from last Sunday's performance. When I have occasion to review a whole concert of his, I shall give him naturally the serious attention that his very serious work deserves. I do think, however, that until such occasion occurs it is more complimentary to him to take the execution of his work for granted than it would be to dismiss him in a polite phrase.

I have made the same omission with regard to Kreisler§ and Spalding‖ in previous reviews where the nature of the music played seemed to have more news interest than the artist's execution.

I thank you for your entertaining letter on the subject and I assure you that I sympathize strongly with your prejudices against the *Herald Tribune*'s political point of view.●

Very sincerely yours,

★(1906–75), American singer and dancer who became the toast of Paris with the Folies-Bergère during the 1920s
†Nathan Milstein (b. 1904), Soviet violinist
‡Fritz Stiedry (1883–1968), Austrian conductor regularly at the Metropolitan Opera from 1946 to 1958
§Fritz Kreisler (1875–1962), Austrian violinist and composer
‖Albert Spalding (1888–1953), American violinist and composer
● genteel Republicanism

*Ernst Bacon (b. 1898), an American composer, pianist, and educa-
tor, was particularly esteemed for his songs. Thomson does not recall the subject of the article referred to in the following letter, but
his advice remains germane.*

To Ernst Bacon

April 1, 1941

Dear Bacon:

Your article is extremely interesting and full of punch, as well as
sense. I find it, however, uneven in tone, and hence less effective
than it might be. There is a certain amount of futility about its indignation and a certain bitterness in the point of view that make me
hesitate to publish it in a newspaper. I am afraid its effect on a large
number of readers would be to alienate the sympathy with its author
that they would normally have if the author himself did not seem to
be so angry. If you feel like doing it over a bit, I think the article
would be greatly improved.

You see, a newspaper is a perfectly good place for controversy,
whenever there is a clear issue to state. It is also a good place for the
exposing of everybody's point of view. It is not a very good place
for the exposing of irritation, however justified the irritation may
be, because such irritation practically always convinces the reader
that the exact opposite of what the writer is saying is the real truth. I
am sending the article back to you with these general suggestions,
rather than with proposed specific corrections, because I never correct anybody's work.

I should like very much to publish an article by you on this or on
any other subject you care to choose. I don't care how controversial
it is; I welcome controversy. But do try to keep the statement of the
issues clear, cold, and deadly as possible.

Very cordially yours,

To a Reader

April 2, 1941

I thank you for your interesting letter. Naturally, everybody can't
like everything. I am very fond of Debussy myself, but I cannot
stomach Sibelius. That a sincere music lover should like or dislike
the work of any given composer of any period is unquestionably his

privilege. I should not think much of him as a music lover if he liked everything.

Very sincerely yours,

In February 1941, an article by Thomson entitled "The Criticism of Music" appeared in Musical America. Among the responses it prompted was one from Carl E. Lindstrom, then the music critic of the Hartford Times. The following letter, however, has less to do with Lindstrom's review than with one of Thomson's pet peeves.

To CARL E. LINDSTROM

April 3, 1941

Dear Mr. Lindstrom:

I thank you for your sending me the *Hartford Times* containing your review of my *Musical America* article, which I should probably not have seen otherwise. I should like to take issue with you on what no doubt seems to you a minor point but which seems to be worth bringing out, since you seem to have read my article otherwise quite carefully.

It does happen that my name is spelled T-h-o-m-s-o-n without a "p." Everything else is a matter of opinion and I don't grudge you yours perhaps quite as much as you seem to grudge me mine. But the spelling of my name is an ascertainable fact, as is, indeed, the dominant role that composers have always played in European musical criticism.

Very sincerely yours,

To a READER

April 3, 1941

Thank you very much for the note about smiling. That a singer's face should light up when he sings is gracious, of course, and is quite correct. That he should walk around the stage grinning when he is not singing at all I find extremely unpleasant.

Very sincerely yours,

To a Reader

April 9, 1941

I agree with you that the Philharmonic boys are awfully hard to conduct. I also agree with you that Mlle Boulanger, whom I have known for twenty years, is not a bad conductor when the circumstances are advantageous. Even the Philharmonic boys will occasionally let themselves be led. Unfortunately, at the Paderewski Fund Concert they did not seem to be cooperating very gracefully. If I had been certain that the nature of their work was due entirely to their natural peskiness and not at all to Mlle Boulanger's inability to get what she wanted out of them in spite of their peskiness, as every conductor with any orchestra in the world has to do, I should have placed the blame on the orchestra. I do not think it diminishes Mlle Boulanger's stature as a musician to admit that she was not perhaps as skillful at bullying an orchestra as some of the professional conductors are.

Very sincerely yours,

To a Reader

April 16, 1941

I too have been wondering what I would think of Horowitz.* It so happens that I have never heard him play. If next Saturday's program were more interesting than it is (it is all Tchaikovsky, I believe), I should certainly go to hear it. I don't know whether I shall get to the Philharmonic on the 1st of May or not. Rest assured that whenever Mr. Horowitz plays in my vicinity a program of piano music that looks in advance even slightly interesting I shall go to it. This season he doesn't seem to have offered anything of the sort.

Very sincerely yours,

---

*Vladimir Horowitz (b. 1904), Russian-American pianist

To Jere Abbott*

June 19, 1941

Dear Jere:

All the friends and all the institutions want records of the *Four Saints*. I am saying no, for the present, although I am not sure exactly why. Chick got a set and I made no objection, considering that he has practically a vested interest in the opera. But I am not awfully eager to spread the work around any further than that in a way that anybody wishing to put out commercial records might think disadvantageous.

I am not sure that this is what I think, but I think it is what I think. In any case, I am replying with a very faint and probably quite temporary no to your telegram.

Best and devotedly,

To Claire Reist†

June 25, 1941

Dear Claire:

Thanks for the nice letter and for the offer of cooperation. The awards which we vote next year will be awards for pieces that have been played during that season. Consequently, if the League plans to cooperate with us to the extent of organizing concerts at which chamber music could be re-heard during May that all the critics have not been able to hear during the winter, it had better envisage in its plans for next season the first New York performance of American chamber music. It would not be appropriate to have the Critics' Circle‡ sponsor a special performance for the purpose of making its final vote by any other organizations than those which were responsible for the first performances, provided those organizations wish to cooperate. We will go into all this in the fall. I just wanted to explain now that the Critics' Circle's plans are not quite as you understand them. We intend to secure during the course of the season a number of works in each musical category which we would like to re-hear.

---

*Co-founder (with Alfred H. Barr, Jr.) of the Museum of Modern Art in 1929, Abbott (1897–1982) was an old friend of Thomson's.
†(1889–1978), author, arts administrator, and a founder of the League of Composers
‡The New York Music Critics' Circle, founded by Thomson in 1941

Then at a concert or series of concerts to be held in May, we will re-hear these works all of us, and vote subsequently our award to the one we think most deserving in each category. We plan also to make an award to American works which have been heard during the season not in a first New York performance. No plans have been made so far for the formal re-hearing of these at the end of the season. None of our award procedures has any bearing on any but the season just ended.

I am glad you like the idea of the whole thing. The critics themselves seem to be extremely eager to function.

Greetings and always faithfully,

To Parker Tyler*

June 25, 1941

Dear Parker:

Your letter gave me great delight and entertainment. You are wrong in assuming that either the author† or myself considers popular music to be wholly different as an art form from the highbrow stuff. Quite the contrary, many of the factors involved, both the psychological and the industrial ones, are identical in the two fields. Certain others, such as the formal esthetics of lengthy symphonic works and the merchandising procedures of the radio companies, are utterly different, though the line of demarcation is not always sharply drawn. In any case the symphonic concert business, both on the air and off, is the subject of other studies by the same author and his associates at Columbia University. I hope to publish from time to time excerpts from those because I consider them of very great interest to musicians. It isn't that I am invariably in agreement with Adorno. It is rather that in the field of radio research, especially insofar as such research departs from strictly empirical procedures and ventures into the field of esthetics and psychology, it is more important right now that all the possible questions be raised than that they be answered with finality. Naturally, a good many of the conclusions stated in these studies are conclusions that persons like ourselves have arrived at many years ago by private judgment or intuition. I think it is not entirely without interest that such judg-

---

*(1907–74), American poet and art writer, biographer of Florine Stettheimer and Pavel Tchelitcheff
†Theodor Adorno (1903–69), German sociologist and twelve-tone composer, deeply suspicious of popular culture and jazz

ment should be given a new form of publicity, not one depending on wit or personal prestige, or one backed up by the sacred mumbo jumbo of scholarly research. At any rate, that is why I printed the excerpts.

On any point where you feel yourself in disagreement with Mr. Adorno's understanding of esthetics, I suggest you write to him personally at the Institute for Social Research. You will find him a very bright little man indeed. He is both a professional philosopher and a trained composer, and his mind has all the best and the worst Germanic qualities.

Always devotedly,

To a READER

September 5, 1941

Not having heard the concert you referred to, I have no opinion about it. I have never heard Mr. Adler* conduct at all. It is very difficult to know whether the excellences and faults of any given performances are to be credited to the conductor or to the instrumentalists. Also, a kind of musical performance which it is difficult to analyze is the one in which nothing seems to be seriously wrong but which seems dull and tasteless all the same.

Very sincerely yours,

To SAXE COMMINS†

September 5, 1941

I have furnished biographies and lists of my works so frequently to the publishers of musical dictionaries that I hesitate to go through the labor of all that over again, especially in view of the fact that somebody always edits half a dozen inaccuracies into them. Consequently, I refer you to John Tasker Howard's book on American musicians and to Claire Reis's.‡ You might just as well have them with the errors already in as to be obliged to do these yourself. As

---

*F. Charles Adler (1889–1959), American conductor who helped found the Saratoga Springs music festival
†(1892–1958), an editor at Random House
‡Howard's *Our Contemporary Composers: American Music in the Twentieth Century* (1941) and Reis's *Composers in America* (1930)

you see, I am extremely disillusioned about the ability of persons who get up such books to put real information into them.

There is a complete list of my works in *Modern Music* for May 1941.

I am sorry not to be of more help.

Very sincerely yours,

To a READER

October 1, 1941

I don't think you will have any trouble finding out the name of the singer that Grace Moore referred to so pointedly.* It is common gossip in New York musical circles. Do forgive me if I fail to pass on to you something that I know only as gossip. The consequences at this time of making public issue out of this singers' quarrel might very well result in grave disadvantages to the one of them that is not American. I am sure you will understand my unwillingness to act as an irresponsible agent in an intrigue which might result so disastrously.

Very sincerely yours,

After the war, Sherry Mangan went to South America, where he continued his work as a correspondent for Time-Life magazines and regularly informed Thomson of musical news abroad.

To SHERRY MANGAN

October 8, 1941

Angel:

Thanks like anything for the musical contributions. They are not, as you have already perceived, exactly hot; but I think I can do a Sunday article, using quotations from various of them. The moral would be: this is the state of musico-intellectual life in Buenos Aires as reported to me by Mr. Mangan of *Time, Life, Fortune.*

I have of your news, in addition to your occasional letters, hoop-

---

*Soprano Grace Moore (1901–47) claimed that a colleague had organized booing at one of her performances and that the same artist had fascist connections.

las of joy and adoration about you from Lincoln Kirstein. After all these years! My own news is simple, records pleasant work in quite considerable quantities. I spent the entire summer in New England, successively at Woods Hole, in Vermont, at Squam Lake in New Hampshire, at Nantucket, and winding up with a week chez Aunt Jessie [Lasell] in her millionaire's so-called camp (how rightly named) on Lake Kennebago. I completely re-orchestrated the Second Symphony, which is being conducted in ten different cities by Sir Thomas Beecham;* and I orchestrated a series of nine or ten (I have forgotten which) of the Paris portraits. I also made a number of new portraits. I start my reviewing season this week, and I live at the Chelsea as before. I miss you like hell.

It will amuse you that whereas in former times no publisher or conductor would even go to the trouble of reading my music, now that I am a famous and terrifying music critic, they are all eager to both publish and play. They used to know in advance that they did not want to encourage it. Now they know in advance that they do. They still don't bother to read it.

Love and kisses to both your halves,

To Paul Bowles

October 15, 1941

Dear Paul,

Nothing would please me more than an article by you. Music schools for Mexican workers do not sound passionately interesting, though they very well may be, if their pattern has news interest or if the results of them are extraordinary and spectacular. Use your own judgment. I presume you must think them interesting or you would not propose an article on the subject. I should also like something, either for print or for my private instruction, about the war between Chávez and the Mexican National Opera Company.

Best,

---

*The wealthy, eccentric, and inspired Sir Thomas (1879–1961) became a good friend of Thomson's.

To Alfred Wallenstein*

November 7, 1941

Dear Mr. Wallenstein:

Your proposal sounds entertaining. I should not care especially about doing anything in the nature of straight program comment, but I think it might be interesting to be interviewed after the program (or after a part of it) about the music played. This plan seems to keep me in my role of free critic, which I prefer to that of a commentator-salesman. This would mean that my speech would have to be partly improvised, or else that I would have to write it out after hearing a rehearsal.

I have no intention of causing you or the Bamberger Broadcasting Service any embarrassment. But I see no reason why, although there is little precedent for this in broadcasting, a professional critic, being interviewed, shouldn't say that he thinks one piece is maybe a better piece of music than another.

Very sincerely yours,

To a Correspondent†

November 13, 1941

It was nice to hear from you and delightful to read your play. It reads to me more like a Federal Theater play of six years back than like anything I can envisage in successful production today. I don't like all that talk about democracy. I don't like it in the press and I don't like it in the political propaganda of our epoch. The word means so many things that it does not mean anything very precisely anymore. The play is lovely, however, and I should like to see it produced.

It is not a good working method to prepare incidental music for a dramatic script before there is a producer and a director has been chosen. It tends to crystallize the production prematurely. When you have a producer and a director, I should be delighted to confer with all of you about what music is needed where and to be of use in any way I can.

Very sincerely yours,

---

*Wallenstein (1898–1983), then American cellist and conductor, was then general music director of WOR radio in New York City.
†a playwright who asked Thomson to compose incidental music for one of his plays

To Edith Behrens*

December 9, 1941

Dear Miss Behrens:

I should like very much to have an article by Mr. Artur Schnabel on the piano works of Schubert. I could not use a digest of his ideas, but I should be only too happy to publish a Sunday article written by Mr. Schnabel on that subject. The article could appear on January 4th or on the preceding Sunday. In any case it should reach my office by Monday or Tuesday of the week preceding the Sunday on which it is to appear. It will be paid for at the *Herald Tribune*'s regular space rates, which are not munificent, but which are unvarying.

Very sincerely yours,

To a Reader

December 10, 1941

I am afraid I cannot help you to realize your life-long ambition to work for *The New York Times.* I could not even do much about you at the *Herald Tribune,* since there is no vacancy in our musical staff. If there were I should recommend the employment of a professional musician with some literary experience rather than a journalist with a deep love of music. Sorry.

Very sincerely yours,

To a Reader

December 11, 1941

I think you exaggerate my inconsistencies, though I must say that I see no great harm in them. If you don't mind, I shall take them up with you one by one in your own order:

1. Claudio Arrau† is indeed a more finished pianist than most, in spite of his unequal trills, because very few pianists have a presentable trill anyway.

2. I see no contradiction between brilliant performance with excellent musicianship and the essentially superficial understanding of

---

*press representative for Austrian pianist Artur Schnabel (1882–1951), who was particularly renowned for his interpretations of Beethoven and Schubert
†(b. 1903), Chilean pianist

repertory. A knife can cut sharp but shallow and still be an excellent knife.

3. An interpretation can be both warm and sweeping without convincing us of its entire sincerity.

4. I find Mr. Arrau's playing of modern music perfectly clear, but I still think that he does not understand the modern rhythmic concept which is one of unvarying small rhythmic units, the freedom of such music exacting rather in the grand accents than in any alteration of the basic tick-tock.

5. I think that an examination of Mozart's D-major sonata* will be sufficient to verify my description of the musical origin of its material. Its emotional origins, like those of all untitled music, are impossible to verify. Any interpreter is free to give the piece whatever emotional expression he wishes, provided that he does not falsify the musical nature of the material. That is to say that it may represent the "calls of a hunted soul" or of anything else, provided that it sounds as much as possible like hunting horns, which seem to me the obvious realistic evocation of the written notes.

I am sorry that my review seemed misleading to you. Its main thesis lay in what appeared to you as an impossible contradiction, namely, that Mr. Arrau, though a very finished musician, is not a very penetrating one. I was not paying off a score against an enemy, because I do not know Mr. Arrau; and I was not log-rolling for any friend, because I mentioned no other pianist. However erroneous you may think my judgment of Mr. Arrau's concert, please believe me that it was not written in any spirit of unfairness.

Very sincerely yours,

To a READER

December 12, 1941

Much as I admire the singing of Mme Rethberg† at its best, and much as I admire her fine musical style at all times, I do not feel that she has been at her best in the past year. Most of the voice specialists whom I know agree with me that her work has passed its prime. This does not mean that we disapprove of her continuing to perform in public. Neither does it mean that we are under any obligation to

---

*(K. 576)

†German soprano Elisabeth Rethberg (1894–1976), much beloved at the Metropolitan since 1922, retired from the stage in 1942.

conceal what we consider to be the true state of her vocal resources. Please believe that there is no bitterness involved in this carrying out what we believe to be our duty as musical reporters.

Very sincerely yours,

To a CORRESPONDENT

December 12, 1941

I thank you for your interesting letter about my Second Symphony and for its loyal criticism. I am afraid that your protest against its being played is evidence perhaps of a not entirely friendly attitude toward contemporary composition. In this case such a protest should be directed to Sir Thomas Beecham, who put the work on his program, not to me who had nothing to do with the matter.*

Very sincerely yours,

To a READER

January 7, 1942

Miss Marian Anderson is certainly one of the finest contraltos now appearing before the public, and many people consider her to be the very finest. I have no way of knowing why Miss Anderson, or any other singer, is not on the rolls of the Metropolitan Opera Company. Neither can I state definitely why that organization draws the color line. So far as I know, however, no colored artist has ever appeared in their productions in a singing role.†

Very sincerely yours,

To a READER

January 15, 1942

I thank you for your charming letter. You are right, of course, that unless a composer speaks through his music to the individual

---

*In his autobiography Thomson wrote of Beecham's performances: "No one else has ever made my Second Symphony sound so glowing, though I do not think he was comfortable with the work."

†Thirteen years later, Anderson (b. 1902) became the first black vocalist to appear at the Metropolitan when she sang Ulrica in Verdi's *Un ballo in maschera*.

listener, he is not speaking to anybody. He does hope, however, that the listener will understand what he is saying in somewhat the way the composer himself feels it. The listener is thus the final interpreter, as you say; but we do hope that his interpretation is not entirely personal and capricious. That is why we use all the means we know to achieve clarity.

I agree with you completely on Music Appreciation courses. I think they are the bunk.

Very sincerely yours,

To Alfred A. Knopf*

January 15, 1942

My dear Alfred Knopf:

Thanks for the lovely note. A compliment from you is worth fifty from the dumb-bells.

Always faithfully yours,

To a Reader

January 16, 1942

We are in agreement that Mahler's Fourth Symphony is not his best work. Don't think for a moment, however, that I form part of any "common front" against his music. I have written much more favorably of the Ninth Symphony and of *Das Lied von der Erde,* and I am ready to speak and to write my admiration for those of Mahler's works (and of those elements in all of his works) which I happen to admire. If there is a "common front" of any kind, it is more like a conspiracy of the Mahler devotees who protest vigorously every time anyone expresses publicly his own lack of the completest devotion to this composer's work. Not that one minds such protests. Quite the contrary. They show that his music means something very deep to the people to whom it means anything.

Very sincerely yours,

---

*Founder of the publishing house that bears his name, Knopf (1892–1984) published Thomson's *The Musical Scene, The Art of Judging Music,* and *Virgil Thomson.*

To Andrew Schulhof*

January 30, 1942

Dear Mr. Schulhof:

As a modernist composer myself and the principal champion in the local press of modernist composition, I prefer not to appear publicly in a disputatious role with regard to it. I am the modernists' natural advocate rather than their opponent. I suggest that one of the more conservative critics would make a better forum appearance in this role than I would. I should think Oscar Thompson or Downes or, best of all, Herbert Peyser† could represent the well-disposed laymen admirably. Thanks for asking me.

Very sincerely yours,

To a Correspondent

January 30, 1942

On reflection, I should prefer not to speak at your Book and Play Luncheon of February 5th, because my attitude about art as a war weapon is not one that I feel like exposing publicly just now. I am inclined to favor for creative artists a policy of keeping art as independent as possible of war conditions and ideologies. A public statement of this position, however, would be more appropriate at some later time when, and if, distinguished artists show signs of turning themselves into propaganda machines. Since I see no such tendency at present, I feel that it would not be appropriate to state my point of view at all. Do forgive me, please, for asking to be excused.

Most cordially yours,

---

*(1900–60), American concert manager; at this time with the Boosey & Hawkes Artists Bureau
†Thompson (1887–1945) was then with the *New York Sun*; Olin Downes (1886–1955), with *The New York Times*; Peyser (1886–1953) wrote for the *Times* and other publications.

To Ernst Krenek*

February 2, 1942

Dear Mr. Krenek:

Thanks for the lovely letter. I am going to use your reference about the "masterful retreat to the heavily fortified Brahms Line." I shall not credit it to you unless you wish.

Conservative as it is, the Hindemith Symphony† has a certain workmanship interest. In view of the kind of contemporary music commonly appearing before us, a Brahms Fifth, as you call it, does present a slightly greater musical interest than the more usual Humperdinck Fifteenth.

Very sincerely yours,

To a Reader

March 6, 1942

The harpsichord-playing world is one of the most disputatious of all musical groups. Its cutthroat antics are only exceeded by those of the vocalists. The pianists are also furious at Mme Landowska‡ for having stated in *The New York Times* that Bach's "Goldberg" Variations were composed, as they were, for a harpsichord with two keyboards and that the work is impossible to execute correctly except upon that instrument. The other harpsichordists are furious at her for playing the work in a more vigorous and lively way than any of them do. I should not pay too much attention to their quibbles. This is not to say that Mme Landowska is incapable of misinterpretations of this work or any other. But her knowledge of the work itself and of the technical possibilities of the instrument is superior to that of any other harpsichord player with whom I am acquainted. They are practically all her pupils, as a matter of fact. Whenever anybody does anything superlatively well, there is likely to be a tempest in the dovecotes.

Very sincerely yours,

---

*Austrian composer Krenek (b. 1900) had emigrated to the United States in 1938 and became an American citizen in 1945.
†Symphony in E-flat (1941)
‡More than any other individual, Wanda Landowska (1877–1959) was responsible for reviving popular interest in the harpsichord.

March 13, 1942

I know the [Max] Reger* score fairly well and still think it more a monument to culture than a work of the imagination. "Getting away from the theme" is one of the marks of a good variation series. Not getting away from it altogether—that would not be truly variation—but getting away from it progressively and going somewhere other than on a jaunt of musical whimsies, somewhere where the theme opens up and flowers unexpectedly. None of the good variation sets by classic masters is a compendium of everything the composer could think of to do, though often the variety of invention is quite large. The Reger Variations seemed to me to lack spiritual coherence and to be consequently, in spite of their cleverness, more like a bit of fancy-work than what we have come to expect in that form from good composers.

Very sincerely yours,

To a Reader

March 13, 1942

I don't follow any special etiquette about applause. I applaud if I feel like it, just as anybody else does, and just as I would if I had paid for my ticket.

Very sincerely yours,

To a Reader

March 1942

When I referred to Stokowski as a possible model from which Mr. Horowitz may derive his style of playing Bach, I meant that Horowitz's Bach bears a closer resemblance to that of the English-trained concert organists (of which Mr. Stokowski is one) than it does to that of either the German or the French tradition of Bach playing.

I don't mind in the least your not agreeing with me that Horowitz's technical abilities are sounder than his musical culture, but I

---

*Variations and Fugue on a Theme by Mozart

regret your unwillingness to believe that my review of his last concert was a sincere statement of my own musical judgment.

Very sincerely yours,

To a READER

[undated]

I thank you for the article "On Music and American Music." I am returning it to you because its literary style is not quite "high-class" enough for the *Herald Tribune*. This does not mean anything except that we have a habit here of using a certain tone in our Sunday articles and are not likely to step outside that unless the material of the article in question is of extraordinary originality.

I do not find your opinions, vigorous as they be, either especially original or convincing. I suppose each of us has his own idea of what American music ought to be like. I certainly do not agree with you that Richard Wagner was the greatest of all German composers.

Very sincerely yours,

To ALLEN WARDWELL*

April 8, 1942

Dear Mr. Wardwell:

Thank you for the delightful letter. The correspondence I recently published about the Metropolitan is typical of a great deal that I receive. Much of it is uninformed and unreflected, but I sometimes think it is interesting for the public to read. As to my own suggestion that a little more youth and energy might be used with advantage in the organizational end of the opera house, it was just a trial balloon. I, too, get a little tired of hearing the musicians blamed for everything. Opera performances in a repertory theater are always hard to make jell. And I know how difficult it is to cast repertory performances when the artists are not under exclusive contract to the theater.

I do hope that my reviews of the Metropolitan performances do not seem carping to you or animated by any but the friendliest spirit of cooperation. As you pointed out, my business is to criticize; and I

---

*(1873–1953), a lawyer and member of the Metropolitan Opera board of directors

know that such suggestions as I have to offer are received with the same good will in which they are made. Nothing is easier, of course, than telling other people how to run their business. If my suggestions seem not practical, please pay no attention. I am not trying to influence you to fire or to hire any given person. I still think, however, that the Metropolitan's insufficiencies are not wholly musical and budgetary. And I can't rid myself of the feeling that better performances can be given with the same artists and for the same amount of money.

If at any time you think there is serious danger of the house closing its doors, that will be another matter. You can count on me in any such eventuality for vigorous support. Because, whether the shows remain good, bad, or medium, you are all we have and you must go on.

Very sincerely yours,

To Alfred Frankfurter*

April 29, 1942

Dear Mr. Frankfurter:

I thank you for the copy of *Art News* with the article about opera decoration. I should have liked very much in happier times to have used it as pretext for a Sunday article on the subject. In the present musical doldrums of the Metropolitan Opera, I do not think it much worth while for a music critic to complain about the lack of taste or imagination in their visual presentations. If the productions were first-class musically, or even in some way vigorous, it would be pertinent for me to point out the desirability of improvement in the designing of scenery and costumes. With the musical productions what they are, to concentrate on their visual investiture would be like recommending a new tailor to a patient dying of cancer.

I am delighted, of course, that *Art News* has seen fit to go into the question, because I think the situation worthy of record and protest. But I am sure you will recognize on reflection that the musical pages need to reserve their ammunition for the musical situation so long as that remains as deplorable as it is.

Very sincerely yours,

---

*(1906–65), art historian associated with New York University

To a Reader

May 27, 1942

You reply to my Toscanini [article] in such detail that to answer your letter in equal detail would amount to virtually re-writing my original. Your main assumptions seem to be

(a) that a composer's idea is wholly clear from the written notes of a score;

(b) that merely giving pleasure to a large audience is the function of philanthropically endowed concerts;

(c) that a musician's general culture and enlightenment are not an important part of his musical performing style;

(d) that attempts to analyze the work of so famous a musician as Mr. Toscanini are of no value to the musical public.

I hope I am not reading your views incorrectly when I put them down in this brief fashion. In any case, I disagree wholeheartedly with the four propositions stated above. They do not seem to me tenable, if music is a major art.

Very sincerely yours,

To a Reader

June 6, 1942

I think that Mendelssohn, though a gifted and charming composer, was a reactionary figure with respect to the Romantic movement. I do not use the word "reactionary" in a wholly uncomplimentary sense. I think Mendelssohn was one, because he was far more interested in where music came from than in where it was going.

Very sincerely yours,

To Theodor Adorno

July 29, 1942

Dear Mr. Adorno:

I find on clearing out my desk of the season's unanswered mail that I have never done anything about your Sibelius article. I am sending it back to you, partly because our Sunday musical space has been so cut down that I would not have room to do much about it anyway, and partly because I don't really like it very much. The article has good ideas and good phrases in it, but there is too much indignation. The tone is more apt to create antagonism toward yourself than toward Sibelius.

Very sincerely yours,

To a READER

July 29, 1942

You are quite right, of course, about the reviewing of my works. For a man to write a criticism or even a review of his own piece is a stunt. It can be got away with once but not often. The chore of covering my works seems to have fallen to my first assistant Francis Perkins. He does it extremely well, I think, being an experienced writer as well as a wholly dispassionate reporter and analyst.

Very sincerely yours,

To a READER

July 29, 1942

I thank you for your charming letter. The stealing of themes from classic composers for use in popular music seems to be a growing habit these days. Classic composers, of course, have never hesitated to steal popular themes for their purpose. So I suppose that whatever is not protected by copyright anybody can use and quote precedent in so doing. All the same, I agree with you that original invention is more interesting in popular music than plagiarism.

Very sincerely yours,

To HARL McDONALD★

October 21, 1942

Dear Mr. McDonald:

I have consulted my colleagues on the *Tribune* and my managing editor and all are of the opinion that there is no objection to my conducting my own pieces in public with any musical organization.

★(1899–1955), American composer and longtime manager of the Philadelphia Orchestra

There is even precedent for such appearances. Mr. Downes of the *Times* has appeared as soloist with the Minneapolis Orchestra, I believe, and has lectured with the Boston Symphony Orchestra. My predecessor, Mr. Gilman, was employed by the Philharmonic Society for many years as program annotator. It is not on record that either of these men was ever seriously criticized for accepting such engagements or that they ever at any time pulled their punches when reviewing the concerts of these societies. Consequently, I am leaving the decision up to you. If you have any reserves about my appearing with the Philadelphia Orchestra, I shall not try to argue you out of them. So far as I am concerned and so far as the *Herald Tribune* is concerned no embarrassment is anticipated.

Very sincerely yours,

To a READER

October 21, 1942

I thank you for your charming letter and I do hope that our unexpected agreement about Shostakovich may be repeated occasionally in the future about other musical matters. I shall pass on to Aaron Copland, Walter Piston, and Bernard Herrmann your complimentary comparison.

There is certainly a possibility that one or both of us may be wrong about Shostakovich. I had an awful moment Sunday afternoon, when my article was already published, at hearing accidentally over the radio the last two or three minutes of the Seventh Symphony. The music did not sound bad at all. I shall hear it all again next month and if I find I have to recant I shall do so. Many musicians have told me, however, that the piece is really the way I said it was.

Most sincerely yours,

To a READER

November 25, 1942

Your letter is a very difficult one to answer. You ask for the name of a musical composer. I am one myself. There are about two thousand or ten thousand others in the United States. If I knew what kind of composer you are looking for and for what purpose, I could possibly advise you better.

Very sincerely yours,

183

To a READER

November 27, 1942

I thank you for your charming letter on the subject of Verdi and Wagner. Nobody but the Germans has ever seriously thought that Verdi was influenced by Wagner. They have pretended so for many years because they can't imagine an Italian writing well without having learned to do so from German models. That is all tommyrot, of course. Verdi has the great distinction of being the only first-class composer in Europe during the nineteenth century who knew Wagner's works and was *not* influenced by them.

Very sincerely yours,

To a READER

December 30, 1942

I thank you for your interesting letter about *Rhapsody in Blue*. I agree with you that last week's rendition of it was stylistically wrong and highly unpleasant. I am not sure that the whole fault, however, was Mr. Iturbi's.* Mitropoulos† may very well have been responsible for some of the maliciousness. This is a piece that is getting a good deal of rough treatment these days. I did not think that Mr. Toscanini's reading of it at the NBC concert a few weeks back was a very happy one, and I have recently heard a two-piano team manhandle it pretty brutally. When they overplay it, as they so often do nowadays, they take the sweetness out of it.

Very sincerely yours,

*José Iturbi (1895–1981), celebrated Spanish pianist and conductor and occasional film personality
†Dimitri Mitropoulos (1896–1960), music director of the Minneapolis Symphony from 1937 to 1949 and of the New York Philharmonic from 1950 to 1958

To Moses Smith*

December 31, 1942

Dear Moses:

I expect that in the Mitropoulos case we are disagreeing about a point of taste rather than a point of fact. I have no prejudice against Mr. Mitropoulos, and I have a pre-disposition in his favor for the large number of new works he has played. I have often said so in print too. His case is a curious one. I find his workmanship more interesting than the musical result. Many people do not agree with me. It may be, too, that he is more at ease with his own orchestra than with the Philharmonic. Please don't think, though, that I am trying to prove anything more than what I have stated in the reviews of his work that I have published in the last two years. I don't even know what you mean by "hitting below the belt." Is it hitting below the belt to admire a man's musicianship without subscribing to his interpretations? And is it not legitimate to make an effort to describe the interpretations in more general terms than would be involved in merely saying that one admired this detail and not that? I have spent lots of thought on the Mitropoulos question, and I have gone to more of his concerts than I have to those of any other visiting conductor at the Philharmonic. I don't pretend that my diagnosis of his case is final for anybody, even for me. But I am beginning to verify what was merely an impression two years ago. I am sorry you question my good will about it.

Very sincerely yours,

To a Reader

February 24, 1943

Nothing would delight me more than to have my antipathies psychoanalyzed. It would be like having one's fortune told by an expert. I am sure you are quite right, also, in thinking that life would be more peaceful for everybody if I continued to neglect the Wagner question. I am not going to do so, however. I have no pretense as a Wagnerian scholar, though I have a long familiarity with the works. I have strong opinions on the subject, too, some of which I think may interest my readers, even those who may differ. I am less inter-

---

*(1901–1964), producer for Columbia Records who supervised many of Mitropoulos's recordings; later a biographer of Koussevitzky

ested, in fact, in convincing people that my analysis of these works is correct than I am in reopening the whole Wagner question for discussion. That question, as I see it, is not whether he was a "great" musical author. It is rather how much sense any given page of his music makes. By "sense" I mean how does it compare as musical and dramatic expression with Mozart, say, or with Massenet. Of course he was a great man and a most original musician. But the cult of his music needs some debunking. My frivolous little review of *Die Meistersinger* the other morning was just a beginning. You tempt me to go on, and I think I shall.

Very sincerely yours,

To a READER

April 22, 1943

I agree with you that Handel's "Open the Gates of the Temple" is a finer piece of music than [Jean-Baptiste Faure's] "The Palms." Unfortunately popularity and usage do not always follow the standards of the highest musical excellence. "The Palms" as music is just so-so. But it has become familiar to everybody as a piece played and sung on Palm Sunday. In this role it has a sort of consecration that musical criticism is powerless to alter.

Very sincerely yours,

To a READER*

May 6, 1943

I thank you for your charming letter about my Easter Sunday article,† and I am delighted that you should find my viewpoint both Christian and Catholic. I must confess, however, that I am technically neither. I was brought up to be a Baptist; but, as you know, that communion does not baptize children except at their request. Since I never made any such request, and since I never joined any other communion, I am to this day not a member of any Christian church. My religious sentiments, however, so far as those things have any value, are, as you put it, Christian and Catholic.

Very sincerely yours,

---

*a Catholic priest
†about a jazz-guitar-playing black preacher

To a Reader

May 26, 1943

You are quite right. My radio is not a very good instrument, though there are worse on the market. I still think I am right that the narrow range of dynamics which any microphone will carry makes Beethoven one of the least effective composers for broadcasting purposes. This does not mean that I consider Beethoven's music, even in its distorted radio sound, to be uninteresting. Quite to the contrary. The way it survives processing is to its eternal glory.

Very sincerely yours,

To a Correspondent

October 15, 1943

Strange as it may seem to you, I am not aware of parodistic intentions in any of the works you named. Perhaps we do not define parody in the same way. I never mind if people find my music entertaining, but I am inclined to credit its risible effects, when they take place, to the surprise of certain listeners at novel uses of familiar formulae. I don't mind laughter, because I am used to it; but I certainly do not seek it or plan for it. The piece that is most commonly associated with parody in many listeners' minds is my opera *Four Saints in Three Acts*. Neither Miss Stein, the librettist, nor myself, however, had any wish to make fun of opera in this work. We wished to write (and we think did write) a perfectly straightforward work on a serious subject—namely, the saintly life. If you consider Mozart's *Don Giovanni* a joke about sacred and profane love, also a parody of Italian opera, then you may legitimately consider *Four Saints* to be a joke about the saintly life and a parody of opera and oratorio. That there is some comedy in both the libretto and the musical score I do not deny, but I *do* deny any wish to kid anything.

Very sincerely yours,

To a Reader

November 3, 1943

My most loyal friends have always protested against my tendency toward a flippant treatment of pretentious musical occasions and my use of slang. On the other hand, I am frequently cited in university courses of English composition for my expressive use of the collo-quial. I am afraid that most of the passages you have underlined in the enclosed clipping fall into that category; though I admit that there is a shade of vulgarity as well in the use of the word "passion-ate" to mean "pseudo-emotional" and in the use of the word "plenty" as an adverb. It seemed to me, while writing the review, that elegant diction would have been inappropriate for this particular occasion. I chose my tone deliberately and my expressions with some care. Perhaps the final result did not justify my procedure. If it didn't, I thank you all the more for pointing my failure out to me.

Very sincerely yours,

To a READER

November 5, 1943

Thanks for the interesting letter. I suggest you listen to some of the old Melba★ records, if you have never heard a convincing trill.

Very sincerely yours,

To a READER

November 5, 1943

It was charming of you to write me in defense of the radio an-nouncers. There is a maxim in the advertising world, "Tell it to Sweeney; the Stuyvesants will understand." There is also a maxim in church choirs, "Never address the music, however simple it may be, to anybody less than the most intelligent person who might be present." I hear a good deal of complaint about radio announcers following the first rule and ignoring the second. That is why I wrote a Sunday article on the subject. As long as the radio gives us good music we will put up with ignorant presentations, but I do think the intellectual tone of these could be raised without endangering that music's appeal to plain people.

Very sincerely yours,

★Nellie Melba (1861–1931), Australian soprano

To Alfred Frankenstein*

November 24, 1943

Dear Alfred:

Thanks for the opera article. Our opera opened Monday night with a fairly ship-shape performance of *Boris*. Beecham is conducting *Tristan* tonight, on account of Walter's† illness. I went to a rehearsal and almost enjoyed myself. He makes it light, if you can believe that.

Best,

To a Reader

November 29, 1943

My references to barrooms in a recent review of one of John Charles Thomas's‡ recitals were intended as in no way derogatory to the character of that excellent artist. There are many styles of singing and the barroom style is one of them. This style is not necessarily a low one any more than barroom conversation is necessarily vulgar. All I meant to imply by my epithet was a certain ease of manner, a combination of lyricism with familiarity in the good sense. I repeated the allusion in order to make it clear that my comparison was not frivolously intended. That you should have so understood it is proof that I did not express my thought adequately. Please believe that I have the highest admiration for Mr. Thomas's work and a sincere respect for my readers.

Very sincerely yours,

To a Reader

December 2, 1943

I am sorry I was not able to go to Miss——'s recital. I sent Elliott Carter,§ who did not care much for her work. She sang for me ten years ago, when I was casting *Four Saints*. At that time she had a

---

*Frankenstein (1906–81), for many years Music Critic of the *San Francisco Chronicle,* was the critical colleague for whom Thomson felt the greatest affinity.
†Bruno Walter (1876–1962), Austrian conductor
‡(1891–1960), American baritone celebrated for his performances of both classical and popular repertory
§American composer Carter (b. 1908) was then an occasional critic for the *Herald Tribune.*

voice of great beauty and phenomenal range, but imperfectly trained. I gather from Carter and from other people who heard her recent recital that she has never succeeded in unifying her out-size scale. A voice like that is from this point of view, as you know, harder to train completely than a more limited one. I wish her all success, because I found her a charming person; and I am sorry that I was not able to hear her.

Sincerely,

To a READER

December 3, 1943

The musical tastes of a four-year-old child are not easy to predict. One child may like *Peter and the Wolf,* another may like nursery tunes, and another will love "Pistol Packin' Mama." I think that in your place I should go to a gramophone shop and listen to some of the records that are supposed to be suitable for children and pick out those that offend me the least. It is grown people, after all, who suffer the most from inferior art products of all kinds.

Very sincerely yours,

To MARKS LEVINE★

December 3, 1943

Dear Mr. Levine:

What I meant by leaders in the musical world is something wholly separate from the popularity of artists or the pleasures they may have given to millions of people. I meant musicians whose work other musicians find it profitable to study. Lhevinne† and Landowska belong in this category. Menuhin‡ and Heifetz,§ by and large, do not. That is the criterion of measurement that made my listings in a recent Sunday article sound arbitrary to you. I do not mean to suggest at all that the glorious career of Marian Anderson is not of value to the Negro race. That is a different proposition. I merely wished to state my opinion that her singing, though pleasant and honorable, is

---

★(1890–1971), of National Concert and Artists Corporation
†Josef Lhevinne (1874–1944), Russian-American pianist
‡Yehudi Menuhin (b. 1916), American-born British violinist
§Jascha Heifetz (1901–87), Russian-American violinist

190

neither a unique achievement of the interpreter's art nor an ideal model of vocal mastery. From the point of view of sheer professional excellence it seems to me that Horowitz, all glamour aside and many faults of interpretation forgiven, is something pretty memorable. So is Rubinstein.* So is Jennie Tourel.† So was Kirsten Flagstad.‡ So was Mary Garden. So was *not* Louise Homer,§ Geraldine Farrar,‖ and many another artist who has pleased lots of people in lots of places over a long time.

Very sincerely yours,

To a READER

January 19, 1944

I thank you for the charming letter. German music has been smelling bad for a long time. It is largely from this fact that I concluded it must be dead. It will take a little time, however, to get it buried.

Very sincerely yours,

To a READER

January 20, 1944

The immunity of critics to legal action is not quite as complete as you make it out to be. If I said in print that a singer has sung off pitch or that a pianist has played false notes, the statement, if correct, is not actionable. If I said that an artist has misunderstood a composer's intention, that is a matter of opinion and consequently not actionable either. If I said that anybody is a bad or incompetent artist, I have made a generalization which I cannot prove and which is capable of being considered by a court as harmful and justifying the payment of damages.

Very sincerely yours,

---

*Artur Rubinstein (1887–1982), Polish-American pianist
†(1910–73), Russian-American mezzo-soprano
‡(1895–1962), Norwegian soprano
§(1871–1947), American contralto
‖(1882–1967), American soprano

January 27, 1944

I am sorry that I don't share your opinion about the "purity" of concert music as opposed to music of the theater. It has always seemed to me that theater music at its best is more specific in its expression than concert music and that the latter might more correctly be compared to an alloy. Of course, if one considers direct meaning in music to be "base," then the opera is certainly inferior.

Very sincerely yours,

To a READER

January 28, 1944

I have known Miss Tureck* for some time, but I have never heard her play a whole recital. I shall do so the first time I am able. I haven't the vaguest idea as to whether Mr. Bowles's criticism of her first Bach concert was just or unjust. Mr. Bowles himself, whom I have known for fifteen years, is a musician of broad knowledge and impeccable sincerity. The members of the *Herald Tribune* music staff make no effort to agree with one another about musical events.

I am sorry Mr. Bowles does not impress you as a competent critic. The *Herald Tribune* considers him rather brilliant. Like many another young critic, of course, he sometimes speaks more harshly in his reviews than he is aware of doing.

Very sincerely yours,

To a READER

February 3, 1944

My remark that you quote, about singing being a sign of expansiveness and dancing a gesture of despair, is based on the simple observation that dancing, among our Negro proletariat and among the Spanish poorer classes, has been the most vigorous and expressive popular dancing of our time. These groups seem to find a release in this way from their hopelessly oppressive conditions of life. The Russian peasantry used to dance a good deal, too, before the

---

*Rosalyn Tureck (b. 1914), American pianist and harpsichordist

Revolution. Economic stability seems to act as a restraint on this kind of expression. The observation, if you wish, is intuitive; but it seems to fit in with a good deal I have seen and read.

Very sincerely yours,

To Alan Carter*

June 8, 1944

Dear Alan:

I thank you for the letter and the programs. It was my hard luck that I did not happen into Bleeck's the night you were there. I do hope you will try me again. I can be found at my own house, which is the Chelsea Hotel in Twenty-third Street, at least as often, believe it or not, as at the bar.

Cordially yours,

To F. B. Stiven†

October 19, 1944

Dear Mr. Stiven:

If you could present me to your friends after the lecture instead of before I should be most grateful. I am not at my best for public appearance when stimulated by intellectual conversation and new people. I like to dine lightly in my own room before these occasions when that is possible.

Very sincerely yours,

To a Reader

December 27, 1944

The artist in question has been reviewed for the *Herald Tribune* in three successive years by three different critics. All these reviews have been on the unfavorable side. None of the critics has any axe to grind in the matter, and I have no reason for supposing them to be

---

*(1904–75), American conductor
†(b. 1909), director of the School of Music at the University of Illinois, Urbana

prejudiced. This artist is known in music circles to consider himself the victim of a conspiracy. I have inquired into the situation as well as I have been able, and I have not found the slightest evidence to support such an idea. It so happens that I haven't been to any of his recitals myself, so that I have no opinion about his execution and artistry. But it might just be possible that he is not as accomplished a player as he imagines himself to be.

Very sincerely yours,

To WALLINGFORD RIEGGER★

February 1, 1945

Dear Wallingford:

Thanks for the charming note. This is the first time a composer has ever congratulated me on an unfavorable review. I am quite willing to believe that your piece might sound like a different one if correctly played. Russians have a way of making everything they touch sound like something they heard at home when they were young. I have always been amused at the way Koussevitzky mistakes Roy Harris for Borodin.

Best and always,

In June, 1945, Thomson visited California, where he wrote and conducted the score for a film called A Tuesday in November, written and directed by Nicholas Ray (1911–79) and produced by John Houseman, "an explication for foreign countries . . . of how in America we elect our president" (Virgil Thomson).

To MARIAN CHASE DUNHAM

Los Angeles
[June 1945]

D.M.

Nice day. All days nice days. Write music, swim and toast my skin. Went to a movie with Rita Hayworth† and was mobbed by

---

★(1885–1961), distinguished American modernist composer
†Film star Hayworth (1918–87) was then married to Orson Welles.

adolescents. They showed their love by throwing burning cigarettes at her and rocks. My address is c/o John Houseman. Write.

L. & K.
Virgil

The big joke on Hollywood is that it doesn't exist. There is no such address in this region, though there is, I believe, a small post office of that name somewhere in Northern California.

To Marian Chase Dunham

Los Angeles
[June 1945]

D.M.

The music is all finished but recording. It is perfectly beautiful. I'm glad it's over, though. I've had no vacation at all. And the weather has been cold and foggy. One day of sun since I arrived. Houseman leaves day after tomorrow and I move over to Chick's house. Fontaine,* who is going away for several weeks, has offered me her house, complete with servants, car and driver. But I don't quite know what to do with it. Chick has no servants and no telephone, but there are guests always. Went to a dinner party at Judy Garland's.† There were lots of people but it wasn't much fun except a Yugoslavian communist colonel and Fontaine, who is a nice girl.

I shall wire when I go to San Francisco.

L.K.V.

To Marian Chase Dunham

Los Angeles
[June 1945]

D.M.

Jack got off this morning after having yesterday a most elegant cocktail party with champagne and lots of hot food that was really a sort of supper. The food was done by Fontaine's cook and was in-

---

*Actress Joan Fontaine (b. 1917) was then romantically involved with Houseman.
†(1922–69), American popular singer and film actress

credibly luxurious. I am moving now to Chick's house. Bette Davis* is coming to dinner tonight and tomorrow we go to a real theater to see Norman Lloyd† in *Volpone*. Sunday we drive with the Antheils to Mexico to see a bullfight. I was mistaken about going to Judy Garland's for dinner. It was Paulette Goddard's‡ I now learn.

lots of K.V.

Maurice is going to visit me in S.F. with his motorcycle. That will be nice, but I don't quite know where to put him.

To Marian Chase Dunham

[Los Angeles]
July 1945

D.M.

I got to Chick's all right and the Bette Davis dinner was fun only I got drunk and talked all the time and the next morning I had early musical engagements at the studio that lasted till middle of afternoon and I got through them fine but felt terrible afterwards so I haven't had anything to drink since, which is a swell idea, anyway that night we went to see Norman Lloyd in *Volpone* and the show was wonderful and yesterday we went to Mexico all day, leaving at eight in the morning and getting back at one o'clock in the night. Mostly it was riding. We didn't stay long and we didn't go to the bullfight because Chick doesn't like them and I was sure the Antheil child aged ten would get bored during three hours of it. So we drove up in the mountains on our way back and cooked our supper at Johnny Goodwin's ranch. Tonight I am going to see *Rose Marie* in Los Angeles, hoping to get some kind of review out of it for a Sunday article. I wired Julia Haines§ to phone you I'm on my way to S.F. Actually I am going on Friday the 6th and Maurice is, I presume, still planning (so he wrote last week) to turn up with motorcycle shortly. Tomorrow I record my film music. It will be a pleasure to leave town on Friday.

KKK
V——

---

*(b. 1908), American actress
†(b. 1914), British character actor
‡(b. 1911), American film actress
§Thomson's secretary at the *Tribune*

To Marian Chase Dunham

[Los Angeles]
Fourth of July [1945]

D.M.

Yesterday I recorded my score at Paramount, conducting myself, and the music is just as beautiful as I thought it was and I got good recordings and I am very happy about it. And then I came home and Johnny Goodwin had won lots of money at the races and took us out to dinner and we had foie gras and pheasant and afterwards we went briefly to a nightclub and then came home and everybody stayed till four but I had only drunk wine and today I am practically as good as new and so shortly we will go down the hill and have lunch and do our daily telephonings (Chick having no telephone) and I shall make my farewell call on the Stravinskys and tonight I go to the Antheils again and tomorrow I shall tend to a few more farewell errands and early Friday morning I shall leave these fogs and vast suburban spaces behind me. Am I glad am I glad am I glad? I've run into lots and lots of people I know, New Yorkers and Parisians and childhood playmates, but so far not a soul who has seen Touche or heard of his being here, though they know all about that musical show on the life of Tchaikovsky. Lenny Bernstein★ was in and out of town briefly and Fontaine does a wonderful imitation of him sitting at a piano and monopolizing a party.

L.K.V.

To Marian Chase Dunham

San Francisco
[July 1945]

D.M.

Now I am here and my whole metabolism is different and I feel wonderful. I enjoy my food and my friends and my sleep and even my work. I had thought I might have a letter on arriving but I didn't. I now think there must be one tomorrow. This is an enormous house built around 1900 or 1910 and vastly comfortable. Schmitz† and wife are away till end of July. Daughter and soldier

---

★Bernstein (b. 1918) was then at the beginning of his celebrity. Thomson admired his conducting skills more than his composing.
†E. Robert Schmitz (1889–1949), French pianist

husband (on leave) are here, though I only see them at meals, which we cook ourselves. There are three or four other people, pupils of Robert, I think, living in the house; but I've never seen them or even heard them, because the place is so large and soundless. There is a fine view of Golden Gate and bridge too. And transportation. Streetcars go downtown quickly. In L.A. there was virtually no transportation at all. I sent you a scarf from Odette Myrtil's. She is an actress, old friend of Chick, and now has a dressmaking establishment. Yesterday I wrote a Sunday article and last night I went to Berkeley with [Alfred] Frankenstein to hear a string-quartet concert. Tonight I go with him to an orchestral one in town. The weather is wonderful.

Love V

To LINCOLN KIRSTEIN★

August 2, 1945

Dear Lincoln:

I seem to have a number of unanswered letters from you. My negligence does not mean that they were unappreciated, for they have served me, in fact, better than any other source of information about musical life in Paris. The big batch of clippings arrived in June while I was in Hollywood. I read them briefly and then lent them to Stravinsky, who has since resisted all efforts to make him give them back. I am going to France myself sometime during the month of August to stay until November. Do let me know if there is any chance of your being around.

Affectionately,

To MAURICE GROSSER

Paris
August 26 [1945]

D.M.

Left New York last Sunday. Got to London on Monday. Stayed till Friday, with two days in country chez Beecham. Flew to Paris in Army plane. London rich still act & think rich, though their food is

---

★written at the end of Kirstein's two-and-a-half-year army service in Europe

bad and their shirts are darned. I think all classes are a little tired. *Tribune* is lending me a car & chauffeur, I believe, beginning tomorrow. Getting around is not too hard, because the Métro works, though nothing else does. Life is difficult but not impossible, prices astronomic, people full of muscular energy, walking all the time, limited food admirably cooked, the city incredibly beautiful all dirty white stone in clean white light. Weather perfect, tempers very sweet. I am moving to the Ritz, I believe, in a few days. I like the neighborhood better than Champs-Elysées. There are only a few hotels where transient Americans can go. Gov't keeps this reserved for missions and business—visiting civilians. Everything else full permanently.

L & K

V

To John Houseman

[1945]

D.J.

Faulkner has written he is pleased* and the name of his lawyer, who is supposed to communicate with me. My publisher (Hans Heinsheimer at Schirmer's) is playing with the scenario, trying to get the party back in. Also to reduce the number of scenes. I must say I always liked the party and that I prefer long plain acts to lots of scenes, but you do what you can with a given plot. Anyway, letting him play around with ideas makes him happy; and I like my publisher to be happy. Myself, I am not touching the show till I finish my cello concerto (now in good progress) and have full permission from Faulkner. Minna has written you, I hear, about Marc's opera.† It seems to go all right in Boston, with the usual hasty changes, of course. Freddie Ashton is here with his ballet troupe, having terrific success as choreog and as character dancer. I must say that when he is on stage nobody can look at anybody else.

Affec.

---

*Novelist William Faulkner (1897–1962) had given Thomson permission to base an opera on his novel *The Wild Palms*. Houseman planned to prepare the libretto, but the project was abandoned.
†probably a revival of *The Cradle Will Rock*

To the GUGGENHEIM FOUNDATION

November 18, 1945

Stefan Wolpe★ is a serious character and a worthy musician. I have been influential in securing for him several times financial aid and professional outlets. I must admit, however, that his work does not interest me personally a great deal. There is nothing wrong with it or with him.

> Always cordially yours,

To a READER

[undated]

I thank you for the correction about Mr. B——'s name. I wrote it correctly but did not notice the printer's error when I read my proof. The fault is therefore mine. I do not think printing a correction would be a very good idea, however. We do not usually do that for errors which do not change the sense of a sentence. If newspapers apologized to me every time they put a "p" in my last name, they would be writing about me all the time.

> Most sincerely yours,

To HOWARD HANSON†

April 24, 1946

Dear Hanson:

I was very sorry to miss the privilege of conducting your orchestra. The trouble all came about through the New York Central, which reserved berths for me on the wrong days and were unable to correct their mistake. At the last moment I found myself faced with a long night's sleep in a chair car, which did not seem the fair preparation for public performance. I particularly regret not having heard the new pieces on the program because I could have got a Sunday article out of those. For five years it has been my intention to cover the Rochester Festival in person, but every year I have had some sort

---

★(1902–72), a modernist composer later influential in New York
†(1896–1981), American composer, conductor, and administrator associated with the Eastman School of Music for more than half a century

of conflicting engagement. I shall get there eventually, I assure you. A thousand apologies and all best wishes.

Most cordially yours,

Having made arrangements to reoccupy his apartment at 17, quai Voltaire (which had been sublet when he was not there), Thomson returned to Paris in the summer of 1946, at which time he also made a conducting and reporting tour of postwar Europe.

To Maurice Grosser

July 17 [1946]

D.M.

Still no mail from you. Trip to Luxembourg and Brussels was fine and my concerts were good. Tomorrow I'm off for Venice. August 1st the army is taking me to Germany. Brussels is a handsome town with lots of food and everything just like no war except for some bombarding. Antwerp is all lacey with bombarding. Luxembourg is almost Swiss-picturesque and also full of good food. Barber and Menotti,* just up from Venice, say that, too, is practically pre-war. I suppose the war gets over in spots.

L. & K.
V.

"As I left for Paris, at the railway station I learned from that morning's Herald Tribune of the death of Gertrude Stein," Thomson recalled in his autobiography.

In Paris I went straight to call on Alice, found her lonely in the large high rooms, but self-contained. Gertrude had been feeling tired all spring, she said, and they had hired a small house near Le Mans. There Gertrude had felt quite ill, had pain, and seen a local doctor. He had said, "You may need surgery. In any case you should go back to Paris."

At the American Hospital, an operation was recommended; but in view of her weakened state, it was thought best to postpone this till her strength could be rebuilt. Ten days later there was no

---

*Composers Samuel Barber (1910–81) and Gian Carlo Menotti (b. 1911) were longtime friends and musical associates.

change in her strength, and she was still in pain. The surgeon, though pressed, refused to operate. So she sent for the director of the hospital and said, "You will send me a younger surgeon, who will do as I ask." And when he came, she said, "I order you to operate. I was not made to suffer."

The words that have been quoted as her last were spoken while she waited for the wheel table that was to carry her to the operating room. As Alice Toklas told me, then and later, Gertrude had asked a little vaguely (for she was already under sedation), "What's the answer?" And Alice, to bring her back from vagueness, said, "What is the question?" It was in reply to this that Gertrude remarked, "I suppose if there is no question, there is no answer." She had earlier remarked, as her nephew's family, eventually to be her heirs, departed, "We don't have to see them again."

She is buried in the cemetery at Père-Lachaise in a double grave under a double stone designed by Sir Francis Rose, the youngest of the painters Gertrude had continued to admire. Half of it awaits to be inscribed for Alice Toklas. ★

Stein had completed the libretto for The Mother of Us All shortly before her death, leaving Thomson the task of composing the score and seeing the work come to fruition by himself, though they had spoken extensively about it during June in Paris. The first performance took place at Columbia University's Brander Matthews Theatre on May 7, 1947, under the direction of Otto Luening.†

To MAURICE GROSSER

Paris
August 7 [1946]

D.M.

Gertrude had a tumor for 20 years and knew what she was doing. When operation was necessary, the doctors didn't think she was in good enough condition but she ordered them to operate and it turned out the tumor had gone cancerous and the heart was weak and she died. She would have died of it anyway pretty soon. Alice is naturally very lonesome. Why don't you write her a little note? She always liked you and talked about you.

LKV

★Toklas was indeed buried there after her death in 1967.
†(b. 1900), American composer, conductor, and pedagogue

To a READER

New York
October 2, 1946

I do not know Richard Addinsell and his *Warsaw Concerto,**
though I am aware that both of them exist. Terribly sorry not to be
of any help.

Most sincerely yours,

To MAJOR JOHN BITTERT†

October 17, 1946

Dear John:

Rodzinski‡ is all for organizing something about the Berlin Philharmonic men. So is Reiner.§ It will require a little tact, however,
since Germans, however virtuous, are still commonly considered
sub-human. We are counting on Nabokov‖ to help when he comes,
probably by speaking directly to the New York Philharmonic men. I
think some serious help for the whole Berlin orchestra can be organized. I have already received several letters from private readers
asking if they could send a package or two.

Thanks for nice letter.

Most sincerely yours,

---

*Addinsell (1904–77) composed this romantic piece for piano and orchestra as part of the
score for the motion picture *Dangerous Moonlight* (1941); it became tremendously popular
and was, for a time, heard regularly in concert performance.
†American (b. 1909), then conducting the Berlin Philharmonic, which was on what
Thomson calls "Nazi rations." With Thomson's and Nabokov's support, each member's
rations were raised from 1,200 to 1,500 calories a day.
‡Artur Rodzinski (1892–1958) was then music director of the New York Philharmonic.
§Hungarian-American Fritz Reiner (1888–1963) was then conductor of the Pittsburgh
Symphony Orchestra.
‖Russian-American composer and conductor Nicolas Nabokov (1903–78) was a good
friend of Thomson's.

To a READER

October 25, 1946

I do not know Thor Johnson* but I hear excellent reports of his work. Leonard Bernstein will probably come out all right eventually: he has too real a talent and too good a mind for me to envisage anything else. But he does require lots of slapping down.

Alfred Wallenstein is a good American conductor. So is Alexander Smallens. Leopold Stokowski and Eugene Ormandy,† though born in Europe, learned their art in this country. Walter Hendl,‡ Mr. Rodzinski's assistant at the Philharmonic, is a bright boy, too, and will probably go far.

Most sincerely yours,

To a READER

November 21, 1946

I see no reason for the Metropolitan Opera Company opening its season with the national anthem. It is not customary in peace times for private institutions to appropriate a work that is conventionally (and correctly, I think) reserved for public occasions of patriotic or governmental character. I deplore the assumption on the Met's part that its annual opening is any such thing, and I don't think the national anthem should be bandied about thoughtlessly now that the war is over.

Most sincerely yours,

To a READER

November 21, 1946

The Editor has passed me your charmingly indignant letter. It would have been a little more courteous, I must say, if you had written directly to me your disagreements with the ideas expressed

---

*Johnson (1913–75), then the conductor of the Juilliard Orchestra, later led the Cincinnati Symphony for two decades.
†Ormandy (1899–1985), music director of the Philadelphia Orchestra from 1936 until 1980, became Thomson's closest friend among conductors.
‡Hendl (b. 1917), then the assistant conductor of the New York Philharmonic, later served as music director in Dallas and Chautauqua.

in my review of *Eugene Onegin,* since those ideas are my ideas and not the Editor's. I am afraid also that you misread my review. It carefully avoids, I think, assuming that my opinion as to the practical nature of this work by Pushkin and Tchaikovsky proves either of these classic writers to be inferior workmen or *Eugene Onegin* to be an inferior work. I consider it to be a great work but not, at least for Anglo-Saxon or Latin audiences, a completely successful one; and I think I am entitled to express this opinion, even though I may be incorrect. You are wrong, of course, in thinking I have a limited acquaintance with the subject. I am afraid that you assume I do not have a "proper knowledge" of it merely because my opinions about it do not agree with yours.

Most sincerely yours,

To NORMAN CORWIN*

December 6, 1946

Dear Mr. Corwin:

I thank you for the courteous letter. I still think that Cocteau's French is more elegant than the English, even though the latter may be based, as is Cocteau's text also, on Sophocles. I also think that the quality of elegance is one not inappropriate to this particular work. I believe it to have been, in effect, the primary conscious stylistic consideration of both Cocteau and Stravinsky. If I didn't find that quality in the English of the text spoken at City Center, that is merely one man's opinion. I grant you that calling the style of that text "radio American" is perhaps not quite clear. It did, all the same, seem to me to lack distinction of language in much the same way that a great many of our more ambitious literary broadcasts do. I should not consider the expressive powers of MacLeish, Benét, and Sandburg† to be characteristic of the radio, since these poets came to the medium fully formed and lend themselves to it only occasionally. They are no more radio poets than I am a radio composer, though I have often written for radio too. Morton Gould,‡ whose style was formed by radio work, could with more justice be said to write, musically speaking, in "radio American."

---

*Corwin (b. 1910), a radio producer, narrated Stravinsky's *Oedipus Rex,* with Leonard Bernstein conducting the New York Symphony, at the New York City Center in 1946.
†Archibald MacLeish (1892–1982), Stephen Vincent Benét (1898–1943), and Carl Sandburg (1878–1967), American poets
‡(b. 1913), American composer and conductor

It may be reactionary of me, but I do deplore the introduction of a public address system to circumstances that do not absolutely require it for clarity. I have heard speakers in the City Center make themselves perfectly clear to the top gallery, and I am sure your excellent diction would have needed no more than theirs a mechanical aid. Electrical devices are part and parcel of radio and of the spoken film, but mixing them with live music gives an effect not unlike that of placing colored reproductions of visual art beside real oil paintings in a museum. In short, wrong as I may be, the public address system did not seem to me the other evening to be either necessary or appropriate.

Since we are on the subject, I also question the value of Americanizing the pronunciation of the leading character's name, since you pronounced all the others in Latin. "Oydipus" would have been more consistent, and if this were judged to be affected, "Eedipus" is the classical Anglicization, since the long vowel preserves the quantity of the original diphthong. "Eddipus" has, to my knowledge, no precedent in any scholastic usage. The point is a minor one. I only bring it up because it is typical of the tendency I reproached you with. I cannot see that folksiness of any sort helps the dissemination of so distinguished a work, since in the case of this particular work it is contrary to the basic stylistic conception that makes that work the kind of work it is.

Most sincerely yours,

To a READER

December 26, 1946

I am sorry to say that the remark you quoted from my review of a recent NBC concert was not an oversight. Wrong as I may be, I consider Reiner a sounder musician than Toscanini and a more complete master of his art than Walter. I may add, I think, that my opinion is shared by many other musicians.

Most sincerely yours,

To a READER

January 6, 1947

The situation you mention arises frequently in both music and ordinary life. The people we love most dearly are not always the noblest characters or the most intelligent. I am fond of the opera

Louise because it reminds me of my own youth and Paris and lots of things that it is pleasant to feel sentimental about, but I realize that it is not an entirely first-class musical work. On the other hand, neither Bach's "Goldberg" Variations nor Hindemith's *Ludus Tonalis* touches me deeply, though I am aware that both are admirable from both a technical and an imaginative point of view. When cases like this arise in the course of reviewing I usually state the facts. Nothing is gained by pretending to be moved by something that merely impresses you or by withholding the fact that a given work, though not perhaps a masterpiece, is not without charm.

Most sincerely yours,

To a READER

January 24, 1947

I am sorry to have forgotten about Brooklyn in my seasonal review. Music critics nearly always forget about Brooklyn. A thousand apologies.

Most sincerely yours,

To a READER

January 30, 1947

Mr. Harrison's★ preference for hearing Bach on the harpsichord rather than on the pianoforte seems to me a legitimate one. The question in his case, since he is not a professional executant on either instrument, seems to me a matter of opinion rather than of prejudice. I agree with you that any musical event is likely to be more interestingly criticized by a reviewer sympathetic to the whole nature of the occasion rather than by one not so favorably disposed in advance. Unfortunately such a casting of all the assignments is out of the question, though we do make an effort in that direction. Reading Mr. Harrison's review, it did not sound to me unfair. Reviewers' opinions, after all, do not have to be right, they only have to be clearly expressed and reasonably defensible.

Most sincerely yours,

★composer Lou Harrison (b. 1917), a good friend of Thomson's and an occasional critic for the *Herald Tribune*

January 31, 1947

I thank you for the extremely interesting letter. By "successful," with regard to Mr. Dello Joio's piece,* I mean that it is perfectly clear, that it has no major faults of workmanship. By "loyally composed" I mean that the author followed his own thought rather than somebody else's. I do not necessarily consider this work to be a masterpiece, but I cannot find anything wrong with it. Also, I find it most agreeable to listen to. This last opinion is personal and does not ask for agreement.

Most sincerely yours,

To a READER

February 4, 1947

Maybe my taste has been brutalized by contemporary opera productions. However, as these go, I assure you that the Metropolitan's *Traviata* is one of the better ones.

The fact that Gluck thought opera ought to be the essence of dramatic art does not mean that it ever has been that, even in Gluck's own work. Actually opera is singing in costume with a little acting added if the performer is clever. Since most of the singers in our opera houses are not clever at all, what usually happens is that their dramatic efforts rarely go farther than the occasional lifting of an arm. The Italians thus do a kind of statuesque performance that is dignified and moderately suggestive. Beyond that nobody at the Metropolitan does anything much that is not inept. There is no Mary Garden working before the public today, nor any Chaliapin.†

Most sincerely yours,

---

*American composer Norman Dello Joio (b. 1913) wrote his *Ricercar for Piano and Orchestra,* to which Thomson refers, in 1945.
†Fyodor Chaliapin (1873–1938), Russian bass noted for his compelling acting

To a READER

February 5, 1947

Aaron Copland is certainly the most famous living American composer, but he is not the dean of anything. That word means, I believe, the oldest member of the profession or the longest in business.

Most sincerely yours,

To a READER

February 14, 1947

I did not notice the misprint "Angus Dei." Theologically the cow might as well have been adopted by the Deity as the lamb. Both are peaceful beasts.

Most sincerely yours,

To a CORRESPONDENT

February 26, 1947

I thank you for the charming letter and the honor of being asked to contribute to your *Mosaic* on Paul Rosenfeld.★ Even if I had time this month, which I haven't, I am afraid that I should not be very good on the subject. I did not know Paul intimately nor greatly admire his writing. He, in return, had low toleration for my music and considered me a "crackpot composer." I am sure that he was a valuable contributor to New York's intellectual life, but I should be hard put to describe the exact nature of his contribution. I must admit that my acquaintance with his writing is limited chiefly to the musical pieces that appeared in *The Dial* during the early 1920s.

It was nice of you to ask me all the same.

Most sincerely yours,

★(1890–1946), American author and critic of modernist tastes

To a Reader

March 12, 1947

Leonard Bernstein's musical abilities, which are high, are one thing; his platform mannerisms are another. In my opinion he has a conducting talent of the first water. Also, and unfortunately, there is a certain personal exhibitionism in his gestures and attitudes. But temperament is rarely accompanied in youth by sobriety. I have confidence in him, because it seems to me that personal exhibitionism is more easily outgrown than mediocrity. Meanwhile, if you close your eyes, you can easily listen to him without tedium. That is something; it really is.

Most sincerely yours,

To a Reader

March 14, 1947

Youth orchestras are not usually my meat unless they are very, very good. I approve of them highly; but I do not find it makes much sense, on the whole, to criticize student work by professional standards. And professional standards are the only thing that makes for reasonable reading in the music columns of a newspaper. If we went in for encouraging students, however gifted they may be, our criticism of professional artists would lose its force. I should be delighted to have information at all times about the work of young groups and talents, but please don't be surprised if I do not use my column for criticizing them. It is not fair to the professional artist or to the reader that I should do so.

Most sincerely yours,

To a Correspondent*

March 21, 1947

I am not too happy at seeing my score called whimsical. Also, I think the idea that Miss Stein and I are primarily wits is, if you will permit me, both antiquated and inaccurate. I should appreciate it if you could refer to *The Mother of Us All*—both the words and the

---

*a young writer for *Harper's Bazaar* who had written a brief article about *The Mother of Us All*

music—as a serious work on a serious theme. That theme is not "the war between the sexes" but woman suffrage. There is comedy in it, of course; but referring to it as witty, whimsical, and charming does not give a resembling picture of it any more than those same adjectives would of *Hamlet*. I am sorry to be so critical, because I know you have spent a great deal of thought on the paragraph which you sent me. But since you have asked for my cooperation, I should be most grateful, and so would Miss Stein if she were living, for some word that would not place us quite so definitely with the amusers.

Always cordially yours,

To a READER

April 2, 1947

Certainly the golden age of singing is over. Everybody is in agreement about that, and the gramophone records are there to prove it. Nevertheless, there are some excellent vocal artists appearing before the public today. I have not heard them all, since I do not go to all the concerts or to all the performances of opera. Consequently, in view of the incompleteness of my information, I do not think that it would be fair for me to send you a list of my personal favorites. It was gracious of you to ask me all the same.

Most sincerely yours,

To a READER

April 21, 1947

I thank you for the warm letter of appreciation. As you may imagine, I have received several expressing the contrary sentiment, though the ayes are more numerous than the nays and all from persons of greater cultivation. The Norwegian Embassy in Washington has sent me a statement to the effect that the Norwegian Government has found "no sufficient basis for instituting legal proceedings against Madame Flagstad."* They have also verified the fact that Mr. Emil Stang, Chief Justice of the Supreme Court of Norway, signed a testimonial to the effect that Madame Flagstad has

---

*Flagstad, who had remained in her native Norway during World War II, was suspected of collaboration with the Nazis because of her husband's political activities, and her postwar appearances in America were picketed.

"shown during the entire period a firm patriotic attitude." Justice Stang has recently revised this statement to cover only the period when she was in Norway, from April 1941 till her recent departure. Prior to that, of course, she was in the United States, where we may presume the FBI kept some kind of watch on her. I do not suppose that she has been a heroine of any kind, but neither has she been a traitor. Certainly she is entitled to practice her profession. Let those who hold her in moral disapproval abstain from patronizing her public appearances.

Most sincerely yours,

To Horace Grennell*

May 22, 1947

Dear Mr. Grennell:

Since I have no child, I have no direct observation of the effects on the very young of any kind of music. Your question implies, moreover, that jazz and "popular music" are the same thing, which I do not believe. Myself, as a child I consumed considerable amounts of both. I am still alive, but I have no idea as to whether my musical tastes would be sounder today had I been brought up in some environment where these things were unavailable. In that case, of course, the classics would have been unavailable too, since music never exists on a single taste level. The question is therefore academic, as well as obscure, since there is no known method for isolating a child from what goes on in his time and country.

Most sincerely yours,

To a Correspondent

May 28, 1947

You did indeed hear an accordion in my *Four Saints* score.

The accordion is a most valuable orchestral instrument. I find it useful in soft passages and incomparable for strong accents. It blends admirably with strings and with the harmonium. The chief inconvenience in writing for it is the scarcity of schooled players who can read rapidly and who are accustomed to orchestral routines. Let us

*A record producer then active with the Young People's Record Club, Grennell had asked Thomson whether jazz and popular music were harmful to children.

hope that in a few more years we shall see the instrument used for ensemble music more commonly than it is at present.

Most sincerely yours,

To Alice B. Toklas

May 29, 1947

Dear Alice:

I have just sent you by regular mail a copy of *Capital Capitals,* which is just off the press. Through some rather absurd errors at the publisher's office, the work got printed before the contract for it was even signed. But that is all right and everything is now being regularized.

Carl [Van Vechten] and Bill Rogers* and others, I am sure, have written you about the performance of *The Mother of Us All.* Their description of it will be more convincing than mine, which is simply that it is very beautiful all the way through from every point of view. The performance of *Four Saints,* which I conducted last Sunday on the radio, was successful also. So much so that I have been invited to record selections from it, amounting to 45 minutes, which is more than half of the whole, for the Victor Company. I shall do this with the same singers and chorus during the last week of June, but the records will not be available commercially for about another year. This is the normal time lag now in the issuing of "serious" music. I must also prepare both the opera scores for the printer, and I have commissions for two orchestral works. All that makes a very busy summer, and so I have reluctantly decided not to go to Paris. I am more regretful than I can say and I am sure you understand how regretful I am that I shall have to delay playing and singing for you the new piece. I shall send a recording of it by the next passenger who seems to have a little baggage space. I have sent the vacuum cleaner by a Madame Joseph Lew, a French lady. I am sending milk and lemon juice by a charming young couple named Monsieur and Madame Aubert. Please continue to ask for everything you want. At this season of the year there are innumerable travellers who would be only too delighted to render both you and me a service.

Lamont Johnson† and his group read Gertrude's Resistance play the other night, and it was delightful. We all laughed a great deal and wept a great deal. It is a beautiful play. If New York were not in such

---

*William G. Rogers, American reporter and friend of Stein's
†American actor

a senseless mood these days it would be produced, and it would be successful. Pavlik [Tchelitcheff] describes contemporary New York as "irrévérencieux et pas intelligent." There is no firm proposal yet for producing *The Mother of Us All* at a downtown theater, but the situation is middling hopeful.

I am terribly sorry I shall not be seeing you as soon as I had counted on.

Always affectionately and yours,

To a READER

October 31, 1947

The subject of castrati would need a news peg to make it appropriate for a Sunday music page. I do not know of any such peg available right now.

Most sincerely yours,

To ALICE B. TOKLAS

November 2, 1947

Dear Alice

I have finished correcting the proofs of the *Mother* score and now it will be coming out. The N.Y. production is still hanging fire but there will be one in Baltimore anyway. That seems to be certain. I went to Pittsburgh, where my niece got married. Now Maurice has come back to town and is repainting his flat. I saw a copy of the letter you received from the Metropolitan [Museum]. It seems there was no sale of the [Picasso] portrait, only a ten-year loan. (The Met does sell, however.) The Met wants the portrait but has no proper place to hang it till they start a 20th-century room. They have made a deal to buy 20th-century pictures from the Modern Museum and elsewhere and presumably by 1953 or 1960 there will be 20th-century paintings in the Met and permanently hung. At present the portrait has been hanging in the main lobby and attracting much favorable comment. I think it also went on tour & Ben thinks that if you insist the Met will keep the portrait though maybe not always hang it. He would like to use it, of course, but not against your wishes. The deal between the two museums (plus the Whitney) seems to be fairly elaborate but all the museum and gallery people approve of it. It is an attempt to make the M.M. a sort of Luxembourg and the Met (with luck) a Louvre. Getting Gertrude and Picasso into such a Louvre, or rather keeping them there, is not impossible, apparently, though the local museum people would all prefer waiting ten years. Don't accept the present arrangement unless you approve of it. Insistence will probably have some effect.

Affection always,

To a READER

November 14, 1947

If I were preserving records in limited numbers for either pleasure or posterity I should begin with my own. If there were any room left, I should choose to preserve the sound of certain singers or instrumentalists rather than mere compositions. Print takes care of these.

Most sincerely yours,

To BETTE ODETS*

November 20, 1947

Dear Bette:

Here is my contribution to the Eisler matter. I am not signing the petition, because it contains statements about matters of which I have no knowledge, such as "establishing the blamelessness of Hanns Eisler's political and human conduct during his stay in the United States." A mutual friend who called on him this summer tells me that Mr. Eisler is hoping for deportation rather than being tried for perjury, since a conviction on the latter charge would send him to prison. I find his situation most regrettable, though I do not know him well enough to understand how he got into the mess. Or rather if his conduct in this country has been strictly non-political, why didn't he dissociate himself earlier from his former party connections? If he was making a play for party support without being really sincere, well, that is exactly the kind of behavior that gets people

---

*Wife of American playwright Clifford Odets. German composer Hanns Eisler (1898–1962) had immigrated to the United States in the mid-1930s. A communist, he was threatened with deportation by the U.S. government and left the country in 1948 after the House Committee on Un-American Activities recommended that he be prosecuted for perjury and illegal entry.

into exactly this kind of a jamb. I am deeply sorry for him, but the best I can do is to certify his musical and intellectual achievements. I know nothing about his character and private life, having met him only once or twice and that briefly.

Always devotedly,

To a READER

November 20, 1947

If I had stood through *Don Giovanni* I am sure I, too, should have found it sour. As it was, I had a good nap. If Miss S—— had committed grave misdemeanors about pitch, I am sure I should have waked up. At musical performances I sleep lightly, and only so long as nothing in any way abnormal, for good or ill, takes place on the stage.

Most sincerely yours,

To the GUGGENHEIM FOUNDATION

December 4, 1947

Edwin Denby is clearly, I think, the best dance critic now writing in any language. His dance reviews are not only penetrating with respect to the subject, they are in many cases literature. The Guggenheim Foundation would make a contribution to civilization by encouraging Mr. Denby's work in this field. He needs, as a matter of fact, some such stimulus or pretext to make him do more work in dance criticism, since he is primarily a poet and does not turn his attention to the dance without some special stimulation.*

Most sincerely yours,

To a READER

December 4, 1947

The Editor has sent to my desk your charming letter about Leonard Bernstein and *The Cradle Will Rock* by Marc Blitzstein. I assure you I did not mean my review to be either sarcastic or a snub. I have

---

*Denby was awarded the fellowship.

known the work for ten years and admire it sincerely. Also, I think its revival at this time a good idea. I am a union man myself, a member of Local 802, National Federation of Musicians; and though I do not believe for one moment that any of us is very much nobler than the rest of us, I have long found in union membership a solid protection in matters contractual.

Most sincerely yours,

To a READER

December 4, 1947

I have been expecting readers to correct me for confusing the Vieuxtemps concerto with the Wieniawski. You are the first to do so, and I thank you. Not that there is an enormous difference in either the style or the musical value of the two works. But the printed program was in front of me as I listened and later, as I wrote my review, I simply made a foolish slip. I made a graver one last year when I mistook Beethoven's Thirty-two Variations for the "Diabelli" Variations, played by Borovsky.* Such slips do happen occasionally, and we do regret them when they do. Reviewing a concert which failed to take place is, however, a lapse from loyalty that I have not yet committed. There are some celebrated cases of this on record, though I do not know of its having occurred in New York City in the last ten years.

Most sincerely yours,

To E. ROBERT SCHMITZ

December 4, 1947

Cher Robert:

Reflecting about your piano concerto, I find the following uppermost in my mind. It is a good piece, interesting to listen to and, in the last two movements, solidly constructed. It has more personality than style, and by this I do not mean that it is entirely lacking in style. I mean that the ideas are good and that the texture of the harmony and counterpoint is not quite as firm as it is in the work of musicians who have composed more extensively. I suggest that before you revise the introduction to the first movement you glance at

---

*Alexander Borovsky (1889–1968), Russian-American pianist

Mozart's E-flat Symphony, No. 39. His thematic material, like yours, needed something in front of it. His solution for the problem is radical, simple, and completely satisfactory.

Thanks for the nice letter from Denver. *The Mother of Us All* will be out by the 15th of this month, unless unexpected delays occur. The publisher and printer are doing their best to make it available before Christmas. Embrace the ladies for me.

Affection,

To ALICE B. TOKLAS

December 31, 1947

Dear Alice:

The Baltimore project blew up because the ladies who found themselves raising money for our opera were unable to make either Gertrude's name or mine unloose the purse strings of that city. So the director of the enterprise resigned; and now Baltimore has no opera for this season. It is a little like the story of *Four Saints* in Darmstadt.

I have made efforts to send you cigarettes. The first one failed. The second is supposed to have succeeded. If it has really succeeded you will receive a carton every week or so. Please let me know the result so that I can take other measures if the present maneuver is not satisfactory.

I have written an orchestral piece that is a view of the Seine at night from in front of my house on the quai Voltaire. The Kansas City orchestra ordered a piece and so I thought it most appropriate that since I had written so much music about Kansas City for Paris, I would write about Paris for Kansas City. Now I am about to do a film that deals with Cajuns and the Bayou country.* It is a very beautiful film. The opera is now published and you should be receiving your copy. Please tell me everything you think about it as a volume.

My mother has been visiting me for three weeks. She spent Christmas with me and it was all very pleasant indeed. One of the smart-aleck friends asked her what she thought of Miss Stein's writing and she replied: "I like it very much when it is intended to be understood. When it is not intended to be understood I do not always understand it."

Louisiana Story, directed by Robert Flaherty (1884–1951), a distinguished American filmmaker, largely responsible for elevating the documentary into an art form

I was made a member the other day of the National Institute of Arts and Letters. New York is in the middle of a huge snowstorm. I hope you have not been too cold in Paris this winter. If you do get cold please come and visit me. Let me know when the tea runs out, so that I can send you more. There is plenty of everything here and I should be unhappy to think you needed or wanted anything there that I could send you.

I have the test pressings of our *Four Saints* records and they are quite wonderful. I have not heard such good choral diction before on discs. Every word is clear. I am having a busy winter and not an unpleasant one. If the opera is not produced again this year I am sure that it will be done next. Interest in it has neither grown nor diminished. We shall see soon what difference publication makes.

Always devotedly,

To a READER*

January 2, 1948

Your first two questions tend to assume that it might be possible to be a good music critic without knowing much about music. This is not true. Nobody ever makes sensible remarks about a matter of which he is ignorant. The chances of making a sensible remark on any subject are in direct proportion to one's knowledge and experience of that subject.

My column is intended for anyone who cares to read it. When I explain a technical point, I try to do so in plain language, avoiding technical jargon as much as possible. I do not hesitate, however, to engage in technical analysis when I find it necessary in order to make my point convincing. In that case, I count on the musicians to understand and the others to give me credit for having explained something whether they can understand it or not.

I have frequently published a change of opinion, though I find that my opinions do not change as often as one might expect them to do. There is no reason for not changing one's opinion.

Correspondents occasionally complain that I have not reviewed a given artist as favorably as the correspondent would have wished. I

_____

*a high-school student preparing a journalism class term-paper on music criticism, who sent Thomson a detailed questionnaire

have even been accused of bad will. Nobody has ever asked me why I wrote as I did. If I were ever asked this question I should reply that I wrote that way because that was my sincere opinion.

There is no special section in any New York concert hall reserved for critics. It is customary, however, to seat critics on the aisle in a good part of the house.

Most sincerely yours,

To Alice B. Toklas

January 28, 1948

Dear Alice:

I am terribly sorry the first two efforts to send you cigarettes did not succeed. The third try, now in operation, may. Please let me know within a week or so whether you have them. *The Mother of Us All* will be produced next November in New York. Meanwhile, Leland Stanford University will do it in San Francisco in March, Tulane University in New Orleans in April, and probably Syracuse University in May. Lincoln [Kirstein] is dickering with Freddy Ashton to direct the New York production. My book★ and Maurice's† have both been sent to you. You should have received the *Mother* score by now. If it is really true that the opera is to be produced in New York for the first of November, I shall not go abroad this summer. I shall have to stay here and get the *Four Saints* score ready for the printer and tend to other unfinished musical work during the first part of the summer. During the last part I shall have to be casting the opera, because we must start rehearsals on October first. That is all the news I have just now.

Always affectionately,

★*The Art of Judging Music* (1948), the second of Thomson's books of collected criticism
†*Painting in Public* (1948), an unsentimental analysis of the art world; later reissued as *Painting in Our Time*, above Grosser's objections to the new title

To Mrs. August Belmont*

February 4, 1948

Dear Mrs. Belmont:

The same mail that brought me your charming letter brought one from another correspondent calling the Guild privileges with regard to ticket buying a "racket." I see no advantage to the Metropolitan in printing either. As to whether the speculation in opera tickets that unquestionably goes on is wholly, partially, or not at all participated in by Guild members is a matter I have no means of verifying. Your belief that "when a member cannot use his tickets, the general practice is to turn them over to the Guild for resale" I am sure is right. That is why I doubted in print, in response to many letters on the subject, that Guild members were involved in any large way in the black market operation that does go on. Neither, certainly, is the box office. It was tactless of me to raise the question of indelicacy, though surely I have rendered a service to the general public, and possibly to the Guild, by explaining just what the privileges of Guild members are with regard to ticket buying. The justice of such privileges existing at all is questionable, but the facts about them are public property. Comparing my resumé of them with your letter, I do not find that I have stated them unfairly.

Much more a matter of concern to me is your belief that I am "a fairly consistent adverse critic of the musical performances at the opera." Consistency is a grave charge against a reviewer, because, unless the performances reviewed conform pretty consistently to some standard, high, low, or medium, which our opera performances surely at present do not, any consistency that appears in the reporting of them, whether favorable or adverse, is evidence of prejudice. Happily, my reviews, as preserved over the last seven years in the music department files, show no such attitude. If they seem to run more to favor than to disfavor, there is not enough imbalance even on that side to make me appear as an indiscriminate supporter of the establishment. The fact that I find more of excellence to report than most of my colleagues do is a result of my having a large staff of assistants. I go only to what I think will make a good evening and an interesting review. I admit trying in advance to pick the best. If you will consult the files you will find, I am sure, that I succeed more often than not.

My Sunday pieces, on the other hand, are often severely critical.

---

*Eleanor Robson Belmont (1878–1979), a former actress, was the founder and guiding spirit of the Metropolitan Opera Guild.

These are not so much reports as reflections. And if the Metropolitan mail is anything like mine, you must know that many another opera lover is deeply concerned about the present downward trend of the repertory houses—a worldwide trend, as I have frequently noted—and about the seeming inability of America, with all its resources, artistic and financial, to arrest this. If the Metropolitan were a minor institution vowed to inferior standards, I would pass it over in silence. Given the degree of enlightened public support and professional excellence involved, it is my duty to share with the public my reflections about it. Some of my readers find these convincing, others not. All recognize, I think, that I cannot treat so respected an institution with neglect or with easygoing tolerance. Either attitude would be discourteous.

My judgment may be faulty; but I should not like to think, dear Mrs. Belmont, that you consider me an enemy of any musical institution. Perhaps criticism is useless. Certainly it is often inefficient. But it is the only antidote we have to paid publicity.

Most sincerely yours,

P.S. The Guild resale service on tickets, if I read your letter correctly, is of benefit only to Guild members. It relieves them of going through a speculator when they need an extra seat and of financial loss in case they cannot use their own. It does not serve the general public or even the Metropolitan itself, insofar as this is a popular institution. It is not a black market, like ticket speculating, but a privileged market. Even the "national" or $10 members of the Guild do not participate. Am I wrong?

To a READER

February 12, 1948

An oratorio is music for reviewing when given in something like its original form, which usually means with orchestral accompaniment. I realize, however, that a great deal of excellent choral music is given in the New York churches in its original form and that the press does not regularly cover it. The reason for our non-coverage is that such music is presumed to be presented in praise of God rather than in quest of public favor. It is not becoming to criticize anybody's technique of worship. Newspapers report on sermons and services, but they offer no judgment. I think there would be a place for the criticism of church music in a periodical devoted to the subject. Occasionally I have even criticized it myself as a "candid reporter." In any case, it is not customary to review church music in newspapers; and any major change in this regard would entail the engagement of a far larger staff than any newspaper has. A further complication comes from the fact that practically all of it takes place on the same day and at the same time.

Most sincerely yours,

To ALICE B. TOKLAS

March 4, 1948

Dear Alice:

I am delighted you like my book and Maurice will be delighted to hear from you about his. I have made another effort to send you cigarettes. The aviator who tried a month or so ago was arrested at Orly. Other friends leaving this spring will do what they can. It is extraordinary the way everything has missed fire. At present I am not planning to come abroad this summer. I should love to have a visit with you but I know now that I do not get much music written as a traveling reporter. So I say to myself, as I did last year, that I am not going abroad. The opera projects are exactly where they were when I wrote you before. Perhaps I can persuade you to come over next fall if it is really going to be done properly. Beecham, who was here a few weeks ago, assures me that he will do it for the BBC in June. This is all the news I have just now. I am still writing my film score. The piece about Paris [*The Seine at Night*] was successful in Kansas City and will be played by Stokowski at the Philharmonic in New York two weeks from now. It will be on the Columbia broadcast at three o'clock New York time, on Sunday, March 21st. This goes to Europe by short wave, but I have never found American short wave easy to get in Paris.

Always devotedly,

To EDWARD ALBEE*

March 17, 1948

Dear Mr. Albee:

Your suggestion of an anniversary piece about Rachmaninoff delights me. Given my own extreme distaste for his music I do not feel

---

*American playwright (b. 1928), then a young man, had proposed a commemorative article on the fifth anniversary of Serge Rachmaninoff's death. He and Thomson would later become friends.

that I am the one to pronounce his eulogy. I have asked a number of musicians if they would care to attempt for this occasion a kind of rehabilitation. So far I have not found anybody reputable who is willing to take it on. It is really extraordinary, after all, that a composer so famous should have enjoyed so little the esteem of his fellow composers.

Most sincerely yours,

To a READER

March 17, 1948

I thank you for the extremely interesting letter. In case you have not followed the career of Hanns Eisler, please let me inform you:

1) The order for his deportation has never passed through a court. He is therefore not convicted of subversive activity in this country. As a matter of fact, no charge has been made against him. His deportation was ordered on an irregularity in his entry visa.
2) He is not to be confused with his brother, Gerhardt Eisler, who is charged with subversive activities of a grave nature.
3) Hanns Eisler is not being deported; he is being allowed to leave of his own free will. He requested and received this solution, being in no position financially to fight his case in the courts.
4) A revision of his case is still possible for some later time when his early political associations, which in the Germany of 20 years ago were unquestionably communist, may seem less dangerous to the American government than they do now. In other words, the case against him, so far as I have been able to find out, is slender indeed.
5) On the other hand, Mr. Eisler is a distinguished composer. That is recognized by his professional colleagues here as well as in Europe. Otherwise I should not have bothered to review his concert or to state in my review that I do not consider his music in any way dangerous to my country.

I should like to add further that I have only the slightest personal acquaintance with Mr. Eisler and that the degree to which my review was gracious was in no way determined by either personal or political sympathies. I consider that I owed him courtesy as a composer and that I owed to the reading public a statement of my sincere belief that his music is not politically subversive. And surely it is permitted to hope that any person suspected of wrongdoing may eventually be cleared.

Most sincerely yours,

To Daniel Gregory Mason*

March 17, 1948

Dear Mr. Mason:

I thank you for the excellent article about atonality. Just how big a jump has to be taken between tertial and secundal counterpoint I do not know. The youngsters seem to feel confident that they can make it. Even if they are right, I should think something not much under a century will be required for the full operation. Myself I do not see atonality, which is our century's chromatic style, as supplanting the diatonic manner of writing, whether this be accompanied or not by unresolved dissonance. I foresee the two existing side by side for a long time to come. After all, every epoch has had its diatonic and its chromatic way.

Most sincerely yours,

To Richard Mohr†

May 13, 1948

Dear Mr. Mohr:

I suggest that the title of each record side be printed either in italics or in quotation marks. These titles have been chosen arbitrarily, being simply the first line of the text in each case. In one case I have used two quotations in order to include the well-known phrase "Pigeons on the grass alas." The phrase "Act Four," which begins Side 10, is also a quotation. I have also taken the liberty of removing the letter "d" from the word "pigeon." My secretary is typing out the text, as sung, of each side. You will have this in a day or so. I am also preparing an introduction. Please be so kind as to see that my name and Gertrude Stein's appear in the labels, at least so far as authorship is concerned, in the same size type. During her lifetime

---

*(1873–1953), composer, author, and music critic of conservative tastes
†(b. 1919), RCA Victor record executive and producer of the 1947 recording of *Four Saints in Three Acts*

we were always careful never to offend each other by assuming that either's work was subsidiary, and I should not like to offend her heirs through an accident in typography.

Most sincerely yours,

To EDWIN DENBY

June 1, 1948

Dear Edwin:

I have read your book of poems [*In Public, in Private*] from cover to cover and back again. I think it is great work in anybody's meaning of the term. So does Maurice. I can't use your piece about Italian ballet in my column, because it is not about music. My new film is being shown to a select preview audience tonight at the Museum of Modern Art. It smells rather successful to me. I am not coming abroad. I am going to Colorado in July and August. All is quiet here and everybody misses you. Stravinsky's new ballet [*Orpheus*] was universally admired from a musical point of view. Opinion is varied about the rest of it. If you are in Paris I wish you would go to see Alice Toklas. You would love each other. There does not seem to be very much news.

Affection always,

To a READER

September 24, 1948

A symphony is like a book in four sections. If you do not read them all you have not read the book. Sometimes acquaintance with one is better than none. Symphonies are normally played in concert nowadays entire. A century ago they would sometimes be cut up into excerpts. The habit is not one condoned now in the intellectual centers.

Most sincerely yours,

September 30, 1948

Much as I should like to do so, I cannot undertake to justify modern music in one letter. My attitude has always been "take it or leave it." It is certain that the history of music in our century consists of the pieces written in our century, not of those written in other centuries and merely kept in the performing repertory. Like every other century, ours has given birth to a great deal that is banal. It has also re-created music in its own image. The best work of our time, like the best work of any time, is that which least resembles the work of other times. Or so it seems to me.

Most sincerely yours,

To a READER

October 21, 1948

I am not much of a believer in scholarship by questionnaires. Also, filling them out takes a great deal of time and thought. And so I have decided, rightly or wrongly, to stop answering them; and I am afraid yours has to be my first refusal. This does not mean that I would not be disposed to answer questions based on some knowledge of my work for purposes of helping a scholar, should he be interested, to elucidate that work.

Most sincerely yours,

To a READER

November 24, 1948

It is a little difficult to explain briefly how a reviewer of music practices his art. One tells the truth, of course; and one tries not to state it angrily. Observance of a courteous tone sugars many a bitter pill. It is important, too, to describe the event, so that your readers can imagine what it was like. Expression of opinion is incidental and will always come through, whether one states it formally or not. A critic does not have to be right about his opinion, because there is no right in such matters. He should, however, be correct in his analysis and description of works, styles, and artists' characteristics. One becomes a music critic by becoming a musician and by learning to write.

Most sincerely yours,

To a READER

December 1, 1948

If Pablo Casals* were still playing in public I should not have referred to Pierre Fournier† as the greatest living cellist. Counting retired professionals among the "living" in the sense of active would oblige me to name Mary Garden and Emma Eames‡ as among the greatest living singers and actresses. I admit my phraseology was far from exact.

Most sincerely yours,

To JOHN W. WORK§

December 17, 1948

Dear Mr. Work:

Please don't get discouraged. Keep on writing and keep on trying to get your music played. You write beautiful music, and one day you will be famous for it. Just keep at it.

Always sincerely yours,

To NADINE MILES‖

December 22, 1948

Dear Miss Miles:

Mr. Shepherd tells me that you are in charge of the production of my opera *The Mother of Us All,* and I am delighted to hear it. If I can be of any help to you, please do not hesitate to write me about

---

*Casals (1876–1973) was not then performing.
†(1906–86), French cellist of impeccable taste and technical skills
‡(1865–1952), American soprano
§(1901–67), a black American composer who had written Thomson complaining bitterly of the difficulty he had obtaining performances
‖assistant to Arthur Shepherd (1880–1958), a composer long resident at Western Reserve University, then preparing a production of *The Mother of Us All*

anything that bothers you. You are certain to run into a nasty set change just before the final scene of the opera. The music at this point is not long enough, and a silent wait is not desirable dramatically. I should like to write a rather noisy intermezzo to cover this change. Will two minutes be enough, or do you need three? I shall try to make it adjustable, so that cuts or repetitions can be operated to make it fit your stagehands' timing.

Mr. Shepherd asked me to tell you about a production idea which we were not able to put into execution at Columbia University but which I have always hoped could be realized. That is to make the opera visually a sort of evocation of a 19th-century photograph album. A permanent frame for the stage would be helpful in this regard, and so would a special curtain designed somewhat like the cover of such an album. Since 19th-century photographs were often hand-colored, one would not need to limit the sets and costumes to gray or sepia tints. Grays and warm browns could give the chief tone to the color composition of the stage but a whole range of pinks, red, purples, and other bright colors could be added in the costumes. In this way a variety of color could be achieved while keeping the spectacle at all times in harmony. The stage movement could be regulated, with or without aid of a choreographer, to suggest photographic poses. I do not mean a series of motionless tableaux vivants, though certain moments might be impressive if held a little. I see the whole rather as a series of such motionless tableaux but with the singers moving constantly from one to another. Each character could move in a different and characteristic way, since each speaks and sings in a different way and since the costumes are also intended to accentuate contrasts of character and decade. All these contrasts risk turning the opera into a costume party unless there is some deliberate overall stylization. It has long seemed to me that the photograph album idea could solve this problem effectively and that the addition of regulated movement would help. Any movement or histrionic effort of a naturalistic character would, of course, interfere.

Do not hesitate to add dancers to any of the scenes where these may seem appropriate to you. Real dancing can only heighten the effect of the movements executed by the singers. The characters known as A.A. and T.T. might very well be Negroes dressed as postillions, serving as sideboys, moving chairs about, opening doors, and being in general attentive to everybody. There is no reason why there should not be eight or ten of these.

The V.I.P. scene can be pointed up perhaps by vaudeville routines of a pseudo-military character. In general, heightening the spectacle by choreographic means seems to me thoroughly desirable. I have even thought of adding a ballet to the opera but I don't know exactly where I could put it.

Most sincerely yours,

To a CORRESPONDENT*

January 3, 1949

I hated Sunday school and everything connected with it till I was twelve. After that, I regularly fell in love with my teachers. One of these was very glamorous, because she held the women's world record for both the 50- and the 100-yard dash and was a great niece of Jesse James.

If you can do anything with the above, you are welcome to it. I am sorry I cannot say anything nicer about the institution. I doubt, under the circumstances, whether you will need the photo.

Sincerely,

To ARTHUR SHEPHERD

January 12, 1949

Dear Mr. Shepherd:

The idea of using a subject from 19th-century American political history was mine; also that of using direct quotation from the oratory of the period. The selection of the characters and their arrangement into a play I left to Miss Stein. She transformed my proposal about the oratory of the period into a method whereby Susan B. Anthony, Daniel Webster, and others speak as they really spoke.

I suggested my ideas to her in the fall of 1945 in Paris, and she wrote the first two scenes immediately. The libretto was finished during the course of the winter and sent to me in the early spring of '46, I being then in New York. In the late spring we discussed it in Paris. She died in July of that year before I had begun the actual composition, which was done during the early and middle part of the following winter.

The Mother of Us All was Miss Stein's last completed work. It represents an attempt to revivify history, to show historical movements and personalities as these appeared to those personalities

---

*who had asked Thomson to contribute a statement for publication about the effect of Sunday school on his life, to be printed alongside solemn testimonials from Fritz Kreisler, Risë Stevens, J. Edgar Hoover and others.

themselves and to others living at the time. That time, of course, was not a specific moment but a whole epoch in the life of our country, the last epoch about which any of us can have, through his own memories or through those of persons he has known in his lifetime, a feeling of having been there.

Always faithfully yours,

To a READER

February 4, 1949

Your letter to the Editor has reached my desk. The whole Gieseking* story is a messy one. The public manifestations were regrettable from every point of view, and Mr. Gieseking's own statements to the press were remarkably lacking in gratitude to the American public for having supported him so warmly during the 13 years when he visited here regularly. Anything I should write about the matter now would tend to aggravate the bad feeling aroused. The less the matter is mentioned the quicker he can come back. Somebody had to be the first previously blacklisted artist of German citizenship to try a New York recital. He took the rap, but it might have been almost anybody else. He took a severe one, because his case was mismanaged, I think, by the Federal officials as well as by his own impresario.

Most sincerely yours,

To EUGENE ORMANDY

February 8, 1949

Dear Gene:

I am delighted that my *Louisiana Story* suite is to be recorded. Lieberson† phoned me that last week. It is going to be hard to cut a piece lasting 18 minutes into four chunks lasting each 4½ minutes‡ and still have any freedom in the matter. I shall see what I can do, however.

Harl [McDonald] wrote me about the English manager and your American music tangle. I still think you should play as much as

---

*German pianist Walter Gieseking's (1895–1956) return engagements in the United States had been the subject of heated protest.
†Composer Goddard Lieberson (1911–77), as president of Columbia Records, was known for his devotion to contemporary music.
‡for the 78 r.p.m. recording format

possible and that you should choose the works for their intrinsic interest rather than for their length. In the case of my own *Louisiana Story* suite, I am inclined to believe that there may exist in England considerable interest in it, since film music is a matter of national concern there and all their best composers have done film scores. Do as you think best but don't forget that the English consider film music more highly than we do here. Also, it does seem to me a little ill-advised not to show the British the best we have in composition, as well as in execution. You don't have to stuff it down their throats, but the best orchestra we have should certainly play in a foreign country the best music we have.

Always affectionately yours,

To ALICE B. TOKLAS

March 10, 1949

Dear Alice:

I heard *The Mother of Us All* in Cleveland. It was a big stylish opera house with lots of boxes and sixty men in the pit. All that was most elegant. The singers, college students, were a little immature, a little feeble for so grand a format. The whole effort, however, was better than what a university commonly can do. Barbara Payne went out to hear it. She is still thinking she might produce it in New York, if and when she finds the money. So far, that is still if and when. Beecham wrote that he was going to do it at the BBC in May and then that he wasn't. It seems to have been turned down by some music committee, the grounds given being that it is too hard to run up quickly. That is not Beecham's opinion, and he is the one who would have to do the running up.

Picasso was elected lately a corresponding member of the National Institute of Arts and Letters, along with Bernard Shaw, T. S. Eliot, and divers other foreign artists. I went to some trouble about this, because some of the older members had political objections to him, thought he was still a communist. Now, of course, he refuses to answer letters and telegrams asking whether he cares to accept. He probably doesn't know what the outfit is and is waiting for someone to tell him. If you see him, will you please tell him that it is a good outfit and certainly the equal in distinction of the French Académie des Beaux-Arts. Also, whether he wants to accept or not, a telegram is easy to answer.

Love always,

To Jack Beeson*

March 10, 1949

Dear Jack:

Thanks for the lovely letter. I like your liking my operas. You touched me deeply when we were doing *The Mother of Us All* by being interested in the key system. I hope all goes nicely in Rome and that you get on with that first opera. Maurice Grosser used to say that it was foolish of composers to write those first four symphonies, that anybody with any sense would begin with his Fifth.

Always best,

To a Reader

March 16, 1949

So far as I know, Hazel Scott† has no standing whatsoever as a classical pianist. I have never heard of her giving a classical recital even though she may have done so occasionally. For her qualities as a boogie-woogie artist you had better consult a boogie-woogie expert.

Most sincerely yours,

To Victor Yellin‡

March 23, 1949

Dear Mr. Yellin:

My early musical education was made in Kansas City, where I had piano lessons from the age of five and organ lessons at twelve. My best piano teacher I encountered when I was fifteen. Her name was Geneve Lichtenwalter, and she is still alive though partly blind. My organ teacher was Clarence D. Sears, also still alive, at that time organist at Grace Church (Episcopal), now the Cathedral of Grace

---

*(b. 1921), American composer and educator, best known for his operas
†(1920–81), a popular pianist and singer of Trinidadian birth; wife of New York Representative Adam Clayton Powell, Jr.
‡(b. 1924), musicologist and composer, then writing a thesis on Marc Blitzstein and Virgil Thomson at Harvard. He later produced and conducted *The Mother of Us All* at Sanders Theater, Cambridge.

and Holy Trinity. I was his assistant at twelve. I played the organ professionally in churches from that time till I was twenty-eight. I largely put myself through college by that means. Before the days of radio, children were not influenced by symphony orchestras; during my teens there was one in Kansas City, however. Brought up in a Southern Baptist family, and being a church organist myself quite early, I naturally became acquainted with American church music and hymn lore in all forms. If you look carefully, you will find as much of Gregorian and Anglican chant in my operas as of Protestant gospel hymns. Another valuable experience of my youth was playing accompaniments for singers, both in the studio and in public concerts. I was thoroughly trained in this technique and earned money by it from the time I was twelve till I went off to war at twenty. I learned about amateur choral singing from Dr. Davison at Harvard, but knew already almost all there was to know about the professional voice, which is after all what one deals with in the opera. I had also read all the opera scores used in current repertory and had heard most of them on the stage. All this means that I went to college as an experienced professional (though not necessarily first-class) accompanist, concert pianist, organist, and conductor. In Boston I had more piano and organ lessons and learned a great deal more about conducting, particularly choral. It was in Paris that my music started going American. Trained at Harvard and by Nadia Boulanger in the impressionist and neo-classic styles current around 1920, it was not till 1926 that I began fishing up out of my subconscious mind musical memories of the old South and the Middle West. This was the result of a working method I had little by little invented for myself, which was to write down the music I heard in my mind, instead of writing music by formula and then trying to hear it, which is the procedure one usually learns from one's teachers. I do not wish to deny the value of that education. I am merely telling you, since you ask, how it happens that I have not employed it systematically in my more mature years.

Most sincerely yours,

To Lawrence Morton[*]

May 12, 1949

Dear Mr. Morton:

I thank you for the extremely interesting letter about Aaron Copland's *Red Pony* music. I have seen the film once but I have not seen the score at all. It is quite probable, and I am grateful to you for pointing it out to me, that the passages in which music depicts pure feeling are not connected with close-ups of Miss Loy.[†] I may be wrong in associating them with her or with the character she plays. I still think, pending a further view of the film, that Aaron Copland has done better work when his music illustrates action or the picturesque than when straight emotion is its subject. I have long suspected, moreover, that the American film industry would get better use out of music by avoiding the musical rendering of straight emotion. Such music causes the characters on the screen to lose dimension and reality. Music more specifically evocative gives them reality by keeping them related to a background. My point of view about this, I realize, is somewhat heretical. Nevertheless, there is something wrong with American film music; and I think the trouble comes from not limiting music's role. Either music is the setting of the story or it is the interior life of the characters in the story. I do not think it can be both in the same film.

Most sincerely yours,

To John Cage[‡]

May 19, 1949

Dear John,

Thanks for the letter and for the two lovely articles. You seem to be in a fine state of exuberance. I liked my trip in Georgia. I am writing music. I think of you. I am worried lest, with the Guggenheim and everything, you might stay in Europe. I would understand that, but I should miss you. I do hope you will write me whenever it

---

[*](1904–87), American music critic and concert organizer
[†]Myrna Loy (b. 1905), American actress
[‡]Thomson greatly admired composer John Cage (b. 1912) at the beginning of his career but dismissed the later works as a "one-way tunnel" to the "gadget fair." For his part, Cage wrote a loving analysis of Thomson's music in *Virgil Thomson: His Life and Music* (with Kathleen O'Donnell Hoover, 1959).

is not a chore. Ajemian★ seems to have played your pieces well at Columbia, but I have heard complaints that [with] noisier music programmed around them they were hard to hear. If I had thought of that, I should have suggested that they be played first. Varèse's† *Intégrales* not too well played, was a pleasure all the same. Ruggles's‡ *Portals* was just plain wonderful.

Affection always,

To a READER

May 20, 1949

I thank you for the extremely interesting letter about the lack of visual taste in concert performances. I think you exaggerate, however. The world that lives by the ear is in general indifferent to what its eye rests on. This applies to the public as well as to the artists. As a matter of fact, a too-stylish visual presentation of music makes the public suspicious. It smacks of commercialism. Nothing gives confidence in the concert hall like dowdiness.

Most sincerely yours,

To ELLIOTT SANGER§

June 28, 1949

Dear Mr. Sanger:

I too have followed the tilting of my colleague Haggin‖ against the windmills of WQXR. I have spoken with Mr. Haggin about the matter several times, and I am convinced that he has no personal animus against the station or anybody connected with it. I merely think he is taking QXR very very seriously, since that is the chief source of high-class musical programs for radio listeners in this vicinity. He thinks that QXR has a good noise filter but does not use the instrument as skillfully as might be wished. This is an opinion,

---

*Maro Ajemian (1920–78), American pianist responsible for the premieres of several of Cage's works
†Of the French-American composer Edgard Varèse (1883–1965), Thomson later wrote that "after Debussy, [he] may well be the century's other great voice."
‡(1876–1971), American composer
§(b. 1897), co-founder and for many years director of WQXR, a New York classical radio station
‖B. H. Haggin (1900–87), a brilliant and vituperative music critic, whose tenure at the *Herald Tribune* as critic of radio music was concluded with the letter of September 20, 1949

of course. It is not our custom at the *Herald Tribune* to dispute with our critics their opinions, so long as the customary amenities have been observed in their expression. The confidence you feel in your engineers is no less justified, I am sure, than the confidence that the Philharmonic Society may feel in its conductors. But if musical criticism is to be independent (which means responsible only to the musical profession and the reading public), we have to leave our critics free to describe any musical event as they themselves hear it. Mr. Haggin's admission of a fault in his receiving machine certainly weakened his diagnosis in the case of the Haydn mass, but it was fair of him, both to QXR and to his readers, to state that he might possibly be in error. This is not the only time, of course, that he has mentioned the noise reducer. I share Mr. Haggin's devotion to your excellent station, though I do not listen to the radio as often as he does. And since, for daily consumption, you offer pretty nearly all the good music we have, I suspect that, were I reviewing radio music myself, my tendency would be toward demanding from you standards of operation far above those that we tolerate from others. You are to New York broadcasting what the Metropolitan is to opera, and we regard any imperfection on your part with alarm.

Most sincerely yours,

To B. H. HAGGIN

September 20, 1949

My dear Haggin:

I sympathize with your distaste for editorial interference and I should like to relieve you of it if that were possible. If your pieces did not go through the music desk, they would have to go through the city desk; and I think you would find that procedure even more irksome. Actually the necessity for finding a satisfactory editorial formula can be postponed for the present, because I am not going to be able to use this season any regular criticism of the radio. The amount of serious music available over the air has fallen so low that its coverage is no longer entitled to even the small space we now give it. I like your work very much and shall regret your absence from the page, but I don't think it fair to the New York musical scene to sacrifice local activities for so meager a field as musical radio is at present. I should like to be able to ask you for a special coverage from time to time if something turns up that the staff is not prepared to handle. I should like also, if you are willing, to continue your

237

articles through October 9. After that, I simply don't know what to do with them. Their sacrifice, for the present, is determined entirely, believe me, by my estimate of the news interest of their subject, and not at all by any dissatisfaction with your handling of it. I shall miss your pieces and so, I am sure, will many readers.

Ever faithfully yours,

To ARCHIBALD T. DAVISON

September 22, 1949

Dear Doc:

Most newspapers do not cover church music for two reasons: (1) There is never a large enough staff for that much church attendance every Sunday, already a heavy concert day. (2) Church music, though often excellent, is not presented to the public as a professional act. It is not presented to the public at all, at least in principle, but to God. And God does not necessarily judge acts of worship by professional standards, since sincerity in His eyes may well make up for technical inefficiencies.

In general, only those musical events are considered appropriate for review that are presented to the public as professional occasions. This criterion eliminates church music along with student recitals and private presentations. Religious music of exceptional novelty or distinction is now and then reviewed all the same. I have covered a musical service from time to time at the Church of St. Mary the Virgin, at St. Patrick's Cathedral, at an extremely primitive Negro meeting house in New Jersey, and at a Jewish temple in San Francisco where a service composed by Darius Milhaud was performed for the first time. One fall I spent all my Sunday mornings for three months going to church services of every faith and sect, in order to collect material for a Christmas article about the religious music of notable quality available in New York City. Religious music presented to the public under concert conditions is regularly covered, of course. In general, however, it is true that newspapers are not staffed for covering the music of worship, also that religious establishments might justifiably object to the public criticism of something not submitted to the general public for its patronage.

A choirmasters' periodical might successfully criticize church music, but the operation would require standards of judgment far more complex and delicate than those commonly employed in the reviewing of concerts and opera performances. My experience indicates that favorable notice of outstanding musical achievement is welcomed by religious establishments but that any assumption of the right to judge their cultural standards unfavorably is resented. Churches are not, after all, primarily purveyors of culture. Their obligations to music are about the same, I suppose, as those they assume toward architecture and toward poetry.

Ever devotedly,

To a READER

September 28, 1949

It has never seemed to me appropriate to display before the public my personal favorites among pieces or artists. Such preferences, anyway, are rarely permanent. Sometimes one grows to like particular works or artists, and sometimes one gets thoroughly fed up with them. In either case, one must describe them loyally in a review. I suppose doctors have their favorite diseases and operations, but they don't talk about them in public.

Most sincerely yours,

To a CORRESPONDENT*

September 28, 1949

If I knew a competent librettist I should be using him myself. Every composer in America is looking for one. For the present the problem seems insoluble.

Most sincerely yours,

To a READER

December 2, 1949

"White voice" is a term used in all the European languages, including English, to describe a kind of singing that lacks vibrancy. It is neither a "heady" tone nor a "chesty" tone nor yet a "nasal" one. It is a little blank, like the voice of early childhood. The term is not used exclusively with regard to the female voice. Tenors also have

---

*a representative of a publishing company who asked Thomson to recommend a librettist

been accused of singing "white." Altos, baritones, and basses are seldom tempted to indulge. There are moments in musical interpretation when it can be valuable, but on the whole it is not considered either beautiful or expressive.

Most sincerely yours,

To a READER

January 12, 1950

Los Angeles is not my bailiwick, and I take no part in its musical politics. I am aware, of course, that it has been the scene, like many another American city, of a local war about the conductor's post. My private sympathies would naturally be with a conductor of American birth and training, provided his musical qualifications were satisfactory. My private sympathies are equally opposed to any group operation which would endeavor to remove a conductor, any conductor, for the purpose of assigning his place to a specific colleague. The constant mention of Steinberg,* excellent musician though he be, in the public and private attacks on [Alfred] Wallenstein have led me to suspect that these were perhaps not entirely disinterested. I am sure that Mr. Steinberg's friends must have embarrassed him deeply by using his name in a manner that might suggest acquiescence on his part.

My own policy as a reviewer is to avoid the comparison of persons and to refrain constantly from recommending to managements and directors the hiring or firing of any given musician. I am engaged by a newspaper to inform the public about performances given, not to serve as an unofficial member of any board of trustees. Some of my reviews may have been influential in causing the New York Philharmonic to change its conductor five or six years ago.† These reviews, however, represented no campaign on my part. They were merely a week-by-week report of what the concerts sounded like to me and what the program policy, if any, clearly was. At no point did I ask editorially that the conductor then in charge be fired or that the one who replaced him be hired. I should have considered any such behavior professionally unethical. After all, it is program policies and standards of execution that determine a conductor's value to the community. And it is the abstention from insis-

---

*William Steinberg (1899–1978), German-born conductor later associated with the Pittsburgh Symphony and the Boston Symphony orchestras
†John Barbirolli had been replaced by Artur Rodzinski in 1943.

tence on personalities that determines a critic's value. I deplore the present state of tension in musical Los Angeles; I take no part in it, and I believe that its maintenance will do harm to music, far more than any mere conductor could do.

Most sincerely yours,

To Lincoln Kirstein

January 26, 1950

Dear Lincoln:

Your letter was a delight to read, but I have no idea what to do with it. I can't publish it, because it is mostly about ballet. And I can't answer it, because you know so much more than I do. I am inclined, however, to consider the musical contributions of the ballet as progressively less weighty since 1914. The three early Stravinsky scores and Debussy's *Jeux* are a mighty lump. The post-war Diaghilev scores were lively but mostly lightweights. Balanchine's musical tastes are even less courageous, being pretty strictly confined to Stravinsky and his diminishing circle. My own impression of ballet nowadays, as compared with those Diaghilev brought to America in 1915 and 1916, is that the number of good dancers in the world is probably larger than at that time, just like the number of competent orchestral musicians. I do not find the spectacles, on the whole, any better executed, if as well, than the earlier ones and I note what seems to me a decline in musical originality. This decline, I may add, is matched by a similar one in the quality of composition available to ballet producers. Several of these, yourself included, have commissioned new works of some quality. I just don't think that the ballet as an esthetic spectacle has shown a rising curve in 35 years. I think its progress has been in breadth rather than height.

Ever affection,

To Arnold Schoenberg

February 22, 1950

Dear Mr. Schoenberg:

I thank you for the charming letter and the answer to Aaron Copland. Convinced that your controversy with Mr. Copland was based on some kind of misunderstanding,* I sent him your reply and asked him if he would agree to answer you directly. He now writes me that he has done so, including a copy of his reply. I sincerely hope that this correspondence can take the place of a public dispute. Two musicians who have enjoyed the confidence of their students cannot accomplish any useful purpose, it seems to me, by questioning publicly each other's good faith. I do not wish to close my column to any musical matter which you take deeply to heart. If you continue to believe that Aaron Copland has spoken disrespectfully of your music and acted disloyally as a colleague, I shall always keep it open for whatever evidence you may have to offer. With cordial greetings,

Ever respectfully yours,

To Sir Thomas Beecham

March 5, 1950

Dear Thomas,

The cello concerto is now long since finished and a complete orchestral score has been sent you. The piano score of the third mvmt went off a month ago. When you have time to read it, I do hope you will drop me a line of opinion. The orch. score in the 2nd mvmt is a little different from the piano score. After the Phila. and N.Y. performances I shall send another piano score and cello part, along with whatever changes may be needed in the orchestral score.

[Pierre] Fournier did not receive the first copy I sent of the 3rd mov't (I have now sent another). He is now trying to imagine that he could not possibly learn it by August, which is merely a French nervous anxiety on his part. I am writing him that he has been engaged to learn it and that he is expected to do so in spite of constant touring. I should like to assure you, however, that if Fournier gets

---

*Schoenberg (1874–1951) took offense at a casual remark Copland made to Shostakovich during the Russian composer's American visit in 1949 (expressing surprise at Schoenberg's considerable following in Los Angeles) and wrote an infuriated public response.

difficult, I shall be more than happy with any cellist of your choice. His proposal to me that the performance be postponed till next year seems to solve nobody's problem but his, since the work has already been accepted by you and by the [Edinburgh] Festival committee. Please do exactly as you like about him. In any case he now has the entire work and has had two-thirds of it since the end of November.

This is a hasty letter about business. I am sorry there is not time for gossip. But my affection for you both★ is in it.

Ever yours,

To Paul Pickrel†

June 19, 1950

Dear Mr. Pickrel:

It would be an honor to be published by the *Yale Review,* and I thank you. Unfortunately, it is not my intention, for the present, to read Mr. Barzun's two-volume work on Berlioz. For the immediate future I am sticking to detective stories. Please understand that my lack of enthusiasm for serious reading at the season's end implies no prejudice against the book.

Most sincerely yours,

To a Correspondent‡

July 7, 1950

I read your script and didn't like it at all. By this I mean that I was unable to make personal contact with the characters or to accept the stylistic conventions. The whole treatment seemed a bit frivolous to me for so powerful a subject as the French Revolution. I realize that many serious-minded persons may have made a similar criticism of my opera *Four Saints in Three Acts.* So please don't take my remarks as anything but a private and personal response. I realize also that I might find other works of yours more congenial. Since you went to the trouble of sending me the *Utopia* script, I had to tell you what I thought of it. If you have any means of picking it up, you will find it

★Thomson includes Beecham's wife, Betty.
†Pickrel (b. 1917), editor of the *Yale Review,* had proposed that Thomson review Jacques Barzun's *Berlioz and the Romantic Century.*
‡Thomson had been asked to read a script for possible adaptation into a libretto.

at my office in the hands of my secretary, Miss Julia Haines. I do thank you for letting me read it.

To Gottfried von Einem*

July 10, 1950

Dear Gottfried:

I don't know where Mitropoulos is; I shall probably not see him until October. I shall be in Colorado myself till about that time. I shall certainly tell him, however, that you would like him to play my Second Symphony in Salzburg. You are right in supposing that it should not be played with other modern works. It sounds beautiful with Haydn, Mozart, Schubert, or Schumann. Beecham used to play it between a Haydn symphony and the "Jupiter." I have done it with Schubert's C-major. I think it might sound well beside the Mendelssohn "Scottish," which Mitropoulos plays particularly well. Stokowski is far from a "dead man," but he is no longer a very young man. His work in recent years, though most carefully rehearsed, has usually sounded to me a little bit devitalized. As for *Idomeneo*, opera is not his specialty and neither is Mozart. He does better with Tchaikovsky, Mahler, romantic afflatus in general. He has also played a great deal of modern music, including Varèse, Schoenberg, Messiaen.

Other American conductors who are excellent are Eugene Ormandy and Efrem Kurtz.† Either could do you a stylish *Idomeneo*, though neither's Mozart is anything like so grand as that of Beecham. George Szell‡ is another good conductor and a first-class opera man.

I shall watch with interest Mr. Krips'§ American tour and report to you on his success. Please remember me to Karajan,‖ whom I met in Salzburg four years ago. Warmest greetings to the Blachers• and to yourself.

Ever cordially yours,

---

*Austrian composer (b. 1918), a director of the Salzburg Festival from 1948. He and Thomson had met in Salzburg in 1946.
†Kurtz (b. 1900), American conductor of Russian birth
‡(1897–1970), Hungarian-American conductor, music director of the Cleveland Orchestra from 1946
§Josef Krips (1902–74), Austrian conductor
‖Herbert von Karajan (b. 1908), Austrian conductor, music director of the Berlin Philharmonic from 1954 and a guiding force behind the Salzburg Festival since the late 1940s
• Boris Blacher, German composer (1903–75), and his wife Gerty Herzog

To a Correspondent*

January 11, 1951

Your recommendation of "The Great Stone Face" might be an excellent one for some other composer. Myself, I don't like Hawthorne much, or New England subjects. All the same, I shall look at it again.

Most sincerely,

To Lucius Beebe†

January 28, 1951

Dear Lucius:

In about 1922, a Swiss composer named Arthur Honegger wrote an orchestral piece (call it a tone-poem if you wish) entitled *Pacific 231*. The numbers, as you are no doubt aware, refer to the order of the wheel sizes in the locomotive type of that time known as "Pacific." The piece is jolly and quite noisy, evokes most picturesquely a ride in the cab of such a locomotive. It was extremely popular for five or ten years but has practically disappeared now from orchestral programs. Somewhere in the gramophone catalogs there should be a recording of it.

Greetings and ever faithfully,

To a Reader

February 21, 1951

I thank you for the extremely interesting letter. Of course Hanslick‡ was entitled to prefer Brahms over Bruckner, but he was scarcely justified on any grounds I can imagine in attacking Bruckner so bitterly and so consistently as he did. These articles were not included in the recently published volume. The story of his really not caring much about Brahms's music I had from Dr. Max

---

*a would-be librettist
†(1902–66), American author, dandy, and train fancier, colleague of Thomson's on the *Herald Tribune*
‡Eduard Hanslick (1825–1904), often regarded as the first important professional music critic, whose works had recently been collected by Henry Pleasants in *Vienna's Golden Years of Music, 1850–1900* (1950). Pleasants (b. 1910) is an American author and music critic long resident in London.

Graf* personally and also from his book *Composer and Critic*. I agree with you that Hanslick wrote charmingly, but I do not find his musical opinions acceptable regarding the composers of his time.

I have no personal motive in writing harshly about Hanslick, since I never knew him or any member of his family. Perhaps I was a little impressed, reading the recent collection, by how easy it would be for any of us who work on the press to take a similar attitude, and how evil it would be.

Most sincerely yours,

To a CORRESPONDENT

February 27, 1951

I regard my chamber music as some of my very best work. Almost any composer's chamber music, of course, is likely to be full of quality. I have no special reasons for writing chamber music beyond the fact that I have always liked to write in all the forms and for all the media. I should not like to think there was anything in music I had not tried. Chamber music is a test of compositional mastery because it is low in color variety. Pure line and harmony have to sustain the composition. There is also something of a test in the fact that most chamber music players will not play a work unless they respect it. They are not like orchestral musicians, who play what they are told to play.

Most sincerely yours,

To a READER

February 28, 1951

I thank you for the interesting letter. I do not know what you mean by "give the opera companies back to the Americans." Were they ever in American hands? I doubt if they ever will be until the repertory consists chiefly of American works. No such repertory is available today. With luck, and with assiduity on the part of composers, it might be in fifty years.

Most sincerely yours,

---

*(1873–1958), Viennese music critic whose book *Composer and Critic* had been published in 1946

To Frank Stanton*

March 8, 1951

Dear Mr. Stanton:

I thank you for the extremely interesting letter and regret your warning that it is not for publication.

I agree with you that tape recordings are excellent and from a musical point of view superior to transmission by telephone wires.† The only thing wrong with them is the psychological factor. The listener knows he is not listening to the real thing, because he knows the real thing has already taken place. You would not use tape on current events, and there is a similar lack of excitement about after-the-fact music broadcasts. However, I do not feel that the coldness (psychologically speaking) of a tape broadcast is grave. There are compensations, as you point out.

As to the cutting down of serious live music broadcasts, you probably regret, as we all do, the CBS Symphony programs that used to be broadcast from May to October. "Invitation to Music" was once part of our fare too. And the "Columbia Playhouse." CBS was for years the intellectual network. Now it is a network like the others. I realize the pressures that have brought this situation about and hope sincerely that when they are lessened, music and other cultural broadcasts may return in quantity. Meanwhile, the summer programs of records (Columbia Records) are not very satisfactory. They seem to be aimed strictly at an audience of modest musical attainments. WNYC and WQXR play a more adventurous repertory.

Here is the $64 question, Mr. Stanton. Does chain radio accept any obligation to offer cultural matter to the cultured minority? One musical number of the kind, and that a rather broadly conceived one, seems to be considered enough for prestige. CBS has its Philharmonic, ABC the Metropolitan Opera, NBC its own orchestra. All three are limited to the winter season. I do hope the present trend away from musical distinction will reverse itself one day. And I do wish that someone as representative as yourself would take the responsibility of informing the musical world about what national radio considers to be our minimum rights. You have given us music;

---

*(b. 1908), president of CBS for many years, second in command only to William S. Paley
†The New York Philharmonic, formerly broadcast live, had begun to tape performances and air the broadcasts at an earlier hour.

and now, little by little, you are taking it away. Certainly television, a visual medium, is not going to do anything very serious about music.

Most sincerely yours,

To Maurice Grosser

Houston, Texas
Tuesday, March 21 [1951]

D.M.

Now the little tour is over and it was good having two letters from you on the way, one in San Antonio and one here. My tour has been pleasant and I have done well (excellent press). Texas in March was always lovely & still is. I suspect that one summer I should show you San Antonio, which has a Mexican section to delight you. All tin-can houses and such. A nice town all round & very pleasant people. Dallas is less interesting. Austin is a nice state capital university town with a lake & hills. Houston is rich, luxurious, hospitable. I enclose photo of its museum of modern art. There is a large brick synagogue in the same style. I played *The Seine* beautifully in San Antonio & now I know it. The *Louisiana Story* here. Good orchestras both places. Sweet Briar, Va. was just a girl's college but beautiful scenery in early spring (near Lynchburg). Am mailing you from here five (no less) new Simenons which Alex Smallens gave me for the trip. Let me know when you need money. I am full of it just now. After this trip I stay here for a while, but on May 15 I go for 2 days to Portland, Oregon, where I make a 20 minute speech at a Bach festival for $400 *plus expenses*. I also get $400 for the Pittsburgh speech. Maybe I am getting into big time lecture prices. Food in Texas has not been interesting except here. Mostly beef and then even that is better when from Kansas City. Here good fish dishes & Southern luxuries like hot breads & proper ham and interesting ways of making chicken hash taste good. Miss Ima Hogg★ gave me an elegant cocktail party. She has a French chateau on a bayou and lovely manners. A childhood playmate from Kansas City gave a party after the concert last night that was stylish and pleasant. She has a New England farm house with early American furniture, and lamp posts around the garden with candles in them. Texas in general seems to have, as always, its special mixture of Southern charm and

---

★(1882–1975), Texas patron of the arts

Western hospitality. And you can talk to everybody about every-thing. Their minds are not set in a pattern and they enjoy the region they are living in. The cities have strong and very different person-alities. The landscape (except here, which is flat as a pancake) is all wonderful and open like Castille, with a high sky; and the soil is the color of the hats the men wear, a pale khaki with no pink in it. And it is not desert; it grows things.

affec

V——

To a READER

April 12, 1951

You should really not use such language in front of my secretary, who is a lady, and who opens my mail.

Most sincerely yours,

To a CORRESPONDENT

April 25, 1951

I thank you for the lovely letter about my *Solemn Music*. The ori-gin of the piece is as follows:

The League of Composers commissioned me to write a work for the Goldman Band. Being very fond of military marches, and also being convinced that that kind of music is the one that sounds best for band, I proposed to Mr. Goldman,* the conductor, that I write one. Mr. Goldman, a fertile composer of marches himself, replied that he would prefer that I did not write a military march. So I chose the other kind of music that has always seemed to me effective in band instrumentation, namely, a funeral march. Two of my oldest and closest friends, Gertrude Stein the poet and Christian Bérard the painter, had died during the year. My *Solemn Music* represented for me a private homage to the memory of both these artists.

Most sincerely yours,

---

*Edwin Franko Goldman (1878–1956), American composer and conductor and founder of the Goldman Band

To a READER

April 25, 1951

My colleague, Mr. Jerome D. Bohm,* who was also at Miss Danco's† recital, told me of his surprise at hearing how very different this artist's voice sounded in a hall and on records. Myself I cannot imagine her in *Wozzeck*. Nor can I quite imagine how she sounded at La Scala. The voice does have, of course, a penetrating upper range; and Miss Danco's enunciation is perfect. I can believe easily in her ability to project musically a dramatic role.

As you know, I am not opposed to French singing. Pierre Bernac,‡ with an inferior organ, delights me profoundly by his artistry. So did Miss Danco at the beginning of the evening. After the first twenty minutes I found that her crooning habits were beginning to weigh on me by their monotony. It may be that further acquaintance with her work may reveal qualities that I did not perceive in one evening. Clearly she is an artist of distinction, though not, it seems to me, so straightforward an interpreter as Bernac or Vallin.§ Please believe that my lack of enthusiasm for her recital had no personal motivation. I do not know Miss Danco, and I had previously heard warm reports of her singing from musicians in this country and in Europe. All one can do in reviewing a recitalist is to describe what one hears. I sincerely hope that I shall hear something more beautiful the next time I have occasion to review her.

Most sincerely yours,

To a READER

May 17, 1951

Please don't worry about Merrill.‖ Nobody is going to stop him from singing. If he broke his contract with the Metropolitan, which he seems to have done, the management has every right to refuse him the use of its name for his own publicity purposes. But he goes

---

*a music critic for the *Herald Tribune* for many years
†Suzanne Danco (b. 1911), Belgian soprano
‡(1899–1979), French baritone long associated with Francis Poulenc
§Ninon Vallin (1886–1961), French soprano

‖According to Sir Rudolf Bing (b. 1902), general manager of the Metropolitan Opera from 1950 to 1972, baritone Robert Merrill (b. 1919) "had gone off to Hollywood to contribute to the national culture by appearing in a film called *Aaron Slick from Punkin Crick* and not until he made a formal written apology... would I accept him back on the Metropolitan Opera stage."

250

right on singing, though not for the present with that company. The incident is of no importance whatsoever and will in no way interfere with his giving deep pleasure to a large public.

Most sincerely yours,

To Ernst Krenek

May 18, 1951

My dear Krenek:

Yours is the most delightful letter of all that I have received about my book.* The Boulez† rhythmic devices are not new: he aspires to codify the whole metrical vocabulary for purposes of achieving a systematic asymmetry. He is considered a heretic by Leibowitz,‡ who thinks that rhythm should remain a free, or expressive, element in twelve-tone-row music, since that was its chief role in the classical twelve-tone works. I take no part in this controversy, since I am not a twelve-tone composer; but my sympathies are toward rhythmic research. I have long considered, moreover, that German music in the last seventy-five years has been generally a little weak in the rhythmic element. I am sure you know what I am referring to. Nothing specific, but just a general lack of sophistication in that domain.

Most sincerely yours,

To the Cincinnati Committee on Human Relations

September 5, 1951

I am shocked to learn that both of Cincinnati's chief institutions of musical learning draw the color line. If I had known this two years ago, I should have refused to speak at the one which I visited. Please use this letter for whatever benefit it may do your campaign to correct this disgraceful situation.

Most sincerely yours,

---

*Krenek had written to congratulate Thomson on the publication of *Music Left and Right* and added, with regret, that it had given him "considerably more pleasure than you apparently have experienced in listening to my music."
†Pierre Boulez (b. 1925), French serial composer and conductor. In 1946 Thomson gave Boulez his first notice in the press; in 1952 they became friends.
‡René Leibowitz (1913–72), French composer and theoretician, wrote *Schoenberg and His School* (1946), an influential, somewhat conservative exposition of atonality.

To Mack Harrell*

October 15, 1951

Dear Mack:

The William Blake pieces are finished, and I would like to show them to you. I need, as a matter of fact, a sort of fitting to be sure that the vocal line is comfortable and becoming. Could you come to my house one day when you are in New York and go over them with me? If you will telephone me any morning, we can make a date. If the telephone operator says that I cannot be disturbed, please say that I have asked you to call.

Your *Dybbuk*† performance was wonderful. Mary Garden thought so too.

Greetings ever,

To John Houseman

October 30, 1951

Dear Jack:

The Lincoln play was planned as a somewhat more highbrow example of the kind of historical pageant that is played in Washington, Virginia, North Carolina, and various places in the South. Louisville hopes that this may be produced annually and form a summer tourist attraction. It will be produced under the patronage of a festival committee already appointed by the University of Louisville. They had originally hoped I would make it into an opera, but I think the text is better adapted to speech than to recitative. The constant introduction of songs, of choruses, of ballet pageantry does seem to me, however, appropriate. I am supposed to deliver the score in time for the production next summer, but if I do not, the production will be made the following summer. The committee is already busy raising a budget, estimated roughly at $90,000. We will have student choruses available for practically free. Members of the Louisville Orchestra will play in the pit for scale. I am planning a small orchestra and a very small number of vocal soloists. I also have some bright ideas about scenery which the Louisville people think are both

---

*(1909–60), American baritone, who sang and recorded Thomson's Five Songs from William Blake which were written for him

†*The Dybbuk,* an opera by David and Alex Tamkin, received its world premiere at the New York City Opera on October 4, 1951, with Harrell as Rabbi Azreal.

distinguished and cheaper than what you call "building bungalows."
The theater is an outdoor one seating between 2,000 and 3,000. It
has a large stage with two smaller ones down front on the sides and
lots of space backstage. There are no flies. This means that scenery is
rolled on. I would like a series of flats painted in literal enlargements
of artists' sketches. The sketches would be somewhat smaller than
the flats themselves. These, completed by a small amount of furniture, should be sufficient for illusion and not cumbersome for stage
movement or for scene shifting. It has been customary to use this
theater in the summertime for light opera. In order to prepare for the
possible flop of the Lincoln production, it is planned to do operetta
next summer only in July and to run the Lincoln piece the first year
for just three weeks. We would need the theater, I presume, for a
week of rehearsals. This means that we will be doing preparatory
rehearsals in July, final stage rehearsals of the production in August.
We will cast in New York, I imagine, and have our scenery painted
here, although it is indicated to use whatever Louisville talent is considered worthy by the director.

The script* that I sent you is very much too long. I have encouraged that because I thought the historical explanations should be in
it. Huge amounts of cutting are indicated. Our contract with the
festival committee allows us to license a New York production at
any time, but Louisville maintains the out-of-town rights for five
years if it produces the work for three weeks every year. I think this
is most of the background material that you need.

A slight complication has recently arrived in the form of a very
serious proposal that I prepare a Negro cast in New York and bring
it to Paris for some festival performances of *Four Saints*. Pavlik has
offered to reconstitute Florine's sets and costumes. The producing
agent is the International Congress for Cultural Freedom, which
Nabokov is working for in Paris. They are also taking to Paris the
Boston Symphony and the City Center ballet.† There is a further
possibility of following the Paris engagement by a week in Florence
and a tour of Germany. Since the sets and costumes, all made in
Paris, will be available, along with the cast, it is even possible that
some New York producer may wish to take the thing over cheap
and run it for a short time next fall.

This is all for now.

Affection,

---

*Lincoln, a proposed opera libretto by Barbara Anderson. When Thomson abandoned the
project, the libretto was set by Norman Dello Joio.
†the New York City Ballet

To Margaret Matzenauer[*]

December 5, 1951

My dear Margaret Matzenauer:

Several correspondents suggested to me that the *Herald Tribune* music page call attention in some appropriate way to the fortieth anniversary of your Metropolitan debut. I am extremely regretful that these suggestions arrived too late for a proper article to be written before November 13. I was not aware myself that this important anniversary was approaching and am deeply chagrined at having missed the occasion to pay you honor and to remind the public of your glorious career.

Most sincerely yours,

To a Reader

December 5, 1951

The Editor has passed to me your interesting and warmly indignant letter. However radically you may disagree with my analysis and evaluation of Mr. Heifetz's violin playing,[†] I beg you to believe I have no personal animus against this artist. I have never met him in my life, and he has never hurt me in any way. I do know his brother-in-law Mr. Chotzinoff,[‡] with whom I have enjoyed a most agreeable acquaintance for many years; and once I encountered his daughter, a charming young woman.

Most sincerely yours,

To a Correspondent[§]

January 4, 1952

(1) I compose a lyrical work when I find a text which pleases me. I am constantly on the lookout for such texts, because I enjoy writing for the voice.

---

[*](1881–1963), German soprano and mezzo-soprano, long resident in New York, an important member of the Metropolitan Opera from 1911 to 1930

[†]One of Thomson's first reviews for the *Tribune* had been a critique of Heifetz entitled "Silk-Underwear Music." A decade later, in the review referred to here, he accused Heifetz of "a certain lightness of mind commonly known as bad taste."

[‡]Samuel Chotzinoff (1889–1964), for some years Heifetz's accompanist, later a music critic and music director at NBC

[§]who had sent Thomson a questionnaire about lyric theater

(2) The poem is the subject; the music is the shape. Either can be emphasized by the composer. I do not think that the best result is obtained when either overpowers the other.

(3) Unless music and words can be married completely and indissolubly there is no point in writing vocal music. The human voice is a most unsatisfactory wind instrument except for the fact that it can really articulate words, and articulate them, moreover, while singing.

(4) I should prefer to state the proposition in the following form: The spoken stage belongs to the speaking actor and the lyric stage to the singing actor. Action and emotion can exist in both. Their primary difference is one of medium. Let us say that one is essentially literature and the other essentially music, though literature is essential to the lyric stage. The speaking stage is more limited and does not necessarily include music.

(5) The traditional forms of the lyric theater are valid and available. I do not consider them essential. Doing without them, however, requires a great deal of invention, and such invention is usually merely transformation. Tradition always makes sense, but so does the reflected violation of it.

(6) Having made certain contributions myself in this domain, I am inclined to leave the awarding of honors to historians, to impresarios, and to the public.

Most sincerely yours,

To a READER

January 18, 1952

I thank you for the delightful letter of disagreement. Our disagreement is purely one of taste, I assure you. I recognize the musical excellences of *Gianni Schicchi* and the serious nature of its continued success in operatic theaters. If I have never cared much for it in performance, that may be due to inefficiencies in the staging of it. It may be due also to the fact that I have always found something elephantine and clumsy about operatic comedies involving a large orchestra. Even grander works like *Falstaff, Meistersinger,* and *Rosenkavalier* have always seemed to me to embody some essential artistic disproportion.

Most sincerely yours,

April 7, 1952

Dear Helen:

I guess the word "stylish" has lost its meaning. It used to mean
well-designed, well-executed and in accord with contemporary fashion. A lady's dress, for instance, could be beautiful, or it could be
stylish, or it could be both, or it could be neither. Applying the
word "stylish" to musical composition or performance is not original with me; but if the meaning is not clear, I should certainly either
explain completely or not use it at all. It is probably Edwardian
affectation on my part and not directly communicative anymore. I
am looking forward with pleasure to our lunch on Thursday with
Mr. Bing. He is loving me again since my article about the picketing
of *Don Carlo*.†

V.T.

To Sherry Mangan

April 8, 1952

If I have not written you in a year, that is not because I don't think
of you constantly. Having your news so regularly from Mina Cur-
tiss‡ has probably led me into supposing that she gave you mine as
well. In any case, I am fine and busy. I have been in the theater again
this winter. Balanchine did for the City Center a ballet on music
from my *Louisiana Story* film.§ Agnes de Mille‖ is doing a longer one
on my Cello Concerto. I did very pretty incidental music for a play
by Truman Capote• called *The Grass Harp*. Just at this moment I
am rehearsing all day every day for the *Four Saints*. That is all for
now. I must be off to my rehearsal. I am asking Julia to sign this and
send it off to you sight unseen. Marc Blitzstein put on the bottom of
such a letter to me "red but not dictated."

Yours ever,

★Mrs. Reid, the publisher of the *Herald Tribune,* had questioned Thomson's reference to a
"stylish" piece of music.

†The Metropolitan Opera's production of Verdi's *Don Carlo* had been the subject of religious controversy; Thomson defended the staging.

‡(1896–1985), translator, biographer of Georges Bizet, and sister of Lincoln Kirstein

§*Bayou,* first performed by the New York City Ballet on February 21, 1952

‖ (b. 1909), American choreographer

•(1924–84), American writer, later a professional celebrity

To a Reader

April 14, 1952

Perhaps I am prejudiced against the piano because I am a pianist myself and against the organ because I spent fifteen years of my life as a church organist. Of the two, surely the piano is capable of greater variety and expression. I have never found audiences really attentive to organ music for more than twenty minutes.

Most sincerely yours,

To Gustave Reese★

November 4, 1952

Dear Gus:

I think I should like to call the new étude set "Second Book of Etudes for Piano." Does this seem all right to you, or have you another suggestion? I did not quite like the provisional title that appeared somewhere on the manuscript, "Nine More Etudes." If we use that, any third volume would have to be called "Nine Most Etudes."

Best and ever,

To Edward A. Weeks†

November 18, 1952

Dear Ted:

It would be lovely to write a piece for the *Atlantic Monthly,* but I have not much to say on the subject of Rudolf Bing. I do not find him very interesting, nor his management of the Metropolitan Opera very novel. It is an honor to be asked, all the same.

Most sincerely yours,

★(1899–1977), author and music historian at this time with Carl Fischer, the music publisher
†(b. 1898), editor of *Atlantic Monthly* from 1938 to 1966

December 2, 1952

Your questions are very difficult to answer. The differences between contemporary music and earlier music would take a book to
explain. Half the book would be needed to explain that many of
these differences are entirely illusory. Contemporary music will, of
course, be found to have produced popular classics. Every epoch
does. Just which works these will be is anybody's guess. Many modern works that are already published will lose their popularity,
though some will not. Also certain works little played now will later
come into their own. Betting on futures is not my game, since I am
not a publisher. Writing music is like giving parties. You make it as
good as you can at the time you are doing it. Making it memorable
is not the main objective. You merely try to make it interesting and
worthy.

Most sincerely yours,

To Edwin Hughes*

December 16, 1952

Dear Mr. Hughes:

I had counted on accepting with delight your kind invitation to
the Olin Downes dinner on December 21. I learn at this moment
that that is the day of the Stravinsky concert in Town Hall, which
includes the world premiere of a new work† by him. Naturally Olin
will have to miss this concert, and that makes it all the more urgent
that I should pay it the compliment of coverage. I am very sorry to
miss the party and very sorry not to be able to be with Olin on this
occasion.

Most sincerely yours,

---

*Hughes (1884–1965) was director of The Bohemians, a New York musical club and
charitable institution founded by Rafael Joseffy, Rubin Goldmark, and others in 1907.
†The premiere was the first New York performance of Stravinsky's Cantata on Anony-
mous Elizabethan Songs.

To John M. Conly*

December 16, 1952

Dear Mr. Conly:

Others besides myself, including Henry Cowell,† have found an affinity between my music and that of Charles Ives. I did not know Ives' music when I was living in Paris. In the last twelve years I have heard a good deal of it. Some of it I find extraordinarily fine, much of it prolix. I admire the New England landscape pieces and find the Second Symphony touching. Sometimes I am tempted to write off his whole production as a supreme case of Yankee ingenuity; but this is not possible in view of the pieces, usually the short ones, that are unquestionably works of art. In any case, the resemblance between Ives' music and mine must come from our having, for similar reasons, followed similar paths. I do not think that Ives ever had any direct influence on me. I do not see how he could have. I do recognize, all the same, that he feels about Connecticut very much as I do about Missouri. His feelings about the Concord literary group do not interest me in any way. I think he was overimpressed.

Most sincerely yours,

To a Correspondent‡

December 17, 1952

I composed while studying with Nadia Boulanger the following works now in print:

Pastorale on a Christmas Plainsong, for organ (H. W. Gray Co.)

Fanfare, for organ (H. W. Gray Co.)

Three Antiphonal Psalms, for women's voices (Leeds)

Tribulationes Civitatum, for mixed voices (Weintraub)

Sonata da Chiesa, for E-flat clarinet, D trumpet, viola, horn, and trombone (New Music Edition)

Passacaglia, for organ (G. Schirmer)

---

*American music critic, an editor of *High Fidelity* magazine
†(1897–1965), innovative American composer
‡writing a master's thesis on Boulanger

I also composed many short works and a Mass for male chorus un-accompanied.

At the time that I studied with Mlle Boulanger, which was in the very early 1920s, her teaching was marked by a great strictness in the disciplines of counterpoint and harmony and great liberty in the approach to free composition. She was not a good teacher of orchestration but that fact did not bother me, since I had already had far better instruction from Edward Burlingame Hill. As for specific instances of her criticism, I remember bringing her a short choral piece one day; when she had finished reading it, she merely said, "This needs no comment; it is completely successful." On another occasion, after I had completed the *Sonata da Chiesa,* a three-movement work of considerable complexity, she remarked, "This is not at all the kind of music I would write myself, but I must admit that it comes off." (*Réussi* was the word she used.)

I must add that I was nearly twenty-five years old when I first went to her and not easily influenceable esthetically. Her attentive efforts to lead me in the directions of Fauré and Mahler were not successful, and she recognized that quickly. We were in accord about Sebastian Bach (I was an organist) and Stravinsky, whose music I knew very well. She did not care for Satie or Milhaud, whom I admired. I did not go to her Wednesday classes, where the students sang sixteenth-century motets, because I also knew that repertory extremely well from my experience as a choral singer and conductor.

Her influence on me consisted of some excellent training in counterpoint, harmony, and organ-playing and in having put me at ease with regard to the act of composition. She taught me to consider it as a natural function of the musical mind, and she wiped away the timidities that had been instilled by previous teachers. These teachers, mostly of German education, had tended to make me feel that anybody writing music was in competition with the classic masters. Nadia made me understand that writing music was like writing a letter. All you had to do was to say what you had to say clearly and stop. I have remained to this day extremely grateful to Mlle Boulanger for this particular service, though we disagree radically on many matters of musical taste and opinion. I suspect that your investigations will reveal some changes in her pedagogical methods over the last thirty years. In 1921 she had three American pupils: Melville Smith,★ Aaron Copland, and myself. For the next ten years, we three sent her most of the others. In the last twenty years I have not recommended her to so many young people as be-

---

★(1898–1962), American organist and pedagogue, later director of the Longy School in Cambridge, MA

fore, though a certain type of American student will find her valuable. I have always deplored her domineering relationship to her women students. She has always worked better with men. She has never had much influence on young French composers, and the Paris Conservatory has never thought her suited for a professorship of composition. Today, in America and in France she is more of a personality than an influence. But from 1921 to 1930 practically every young American composer who has since attained distinction passed through her hands and got something valuable from her.

If you can think of any more questions to ask me, I shall be delighted to write you again.

Most sincerely yours,

The following letter, to John Marshall (1903–80) of the Rockefeller Foundation, concerns a proposal by the Louisville Orchestra to support the work of contemporary American composers through commissions, performances, and recordings. Once approved, the project became a landmark event in American music as the orchestra played literally hundreds of new compositions over the next several years.

To John Marshall

January 8, 1953

Dear John:

The Louisville project seems to me extraordinarily well thought out. In practice, of course, neither the program nor the project will follow quite so neat a plan. This is of no importance, since a certain flexibility is part of any project's intelligent execution. This project seems to me most intelligently conceived, and certainly Mayor Farnsley* is capable of making it work. I can find no flaw in it. It seems to me designed to strengthen the weakest element in the contemporary musical scene, which is contemporary repertory, and also to strengthen the symphony orchestra at its weakest point, which is its dependence on "name" soloists for attracting the public. Louisville's present patronage of contemporary composers has proved the feasibility of doing without name soloists. The new project, which is the extension of an already successful policy, cannot fail to provide a model of policy for other orchestras, if it is at all successful. Under

*Charles P. Farnsley (b. 1907), publisher, arts patron and Mayor of Louisville from 1948 to 1954

the administration of Mayor Farnsley and his close associates, I cannot imagine it not being successful. My recommendation for its adoption is therefore one hundred percent favorable and with all flags flying.

Ever yours,

To a READER

January 29, 1953

We all regret the incident which took place in Washington recently with regard to Aaron Copland's *A Lincoln Portrait*.* We have taken no notice of it, however, in the columns of this newspaper; and I am advising Mr. Copland's friends to do likewise. I very much fear that public protests and similar manifestations might result in merely publicizing the incident to Mr. Copland's disadvantage. There is, after all, no possibility of changing a program that has already been played. There was not even much possibility of winning the case at all, since there was only a day or two to fight it. With a week or ten days to mobilize the defense, the result might have been different.

Most sincerely yours,

To CHARLES DENBY†

February 3, 1953

My dear Charles:

Many thanks for the letter. Roy [Harris] tells me his "Red" scandal in Pittsburgh is not over. My policy with regard to it and with regard to Aaron Copland's unfortunate rebuff in Washington is to give no publicity to the incidents, since such publicity seems to me possibly dangerous. I am hoping that the indiscriminate baiting of innocent liberals will die down. If it does not, then we shall all have to do something; but I have no idea at present what that will be.

Greetings and ever sincerely yours,

A Lincoln Portrait had been scheduled to be played at the Eisenhower inaugural, but after Congressman Fred Busby denounced Copland for alleged left-wing connections, the piece was dropped.
†(1883–1961), brother of Edwin Denby and president of the Pittsburgh Symphony Society, which had come under pressure to drop works by Copland and Roy Harris from its programming

To John Marshall

February 5, 1953

Dear John:

Answering your questions about the Louisville project:

1. Its operation, being novel, is bound to get a great deal of attention in the national press, both daily and weekly.

2. This attention can be channeled toward the critical columns or toward the news columns, as desired, or toward both.

3. The channeling should be guided by the advice of a responsible public relations office experienced in music and in other intellectual enterprises. I think it should be a New York office, and I suggest either Carson-Ruff Associates (who handle the National Institute of Arts and Letters and the Metropolitan Opera) or Margaret Hartigan (formerly of the New York City Center) or Muriel Frances, or the firm of Isadora Bennett and Richard Pleasants. It is not a full-time job or an expensive one, but it needs an experienced hand.

4. For news coverage the daily press, excepting that of the Louisville region, is less valuable than the national weeklies (*Time, Newsweek, Life, Look,* etc.). Constant coverage is not necessary; an occasional feature story is quite sufficient. Several of these, dealing with Louisville's present system of commissioning unusual works, have already appeared and have been valuable toward building up in Louisville itself confidence in the operation and support for it.

5. Critical coverage should be sought on all the levels:

    a. Local and regional. This presents no difficulty.

    b. Out-of-town newspapers. This is complex. No out-of-town paper will be able to cover every month with its own staff a musical series taking place in Louisville. Papers with space for coverage will be obliged to use reviews by Louisville critics or by employees of the national news services (AP, UP). I suggest that a sort of festival be held every spring, perhaps just before Derby week, to which distinguished critics would be invited. In the course of a few days the orchestra could review the highlights of the season, and recordings would be available of all the new works. I suggest also that once a month one critic be invited to Louisville, a representative of, say, the *Dallas News, San Francisco Chronicle, Christian Science Monitor, The New York Times, Chicago Tribune,* etc. It could be arranged by the public relations office that other papers print the visiting reviewer's article each time. In this way the project will become known in other cities to which it might offer a model, and constant reviewing of the new works will be available nationally through the papers that give space to contemporary composition.

6. Recordings of the commissioned works could be furnished (with permission of the American Federation of Musicians and ASCAP) to schools, colleges, and educational broadcasting stations. Also to selected foreign periodicals, to the Pulitzer Prize committee (which works from recordings), and to music publishers (who will certainly wish to keep an eye out for viable new works).

7. A series of awards (like those voted annually by the N.Y. Music Critics' Circle) could be made at the May Festival by a panel of critics appointed each year. This panel could include foreign critics as well as Americans.

8. The Louisville Orchestra should continue to visit New York periodically, and also other cities, with its vigorously up-to-date repertory. Such tours are not costly, if efficiently organized, and are of enormous value to back-home support, as well as to propagation of the Louisville idea.

9. The orchestra should expand its present arrangement for issuing commercial recordings of selected items from the new repertory.

As you can see, the opportunities are infinite for publicizing the enterprise and for submitting it to constant criticism. I do not recommend the seeking of indiscriminate publicity or irresponsible criticism, either of which might jeopardize its success. I do recommend a professionally directed policy which will maintain the dignity of the Louisville Orchestra while securing to the society, to the city, and to the composers commissioned the advantages of a national and even of an international interest in the project. As a newspaper man, I do not view such a policy as a difficult one to carry out. The project itself is a "natural" for publicity; its unusual character assures that. But publicity left in amateur hands is likely either to die or to get quite out of hand. Professional guidance is always necessary unless it is desired to operate in obscurity. It is especially necessary for preserving the dignity of intellectual institutions operating in public.

I am rather fond of the May Festival idea. It would come at a time when reviewers are footloose and when Kentucky is at its most delightful. It could be built into a charming occasion valuable to composers, publishers, reviewers, heads of symphony orchestra boards and of auxiliary committees, music librarians, music patrons, and students of cultural sociology, a meeting ground for North and South.

Yours faithfully,

To a Reader

February 12, 1953

I wish I could help you, but unfortunately the influence of jazz on classical composers is a subject about which I am relatively ignorant. We all know a half-dozen famous cases in which classical composers have imitated the jazz style—Stravinsky, Milhaud, Copland, myself, and others. Whether jazz has had a large influence on classical methods of writing in general I do not know. I am inclined to think that the influence of the classical composers on jazz has been greater.

Most sincerely yours,

To a Reader

February 18, 1953

I am at some difficulty trying to explain further what I meant by the paragraph that you quote from my Birthday Salute to Toscanini.

The idea that Toscanini is not a conductor of marked personal characteristics is acceptable, I think, to most musicians who know his work well. You have only to compare it with that of Beecham, Stokowski, and the late Koussevitzky to realize what I mean. His orchestras do not even have a characteristic sound, as the orchestras of Monteux,* Reiner, and Ormandy do. He has not the cultural enlightenment of Mitropoulos or of Ansermet.† His power over the public comes rather from his determination to make every piece "work." His reputed fidelity to the written notes is both a virtue and a fault. It protects him from interpretive bad taste, but it also blinds him to many expressive intentions on the composer's part that musical notation is incompetent to record. Toscanini's greatness lies, I think, in his ferocious loyalty to high standards of musical execution. Clarity is his passion, and he never wavers in his pursuit of it. To return to the matter of his "culture," he seems to view musical performance as the central objective of the whole music world rather than as a mechanism for transmitting the composer's enlightenment. The paradox in what I am saying lies in the curious fact that with an attitude toward music so completely that of the typical star-performer he is not on the platform a star quite like any of the others. His star-quality is that he gives an illusion of not being a star. The effect of all this on the public is phenomenal.

---

*Pierre Monteux (1875–1964), French conductor
†Ernest Ansermet (1883–1969), Swiss conductor, founder of l'Orchestre de la Suisse Romande

I do not know whether the foregoing is any clearer than the paragraph you quoted. If it means anything to you, that will be because you have already sensed in this conductor's work the anomaly I am describing. I doubt very much if it would communicate to persons who do not already know, at least a little bit, what I am talking about.

Most sincerely yours,

To Ernst Bacon

February 24, 1953

Dear Ernst:

The New York Times carried the story about Aaron's *Lincoln Portrait*. We did not, because I thought that publicizing the incident might be more disadvantageous to him than protesting about it. It all happened so quickly that no practical advantage could be derived from offering more support to the conductor who had chosen to program the piece. Roy Harris has been having similar troubles in Pittsburgh all winter, and I have not publicized them either. If this sort of thing diminishes, my policy will have been proved to be the right one. If it increases, then we must all get together and do something effective. We might even, if necessary, boycott the organizations guilty of discrimination. I do not think individual action is ever very effective and I know that agitational or editorial protest can be a two-edged weapon.

Ever yours,

To a Reader

February 24, 1953

I am sorry to have disappointed you in my review of *The Rake's Progress*. Perhaps, if you hear it often, you may find some of the enchantment in it that I did. Perhaps, too, on further hearing, I may find it "frustrating," as you did. One can never tell.

Most sincerely yours,

March 12, 1953

I don't know what I could write you as a blurb for Roger Dettmer.† He is good but green. Under your guiding hand he may even become brilliant. Just now he is mostly promise. If you wish to promote him as my pupil, you can say that he has written reviews for the *Herald Tribune* and that I recommended him to your attention. "A young reviewer distinctly worthy of your attention," or something like that, could be quoted.

Good luck with him!

Most sincerely yours,

To Joseph Herzberg‡

March 18, 1953

Dear Joe:

If I had more Sunday space, I would:

1. Enlarge the photo layout.
2. Add small photos among the agate listing of the week's programs.
3. Feature weekly a small biog-in-box, a musical man-of-the-week, with photo.
4. Print a weekly column by Arthur Berger§ featuring news notes. Our Sunday page at present badly needs informative matter. I have already asked the music editor to classify musical news items as A, B, and C; and you have assured me you will get class-A notes into the paper. A little space would make this easier. Dance and art get notes printed; why shouldn't ours? The *Times* at present beats us on two counts: musical news items and gramophone records reviewed. The first can only be changed by more Sunday space.
5. Amplifying the record coverage. Cover popular records only where advertising justifies that use of the space.
6. Publish monthly a column on radio and television, especially on television opera.
7. Print articles by famous musicians. We can always get these with newspegs. I can also get special pieces from Europe by name writers, because they know about us. (We are the music page that Europe reads.)

---

*executive editor of the *Chicago Herald American*, and later the *San Francisco Examiner*
†(b. 1927), American music critic, long based in Chicago
‡(1907–76), then the city editor of the *Herald Tribune*
§(b. 1912), American composer, critic, and writer

8. Return to occasional coverage of jazz.

9. Stimulate controversy by printing letters from readers.

Respectfully (and hopefully) submitted,

To Nicolas Nabokov*

May 12, 1953

Dear Nicolas:

I have consulted with Sam Barber and wish to propose the following list of composers and performers to be invited to Rome with all expenses paid:

Carlos Surinach, composer and conductor

Joseph Fuchs, violinist

Leontyne Price, soprano

Arthur Gold and Robert Fizdale, duo-pianists

The Harpsichord Quartet (Sylvia Marlowe, harpsichord; Bernard Greenhouse, cello; Claude Monteux, flute; Harry Shulman, oboe).†

In addition to these, there will be, of course, Lou Harrison, Ben Weber, Samuel Barber, and myself. If this list is considered too large, it would be possible to bring Sylvia Marlowe alone and let her play her 20th-century repertory with good chamber musicians from Italy. She assures me that this would be perfectly possible if there was a little time for rehearsing and particularly if the players would learn their parts in advance for the difficult works, such as Elliott Carter's piece. It would also be possible to bring only Sylvia Marlowe and Bernard Greenhouse to rehearse in Rome with the flute and oboe players or with a string group. The Harpsichord Quartet has a fine 20th-century repertory, including works by Harrison, Weber, Carter, Haieff, Rieti, Lessard, de Falla, and others.‡ Also rare 18th-

---

*Nabokov was then assembling a series of concerts in Rome under the auspices of the Congress for Cultural Freedom.

†Surinach (b. 1915); Fuchs (b. 1900); Price (b. 1927); Gold (b. 1917); Fizdale (b. 1920); Marlowe (1908–81); Greenhouse (b. 1916); Monteux (b. 1920); Shulman (1916–71). Marlowe, in particular, was a close friend.

‡composers Lou Harrison, Ben Weber (1916–79), Elliott Carter, Alexei Haieff (b. 1914), Vittorio Rieti, John Lessard (b. 1920), and Manuel de Falla, (1876–1946)

century works such as the Couperin *Apothéose de Corelli*. They play very beautifully together, but it would also be perfectly possible for Miss Marlowe to perform this repertory with Roman chamber music players. Greenhouse will not be available for any work in Europe before April 1, which eliminates the possibility of using him as soloist in any of the orchestral concerts Surinach has organized for Barcelona and Madrid in March. The availability of Leontyne Price will depend on whether *Porgy and Bess* is still playing at that time, since her contract runs until June 1954; but the chances of her being excused seem favorable, even if the opera should still be running. I am asking Lou Harrison to write his piece with her in mind as soloist.

Here is a tentative list of distinguished music critics. Unfortunately I am not acquainted with the profession as practiced all over the world.

Olin Downes, *New York Times*
Alfred Frankenstein, *San Francisco Chronicle*
John Rosenfield, *Dallas Morning News*
Manuel Salazar, Mexico City
Cecil Smith, London *Daily Express*
Domingo Santa Cruz, Chile
William Glock, London
Fidele d'Amico, Rome
Gerald Abrams, London
Marcel Schneider, *Combat*, Paris

The latter was recommended by Samuel Barber. Among the others, the least distinguished intellectually are Olin Downes, John Rosenfield, and Gerald Abrams; but all three are influential. I know nothing about the press in Germany, Austria, Switzerland, or Spain except that I have little faith in the perspicacity of Stückenschmidt.* Claude Rostand in France is not without a certain common sense.

The concerts which Surinach and I will direct in Spain seem now to be quite a festival. There will be two orchestral programs in Madrid and three in Barcelona, all with soloists. We would like to use Joseph Fuchs and Leontyne Price, also Leo Smit† if he is available. He could play the Haieff Concerto with Joseph Fuchs, and a whole program of modern American sonatas. It might be valuable to take him to Rome for this performance. In this case, let us consider

---

*Hans Heinz Stückenschmidt (b. 1901), German music critic and musicologist, wrote extensively about Schoenberg, Stravinsky, Busoni and others.
†(b. 1921), American composer and pianist

bringing over Sylvia Marlowe without the other three members of her quartet.

Please let me know as soon as possible whether my list of soloists is acceptable, because the Spanish engagements are being made at this time. Also because American engagements for next March and April will have to be refused by this time. Since you have no other Spanish conductor on your list, Surinach should be asked to conduct whatever Spanish works are played at the Congress. I have heard him work frequently and he is first-class.

As to the conductors, if Bernstein and the other American big boys turn you down, consider Walter Hendl, who conducts modern music very well and who would profit by the Roman experience.

This is all for now. I hope and presume you are happy.

Affection ever,

To a READER

October 12, 1953

Whether musical criticism is of service to the progress of the art I have never known. But if one is to do it at all, one must tell the truth as one believes that to be. I do not know whether my review of last Thursday evening's Philharmonic concert will or will not lose me a friend and a valued interpreter,* but that is the chance I have to take. Don't think that I write articles like that just for the fun of throwing my weight about.

Most sincerely yours,

To A. H. FRISCH†

October 21, 1953

Dear Mr. Frisch:

I remember you well and was glad to hear from you. What you are doing with musical tapes is not dissimilar to the experiments

---

*Thomson's review concluded: "The impersonal, the objective involvement in a piece of music and all the ways and means of making it sound that are the mark of great and civilized conducting were further away than I have ever heard them in any performance by Dimitri Mitropoulos. Let us hope he settles down soon to work *with* his orchestra instead of against it. Last night they played *in spite of* him, rather than *for* him."
†Abraham Herman Frisch (1900–82), a Harvard acquaintance and lawyer with an interest in tape music

being operated in Paris, Frankfurt, and New York under the name of *musique concrète*. May I suggest that you might be interested in the efforts of Otto Luening and John Cage. Mr. Luening is a professor in the music department at Columbia University. Cage is a composer who has long specialized in percussion music and mechanical devices.

Most sincerely yours,

To Nicolas Nabokov

November 15, 1953

Dear Nicolas:

Sam Barber and I have gone over the programs pretty carefully several times and feel that they might be more distinguished. If there are not enough unusual modern works available to liven them up, perhaps some rare ancient ones might do the trick. I realize that the twelve commissioned ones may change the effect considerably from what the programs looked like on paper. As for my own piece on them, I have not liked the idea (and Sam supports me in this) of being represented by *The Seine at Night*. I am still hoping that all three of my Orchestral Pictures (20 minutes) can be played and that I can conduct them. If this last is not possible to arrange, then perhaps the pieces could be played by someone else; but all three of them *please,* especially the *Sea Piece with Birds,* which is rather unusual.

About travel money. Barber thinks he may be able to get himself sent by UNESCO, which would save his passage. Carlos Chávez will almost certainly not be able to come; that saves another. I regret that there is no room now for Greenhouse and beseech you to invite him at the first opening possible in your budget.

About Barcelona. I do not expect the Roman conference to underwrite with expense-paid invitations the whole of the Barcelona personnel. Surinach is enough and will be good for Rome too, though Barcelona and Rome would both profit also from Greenhouse, if he can be squeezed in. In general Barcelona will use people already going to Rome—Fuchs, Leontyne, me, and if possible Copland. However, Barcelona needs to know whether Copland is to be available. Will you please write me *immediately* or *wire* whether Copland's passage is being paid to Rome. He thinks it is, and his name has three stars in the big list. But he is not on any other list, any committee, or any panel. So I am wondering whether the budget restrictions will really allow his being invited. If you can tell me about this

271

right away, I can either make an engagement for him in Barcelona or abandon it. But I cannot ask Barcelona to wait beyond December 1.

Affection ever,

To Ernst Bacon

December 22, 1953

Dear Ernst:

How well I know your feeling! I often write an unfavorable review, but when anybody writes one about my work I am absolutely convinced that he is ignorant, stupid, and probably in the pay of my enemies. I must say that Peggy Glanville-Hicks'* review of your choral piece (I was out of town myself) seems a little severe to me, but she did say that the audience liked it, thus attesting, as a good reporter, that the work was a success with the public. As for her opinion of the work, I do not feel that it would be right to scold her, since she is a responsible musician, an excellent composer, in fact, and has a right to express her own judgment. I do not try to influence in any way the opinions of my staff. I correct them if they express their opinions badly. It is quite probable that some other member of the staff might have written quite differently about the occasion; but I do not know how to insure artists against an unfavorable review other than by engaging only musicians to write reviews and demanding of them that they express their honest opinion in correct English. I am sorry as I can be, but glad you wrote me about the matter.

Yours ever,

To a Correspondent

January 19, 1954

Musical ideas come to my mind in all sorts of ways, some provoked by an experience and some seemingly spontaneous. Many of these ripen into works and some do not. The important thing about a musical idea is not where it came from but where it is going, whether it is strong enough to become a piece. I imagine that some connection, conscious or unconscious, between the idea and one's

---

*Australian-American composer (b. 1912) and occasional contributor to the *Herald Tribune*

own emotional patterns is necessary if one is to work well with it. This is particularly necessary in the case of long works. If something about their theme does not "inspire" the composer, he is not likely to carry them to a successful, or convincing, conclusion. As for my own works, I do not think that I remember the precise moment when any single one of them was conceived. Even my musical portraits, though composed in front of the sitter, have an earlier conception, though not precisely a musical one, at the moment of my inviting the subject to sit. At this moment I have no idea what my portrait is going to be like; I merely think that I would like to try a sitting and see what happens.

Most sincerely yours,

To a CORRESPONDENT

February 2, 1954

I thank you for the interesting letter about my orchestral pictures. Your disappointment with them I cannot dispute. Your resistances, however, I cannot accept, since they are based on comparisons. I assume by these comparisons that [you think] I am emulating the musical landscape painting of Debussy. You might have mentioned Mendelssohn or Smetana and been equally unjustified. I once had a teacher of composition who complained that my symphonies were not as satisfying to him as those of Brahms. The fact that they were not intended to express the same things as the symphonies of Brahms escaped him. If my *Pictures for Orchestra* have any individual quality of their own, that is an achievement, no matter how grand Debussy's achievements were in musical landscape painting. If you find them weak as music and as evocation, I can regret your opinion; but I cannot dispute it. It is valid as the reaction of an experienced listener. But when you assume that they are imitations of Debussy I resist. It is like considering any fugue as an imitation of Bach. Musical landscape existed long before Debussy and will surely exist long after him. His work may well represent a high point in that tradition, as Bach's does in that of the fugue; but I still do not feel that comparison is a proper method of musical criticism. It is a method of description, not a basis for estimate.

Most cordially yours,

February 22, 1954

I thank you for the charming letter. I am afraid our Metropolitan Opera is very much like the little girl who had the curl right in the middle of her forehead.

Most sincerely yours,

To a READER

March 4, 1954

I happen not to have read Mr. Haggin's remarks about me. Sometimes he approves of me and sometimes he doesn't. I have long considered that the criticism of criticism was fruitless. Still less do I care to engage in polemics with any critic on the subject of myself.

Most sincerely yours,

To MAURICE GROSSER

Rome
April 19 [1954]

D.M.

It was nice hearing from you twice and I thought to write you in Athens so it would wait for you, but the congress has been a 24-hour affair. Now it is over and I am staying another week to rest up and buy neckties. My Barcelona concert was a big success with rave notices in the papers. Saw Senabre, bought a small picture, so did Roger.* Here, I appeared in one day as a speaker, composer & conductor and seem to have been pretty impressive too. No press, as everything has taken place by invitation. Sylvia, Joe Fuchs, Leontyne, & Surinach all performed better than the Europeans. Sauguet, Poulenc, Auric were all here. Also Sam Barber & Aaron. I stayed with the R——s, Roger nearby at the Academy. Did not like the sterilized American atmosphere. Lou Harrison's competition piece won half a prize. The French insisted on dividing it with their boy, whose piece was not good. And the Germans had to have half a prize for an orchestral piece, though the Swiss that got the other half

---

*American artist Roger Baker (b. 1925)

was better. As soon as the congress was over I moved in town to the Hotel Inghilterra, which is grubby & homey like a French hotel. Weather has been *very* cold. Today a bit of sun. On Friday I go to Paris, stay till May 2; write to 17, quai Voltaire. Have been seeing Massimo★ & his timid fat wife and six children. He has written piles of music, some of it pretty, all of it a bit amateurish. He is sweet as always, sends you greetings, would love a photo of his portrait when you can, hopes you will come to see him when in Rome. I'm enjoying the outside of Rome, haven't looked inside the churches or museums, though Roger has been chasing Caravaggios. Food & wine fair, fresh peas wonderful. Hope Greece is warmer than Italy. The Matts† went to Sicily and came home with terrible colds. Gertrude's eye trouble is just cataracts. Matt's brother is dying of cancer. Write me of Greece.

love

V——

To a CORRESPONDENT‡

April 23, 1954

The Committee read your music in all friendliness and decided not to record it at this time. We do not encourage composers to submit unrequested manuscripts, but we always read them carefully. If there is any prejudice in any member regarding the style of a work, the nature of its inspiration, or the celebrity of its composer, I am not aware of it. Any composer whom we neglect to record is, of course, entirely free to consider us as acting unfairly; and I understand most sympathetically your feelings of bitterness in the face of a rejection. All the same, I do not think it a good idea for you to submit the same work again at this time. Our recording schedule is virtually complete for the next two years, and it is not probable that the Committee will meet again to select other works until some time next season.

I am sorry that I cannot give you any immediate consolation for your disappointment, nor would it be proper for me to divulge to you what was said at our meeting in your music's favor and disfa-

---

★Composer Leone Massimo (b. 1911), a Roman prince
†Historian Garrett Mattingly (1900–62) and his wife, Gertrude
‡a composer whose work was rejected for the Columbia Masterworks Modern American Music recording series, of which Thomson was the chairman. Others on the Committee were Copland, Barber, Cowell, and Lieberson.

vor, since it is not the custom of editorial boards to enter into polemical discussions with authors about their own work.

Please believe that our Committee acts in good faith and that our
decision not to record a given work in a given series at a given time
is not offered to the composer as any definitive judgment of the
artistic qualities of the work.

Cordially and sincerely yours,

To Maurice Grosser

Brussels
July 14 [1954]

D.M.

Off to N.Y. this afternoon for my stadium concert. Luxembourg
show was good and my concert here, I gather, pretty brilliant. Anyway, the Paris orchestra boys were adorable, worked for me like
lambs, and the Radio-Symphonique is a first-class orchestra, and
Maurice Gendron,★ who had also played the Cello Concerto in
Vienna, is first-class too. There were 20 people present, all distinguished—Alice T. & the Manuel Rosenthals† and the Boris Blachers
etc. The orch. boys all crazy about the concerto. Everybody hates
Appalachian Spring—some very pretty material in it but a choppy
piece and quite unnecessarily difficult. I'm glad you think of coming
back next winter. Six months is a lot of Europe these days. R.
[Roger Baker] moves today to his old rooming house. He seems to
have started painting finally. In August we will be in Austria, at
Kitzbühel, then Venice for my flute piece (I finished it at Chexbres).
And maybe I go to Ankara from Sept. 1 to 10. I'm invited by the
Turkish gov't. If I do, would you like to come to Istanbul? Or
maybe I could stop a minute in Athens. I'll be back at quai Voltaire
from July 30 to August 4. My flat is painted yellow again & I've new
curtains, 2-inch gold & white stripes.

Anyway,

love,
V——

★(b. 1920), French cellist
†(b. 1904), French composer and conductor, best known for his ballet of Offenbach arrangements, *Gaîté Parisienne*

To a CORRESPONDENT*

July 22, 1954

If your editor does not wish you to judge music and its performance, but only to report on it, then that is your assignment. Independent music criticism is only possible with the support of your
paper. If you do not have that support I think you are ill-advised to
attempt it. If you feel that you must attempt it, then my advice is
that you describe the music precisely and avoid all words implying
"good" or "bad." Just let the facts speak for themselves.

Most sincerely yours,

To GEORGE CORNISH†

July 27, 1954

Dear Mr. Cornish:

As I have previously informed you in several conversations since
May 1953, I wish to resign my post as Music Critic of the *New York
Herald Tribune* on October 1. As also agreed between us in conversation, I shall send to the music editor a few Sunday articles covering
European events, probably the festivals of Salzburg and Venice, before that time. The Sundays during August and September in which
I do not appear in the paper are to be considered as my 1954 vacation. If you will be so kind as to sign one copy of this letter and
return it to me, I shall understand that my resignation has been accepted.

Ever faithfully yours,

To the NEW YORK NEWSPAPER GUILD

July 27, 1954

Gentlemen:

I enclose a copy of my resignation to the *New York Herald Tribune*.
I am leaving the paper as of October 1. Since I do not plan to take
another newspaper position at this time, I should appreciate it very

---

*a young music critic who had written for advice
†(b. 1901), then executive editor of the *Herald Tribune*

much if my membership in the Guild could be transferred to an inactive list, so that, should I ever take up newspaper work again, I could be reinstated without payment of back dues.

Very truly yours,

Part Four
EVERBEST

(1954–1985)

*F*rom 1954, when he retired from the *Herald Tribune,* through 1988, when these words are written, Thomson has kept himself busy with numerous composing projects, revivals of earlier works, conducting and lecture dates, trips and tours abroad, faculty appointments at educational institutions, writing books and the occasional article—all the time keeping up with an extraordinary social circle.

Thomson's freedom from the constraints of newspaper writing did not immediately yield an abundance of new compositions:

As after my return to Missouri from World War I, after my return to Paris in 1925, my return to America in 1933 for producing *Four Saints,* my return to New York in the fall of 1940, whenever I have closed off an epoch in my life and opened another, it has taken a little time before the music flows. Relieved from deadline pressures and with nothing I had to do (evenings, at least) I seemed to write less music than before. I wrote songs to old English poetry and to Shakespeare, also songs in Spanish. I did six Shakespeare plays, three films, and a new ballet, *The Harvest According,* by Agnes de Mille (to excerpts she had chosen from existing works, with filling added). I traveled too, to South America, lecturing in Spanish and conducting; to Venice for two festivals, to Berlin for another, eventually to Japan. But I was not content with just moving about, nor with merely composing films, plays, and short recital pieces. It was not until I had completed a forty-five-minute work, the *Missa Pro Defunctis,* and in 1960 brought that through its birth pains in Potsdam, New York (with an orchestra *of ninety, a chorus of three hundred), that I knew my reconstruction time was over.*

Soon after the premiere of the *Missa*—a sophisticated work reflecting Thomson's lifelong interests in both church and popular music—he set his sights on writing a third opera. After a difficult search for a new collaborator, Thomson finally settled on Jack Larson (b. 1933), an actor and poet. They chose the life of George Gordon, Lord Byron, as their subject and entitled the work *Lord Byron.*

The opera tells of the dean of Westminster Abbey's refusal to bury Byron because of the poet's radical politics and many scandalous affairs, then recalls Byron's life through a series of flashbacks. The music displays Thomson's familiar gift for prosody but is couched in a more complex harmonic and rhythmic language than the two Stein operas. Completed in 1966, *Lord Byron* was first performed at the Juilliard School in 1972, with a subsequent revival in 1985. However, it has yet to be performed by the Metropolitan Opera, for which it had been commissioned by the Koussevitzky and Ford foundations.

Other important works from this period include the Cantata on Poems of Edward Lear (1973); the ballet *Parson Weems and the Cherry Tree* (1975) for chamber orchestra (written for Erick Hawkins); and, of course, numerous portraits of various friends and colleagues, including Eugene Ormandy, Lou Harrison, John Houseman, and conductor Dennis Russell Davies.

Although he did not write with the prolix intensity that had characterized his days with the *Herald Tribune*, Thomson continued to furnish articles to a variety of publications, including *The New York Review of Books, The New York Times, HiFi/Stereo Review, Musical America,* and *Vogue.* He also produced an autobiography, *Virgil Thomson* (1966), and a history of contemporary domestic composition, entitled *American Music Since 1910* (1971). Two further collections of Thomson's writing were also published: *Music Reviewed: 1940–1954* (1967), an anthology of articles from the *Herald Tribune,* and the more encompassing *A Virgil Thomson Reader* (1981).

His teaching positions included a professorship at Carnegie-Mellon University (1966) and residencies at the University of Bridgeport (1972), Trinity College in Connecticut (1973), Dominican College in California (1974), Otterbein College in Ohio (1974), California State University at Fullerton (1975), and UCLA (1976). He was also awarded many honorary doctorates and a host of other honors, including the Creative Arts Award from Brandeis University (1968), the Handel Medallion of the City of New York (1971), the Henry Hadley Medal of the National Association for American

Composers and Conductors (1972), the Edward MacDowell Medallion (1977), and a Guggenheim Fellowship. He was the subject of numerous festivals and tributes, including one in his native Kansas City on his eighty-fourth birthday and one at Yale University when he turned ninety.

In this last set of letters, we find Thomson perpetuating lifelong personal and professional relationships while establishing new ones; following his business matters carefully; answering admiring (and some not-so-admiring) letters; voicing support for such disparate creators as Milton Babbitt and Yoko Ono, and exchanging a recipe or two.

Today Thomson lives in the same suite at the Chelsea Hotel he has occupied since 1943. He does not hear well and has curtailed his composing and concertgoing, although he does both on occasion. But he goes out often, entertains friends at home, and continues to play an active role in the intellectual life of his time.

To MAURICE GROSSER

Tennerhof-Kitzbühel, Austria
August 22, 1954

D.M.

All goes quietly here. It rains almost every day and on the others there is not much sun and the whole place is nicely boring and so we work. I've corrected proofs 3 times on the flute concerto and done various other musical odd jobs, waiting for a proper inspiration about a piano concerto, [which] now forms itself slowly in the mind but which is not ready to really work on yet. R. [Roger Baker] has been painting still lifes in all sizes, several very small, almost miniatures, and pretty as anything. We went to Salzburg for 4 days and heard some operas and I worked with my flutist on the concerto and we had a nice time. It rained there too. I wrote Jay* that Salzburg was a cage of lions, all buying and selling one another. But the food is better here. My *Tribune* resignation and the excellent *Time* story about it have brought me lots of mail.

Affec——— ever
V.T.

---

*Jay Harrison (1927–74), music editor and critic for the *Herald Tribune*

To Manuel Rosenthal

November 16, 1954

Cher Manuel,

Last night Leontyne Price sang your early songs at the Town Hall, and I adored them. She sang them charmingly too. The whole evening made me miss you and Claudine very much. Just before Leontyne's concert, I had conducted one myself which included the *Socrate* in English (my own). I had all the first-desk men from the NBC orchestra, and they played it divinely. I also did some vocal pieces of mine, a Mozart symphony (No. 33) and the Bach B-minor Suite (with Julius Baker playing flute). The concert seems to have been a great success, because the press was tremendously enthusiastic. Leontyne's reception, of course, was the kind of demonstration that happens once in ten or twenty years. Flowers all over the stage and all that.

I had intended writing you earlier about my Flute Concerto which had its premiere in Venice on September 18th. The piece seems to be perfectly successful, and my soloist, Elaine Shaffer,★ is quite a wonderful artist. She had asked me at the time if I cared to speak about her to Henry Barraud;† but I told her I preferred not to recommend artists to Barraud, since he so easily feels embarrassed in such a situation if he cannot use them immediately. I suggested that I write you instead. If you care to pass on to Barraud or anybody else my admiration for the technique and musicianship (plus utterly charming platform presence) of Miss Shaffer, who is having considerable success as a soloist, I should be grateful. If you would care to use her in any of your own programs, with or without my concerto, I don't think you would find her disappointing.

Also, I shall be sending to you next spring a pianist named Charles Rosen.‡ Please give him advice, engagements, anything that seems appropriate. He is extremely intelligent and a very extraordinary pianist, particularly in French music. He plays the Debussy Etudes like nobody else.

Theodate [Johnson] is divorcing and madly happy. I must say it is a great pleasure having her in New York again. She is working for *Musical America*. Weather is sunny and pleasant. I adore not working nights. All New York needs right now is you and Claudine. I embrace you both with affection.

Ever,

★(1925–73), American flutist for whom Thomson wrote his Flute Concerto
†(b. 1900), French composer, music director of the French National Radio from 1948 to 1965
‡(b. 1927), American pianist and musical scholar

To Frederick Fennell*

November 16, 1954

Dear Mr. Fennell:

I have received your recording of the band pieces and have played it with great delight. My piece† comes out beautifully and harmonious as to sonority and balance, in every way clean and handsome.

Your tempo, which is more than twice as slow as the one I use, has convinced me completely. I shall adopt it from now on, whenever I get a chance to conduct the piece. At that slow pace, however, I shall try to maintain the rhythm a little more rigidly than you have done. Whether this will be possible I do not know, but I should like to preserve as much as possible of the march feeling.

So please accept all my thanks and my sincere compliments. I am delighted with your reading of the piece and with the recording.

Ever faithfully yours,

To Allen Hughes‡

January 4, 1955

Dear Allen,

Thanks for the greeting and brief note. I am delighted that you have your fellowship but a little sorry that you are not here. So is Jay Harrison, who would like very much, now or later, to have you review for the *Herald Tribune*.

I would love it, and so would other friends of Francis Poulenc, if you could tell me what is the real state of his health. Has he gone really mad, or is he just upset about the stage rights to his libretto?§

Roger's show came off fine. Now he has moved to a new apartment and is slowly painting that.

I wish you would write me oftener.

Affection ever,

---

*(b. 1914), American band conductor, who made many recordings with the Eastman-Rochester band for Mercury Records
†*A Solemn Music* (1949); see p. 249
‡(b. 1921), American music and dance critic, later associated with *The New York Times* for a quarter-century. Hughes then had a grant from the French government to write a book (never completed) on Poulenc.
§Poulenc was then working on *Dialogues des Carmélites;* he arranged his own libretto from the play by Georges Bernanos.

March 3, 1955

Dear Gottfried:

Here is a lovely tune, rare, beautiful, and unfamiliar. It is clearly of folk origin, adapted to religious words, and much older than 1805, though nobody knows where it comes from. Its publication in a New England songbook of that date seems to have been its last. Already the "modern" or Handelian style of tune and harmonization, as practiced in the Boston churches and taught in the schools, was pushing the older tunes back into the less "enlightened" farm and frontier regions. Anyway, I love it and hope you can use it. I got it from *Down East Spirituals* by George Pullen Jackson, a scholarly collection published in New York about 10 years ago.

I heard Kempe* conduct *Arabella* yesterday at the Metropolitan Opera. He was wonderful. Karajan opens Tuesday with Berlin Philharmonic. The Veterans of Foreign Wars are protesting and will probably picket Carnegie Hall, but I don't think there will be any serious trouble. He has Washington support.

If Charles Rosen turns up, please be nice to him. He is a wonderful pianist and a wonderful musician. Also useful, because he can learn anything in no time.

My best to all, including your wife.

Ever yours,

To Allen Hughes

April 16, 1955

Dear Allen,

I am not moving out of New York for the present, though I may go to South America in June or July. Whether I go to Europe at all this summer is problematical, and I do not seem to care very much. Here I work quietly on a long piece, and the weather is pleasant.

Henry Pleasants's book† is a horror and is getting lots of publicity. Marc Blitzstein's comment was that three-fourths of it is true but we are not taking it from *him*.

---

*Rudolf Kempe (1910–76), German conductor especially esteemed for his performances of Strauss and Wagner
†*The Agony of Modern Music* (1955), a scathing attack on musical modernism

Do give Poulenc my love and tell him how happy I am that he is recovered. I always thought he would get well when the rights to his libretto were settled.

Do write often, and do come home sometime.

Affection ever,

To Maurice Grosser

[Santiago, Chile]
June 29, 1955

D.M.

My departure for Buenos Aires was delayed by a slight revolution there, so they organized me a concert of my works which I conduct tomorrow. Then go on to B.A. the next day, since now the planes are flying again, and also my concert there, though postponed from June 24, will really take place on July 11. Then I have others in Montevideo, São Paolo, and Rio. This town is cool and foggy and the oysters heavenly. I have been discovered here by press and faculty as the great American composer, so I guess I can come back if my concert goes good. Bought vicuña mufflers and tried to have a coat made, but the cloth was out of stock. It comes from Bolivia, so maybe I can get it in Buenos Aires. Nothing else to buy unless you want copper objects or peasant art or real chinchilla pelts. I am hoping to have letters from you in B.A. though they sent some mail to me from there which has not arrived here because stopping the planes for a week messed up everything. But do write. And Leonid [Berman] complains you haven't written him. They are liking Northeast Harbor and have asked Roger to visit them. He is still in N.Y. because he couldn't rent his flat. Life here is a bit intellectual, very serious about art and music and such, but socially agreeable. Concerts are at 7. So are parties and lectures. Dinner is 9 or later. The country is like France in winter, lots of golf and riding and ski things very close to town. There is a very devout Jazz Club and lots of "little theater." Sex is active in the Spanish way but also sort of discreet in a British way or Swiss way. The embassy people are serviceable and generally quite adorable, nice married couples of 35 to 40 and enjoying living here. There is energy and nobody has nerves. I've enjoyed being admired but after 3 weeks of it shall be glad to move on. And I do miss not having your news.

love ever
V.

To Margareda Guedes Nogueira*

September 20, 1955

Dear Maggie:

I miss your news. What are you up to? I am not going to phone you to find out, because the excitement of telephoning such a distance sort of hinders the flow of information. All the same, I was terribly impressed at being telephoned from Rio, especially since I had company when the call came through. It was all very showy.

Weather here remains stormy and sticky and mostly hot. One hurricane after another destroys some part of the eastern seacoast. We have been expecting one named Ione for the last 12 hours, but I am afraid it is going to be a dud. Myself I like a little destruction from time to time.

My life is quiet. I do a little housekeeping and I write music. I have a new cook, a most agreeable woman who also knows her business. As you can see, I also have a secretary, part-time, who is a virtuoso typist.

I have had great success with my story of how the Brazilian Ministry of Education had arranged everything else about my concert in Rio but forgot to hire the hall. I still suspect that the American embassy interfered secretly on account of my Picasso portrait.†

Please give my greetings to all the nice little friends. And please write me a nice letter. I am sure you must have a secretary at the office and that you can dictate to her in English. If not, I shall read it in Portuguese with my dictionary.

Affection ever—

Yours,

To Jorge d'Urbano‡

September 20, 1955

Cher ami:

At last I have procured for you a copy of *The State of Music*, which has been out of print for some years. I was about to mail it to you today, when I learned through the press of the somewhat agitated state of your country. So I think I shall hold it a little longer and wait

---

*Brazilian diplomat, second wife of English composer and pianist Stanley Bate (1911–59) Bate's first wife had been Peggy Glanville-Hicks.
†because of Picasso's alleged communism
‡Argentine music critic

for a quieter moment, when the delivery of mail is less likely to be delayed; I do have it for you, however, and it will be sent to you.

I was very much impressed with the high level of music reviewing and commentary in Buenos Aires. There is nothing comparable to it elsewhere in South America, or for that matter in North America outside of New York. Even here, since the death of Olin Downes and my own resignation, the profession has lost some of its brilliance. I was impressed also by the discriminating enthusiasms of the music audiences in Buenos Aires. Clearly this is no provincial music center.

With cordial greetings and happy remembrances,

Ever sincerely yours,

To James S. Pope*

September 27, 1955

Dear Mr. Pope:

Your invitation is tempting, but I swore off writing music criticism last fall and I am still on the wagon.

Many thanks all the same.

Most sincerely yours,

To William Walton†

November 8, 1955

My dear Sir William:

It was a disappointment to me that you had been obliged to return to London before it became possible for me to have a little visit with you. I do want to tell you how highly I esteem your opera *Troilus and Cressida,* which I saw in its second performance here. It is a noble work and a rich one; and I found the ending, from the beginning of the sextet through the final curtain, extraordinarily powerful both musically and dramatically.

The work will have, has already had, success in many parts of the world and I am delighted. Making English-language opera is a major aspiration of our time, and yours is a notable step.

Most sincerely yours,

---

*editor of the *Louisville Courier-Journal;* had asked Thomson to write an article
†(1902–83), British composer, best known for his symphonies and film music. The New York City Opera had just given the New York premiere of *Troilus and Cressida.*

To MARGAREDA GUEDES NOGUEIRA

November 8, 1955

Dear Maggie:

Willy Walton was here for performances of his opera in San Francisco and New York. It got good press everywhere. Some musicians, including myself, found it highly professional but not remarkably communicative. It is a successful piece and will do us all good, but I did notice at the City Center Theater that the other composers present showed no signs of worry.

Don't ruin yourself with telephone calls from Brazil, though I must say they are enormously exciting to me and impressive to any friends who happen to be around.

Love, and yours ever,

To ALICE B. TOKLAS

November 15, 1955

Dear Alice:

My South American tour is long since over; and I don't ever have to do that again, though I can if I want to. I did like Argentina and the Argentines, and I always like Caracas. Brazil is a madhouse. The other countries are just provincial countries, picturesque enough and all that. And I do like places where Spanish is the language.

Maurice is on his way home from Greece, will arrive at the end of this month. He has painted more pictures of it and will show them in spring. He also writes that he is now finished with Greece and glad of it. It will be nice having him back.

Meyer Kupferman* tells me that he has finished [Gertrude's] Faust opera. I heard a concert of his works recently and found him to be a very interesting composer, much more interesting than I had thought from hearing his little opera *In a Garden,* which had seemed to me chiefly delightful because of the text by Gertrude.

We have had no winter at all here yet, just balmy fall. I hope Paris will not be cold or that, at least, your heating arrangements will be more satisfactory than before.

I have just received a check from Columbia Records for $1.00.

---

*(b. 1926), American composer, had just finished *Dr. Faustus Lights the Lights*

This represents the author's and composer's royalties on 25 copies of *Capital Capitals* sold since their last report. One half of this princely sum belongs to you.

Love ever,

To Nicolas Nabokov

December 8, 1955

Dear Nicolas:

Juan José Castro★ has accepted the National Orchestra in Buenos Aires and returned in glory. I am very proud of my Argentines for running a major revolution with so little breakage. They are a stiff people and not jolly at all, rather like Swedes; but they are intelligent and serious-minded in a way not at all usual for Spanish Americans.

New York has been having chiefly a French season, what with the Comédie Française being an enormous success and a French clown named Marcel Marceau wowing everybody. Also Maurice Chevalier, Edith Piaf, and the Casadesus family all over the place.

Maurice is just back from Greece with another batch of pictures. Roger paints busily. Sam Barber stays mostly in Mt. Kisco and writes his opera.† Aaron refused to attend the first New York performance of his piece for chorus and orchestra, which Lenny Bernstein played with the Symphony of the Air, because he was mad at Lenny for sacrificing too much of his rehearsal time to a Mahler symphony.

Everybody, including the United States Government, is mad at the Philharmonic for playing too much Soviet music in Europe and not enough American. The Philadelphia Orchestra tour seems to have pleased everybody here. I must say that Ormandy behaved very well about playing American music. He played 10 sizeable American pieces in 22 concerts.

Poulenc writes that his opera is finished and that he finds it *très beau*.

Affection ever,

★(1895–1968), Argentine composer and conductor
†*Vanessa*, which would win Barber the Pulitzer Prize for music in 1958

To J. Douglas Brown*

January 17, 1956

Dear Mr. Brown:

It is an honor to be asked my opinion of Milton Babbitt, whose work I have long admired. I consider him an original and striking composer, as well as a musician of impressive intellectual attainments; and the already remarkable distinction of Princeton's music faculty will certainly be enhanced by his becoming a permanent member of it.

I should like to add further that, in addition to the high esteem in which I hold Mr. Babbitt as a composer and musician, I cherish for him also a warm personal regard, for he is a gentleman as well as a scholar.

Most sincerely yours,

To Alice B. Toklas

May 4, 1956

Dear Alice:

Yes the opera† was lovely very lovely. It was beautifully sung and it looked well too. Now for the first time it has been presented in a completely professional manner. And it has been accepted as a classical work just like *Four Saints*. I have not been able to secure a recording, but the success of the work was so great that I am sure recordings and other performances will be coming along within the next few years. Mother who has been here a few weeks is going back to Pittsburgh next Sunday.‡ She is ninety and in full possession of her faculties, good wit, and good manners. She has been a delight to everybody, including me. My own summer plans are still obscure. I am staying on in New York for a while. With the weather as cool as it is, there seems to be no emergency about leaving town yet.

Love ever

---

*Dean of the faculty at Princeton University, who wrote Thomson regarding tenure for Milton Babbitt (b. 1916). Over the next thirty years, Babbitt would help establish Princeton as a center for the American musical avant-garde.
†*The Mother of Us All,* at the Phoenix Theater in New York
‡Thomson's mother spent the winters in Pittsburgh, where her daughter, Ruby, lived.

To Frederick Dorian*

May 4, 1956

Dear Fritz:

The performances of *The Mother of Us All* were very lovely and very successful. I do wish you could have been here. My season is now over except for one lecture at Drake University in Des Moines and an honorary degree at Rutgers. Mother who has been visiting me for three weeks is going back to Pittsburgh Sunday. I may be passing through Pittsburgh myself on May 30. If so, I shall phone you. Do send me a little scribble saying how you are and what your summer plans are. At your good advice I studied the Tchaikovsky Sixth and Beethoven Third. To my great regret I find them both hugely boring.

So I have put the Mozart No. 33 in B-flat on my Detroit program. That delights me ever and will be a pleasure to conduct.

Affection ever,

To Lou Harrison

May 26, 1956

Dear Lou:

Thanks for the beautiful music: and I love your instructions included for building the instruments to play it on. As for the tuning fractions, I am not sure that I could carry those out, conditioned as I am by the crudities of ordinary music life.

John has finished his book about my music and it is quite wonderful.† He has analyzed every single piece and scrap with penetration and mostly with love. And he has written about it all in the most elegant language. He is producing a concert on May 30 at the Carl Fischer Hall with some of his friends.

Landscape here is finally spring but weather is still cold and bright like late winter. Last week I went to Des Moines, Louisville, and Pittsburgh. It was cold everywhere except Louisville. Northern Kentucky seems to me the only Arcadia left in America.

Though I swore last time that I would never again write music for a Shakespeare play, I am now doing two for John Houseman at the

---

*(b. 1902), American musicologist, longtime professor at Carnegie-Mellon University
†*Virgil Thomson: His Life and Music* by Kathleen O'Donnell Hoover and John Cage

Stratford Festival—*King John* and *Measure for Measure*. These will keep me here for another month. I do not mind not going away because there is no summer yet. Later I suppose I shall go somewhere. I have promised to spend August in France with Nicolas Nabokov. I have also promised to spend August in Brazil with Maurice. Maybe I shall do one or the other.

In spite of my none-too-well-tuned ear, your symphony is very beautiful as I listen to it from the page.

Affection ever,

To the KNOEDLER GALLERIES*

May 26, 1956

I have gathered from friends who have visited Alice Toklas that her objection to accompanying Gertrude Stein's pictures to New York actually is one of not wishing to appear at the gallery at any time as part of the show. She considers her long friendship with Gertrude to be a purely private matter and no part of Gertrude's life as a poet or as a picture collector. If she understood clearly that the gallery asks no service from her in the way of personal presence, she might be induced to accept the invitation. Even so, however, she would have difficulty in accepting so great a favor without being able to return it. And returning it in the form of a public appearance she would not think appropriate or becoming. Her position with regard to the pictures is that Picasso painted them and Gertrude bought them and that she herself has no right to participate in any showing of them beyond the private gesture of lending them so that the public can look at them. If you can get around this principle you will be lucky. I do not think there is much chance.

Ever sincerely yours,

To ELAINE SHAFFER

June 8, 1956

Dear Elaine:

Our Flute Concerto has had a good season. Everywhere the public reception was enthusiastic, and everywhere but New York the press was fine too. Here the press was very poor. Everybody seemed to

---

*The gallery was then planning a Picasso exhibit that would incorporate much of Stein's collection.

think it a negligible work. My theory is that none of them could listen to a quiet piece by April. Anyway, it will be played some more next year. And I am hoping that you will be able to record it sometime somewhere.

Meanwhile affection to you both and all good wishes,

To Elliott Carter

June 11, 1956

Dear Elliott:

I have received your String Quartet* and am as delighted with its pages as I have always been with its sound. Many thanks for thinking of me. If I see you before summer sets in, I hope you will write in it for me. If not, I should rather like to have back, at your convenience, the copies of *Buenos Aires Musical*.

Best and ever yours

To Maurice Grosser

Paris
August 21, 1956

D.M.

I've been always in the country chez Nicolas since I arrived, except for a weekend in Belgium fraternizing with Queen Elisabeth.† I seem to be going to Tokyo with Nicolas in 1958. I've seen through the 12-tone music and rhythmic abstraction world. It is, like the painting, *applied art,* as such very good. Jackson Pollock died the other day of a motor accident. Maybe in Sept. I'll go South for a minute and see Iris Barry.‡ Depends on Paris weather. Maggie Nogueira doesn't seem quite sure when she moves to Bordeaux. Letters very vague with Stanley [Bate] around. She must be tight *all* the time.

L.V.

---

*No. 1 (1951)
†Queen Elisabeth, an admirer of Thomson's music, had recently become a friend.
‡novelist and film critic (1895–1969), founder and director of the Museum of Modern Art Film Library

To Mary Garden

January 12, 1957

Dear Mary,

It was a delight to get your letter and to know that you may be coming over.

You will not be able to hear the new diva* since she is not singing anymore this season. I have not heard her myself; but most of the musicians for whose opinion I have respect consider her a big hoax vocally, with some ability to project roles. If she is really any good, she will be around long enough for both of us to hear and see her eventually.

Love,

To Sherry Mangan

February 6, 1957

Dear Sherry:

The "tranquil music"† was a silly idea and I knew it was; but I accepted it in return for a conducting date in New Orleans, as well as the commission fee. I have produced, apparently to Mr. Benjamin's satisfaction, the most tranquil thing in the world, which is an orchestral transcription of the Brahms Chorale Preludes. I shall conduct the premiere on March 26.

I have been in New York since the middle of November (after a California trip), but now I am starting to travel a bit. Health good, spirits good. I like the idea of a good biographical book on Artaud‡ and should like to see you undertake it. You are not so cuckoo that writing about somebody who really was would send you off.

Affection ever,

---

*Soprano Maria Callas (1923–77), who had made her Metropolitan Opera debut in October 1956
†Edward Benjamin (1897–1980), Louisiana patron of the arts, had commissioned works of "tranquil music" for the New Orleans Philharmonic Symphony.
‡Antonin Artaud (1896–1948), French poet, actor, and director who originated the concept of a "theater of cruelty"

February 23, 1957

Thanks for sending me the press.* I always want to know the worst, no matter what it is. When my notices are overly favorable, I always think there must be something wrong with me, and when they are unfavorable I am sure there is something wrong with the reviewer.

Ever yours,

To EDWARD BENJAMIN

[Caracas, Venezuela]
[Summer, 1957]

Dear Mr. Benjamin,

I was pleased with the orchestra's performances the other evening. I was also pleased with the sound of the Brahms preludes. Whether they are restful or tranquil is for others to know. Myself, I resist verbalizing a musical act. All the same, your idea is a good one. Music has long been used to activate the legs (as in dancing), to elevate the spirit (as in church), and to produce (in the theater and elsewhere) dreams of love. Eventually it might come to cure a cold or allay a fever. Certainly your present use of it to repose the nervous system is salutary and may carry far.

All the uses of music are beneficent. It is not a poison, though professionals, when subjected to it involuntarily, can experience a definite irritation. A certain irritability, as a matter of fact, seems to be the one thing that characterizes the musical temperament. And it is exactly in the presence of music (as at rehearsals, for instance) that musicians throw their biggest tantrums.

I suppose we can't ever listen passively, as the layman can. Consequently, we seek elsewhere than in music the restful function and the tranquil state. But if our music comes to do for others what it cannot do for us, naturally we are pleased. We can even try to achieve the effects you describe, unaccustomed as we are to writing with the listener's private needs in mind.

So here is my answer to your question. Yes, the composers will try to fulfill your requests. They will be self-conscious about it, but they will work sincerely to produce for your need. Some may even

---

*after an appearance with the Detroit Symphony Orchestra

succeed. After all, the "Goldberg" Variations were composed to cure an insomnia. And surely Bach did not intend to bore his patron into sleep, but rather to tranquilize him so that sleep could come in its own time.

Very sincerely yours,

To a Correspondent

September 6, 1957

I shall be delighted to write "kind words" about you to your manager, if he feels the need of my opinion. I should not like, however, for him to use any such statement as publicity material.

During all the years that I worked on the press I made it a rule not to write publicity except insofar as quotations from articles already printed might be useful to musicians and their managers. By declining on all occasions to write material especially destined for advertising I managed to refuse courteously any such service to artists about whose work I held grave reservations. I am sorry that this rule, which I still follow, prevents me from writing nowadays about artists I admire.

I shall be glad to reply to your manager in the same terms in which I spoke to you about your work, but please do not ask me to write anything destined for commercial use.

With best wishes and my greetings,

Ever sincerely yours,

To Maurice Grosser

Paris
June 15 [1958]

D.M.:

The car works wonderfully and Wendell* has now learned the non-automatic gear-shifting and I am learning the one-way streets and I have had all the chairs re-upholstered and I've seen practically everybody and I wrote a preface for the Hoover-Cage book and in general I've done everything but buy the flat. I gather from the femme de ménage that Bélard wants to sell and Mme Ovize does not

---

*Wendell Dorne, Thomson's cook and valet at the time

or at least that she is holding out for higher prices. In any case, they are at war about that and about everything else, so I just wait till he tells me what's to be done. I gather Portugal did not greatly amuse you or impress. I doubt also whether Tangier will. If you end up in Spain I should be inclined to visit you in August, but don't go to a country you don't like just on my account. It might also be pleasant to take a little house in the Dordogne, which is cheap, and with Wendell and two cars keep house a bit. It is a region not much painted. As for your idea that painting is not general culture, you may be able to get away with it in America, but here it is exactly that. Here literature is basic education, painting is real culture, and music a special sensitivity of certain people, who are none the nobler for having it either. This way too: reading is for enjoyment, but literature is to be understood; painting can be enjoyed, buying it is a compulsion (& maybe not a bad idea); listening to music is a compulsion but supporting it is a folly and learning it is painful for all concerned.

yours

To Lou Harrison

November 21, 1958

Dear Lou,

I miss you vastly and was very happy to have your card. I am on a film now (for United Nations)—all chunky and fugal. I don't seem to be going to California this winter. But I shall be going to Europe in May. Please send text of your political primer (in English).★ John [Cage] is in Milan for the winter, making tape-music. He upset everybody (and impressed them no end) in Darmstadt. The book about my music will be out, I'm told, in January. I see Ben [Weber] some. He has reduced by 45 pounds and still going. I've lost 12.

Having wonderful time wish you were here.

L.V.

★Harrison was devoted to Esperanto, the would-be "global language."

February 2, 1959

Dear Alice:

Elizabeth Bishop★ wrote me that she had written to you and that she would be very glad to see you in Brazil. She did insist that Rio is awfully hot in January and February, but that Petropolis, where she lives, is much cooler, being in the high mountains. I do hope it has not been too awfully cold in Paris. The winter here has been fairly severe. I don't notice the cold much in New York.

I have been cooking with great delight out of your cookbook. The green mashed potatoes, and the fresh fruit mashed up in a blender, are pretty successful. I may have to give up the green mashed potatoes soon, because I suspect that they are about to become familiar in New York.

After I finished my film, I went to New Orleans for Christmas week. Since that time, I have been making a suite out of the music and doing other jobs. Now I shall begin travelling again. I am speaking at Wellesley in a few weeks. Also in Kansas City, on the same program with Harry Truman. The Missouri Music National Association had the idea of inviting two Kansas City musicians to participate. Somewhat later, I shall be going to Vermont, Maryland, Michigan, and maybe California. I hope to California, because I never like to allow a season to go by without spending a few days in San Francisco.

I shall arrive in Paris toward the end of May. There have been invitations to lecture at Oxford, which I should very much enjoy doing; but the correspondence is so steadily irresponsible that I'm not quite sure whether they mean it.

Love ever,

To a Reader†

February 28, 1959

Your charming letter to *The Atlantic* seems to me more a cry of pain than an argument. Actually, it assumes that I accept the very conclusion my article was written to refute: namely, that when an evolution is complete, the subject of it may as well be abandoned.

★(1911–79), American poet
†who had written to the *Atlantic Monthly* in response to Thomson's article "Music's Tradition of Constant Change" (February 1959)

Believe me, I do not hold that; and I don't think I said it. I don't think, either, that I said anything to justify the idea that music is "doomed," or that all the tunes have been written.

I did say that "our musical *language* is complete," like an atomic table that has been filled up. This statement is not a matter of opinion; it is a judgment about the facts of music history. It may be wrong, but it can only be disputed on technical and factual grounds. An emotional view of its implications will not invalidate it.

Those implications are not nearly so grave in my view as in yours. I can face music's continuity after Beethoven and Debussy as easily as Milton faced English poetry after Shakespeare. Once a language is complete, as grammar and vocabulary, it does not change much; but its expressive possibilities remain. This is why Bartók and Sibelius and Brahms and Tchaikovsky could write music that is intensely expressive without embodying either technical innovation, like Chopin and Berlioz, or compactness of structure, like Beethoven and Haydn and Mozart.

By Debussy's "verbal-musical amalgams," I mean the extreme sensitivity of his words-and-music union, as in *Pelléas* for instance.

One-hundred-percent dissonance in the organ music of Bach was not produced entirely by contrapuntal textures. A large part of it came in performance, and still does, from the use of mixture stops, which produce, in the upper octaves, a full major chord for each fundamental tone. A simple chord of the diminished seventh—say C, E-flat, F-sharp, and A—will therefore give out also E natural, G natural, B-flat, A-sharp, and C-sharp. Here we have seventy-five percent of the possible maximum of twelve tones; and a cruciform church with stone interior can be depended on, through its own reverberation characteristics, which include complex echoes and sound survivals several minutes long, to produce all the rest, along with some not in the tuned scale—an effect of maximum dissonance utterly dazzling.

As for Soviet Russia, I do not find there much "musical ferment," though there is, of course, massive distribution for officially acceptable works.

Naturally, when you make complimentary reference to my own music, I do not feel the need of defending a contrary position.

Most cordially yours,

To Nicolas Nabokov

New York
March 3, 1959

Dear Nicolas:

There isn't anything at all that one can do to influence the Pulitzer committee, since their names are not announced. I shall speak a little about the matter with Douglas Moore, however, just on the chance that he might be disposed toward rewarding an opera.* (Whether he is on the committee or not, he is a little bit on the inside, since the Pulitzer Award is given [by] Columbia University.)

Do send me plenty of postcards from Japan.

Affection ever,

To Maurice Grosser

Paris
Monday, September 7 [1959?]

D.M.

I now have a crystal chandelier and a rug with lots of pink and white in it. That does the trick. Now the flat is bright & warm & quite grand. After lots of reading the Kenneth Koch† libretto, I find it on the whole silly and terribly monotonous and I don't think I want to use it. I'll break that to him in N.Y. The papers announce the [Paul] Bowles opera with Libby Holman‡ for fall production. I don't go out much. I enjoy staying home evenings in the flat. I go to Venice Sept. 16–19 for a meeting, trip paid. I keep thinking of spending a winter in Paris, maybe next after this one. It would be nice if you were around too. And if you had a car we could go places.

love——

---

*The Holy Devil, Nabokov's opera about Rasputin, had received its world premiere in Louisville in April, 1958.
†(b. 1925), American poet, now professor at Columbia University, had written a libretto called Angelica, part of which was later published in A Change of Hearts (1973)
‡(1905–71), American singer and actress, a friend of the Bowleses, who were frequent guests at her home in Connecticut. The opera Yerma was based on a play by García Lorca.

To Maurice Grosser

New York
July 10, 1961

D.M.

Alice T. has broken her knee (spent all night on the floor) and is in a cast, bored stiff and (says Jo Barry)* cross as a bear. She asks where you are, which means she would like to hear from you. She has bad eyes and can't read or write much, but Barry seems to be around & serviceable. He wrote to me at her dictation.

I've orchestrated *A Solemn Music* for N. Boulanger to conduct. And written 4 or 5 mag articles because I needed some money. I've lost about 17 pounds. Feel marvelous. Weather heavenly.

Embrace all

love
V.T.

To Maurice Grosser

November 9, 1961

D.M.

I have no Wendell [Dorne] but I have a full-time secretary, a young composer who takes dictation, types, and copies music. He is 23, six feet tall, with a wife about four feet tall, and thoroughly nice. He is organizing my papers so I can eventually get at the book of memoirs I signed with Knopf to write in three years. For Nadia I orchestrated the *Solemn Music* and she will play it at Philharmonic. Lenny played *The Seine* beautifully. Another time at the Philharmonic I made a speech about French music. And still another time my Blake songs were sung at Town Hall with a good baritone & orchestra & wowed all the young downtown group. So you see I am doing all right. Orchestrating my Whitman piece about Brooklyn Ferry. And in December the Town Hall gives me a concert for my being 65 and a medal and all that. It is on Dec. 18 and I am sort of hoping you will be back by then. Ruby visited in Missouri & loved it. Alice T. broke her arm, is better now. I am dining at the White House next Monday. All for the governor of Puerto Rico & Mr. Casals plays cello & lots of composers are invited. Then I go to

---

*Joseph Barry (b. 1917), author and journalist close to Stein and Toklas. He was labeled "Jo the Loiterer" in the *Mother* libretto because of an arrest during his student days.

Boston, because King's Chapel has an anniversary (275th, I think), and I conduct my percussion Mass, also record it, and dine with Mrs. Foote. Theodate got married to her young man, the dentist twenty years younger who loves her, and they will live at the Dakota with your eggs.*

LKV

To a CORRESPONDENT†

November 28, 1961

My dear Patricia,

I am complimented that you should want me to write a school song. I am afraid that I should not know how to begin without words, and I am not a writer of verse.

Also, the best school songs have nearly always come into existence by the choice of some old and beautiful melody to which words about the given school have then been added.

Most cordially yours,

To ROBERT L. SNYDER‡

December 14, 1961

Dear Mr. Snyder:

As you know, I worked with Pare Lorentz on his first two films, *The Plough* and *The River*. In both cases, if my memory is correct, Thomas Chalmers§ recorded the spoken text. I had nothing to do with this and did not see Chalmers in connection with either film, except possibly at some social meeting with Lorentz. I saw a great deal of Chalmers later in 1937 in connection with a theatrical production of Shakespeare's *Antony and Cleopatra*.

If in my preliminary discussion with Lorentz of music for these films any pecking was done at a piano, I did it. I never saw Pare touch the instrument. Pare did have an extreme sensitivity to the expressive powers and dramatic uses of music. We did discuss, at

*a painting of eggs by Grosser
†a student at St. Joseph's College in North Windham, Maine
‡then an assistant professor of radio and television at Kansas State University, preparing a dissertation on Pare Lorentz
§(1884–1966), American actor, singer, director, and writer

length and often, the melodic material and kinds of material that we both thought proper to use with the films. In both cases I did some research. For *The Plough* I looked up all the cowboy and Western settler music available through books. For *The River* I made an investigation of old Southern hymns, the kind known as "white spirituals," through books not available in all libraries.

I played to Pare on the piano all the material that I planned to use and got his acceptance of it before composing with it.

After Pare had cut his film, I composed my musical sections in accordance with his timing and played them for him on the piano in front of a projection of the film. After acceptance by him in this form, I orchestrated the complete music and it was recorded, in both cases, at a sound studio in Astoria, Long Island, by an orchestra consisting of some 32 or 33 members of the New York Philharmonic, conducted by Alexander Smallens.

At this point arrived the event which Pare had been working toward and waiting for all the time. He likes to cut his film to an existing musical background. But since a background cannot be composed, orchestrated, and recorded (that is, a background specifically designed for a given film) until the film has been cut and the lengths of the shots and sequences fixed, Pare has to go through a cutting for the visual narrative, but his heart is not fully in it. When he gets the final recorded music track, then he goes back to the cutting room, finds inspiration for expressive visual narration through the musical detail, and wholly recuts his film. At least, that is what he did on *The Plough* and *The River*.

In the case of *The River,* the original version, still available through the Museum of Modern Art Film Library in New York, is in four reels and lasts 36 minutes. Several years after the launching of this version, Pare cut the picture down to three reels, lasting 27 minutes, in order to render it available for use in schools, where the half-hour limit on film showing is practically universal. In recutting his film for this purpose, he was naturally obliged to re-cut the music track. This he did without consulting me, and he did it very well. Nevertheless, the three-reel version is not as advantageous musically, in my opinion, as the original one. I suggest strongly that you take a look at the original before forming firm judgments about the musical contributions of the other.

That should do for now. If you want to know more, ask me specific questions. And good luck with your dissertation. Pare's films are unique, powerful, and very important.

Very sincerely yours,

To Ruby Gleason

December 23 [1961]

D.R.

The [Town Hall] concert was very grand and I got academic medals from N.Y. University and a scroll from the Mayor and telegrams from Gov. Rockefeller and Pres. Kennedy and about 100 others and they were all stolen three days later along with my hat and my new Paris overcoat from a box in Carnegie Hall. Coat insured, medals and scrolls can be replaced, I think—not the letter and wires. Unless they get sent back by mail. Certainly my name and address were on them all. Dinner tomorrow for Maurice and the Garrett Mattinglys. Sent in. Soup, ham with cherries, mince pie. Christmas night I dine with Chinese food (a Russian composer with Chinese wife).* On Sat. I have a party. On Sun. Dec. 31 I go to Los Angeles.

love and Merry Christmas

To President John F. Kennedy

December 27, 1961

Your Excellency:

Your telegram sent to my recent Town Hall birthday concert was impressive to all present and deeply touching to me. In thanking you for your very great attention may I also wish to you and yours as joyful a New Year as is possible in view of your father's health.

May blessings follow you always.

Most respectfully yours,

To Flowers of the Week

March 12, 1962

Gentlemen:

I find that receiving flowers on Friday afternoon serves no practical purpose in my life. Consequently, I accept your offer to refund

---

*Alexander Tcherepnin (1899–1977) and his wife, Ming

the advance on the remaining portions of my $16 subscription. $12 will be therefore the sum that you owe me.

Very truly yours,

To a CORRESPONDENT*

March 12, 1962

If you wish to send along your libretto, with postage for its return, I shall be pleased to read it. I must warn you at the same time that I am at this moment highly resistant to biblical subjects.

Most sincerely yours,

To a CORRESPONDENT†

March 26, 1962

I suppose that the reasons why artists have for so long frequented the Chelsea Hotel begin with the fact that the hotel is both cheap and reasonably well run. There are apartments with kitchens to be had by the month or by the year. The rooms are large, the ceilings high, the walls thick. Everywhere there is a Victorian spaciousness that is most agreeable, as indeed are also the colored bellmen who run our errands.

As for "keeping itself to itself," old residents here tend to bow in the elevator, but they do not impose on one another.

It is also interesting, and part of the charm of this building, which was opened in 1884, that the iron balconies on the outside of it and the bronze and mahogany staircase on the inside are museum pieces —the latter from the William Morris studio in England.

My own apartment has woodwork of that time, very beautiful painted tiles in the bathroom and around the fireplaces, also brass hinges and doorknobs extraordinarily handsome.

Most sincerely yours,

---

*a would-be librettist
†who had asked Thomson why the Chelsea Hotel was popular with people in the arts

To Eugene Ormandy

March 30, 1962

Dear Gene,

Schirmer is sending you today or Monday my *Solemn Music* with Fugue to follow.

I did not send you the recording of the *Solemn Music* because I did not like the sound of it. It does not resemble very closely what took place in the hall.

I am very grateful to you for being firm with Mr. Benjamin. I had already written him that he really should not give you instructions on how to play my pieces, since that kind of thing takes place better in the purely professional communications between the composer and the conductor. I read in *The New York Times* that you were going to do a little more resting than is your custom, and I am very glad. A quiet summer in the country will do you and Gretel far more good, I am sure, than all the "restful" music in the world.

I do hope you can manage to achieve your usual success on the orchestra's tour without your usual overstrain.

Very very very much love to you both,

To William Schuman*

May 3, 1962

Dear Bill:

Here is the piece.

I have marked the registration in terms of the new organ, specifications for which I had from an organist friend.

A small voice, say one vote, in the choice of organist would be appreciated by yours truly, since the piece is a little special and requires rhythm (a musical element not cultivated by all organ virtuosos).

I hope you like it. I do.

I tried it out on a largish instrument and it does make a jolly row.

Yours in affection ever,

---

*(b. 1910), American composer and music administrator, then president of Lincoln Center. Thomson had been commissioned to provide a commemorative organ piece for the opening of Philharmonic Hall; it was entitled *Pange Lingua*.

To Mary Hazard*

May 23, 1962

Dear Mary,

The Spanish things and places I like most are the Prado itself and the Goya church in Madrid (San Antonio de la Florida); the cities of Old Castille (especially the University at Salamanca and the museum in Valladolid); Avila itself, which my *Four Saints* is largely about; Compostela, unique for Romanesque sculpture; the Gaudí church and houses in Barcelona; Montserrat nearby and its pictures, which one must ask to see; the irrigation and the tree planting in Andalusia; beautiful Cádiz (which seems to be where Jonah was going when the whale swallowed him and brought him back); the sherry wine manufactories in Jerez (also the Portuguese wine making in Oporto); the shellfish at a Madrid restaurant named Korynto, near the Plaza de Callao; and in general the lightness, dryness, and openness of all the Spanish landscape, like our own Southwest. This landscape is best enjoyed, I find, in the hot weather and by car. The roads are good and traffic not crowded. I do not care for the Costa Brava or the beach life around Málaga and Torremolinos. The corniche drive from San Sebastian west is pretty spectacular. So is the mountain road from Córdoba to Málaga and the chasm-straddling city of Ronda. All this and more, which you no doubt know already.

Affection ever,

To Maurice Grosser

Santa Fe
August 6 [1962]

D.M.

Still loving it. Swimming pools and wild orange jam and heat without heaviness and a sign in the desert says "Opera traffic use left lane." Sauguet spent 5 days, all the West a marvel for him. Went to Indian dances & Albuquerque & all the museums of matters indigenous. Am tanning nicely. Am writing every day—articles and things I had promised. A good place for work. Shall go to Los Angeles on Aug. 17 for seeing *4 Saints* done by carefully selected high-school students. L.A. region hopeless for being alone and no car or

---

*Mrs. Leland Hazard, a family friend from childhood

driver. I might come back here. A. Toklas at Italian baths then going to the inn near Paris as once before, a country *maison de rendezvous* with good food. [Nicolas] Nabokov had a heart attack, is better, resting, going to Brazil next week all the same. You seem not to be liking painting Greece anymore. Why don't you try Israel and hit the jackpot? All those sacred sites!

Love,
V——

To a CORRESPONDENT*

October 12, 1962

My dear Neil,

If you want to find out about my life and works, you must go to a reasonably good library and look up my name in the catalogue. Then you must ask for all books listed in that catalogue as containing material about me. Next you must examine that material until you find the information that you need for your report.

I am not sending you this information myself, simply because I do not think it right that I should do your schoolwork for you. If you have specific questions that you cannot find answers for in the books you consult, I shall be glad to answer them. But they must be very precise questions that can be answered briefly and factually.

Good luck to you.

Most sincerely yours,

To a CORRESPONDENT†

October 12, 1962

When I heard you sing last year at Mr. Gruen's‡ house I was not at all displeased with your work. I do not feel inclined, however, to recommend you unreservedly for concert appearance. It was my strong impression at that time that you would appear to more advantage in operetta than in recital.

---

*a young boy working on a school report about Thomson
†a young singer who requested Thomson's endorsement
‡John Gruen (b. 1927), critic, composer, memoirist, and biographer of Gian Carlo Menotti and Leonard Bernstein

Since you have asked me frankly, I have answered in the same manner.

With the best good wishes for a successful career,

Most sincerely yours,

To a CORRESPONDENT*

October 15, 1962

One has eaten memorable dishes, quite several of them. I remember vividly at Bourg-en-Bresse in 1938 an ice made of wild strawberries.

The recipe for this is simple. All you need is to catch the wild strawberries, plenty of them and preferably the French kind, highly fragrant. Then you simply mash them, put them through a colander to remove the seeds, add a little sugar, and a small amount of lemon juice to underline the flavor, and freeze in an apparatus that has a dasher (an old-fashioned ice-cream freezer is always best). No water or milk is used.

This is also the correct way to make an ice out of any strawberries or raspberries.

Yours and best ever,

To BORIS I. BARONOVIC†

October 24, 1962

Dear Mr. Baronovic:

If it is decided to perform *The Mother of Us All*, your designing problems will be far simpler than for *Four Saints in Three Acts*. *The Mother* can be done very well on a stage without proscenium and with little scenery. It needs rather elaborate costumes, derived from different decades of the nineteenth century (running from John Adams, who is 1830, to Lillian Russell, who is pure 1900). The scenery and props will benefit by being very simple. I like to individualize the characters through their costumes and leave the backgrounds against which they move almost abstract, as if they were images out of an album of ancestral photographs. You will find

---

*a friend who asked Thomson to describe his most memorable meal
†(b. 1927), theatrical designer and instructor at University of Buffalo, later at American University

explanations in the piano-and-vocal score that will help you to design the backgrounds. *Four Saints in Three Acts* requires stylized movement, stylized costumes, and ornamental backgrounds suggested by Catholic altar decoration. These may be as tinsely as you wish (and under no circumstances Gothic), for they need to be constantly present as excitement to the eye. The costumes, on the other hand, since we are dealing with members of religious orders, are not individualized very much, though they may be sumptuous in effect and bright in color.

When the opera has been chosen, I suggest that you make some acquaintance with the musical score and read the introduction. After that it will be necessary to have a conference with the musical and stage directors. I could not possibly at this time suggest the materials that you may be using. If *The Mother of Us All* is to be given, you may find it advantageous to hire period costumes from some establishment such as Brooks or Eaves in New York.

I do not know what date is being envisaged for an opera performance. Certainly I shall be ready at all times to help you and your colleagues with such experience as I have in dealing with both of these works.

Most sincerely yours,

To Gertrude Mattingly*

October 30, 1962

Dear Gertrude:

My New York summer disappeared when in early July I went to Aspen, Colorado and then Santa Fe and then Los Angeles and did not come back till the middle of September. When I telephoned you there was no answer and so I presumed that you had already gone to England. The fall has been warm here and most agreeable. Now I am going for two weeks to Brussels and Paris, where I imagine all will be cold and wet. I am going chiefly to look into Alice Toklas, who is 86 and none too well, though the mind sparkles and she has just written a book of memoirs.

Beginning February 1 I shall be for four months at the University of Buffalo as composer-in-residence with no teaching duties. I shall be back and forth to New York, of course; but I am supposed to be more or less in residence there. They seem to have found for me

---

*Garrett (Matt) Mattingly and his wife, Gertrude, were then in residence at Oxford, where he taught history.

already a nice flat in the same building with what they say is the best restaurant.

Yesterday's *New York Times* carried the information that Matt's successor in Oxford is to be your neighbor Trilling.*

I do hope that Matt is well enough to enjoy Oxford. I envy your being there. Its beauty can be almost unbearable, at any rate quite unbelievable.

My love to you both,

To RUTH FORD†

November 1, 1962

Dear Ruth,

November 29 is perfect and so is 9:30. I am going off to Paris today, returning on the weekend of November 17. That is a little late for cooperation on the invitation list, and I am afraid there is no time to do it now. My friends are your friends, after all, and vice versa. We can confer that last week about insults and omissions. Just go ahead and ask whomever you like. I would suggest, if you don't mind, Edward Albee, who is an old friend and, being particularly stylish just now,‡ adds brilliance to an evening.

Kisses and looking forward to more.

To GERALDINE OBLETZ§

November 28, 1962

Dear Miss Obletz:

The change of the first lecture to February 14 would seem to have been made without any consultation of either Mr. Charles Rosen, who is going to play the piano, or myself. He tells me that he can manage; so can I, by taking the midnight train from New York, since I am obliged to be here on the 13th. I have no idea why the

---

*Lionel Trilling (1905–75), American critic and essayist, long associated with Columbia University
†(b. 1920), American actress, wife of the actor Zachary Scott and prominent in New York intellectual circles
‡*Who's Afraid of Virginia Woolf?* had opened on Broadway on October 13.
§secretary of the University of Buffalo music department

313

change was made, but I presume it must have been for somebody's convenience.

Most sincerely yours,

To the NATIONAL SOCIAL DIRECTORY

January 17, 1963

Gentlemen:

For many months you have been billing me regularly for a book which I have never ordered and never received. This morning I find in my mail a package which is probably that book. I have still never ordered it. I am spending a five-cent stamp to request that you cease billing me. Further than that I am not inclined to continue the correspondence.

Most sincerely yours,

To the MARQUISE DE CASA FUERTE*

[Buffalo, N.Y.]
February 11, 1963

Dear Yvonne,

We are all very much shaken by Poulenc's death. A grand memorial is being prepared for April at the time when Schippers† will conduct his *Tenebrae* service in four concerts with the Philharmonic. There will also be a concert in Philharmonic Hall where Benny Goodman‡ and Leonard Bernstein will play the new Clarinet and Piano Sonata. Gold and Fizdale will also play things, and Jennie Tourel will sing things. Robert Shaw,§ conducting the Mass that same evening in Cleveland, will be piped into the hall by radio. There will also be a New York chorus singing something else and even, probably, Artur Rubinstein playing things too. It will all be very very impressive. Doda Conrad‖ is organizing the program.

I am in Buffalo now but have come to New York for rehearsals

---

*French violinist, née Yvonne Giraud, married to a Spanish grandee. A friend of Poulenc's and of Thomson's, she was the subject of a 1940 musical portrait.
†Thomas Schippers (1930–77), American conductor
‡(1909–86), American clarinetist and popular band leader
§(b. 1916), American conductor and choral director
‖(b. 1905), French bass of Polish birth, a close friend of Poulenc's

and the concert that includes my opera *The Mother of Us All*. I shall be back and forth from time to time but on principle I am in residence there. The weather is very cold, but I like the town and the people.

I am invited to speak and conduct in Berlin from May 18 to 25. After that I shall come to Paris, maybe briefly, maybe for longer. Meanwhile I shall send you programs of my Buffalo manifestations, of which there are a good many.

Love ever,

To Leopold Stokowski

February 11, 1963

Dear Mr. Stokowski:

Being seated at the Baltimore concert in the manager's box, which is under a balcony, I could not be sure that I was hearing the balances right. The whole piece,* moreover, sounded to me to lack volume. It also sounded to me a little slow, as if you had observed punctiliously my metronome markings, which are themselves a little on the slow side.

Having finally acquired a tape of the previous night's performance, which was broadcast, I have checked the whole thing against the score.

The balances and volumes, so far as I can judge these from a tape, seem perfect to me. The tempos, on the other hand, seem to me almost everywhere a bit slow. This is my fault, because I seem to have preserved in the concert suite tempos that were designed for film accompaniment. I find that the whole suite, as a concert piece, needs to move forward with more ease and urgency than my marked tempos allow. Consequently, should you again have occasion to play the work, I suggest that you prevent it from becoming viscous or static by simply letting it move forward constantly. The jungle section is the only one which does not absolutely require such movement, and even that one will permit some lubrication through tempo, if your own instinct seems to indicate that.

I enclose the notes exactly as I wrote them down on listening to the tape.

I am ever so grateful to you for having played the work and thus allowed me to hear it at leisure. Having never heard it before except

---

*the suite from *Louisiana Story*

when conducting it myself, I had not realized that I had underestimated everywhere the speeds required.

Thankfully and ever sincerely yours,

To Mary Priscilla Rea*

February 11, 1963

My very dear dear Mary Pris,

After discussing with Carol Truax† your late supper problem, we both decided that an easy and elegant thing to have would be quiche Lorraine. If you have a good bakery caterer who can make them for you, they can be reheated in the oven and served either alone or with a mixed green salad. Supplementary foods not requiring utensils would be bowls of apples and plates of chocolate cookies. For a dead-of-winter supper I suggest also offering coffee as well as booze.

If quiche Lorraine turns out to be impractical, a very good winter dish is Boston baked beans with hot brown bread and slices of ham.

As another alternative, one could have ham (hot or cold) with hot macaroni and cheese.

I don't think that a wholly cold supper would be as nice as one that has at least one dish hot.

My love to you,

To a Correspondent‡

March 15, 1963

My Paris flat consists of one large room with high ceiling, supplemented by an entrance hall, a modern kitchen, and a bath–dressing room with closets and drawers. The living room has two couches that serve as single beds. The locale is a little small for two persons who may both be there most of the time. If one goes out a good deal, the other can work more peacefully. For two persons working at desks or typewriters, one of them often finds it more convenient to work at a table in the kitchen, which is well lighted and perfectly comfortable. The place has lovely eighteenth-century proportions

---

*daughter of Esther Goodrich, a childhood friend from Kansas City
†(b. 1900–86), author of several cookbooks, wife of Gustav Reese
‡a would-be sublettor of Thomson's Paris flat

and is furnished with good pieces. There are also dishes, glasses, linens, and silver. There is a large electric icebox and a vacuum cleaner. The place is quite easy to keep.

The price is $150 a month. In addition, the people who live there pay their own gas, light, and telephone bills. The heating is electric, and that comes also on the light bill. I am not at all sure that the two of you would be happy there, though Leo Gershoy (historian from New York University) and his wife were very happy there. Also, I like to rent it for the full winter, which makes the cost higher for you, since you are not to be there till January. If you wanted to take it from the first of October, and if I find anyone wishing to use it for the first three months, that would be more satisfactory to you. While you think over the information that I have given you here, I shall look around for a fall occupant. I shall be there myself during June.

Very sincerely yours,

To Maurice Grosser

July 2, 1963

D.M.

It is very hot & I feel terrible. Nothing wrong, however. I week-ended chez Gruens and cooked dinner for 12—roast chicken tarragon, onions with zucchini, à la Wendell, & fresh things like garden lettuce & red strawberries. I put tarragon under the skin & roasted the chickens with no butter & no basting. It was wonderful. Chicken fat & jelly ooze out and make pan gravy. Try it. Medium oven, around 325–350. Just tie up the feet, salt & pepper a little, put bird upright in dry pan, & never touch. A sizeable one takes about an hour & a quarter. I am sorry about your father. Had a letter from you in London. And some shows. Also the museums. Here terribly hot & I feel terrible, as I said before.

LV

To ROY ANDERSON*

September 25, 1963

Dear Mr. Anderson:

Thank you for the two reviews and for your general esteem of my talents. Your reaction of distaste for my *Pange Lingua* is one I have encountered before among church musicians, though it is by no means universal. You are wrong, of course, to imagine any parallel between my fees and my music. I was quite well paid for this organ piece, actually more than I have ever received for a film, when you take into account its playing time and its scoring for a solo instrument (no orchestration involved).

Does your lack of enthusiasm for Baroque organs extend also to the Baroque musical forms? My *Pange Lingua* is a chorale with variations and fugue.

Anyway, you don't have to like the piece, as you know. And you did, after all, get up some quite warm indignation about it. Your heat alone should tempt organists to look into the work.

Most cordially yours,

To MAURICE GROSSER

Yaddo (Saratoga Springs, New York)
June 8, 1964

D.M.

Here I like it. I work all right and there is comfort. I have a large parlor, bedroom, and bath in the main house (post-Richardsonian circa 1890). The food is lovely, American at its best. The estate is large, with tennis, swimming pool, rose garden, woods, & lakes. Also mosquitoes. Weather has been cold. The other guests not very interesting (which is just fine). The town real tacky. Hundreds of dim boarding houses and fifth-class hotels, large bath establishments, no nice stores, everything for hicks. Nearby at Glens Falls is a famous museum that I am going to see today. Yesterday there was a country circus with mangy lions, some elephants, and a hippo. There is night sulky racing. The big-purse jockey races come in August. Your letter of June 4 came today. It would be nice doing

---

*then editor of the *Choral and Organ Guide*

318

Madrid together again. First I must write the harp piece. I told you Marrakesh makes pink pictures. Have been reading lots of Max Jacob.* It gets more & more wonderful.

love,
V.T.

To a Correspondent†

June 9, 1964

I know nothing about W. C. Williams and painting. His desire to hear his own lines sung, universal among poets, brought him to me with the G. Washington play. I took it he had been encouraged by my opera (text by Gertrude Stein) *Four Saints in Three Acts.* I declined the collaboration not at all on poetic grounds but because I found his work short on stage instinct. (Most modern poets lack a *sens du théâtre.*)

As for Pound,‡ I imagine he came naturally through Provençal poetry to wonder whether the modern poetry-and-music divorce was permanent. His opera on Villon's *Testament* essayed reconciliation. Antheil may have helped him some, though neither ever told me that he had. Antheil was the literary man's ideal of a composer. Pound must have known him through Sylvia Beach. *[Antheil and the] Treatise on Harmony* is not very deep. The opera, on the other hand, is verbally sensitive and melodically not stupid. Pound did lack, of course, musical preparation.

Williams's idea (or anybody else's) that the "natural" material of music is noise shows ignorance of acoustical phenomena. The "natural" material of music, the most ancient and the most universal, is the overtone series sounded selectively—together, in sequence, or both ways. It is exactly this material, which is "pure," being based on one fundamental, that distinguishes music from noise, which is "impure," since it consists of interfering overtones based on more than one fundamental.

I never trusted Williams's musical instincts or his theorizings about aesthetics. He was a poet, not a philosopher. Not even a very dependable critic. He was warm of heart and a very gifted writer

---

*(1876–1944), mystic poet and painter, close to Thomson during the latter's years in Paris
†who had asked Thomson about the American poet William Carlos Williams (1883–1963)
‡American poet Ezra Pound, "past master at launching careers," was, according to Thomson, responsible for launching George Antheil in Paris.

(maybe an almost "great" one), but he was not in the Ph.D. sense (no slap intended) an intellectual.

Most cordially yours,

To Jan Popper*

December 18, 1964

Dear Dr. Popper:

If the opera situation is worrying, Course 20-D worries me even more.

Your letter of June 19 described it as "dealing particularly with the simple analysis of contemporary music." Now it is "primarily an intelligent listening course" and "will include Romantic and Impressionistic music for approximately two-thirds of the semester."

Obviously such a course is needed for filling up gaps in the musical experience of future music majors, but I seriously doubt my ability to direct it properly. It involves material I have never taught, nor even studied with pedagogy in mind. Teaching appreciation requires experience that I do not have and that I should be reluctant to acquire at the expense of thirty students, however "interested and stimulating."

I should have accepted, all the same, to improvise such a course with the aid of my assistant had not the *Mother* project also received alteration.

Financed by Extension and Drama as well as Music, aided by Houseman, with myself in some control of the visual presentation, and with the possibility not denied of professional voices for the major roles, this project seemed to justify to both you and me that I join your department for the semester.

In its present state, you do not need my help. Your department surely does not need me to give a "listening course." And I should be embarrassed to be on campus a whole semester with nothing more to do than to talk about my own music and to cooperate on an abridged concert version of my *Four Saints*.

I realize that my presence at casting and rehearsals might be helpful, but what bothers me is that it is not essential. And the projected concert involving *Four Saints* remains a bit uncertain in my mind,

---

*(b. 1907), then the chairman of the U.C.L.A. music department

320

since the work is more difficult to prepare than one might imagine and certainly, with seven soloists, more expensive.

What can we do about any of these problems? I am feeling thoroughly discouraged. And for your sake it must be decided right away whether my coming to U.C.L.A. at all is justified.

Ever sincerely yours,

To Joanne W. Peyton*

January 13, 1965

Dear Mrs. Peyton:

I have no lecture in my repertory that would even faintly pass for being about Beethoven, but there is a brilliant one called "Stravinsky's Operas."† Could you possibly use that?

My guess is that we call off the whole thing—that is to say, the idea of my appearing at all in your Beethoven series.

Ever sincerely yours,

To Maurice Grosser

Los Angeles
May 15, 1965

D.M.:

The Mother here a remarkably good show—especially the scenery, which I shall have photos of. Anne and Chris were Negroes. SBA a fine voice. Jo a young Filipino. Orch. excellent.

The libretto about Byron‡ gets extended and finished and will be good. And I think I've solved the problem of Byron's death. He had to die before 40 (like Harry Dunham) and it was the only way of being successful in politics. His other messes all came from having to humanize himself. As a lord, a millionaire, a genius, and a beauty, life would have been impossible without constant misbehavior, cutting himself down to size so he could work. And the Italian contessa's family was politically active (against papal states and with

---

*Program coordinator, Letters and Science Extension, University of California, Berkeley.
†Thomson eventually delivered his Stravinsky lecture, calling it "A Twentieth-Century Beethoven."
‡Thomson had begun work on *Lord Byron*, to Jack Larson's libretto.

Greek liberation). With *Don Juan* the poetry career was probably ending; certainly the beauty was mostly gone; love he'd had; the political apotheosis (with House of Lords impossible from the sister scandal) was available. So he had to take it in Greece and succeed by dying before he messed it up. I'm delighted with this tragical view. He's like Marilyn Monroe or James Dean—romance and violence, drunkenness and early death.

L & K

To JOANNE W. PEYTON

June 3, 1965

Dear Mrs. Peyton:

O where, O where has my little check gone?
O where, O where can it be?

Anxiously,

To a CORRESPONDENT★

July 14, 1965

I do not give regular music lessons, but I do sometimes serve as what might be called a musical consultant. And that, I gather, is what you are looking for.

In any case, I should like to be prepared for the interview by an advance view of your music, if you could send me some.

The cost of the interview, by the way, would be one hundred dollars, and this includes whatever time I spend in advance.

Most sincerely,

To BENNETT CERF

November 8, 1965

Dear Bennett Cerf,

At the recent Knopf dinner you informed me of your resentment regarding something I had said about you three years earlier. There was not time to let me know what was the unfortunate remark, to

★a composition student

322

whom it had been made, and by what means you had been informed of it (or possibly misinformed).

Without asking for an explanation now, I do regret the pain you have been caused. To make disobliging remarks about a person one does not know is not pretty behavior, and with regard to you I even feel a certain gratitude for your having published books by my good friend Gertrude Stein.

Please believe I feel no malice toward you (how could I?) and that I find unfair to you whatever careless hurt you have received. The quote may have been false, part true, or merely out of context. In any case you are its victim, which I regret.

Sincerely yours and very cordially,

To MAURICE GROSSER

Los Angeles
April 25, 1966

D.M.:

It has been all right here and I was occupied with divers literary labors and the libretto. The thing goes through now a final draft and re-shaping.

More commissions—one from NY Philharmonic for 1967 and one from a man in KC for a cello piece. I have no summer plans at all beyond June 1.

I've been seeing Oscar Levant* every day. Withdrawal from being hooked again on sleeping pills. Was in hospital, now home, was awful, now improved. Saw Leland [Poole] too; he seems fair, though much slowed up. I think he has a cancer somewhere but it is not over-active. Isherwood thinks my book a masterpiece.†
Bachardy‡ arrived yesterday, most grateful for your New York flat.

love
V——

---

*(1906–72), American pianist, composer, and media personality
†English-American writer Christopher Isherwood (1904–86) had read the manuscript of Thomson's autobiography, which would be published later that year.
‡Don Bachardy (b. 1934), American artist, longtime friend of Isherwood's

To Maurice Grosser

New York
July 25, 1966

D.M.:

This will mostly be about disaster. Creekmore's* death, according to *NY Times,* was from a heart attack.

The Bowleses are here. Paul's mother and father have both died. In Florida. Paul now goes to Bangkok to write a book, but greatly fears he will not be able to stay, since Thailand, according to Libby [Holman], will not give long visas or renew. Jane goes to Florida for 3 weeks with her mother, then back to Tangier, where she doesn't really like it alone with Cherifa† but fears her French friend (of 60) will have got off with someone else.

I spent the weekend with Golde‡ at Water Island; and Frank O'Hara,§ also a house guest, was run over on the beach by a jeep. A broken leg and facial plus other lacerations are not important, but a liver injury which caused the loss of a quarter of it (most of the left lobe) give him, it seems, less than a 50–50 chance to live. He is in a small hospital, Bay View, at Mastic Beach, L.I.

I hated the hot weather in NY. Then bought a 24-inch fan, which helps. It has 3 speeds. Also the weather is a bit better. End of disasters.

L.K.V.

To Jack Larson

Pittsburgh
October 3, 1966

Dear Jack,

The triumph scene is wonderful. Also the ball.
The double scene will be hard to handle, but I shall try.

---

*Hubert Creekmore (1907–66), poet and translator
†(b. 1928), a Moroccan woman close to Jane Bowles for many years; their relationship was passionate, mercurial and, according to some friends, destructive.
‡Morris Golde (b. 1920), a friend of Thomson's, was later a founder and president of the Frank O'Hara Foundation, which fostered the work of unpublished poets in association with the Columbia University Press.
§(1926–66), American poet and art critic. He died of his injuries.

I had imagined 3 sections—one for the women alone, one for the men alone, and then a finale using both at once. This with a buildup of worry and tension till at the end the public would be sure of impending disaster.

The scene you have written is not quite certain of disaster. And the constant shiftings back and forth will loosen the tension that is there.

It moves too often to be played with blackouts; they would get monotonous. Keeping the lights on but freezing the actors when the scene shifts would probably be best; but if done too often, that also loses tension.

Annabella's last speech needs an addition that says she is not nearly so confident as she seems but in spite of her best intentions fears disaster and is prepared to face it. That is her decision.

And Byron's first speech on page 50 needs something wild and drunken and quite horrid.

Up to this point I should need a few pages in counterpoint, for example:

Annabella continues to declaim, repeating her faith, worries, and decision while Lady M. and Augusta strive to calm her, then lead her from the room	while at the same time	Byron gets drunker and wilder, till the others interrupt. "It's late. Let's all to bed." At which point he is helped from the room.

This material could be largely repetition of the previous tirades, since it is all sung at once.

For a 2nd-act finale, I need more text and especially a higher degree of violent statement and explosive admission of truths that forecast the disaster we come upon in the next scene.

This scene, beginning all sweet and charming, should actually be prepared by the 2nd-act finale.

In that scene, if possible, I should like to show Annabella at her most divided-minded—a wish to save him thru love and the knowledge that she may ruin both their lives by trying. And Byron at his most cynical and self-destructive, really Byronic and terrifying.

Do you think this is possible?

If not, I shall do what I can with what is there. But it is all pretty tame for the play's most dramatic curtain. And it does not lead inevitably to the controlled fury of the Six Mile Bottom revelations—a wonderful scene.

If Houseman is in NY when I go there on the 7th, I shall show him the new scenes and this letter.

> love and everything grateful
> V.T.

To DONALD SUTHERLAND*

August 30, 1967

My dear Sutherland:

[Eugene] McCown's death was in no way parallel to that of E. Faÿ. He was old, ill, gaga, and virtually starving. Also, suicide is more than doubtful. I shall get you the details in a few days.

B. Faÿ escaped from a prison hospital near Le Mans with the aid of Jesuits and the complicity of a fellow-prisoner, to whom he furnished the necessary funds through his New York banker (funds held secretly, since they were outside France). If the banker chooses to give you the details, I can arrange a meeting. I shall inquire into that.

The death of Max Jacob can be had, as I did, from Henri Sauguet. I also had some facts from a monk at Saint-Benoît-sur-Loire. All of which I shall share with delight.

I am in Europe from September 21 for about a month, then New York. Pittsburgh† is over, a one-year deal. This year I do second half at Trinity, Hartford.

Alice [Toklas]'s death and funeral, via [Janet] Flanner and [Doda] Conrad, are detailed and rather gruesome.

> Virgil

To a CORRESPONDENT‡

June 25, 1968

The address is 17 *bis,* quai Voltaire.
You will find the key at 19, quai Voltaire (Hôtel du quai Voltaire).
You enter 17 *bis* at 17 (there is a well-marked electric light), walk straight ahead, turn right in the courtyard, and go to Stairway B.
There you will find more electricity.
Mount two flights.

---

*(1915–78), literary scholar, author, and translator best known for his modern adaptations of Greek plays. Thomson determined to interest Sutherland in the works of Jacob.
†where Thomson had been a visiting professor
‡a Paris sublettor

My door is the one on the right.

The key pushes in before it turns.

Inside, electricity to the right.

Bathroom electricity just inside the bathroom door to the left.

Beds will be made.

If you wish to send me a check for $150 before you leave, send it to this address. This will cover everything for two weeks—gas, light, heat, telephone—except long-distance calls.

I am writing the concierge and present tenant.

Very sincerely,

To a CORRESPONDENT*

October 25, 1968

I went to Nadia Boulanger in the fall of 1921 at the suggestion of Melville Smith, a fellow-student from Harvard. Aaron Copland was also a student. We three were her Americans at that time; and we later sent others, as did Walter Damrosch, a patron of the American Conservatory in Fontainebleau.

I had lessons in composition, organ, and counterpoint, chiefly, a bit of harmony later and a bit of orchestration.

I returned to Harvard in fall of 1922, returned to Boulanger fall of 1925, and went on with my compositions under her counsel (some fugue, too) till spring of 1926.

Boulanger influenced American composition in the directions of:

1) a Bach-based neo-classicism
2) a Fauré-based harmony
3) a self-confidence in making the needed break with German models
4) an indifference to noise-music and 12-tone music.

For the personality, as I knew it, see my article in *The New York Times Magazine,* 4 February 1962, and the references to her in my memoirs *Virgil Thomson* by Virgil Thomson (A. Knopf, New York, 1966).

With every good wish for a successful study,

Sincerely,

---

*a student who inquired about Boulanger

May 14, 1969

D.M.:

The Met's (in effect) refusal of my opera* has been a shock. [Rudolf] Bing himself seems to have been pleased with it till a rich trustee said no. It seems that *both* incest & pregnancy (and among the high-born) are considered bad taste. Anyway, I now know from the unanimous (but one) enthusiasm that the piece is sort of dynamite. Nicolas N. is taking a tape of the reading-audition to East Berlin, where they do handsome productions and where corruption among the high life is believed to be true. We may have to wait a bit for a production. San Francisco and others are approached. The tape is excellent.

Meanwhile I am back at my book.

love,
V——

To Friede Rothe†

July 8, 1969

My dear Friede:

I thank you for your charming fan letter.

If we were again in seminar, it might be fun to open the question as to whether Mozart is or is not one of us.

He wrote such pretty music that one would like to let him join. Mary Garden, however, who was certainly a modern-minded musician, would have none of it.

"I can't bear infant prodigies," was the way she put it.

My best to you.

Sincerely,

In the late 1960s and early 1970s, Thomson hosted a weekly show devoted to American music on the New York radio station WNCN. The program inspired correspondence from listeners; the following

---

*Lord Byron

†(b. 1917), press representative long associated with Claudio Arrau. She had asked Thomson whether Mozart was "the first of the modern self-expressors."

response was to an admirer who expressed befuddlement at the appeal of Charles Ives.

To a CORRESPONDENT

January 20, 1970

Your letter of December 9 made me happy. I realize that Ives is a very interesting composer but his carelessness and volubility are sometimes hard to take.

Your remark that his music does not have a characteristic sound I can agree with easily, though the fact is surprising in a composer who wrote so much. One would expect a strongly identifiable personality to develop.

The recording of my *Five Songs of William Blake* has been out of print for some years. I have been told that copies sell for as high as $75.

At some time later this year I intend to broadcast it again over WNCN. At that time there would be no objection at all to your having it taken off on tape or on an acetate disc. This form of recording is called an air check and is perfectly legal so long as it is not offered for sale or used commercially.

Very sincerely yours,

To DONALD SUTHERLAND

May 4, 1970

Dear Donald,

The trick of keeping my temper in a polemical situation I learned at the *Herald Tribune*. It is part of what was called there "the amenities of controversy." And it enables one to make the deadly thrust without seeming to be *interessé*.

Yours ever,

To a CORRESPONDENT*

November 17, 1970

Paul Bowles knew Gertrude Stein very well, and there is correspondence (from him at Yale Lib., from her chez him). He once set to music a letter from her, charmingly.

His "status" in her house was merely that of an interesting young man. Gertrude refused to take his poetry seriously, and so did I. I liked his musical talent and encouraged it. G.S. did not venture musical judgment, probably never heard any of his pieces.

P.B. worked under me at *N.Y. Herald Tribune* as a music reviewer (1942–43) for a year and a half during the war. His musical knowledge of folkloric and modern repertory and his judgments were sound. He wrote clear prose, having been previously trained in this by Minna Lederman, editor of the quarterly *Modern Music,* for which he had written considerably in the middle and late thirties.

After the early discouragements I mentioned, I never heard of Bowles writing poetry again. But he wrote about music and later was successful in fiction. English friends had encouraged that.

I taught him to write incidental theater music (orchestrated for him his first show, *Horse Eats Hat* for John Houseman and Orson Welles). He later worked with Houseman, Oliver Smith, and Tennessee Williams.

An opera, *Denmark Vesey* (text by Charles-Henri Ford), was given in concert form (early 1940s) but never staged.

There are a zarzuela to a play by Lorca and a full opera to another. Both were performed.

Young people do not go places merely to "practice their art" or to advance their careers. Paul loved travel, spoke French and Spanish, eventually learned Arabic. He has long written for *Holiday* magazine. The Panama honeymoon is described by his wife, Jane Bowles, in her excellent novel *Two Serious Ladies.*

P.B. still writes music, but his chief breadwinners are travel articles and fiction.

Please try not to view his life as a planned career. He had more spontaneity than that, and he was always resistant to pressure, both from others and from his own convictions about "duty" or calculations about "advantage." He is as "free" a man as I have ever known, even when accepting an obligation, which he does strictly on his own, never under pressure.

---

*a graduate student preparing a doctoral dissertation on Paul Bowles

In the mid–1930s Bowles had political predilections of a Marxist color, but I doubt that they determined his travels.

Very sincerely,

To a CORRESPONDENT*

November 25, 1970

The behavior of Kafka's executor is typical. Also, nobody will destroy an artist's work merely because he asks that.

Families, of course, are likely to destroy anything that might tend to be found embarrassing in front of their friends and neighbors. In view of these facts, which are commonly known, any artist who wishes his work destroyed would be wise to do it himself, and those who wish relics preserved should never let close relatives get their hands on them.

Anyway, asking your friends or executors to destroy the record of your thoughts is a little bit like asking your doctor for a lethal dose. If killing is to be done, suicide is best. Anything else is, to say the least, an imposition.

Very sincerely yours,

To a CORRESPONDENT

December 4, 1970

I thank you for the interesting and highly complimentary letter.

In answer to your questions:

1) My present activities are writing music, and occasionally a book. Actually a book called *American Music Since 1910* will be issued in January by Holt, Rinehart & Winston, and I have just completed the scoring of an opera, *Lord Byron,* which will be produced next season.

2) Major influences on my musical life have been certain teachers,

E. Geneve Lichtenwalter, pianist
Clarence D. Sears, organist
Archibald T. Davison, conductor

---

*an English professor who asked whether Thomson would, like Kafka's executor, disobey a deathbed request to destroy an author's manuscripts

Edward Burlingame Hill, composer
Nadia Boulanger,

and certain composers, chiefly,

Debussy
Erik Satie.

Naturally, like everybody else, I have found the classical masters a gold mine.

3) My operas are commonly thought to be my most original contribution, though posterity may think otherwise (you never know). As for personal favorites among my works, I seem to find myself at any given moment absorbed by the latest among them. Also by some pieces that have been less successful than others with the public. These would include certainly my Second Symphony and my String Quartet No. 2.

Again thank you for your letter.

Very warmly,

To Tanaquil Le Clercq*

December 18, 1970

My very dear Tanaquil:

Your sending me the Mary Garden box was a most happy thought.

It seems to be a container for some form of cosmetic. The house of Rigaud put out well before World War I a perfume named for the singer, offering her $35,000 for the name. Since she did not care much for the odor and had no confidence in its success, she accepted this sum rather than a royalty on sales. She later regretted having done so, since the scent was such a vast success that it sold all over the world for twenty years or more.

This little box was clearly a part of the line, and I am ever so happy to have it since it reminds me both of Mary, who was a neighbor of mine in Paris and a good friend, and of my sister, who as a young girl loved and used the perfume.

Ever warmly yours,

---

*(b. 1929), New York City Ballet ballerina and fourth wife of George Balanchine

To a Correspondent*

January 26, 1971

I enormously admired your finger work and the control that enabled you to produce a large variety of colors and articulations.

What seems to have lost you the chance to play again is the erratic and seemingly irresponsible nature of your approach to Beethoven. Tonal variety and an orchestral way with the classical masters are valuable, but tempo and phraseology in these works do not admit idiosyncratic treatment. They cannot deviate widely from the norm, as this is understood by today's (and yesterday's too) great pianists.

Your Debussy was lovely, because you are close to its time and "understand" its ways. But for Beethoven I suggest that you "orchestrate" with your fingers while observing a "general line" definitely modeled on that of someone's recording, someone who appeals to you as being authentic, that is to say, traditional without stuffiness.

Busoni and Rachmaninoff had that quality. Rubinstein often does. Clifford Curzon† can open up the long works of Schubert and Schumann by giving them a "line." Landowska could do it with Mozart piano sonatas.

I strongly advise you to follow these artists by imitating their way of treating classical structures.

At present you are a fine pianist and play modern music beautifully, but in the classics you are, interpretatively speaking, off-center.

I like very much, I may say, the way you control piano sound.

Good wishes ever,

Sincerely,

---

*a pianist who was eliminated early from a competition on which Thomson served as a judge
†(1907–82), British pianist, once a student of Boulanger's

To Francis Thorne*

Aspen
August 3, 1971

Dear Francis,

Aspen Music Association gave me a birthday concert and I conducted and it drew a large audience, was reviewed in Denver, pleased the management no end.

Willie Masselos† came to dinner with Alicia de Larrocha‡ and was not eager about the MacDowell benefit dinner. He doesn't want to have to learn anything, considers the whole affair a chore. I find his attitude unpleasant. Would you mind greatly if I got someone else to play my portraits? John Wustman§ does them beautifully. Also the Fennimore boy.‖ Maybe your friend Robert Helps.• Almost anybody would be glad of the MacDowell date. And Willie is a pain, as I knew he would be. He dislikes my music and doesn't conceal that.

Peter Mennin** has been having a foot operated on in Iowa. But pressed by Houseman he did set a *Byron* date—April 14–15–16.

Best to both ever,

To a Correspondent††

January 25, 1972

Not another Faust opera please.
There are already fifteen or more.

Very sincerely,

---

*(b. 1922), American composer and music administrator, a co-founder of the American Composers Orchestra
†(b. 1920), American pianist who played many new American works, including the premiere of Copland's Piano Fantasy
‡(b. 1923), Spanish pianist
§(b. 1930), American pianist, best known as an accompanist
‖Joseph Fennimore (b. 1940), American pianist and composer, briefly one of Thomson's pupils
• (b. 1928), American composer and pianist, a specialist in twentieth-century repertory
**(1923–83), American composer; then president of the Juilliard School, which presented the world premiere of *Lord Byron* in 1972
††a would-be librettist

February 29, 1972

Miss Yoko Ono is a poet and graphic artist of international reputation and unquestioned distinction.

Having known her and her work for upwards of ten years, I hold both in high admiration.

As a resident of the United States she would certainly enrich the intellectual life of our country and contribute to its vigor.

Very sincerely,

To Alvin Ailey†

April 25, 1972

Dear Alvin,

I loved it all.

The skylark ballet is very original. You have turned away from the angular, fast movements used ever since Fokine (instantaneously from one pose to another) and returned to the Romantic curvaceous movements without loss of speed. Very refreshingly sensual. And your people are good with hands, which the New York City [Ballet] and the [American] Ballet Theatre are not.

A million for all you did for *Byron*.

Yours,

To Maurice Grosser

Washington, D.C.
August 31, 1972

D.M.:

I am doing criticism classes for the Music Critics Association, which is having a convention. Wash. is very pretty in the summer, like a college campus full of unlabeled bldgs. I go to Paris on Sept. 3

---

*A letter of reference provided to Yoko Ono (b. 1933) when she and her second husband, John Lennon, were threatened with expulsion from the United States. Thomson had known her since the early 1960s.

†Ailey (b. 1931), American dancer and choreographer, worked on the Juilliard production of *Lord Byron*.

to paint and fix up the flat. If it goes fast I shall move over to London on the 15th. If not, I shall stay on a bit. The Met Opera is to do *4 Sts* after all, in a small round theater seating 300. *The Mother* has still not found a small N.Y. theater but I think will open end of October. *4 Sts* is for February, 2 or 3 weeks of it. Patrick Smith,★ a young man who wrote a fine book about opera librettos and who reviewed *Lord Byron* as "a masterpiece," wants to buy the pencil orch. score. No price yet mentioned. Nat'l Portrait Gallery has not yet found the money to buy Alice Neel's† portrait of me, but they likely will. She wants $8000. I visited the place. It is nothing like as grand as the London collection, but there are some tasty items. I wrote portraits again in Aspen. As you see, I am doing all right.

L.V.

To the HAMILTON WATCH COMPANY

October 2, 1972

Gentlemen:

I am sending you by separate post a gold presentation watch which I was honored to receive from the Lancaster Symphony Orchestra in April of last year. It kept perfect time for one year, then began losing five minutes a week.

After I took it to the watchmaker recommended by your New York office, who changed the battery, it ran for about three more weeks, still losing time.

The technical specialist in your New York office thereupon oiled it a little, and it ran for one more week.

At his suggestion I am sending it to you for whatever it may need, possibly a thorough cleaning. When he pointed out that the guarantee was good for only a year, I replied that the circumstances under which I had acquired the watch had made it precious to me and that I was hopeful that it might enjoy a long life.

It is with that hope that I now entrust it to your Repair Department.

Attached to the beautiful watch is a handmade lizard-skin strap which cost me $40 in Paris. Please do not lose it but return it with the watch. I would have removed it myself had I known how.

★(b. 1932), author of *The Tenth Muse: A Historical Study of the Opera Libretto* (1970) and a president of the Music Critics Association
†(1900–84), American painter esteemed for her portraits

Should the cost of the repair seem to you surprising, you might let me know in advance.

In any case do please make it work for me. I miss it.

Very truly yours,

To the HAMILTON WATCH COMPANY

November 1, 1972

Gentlemen:

On October 2 of this year I sent you a watch to be repaired.

It was received on October 6 as registered mail no. 415534. On October 13 I received and paid by check a repair bill of $22.95. This sum includes a New York City sales tax, charged without explanation, but which I paid in order to facilitate the return of my watch.

The repair bill did not mention the nature of the repair, but it indicated that I would receive the watch in a week or ten days.

This letter is to remind you that I have still not received the watch and to request that you expedite its delivery.

I should also appreciate a letter stating the nature of the repair done and, if this included a cleaning, how long I may expect the watch to remain in service before it will need a further cleaning.

I should also appreciate, since we are still in correspondence, either an explanation of the charge for New York sales tax or a return of the amount erroneously so charged.

Above all, I should like my watch back as soon as you can send it, and a statement of what repair it has undergone.

Your silence gets me down.

Very sincerely,

To JOHN HOHENBERG★

December 2, 1972

Dear Mr. Hohenberg:

I learned of my Pulitzer Prize from a telegram of congratulation received while I was on tour in the South, a wire from my managing editor at the *New York Herald Tribune*.

I subsequently received a large number of such messages, includ-

---

★(b. 1906), secretary, Pulitzer Prize advisory board. In preparing his book *The Pulitzer Prizes* (Columbia University Press), Hohenberg sent questionnaires to recipients of the award.

ing a letter from the White House. The volume of these, easily twice the notice attracted by any other of my professional recognitions, either previous or subsequent, has led me to suspect that the high prestige of this particular award is associated with the Pulitzer name, one of the grander ones in American press history.

Not that there is anything wrong with the Pulitzer award or with the choice of its recipients; on that score it has been impeccable. But there is nevertheless an unexplained vast difference on the publicity level between receiving a Pulitzer Prize and receiving a Guggenheim fellowship or even a gold medal from the National Institute of Arts and Letters.

Whether the Pulitzer has helped my career I cannot say. I was already fifty-two. But I do know that press agents always mention it; it has unquestionable publicity value. Naturally, I am proud of it as well, and of the fact that it is still the only one ever awarded for a film score.

I do not know whether Roger Sessions ever had a Pulitzer; but offhand I should say the recipients constitute a pretty sound list of the Americans who have written distinguished music. Ives seems to have got it after death; I do not remember about Ruggles or Varèse. And John Cage is still up for grabs.

With all good wishes for an interesting and entertaining book.

Very sincerely,

P.S. Works are brought to the attention of the jury by a procedure that does not seem to have varied much in the last thirty or more years. This does involve, being national in scope, many individual recommendations. In my case, I was not aware of being considered at all. I was aware, however, that somehow or other the prize got passed around, that everybody reputable was considered but had to wait his turn, and that nobody could be honored without having produced a meritorious work that year.

To a Correspondent*

January 20, 1973

I have long disapproved of American poets working for the Modern Art establishment, whether this is done as an employee of the Museum of Modern Art or as a contributor to any of the periodicals controlled by or connected with that museum.

---

*who had inquired whether Thomson felt Frank O'Hara's association with the art world had compromised his poetry

I am aware that the modern movement in painting was launched in Paris and continuously supervised by poets. This includes almost every poet working there from Apollinaire through Gertrude Stein and the surrealists.

The practice was an informal one, and the poets were informally, but more than adequately, recompensed by illustrations for their books and the gift of pictures.

The practice here is underpaid and overorganized.

As a result, the poets who advertise painting become very quickly a part of the Modern Art mafia.

I consider this situation beneath them and injurious to their intellectual integrity.

O'Hara is not the only poet in America who has got involved in what we know to be a name-and-price racket.

That is all I have to say on the subject.

Very sincerely,

To Carole Lawrence*

March 17, 1973

Dear Mrs. Lawrence:

I wish you well regarding the *Lost Generation Journal*.

I am sorry I have not the leisure at present for answering your many questions, though I am grateful for your interest.

I may add that I have never really liked the term "lost generation." Nobody involved was any more "lost" than young people are at any other time. And anyway, the term was from the beginning without much in its favor save as personal publicity for Ernest Hemingway.

Very sincerely,

To the Spence School

April 7, 1973

Gentlemen:

This is to recommend for acceptance in your school Amy Bernstein, now ready for the eighth grade.

I have known her parents for twenty years; they are intelligent and good people.

---

*editor, *Lost Generation Journal*, who had sent a lengthy questionnaire to Thomson

The child I have known since birth. She seems to be unusually intelligent and a self-contained personality.

By this I do not mean that she is unduly introspective, merely that her ways are neither violent nor unreflected. Thoroughly in command of herself, that is the way I would describe her.

She is also cheerful, good humored, and companionable.

Very sincerely yours,

To Paul Bowles

June 2, 1973

Dear Paul,

It was good of you to write me the details of Jane's death.* The fact of it, especially its coming after so long an illness, is a sadness for us all who loved her. That she loved me too I have never doubted.

And your adaptation to the change, whether or not you may have reflected about it, will inevitably make a great difference in your life. I send you my sympathy.

Maurice had written me over a month ago, while you were still in Malaga, I think. I telephoned at that time to Allen Hughes and asked him to inform the obit people at the *Times,* suggesting also that he speak to the book page. Since you were not available by telephone and since nobody around here seems to have had much biographical information about Jane, what the paper finally published is the enclosed notice, which is chiefly literary.

I have been in touch this last winter fairly continuously with Dan Halpern.† I find his magazine quite interesting. At the moment he is in England where he will try to see Mary Butts's daughter. He hopes to reprint certain books of hers, along with an original volume of her poetry. I hope he will be able to do this, since I have always held her work in high esteem. I loved her too, as I loved Jane, and both were, for all their enormous talent, frighteningly self-destructive.

My love to you, dear Paul, and do tell me what I can do to be of help to you or to Jane's posthumous glory.

Ever yours,

---

*Jane Bowles had died at a convent in Malaga in May, 1973, after a series of strokes, at the age of 56.
†(b. 1945), editor of *Antaeus*

To a Correspondent*

June 2, 1973

I first heard Eva Gauthier sing at the Lowell Institute in Boston, 1923. I subsequently heard most of her Boston and New York concerts until I moved to Europe in the fall of 1925. This means that I knew her work in the finest period of her vocal powers.

In 1936 I engaged her, along with Colin O'More,† to sing in Hartford the *Socrate* of Erik Satie.

I prepared and coached this performance, the first full orchestral one ever to be given in America. Alexander Smallens conducted and a mobile stage-set was designed and built for this performance by Alexander Calder,‡ to my knowledge the sculptor's only formal stage work, unless you count his Toy Circus.

From 1933 till her death I was a close friend of Eva Gauthier and knew well, through various of her pupils, her work as a teacher. She seems to have been most remarkable as an advisor on repertory and as a coach. She was less distinguished, I think, as a voice trainer, though her own vocal technique was secure and accomplished.

In her last years, as you know, she was far from well and chronically in need of financial help. Various friends seem to have contributed, but none of them really took care of her.

I do not consider her to have been a "neglected artist." Any singer making her career through modern music and through rarities was certain in those days to have a limited public, however devoted. Eva Gauthier was a first-class musician and a great artist. But her voice was not powerful enough for the opera houses, and her distinguished repertory was not for the boob trade. An account of the *Socrate* performance and its decor is to be found in my autobiography, *Virgil Thomson*. If I can help you with any further information I shall be glad to do so.

Very sincerely,

---

*who had asked Thomson about his association with the soprano Eva Gauthier (1885–1958)
†(1890–1956), American tenor
‡(1898–1976), American sculptor and painter best known for his mobiles

To a Correspondent

August 1, 1973

I am ever so pleased that you are interested in my portraits. I have been doing these off and on for the last forty-five years, always in front of the sitter. There are upwards of two hundred by now.

They are neither casual nor intentionally humorous. Some were written in Paris and some here, occasionally in other places too.

The bitonality in the Sophie Arp* was not a calculated effect; I never calculate these pieces in advance, but count rather on the discipline of spontaneity to keep the music alive; anything can happen.

Hans Arp (later known as Jean)† was actually something of a poltergeist, though that title for his portrait was invented by me. But he did love playing tricks and secret games. His portrait, I may add, is of the man, not of his work.

If you can find in your local library a copy of my autobiography, you will read there an extended explanation of these pieces.

As you know, I did not invent the musical portrait, though I may well be the only composer to have consistently drawn them from life.

Most sincerely yours,

To Paul Bowles

Travellers Club, London
October 1973

D.P.

Maurice will be in Tangier about the 10th for one month. I have been here for three weeks, going now, by way of Berlin, to you know where. Home on Nov. 1. Here I bought a pair of shoes and finished a piece—a Cantata on Poems of Edward Lear. It would be nice if you came sometime to New York but I know one needs a reason for trips. The friends are under control and Jim Bridges has what seems to be about to be a successful film with Jack Houseman playing a big role as a professor at Harvard Law School and very good he is really.‡ Maurice will go to Marrakesh to be seventy. I

---

*Sophie Täuber-Arp (1889–1943), Swiss artist and sculptor, married to Jean Arp
†(1887–1966), poet, sculptor, and painter who helped found the Dada movement
‡The film was *The Paper Chase,* directed by James Bridges (b. 1936), for which Houseman won an Academy Award as best supporting actor of 1973. Later he replayed the role of Professor Kingsfield in a television series based on the film.

342

shall be seventy-seven in New York. Nothing wrong but one ear is a bit deaf. I suppose you must be well; you had everything there was when you were young; nothing left to have. I suppose Maurice will keep his flat in Tangier. Unless it really seems everyone is moving. Where would you go?

affection ever
Virgil

To Leonard Bernstein

March 14, 1974

Dear Lenny,

My warm congrats on the success of *Candide*.* Way back in 1945, when I used to help out the French radio with broadcasts of American music from discs available through U.S. Information Service, by far the most popular with the public were excerpts from *On the Town*. And the French musicians around simply could not get over their astonishment that in New York an *opérette* composed in such a sophisticated musical style could be successful.

So still, with *West Side Story* and *Candide* you remain world master of the "musical." All honor to you!

Now that I have been through the Norton lectures† (three by video, all six by reading) it is clear that your skill in explaining music is also tops, as indeed it was when you used to do it at Carnegie Hall.

I find nothing reprehensible about your bringing in linguistics. You needed an authority to support an "innate musical grammar" and Chomsky's‡ heavy artillery is surely that. Especially since post-war researches in the physiology of hearing, though they do support a syntax based on the harmonic series as unquestionably built into the human ear, are being treated by the Germanic twelve-tone world and the French-based solfeggio world as "controversial."

So the linguistic argument, though merely an analogy, as you pointed out, does carry weight. And it enables you to bypass vested musical interests.

I am sure your conclusions are valid, and I see no reason why you should not have used any material conveniently to hand for ex-

---

*Bernstein's *Candide*, a failure when first performed in 1956, was revived in New York in 1973 in a much-altered version with a new book; the production was a success.
†delivered at Harvard University, recorded, and later published in book form
‡Noam Chomsky (b. 1928), American linguistic theorist

pounding them. All the more so since that material is relatively familiar and hence easily acceptable. I enjoyed everything.

Many thanks for the courtesies of your office. I am returning the borrowed scripts with gratitude.

Ever warmly your admirer,

To Rachel Gallagher*

June 5, 1974

Dear Miss Gallagher:

When I have visitors from out of town I take for granted that they can find their way to the museums, theaters, and similar places of interest. As special treatment I have them to dinner with appropriate friends and take them to dinner at other friends' houses, appropriate or not.

Nothing is so interesting to out-of-town Americans and to foreigners as seeing the way New Yorkers live.

Very sincerely yours,

To Maurice Grosser

Travellers Club [London]
October 5, 1974

D.M.:

I went to Brussels and gave a French lecture with piano recital. Had sensational lunch in the country. Drank a magnum of '59 claret & ate home-grown lamb with fresh-picked vegetables. Coming over a Negro girl at Pan Am who likes my music abolished my overweight charges and put me in first-class. Dinner was ceremonial—at tables—with caviar, foie gras, roast beef (cooked there), and multiple wines. We ate from 11:30 till one, were awakened with breakfast at 3 (8 in London).

L & K

---

*who had asked Thomson how he entertained guests in Manhattan for an article in *The New York Times* travel section

To Wye Jamison Allanbrook*

February 10, 1975

My dear W.J.

Your rhythm and meter piece is *very remarkable*.

I had known about the prevalence of dance-meters in eighteenth-century music and delighted in Wanda Landowska's quick ear for them. Nobody like her for unmasking an allemande. But I had not dreamed of their elaborate use in characterization as you have exposed that in the *Figaro* chapter.

Now we *must* have a *Don Giovanni* analysis, which will be more difficult, but which is absolutely necessary for establishing the tempos. Even Beecham was uncertain about some of these; the best to date are those of Karajan.

There is more in Mozart than dance meters, of course. I can show you the instrumental imitations in about half the piano sonatas, and it is these that determine the tempos, along with the dance meters and the operatic evocations. I do not begin to understand the concertos or the violin sonatas. But I do want to show you my "solutions" for certain piano sonatas and for at least one of the fantasias. I suspect that between us we might solve all the works for piano solo and publish our findings in a book.

I suppose you know the brochure of Jacques Chailly† on the *Magic Flute* libretto. And by whatever means arrived at, the tempos in Beecham's 1936 recording of that opera, made in Berlin, seem to have become, over the last forty years, final.

Figaro, thanks to its dance meters, is not difficult in this respect, and never has been. But *Così* still is. And *Don Giovanni* is a giant problem. If you can take on all three of the da Ponte operas, you will have a life's work laid out, and the music world will be grateful.

When can we talk together of these matters? Do you ever come to New York? Where will you be in the summer?

Again, let me say it, *a very remarkable book*.

I shall send it back later, must keep it around for a bit.

Ever admiring,

---

*(b. 1943), musicologist, whose studies mentioned here were later incorporated into *Rhythmic Gesture in Mozart: Le nozze di Figaro* and *Don Giovanni* (1984)
†(b. 1910), French musicologist. The work referred to is *The Magic Flute, Masonic Opera* (1971).

May 28, 1975

Dear Sandy,

Mr. Perls* will no doubt have told you that I phoned him for your next year's schedule and that he informed me of the Whitney show to take place in the fall of '76.

A musical associate of mine, a young conductor named Joel Thome,† has been planning for 1976 a performance of Satie's *Socrate* with orchestra, in my English translation. And it has occurred to me that if you are willing to reproduce the mobile set that you designed for Hartford back in 1937, I think it was, the performance might be of considerable interest to expose at the same time as your Whitney show.

If you think the idea impractical do let me know through Mr. Perls.

But if it interests you to repeat this historic stage set, perhaps we could make plans for that when you come to New York this year.

Meanwhile, all my affection, and to Louisa.

Long time no see.

Everbest,

To a Correspondent‡

September 8, 1975

Louis Gruenberg was a distinguished and successful New York composer during the 1920s and '30s, but it so happens that living abroad most of that time, I did not come in contact with his work.

He actually wrote music for a film by Pare Lorentz, *The Fight for Life,* which had been originally reserved for me and which I would have composed had I not been absent.

He remains a curious case, but there is no assurance that his work will not be revived at some later time.

Very sincerely,

---

*Klaus Perls (b. 1912), art dealer who represented Calder
†(b. 1939), American composer and conductor, who later led the complete recording of *Four Saints* on Nonesuch
‡Thomson had been asked to assess the importance of composer Louis Gruenberg (1884–1964), whose opera *The Emperor Jones* was much discussed in the 1930s. Gruenberg also wrote a violin concerto for Jascha Heifetz.

To Alan Wald[*]

January 16, 1976

Dear Mr. Wald:

I am very happy that someone at last is taking an interest in Sherry Mangan.

As one of his longest and closest friends, I probably know more about him than anybody else. Certainly I can answer your questions easily, though I do not have too much time for those requiring length.

1) His family were well-to-do Irish Catholics with good background. His mother, née Sherry, came from gentle people. His father, a nephew or grandson of a well-known Irish poet, was a pediatrician (studied in Vienna) and the author of a two-volume life of Erasmus. He read, wrote, and spoke Latin with ease.

2) Sherry's literary influences were his own classical studies in Greek and Latin, along with his admiration for e e cummings and James Joyce.

3) He had few literary activities among expatriate writers in Europe, though he wrote a certain amount of poetry there between 1925 and '27.

4) His taking up of the Trotsky faith was influenced by Wheelwright[†] (a lapsed High Anglican), but psychologically determined by his own position as a lapsed Catholic. Like many of the Jewish communists who could no longer support their tribal beliefs but replaced these with a faith in Lenin as Moses and Russia as the Promised Land, Sherry found in the Trotsky position exactly those opportunities that he needed for behaving like a Jesuit theologian.

5) At this moment I cannot think of any associates of his still living who might be of value to you.

You should look for access to all the copies of his own hand-set and hand-printed magazine *larus* (Sherry was a master printer as well as a classical scholar and poet) and also of the magazine *Pagany,* for which he acted as a sort of European editor and to which he sent contributions by particular friends of mine (Gertrude Stein, Mary Butts, Georges Hugnet) and an American writer of prose and poetry whom he enormously admired, Robert McAlmon.

If you ever come to New York we could go into his life and literary activities at greater length. I presume you have seen his vol-

---

[*](b. 1946), American literary scholar and biographer, associated with the University of Michigan. His research led to *The Revolutionary Imagination: The Poetry and Politics of John Wheelwright and Sherry Mangan* (1983).
[†]John Brooks Wheelwright (1897–1940)

ume of collected poems and a poem of some length called "Ave," printed by himself in pamphlet form, actually his farewell to poetry.

If you wish to ask me things by telephone some Sunday morning at the cheap rate, give me a call.

I have several hundred letters covering the period from 1922 till his death in, I think, 1959.

All good wishes to you in this badly needed enterprise.

Very sincerely,

To Richard Gaddes*

February 19, 1976

Dear Mr. Gaddes:

It was most courteous of you to send me a cast list for *The Mother of Us All*.

Being out of touch with rising careers, I know the work of only two soloists, Mr. Lewis† and Miss Dunn.‡ The latter, though an admirable artist, is in my memory of her a mezzo-soprano. Unless her range and vocal color have recently changed, this fact presents certain inconveniences:

- Her confidante in the opera is also a mezzo-soprano, offering thus a minimum of contrast with the leading singer.
- The role of Susan B. has been designed for the range and vocal registers of a dramatic soprano, its culminating point vocally being the held high C at the end of Act I.
- The tessitura (or lie) of the vocal line with regard to the registers of head-voice and medium-voice is almost certain to be uncomfortable in the final solo, and this discomfort, if present, is certain to be communicated to the audience.

If I am wrong about Miss Dunn, pay no attention to my worries.

If I am right, and she really is still a mezzo, I would like to urge a reconsideration of her casting in this long, high-lying, and tiring role.

Regarding the possibilities of a full-length overture, I presume you have the prelude to Act I, the prelude to Act II (which actually

---

*Gaddes (b. 1942) was artistic administrator of the Santa Fe Opera, which was then planning the summer 1976 production of *Mother*.

†William Lewis (b. 1932), American tenor cast as John Adams

‡Mignon Dunn (b. 1931), American mezzo-soprano cast as Susan B. Anthony. She sang in the performances and the recording with alteration(s) to the vocal line.

constitutes an overture), the prelude to Act I, scene 3, and of Act I, scene 2, to be used in case more time is needed for changing the set.

G. Schirmer has all of these materials, which are not in the regular score. I should be happy to discuss the matter with Mr. Leppard,★ should he care to write or telephone me.

Regarding your stage director, whom I also do not know, I should like to suggest that this opera is most effective when the stage movements are completely planned, like a choreography, and when all temptations toward playing for laughs are under control.

I should be happy to meet with your director, if he is so inclined. I am speaking, both vocally and dramatically, not from a mere composer's fantasy, but from a twenty-year acquaintance with the work in rehearsal and production.

Luckily, the opera is foolproof; no matter how it is staged, it always comes off. Need I add that I am looking forward with the greatest of confidence to the Santa Fe production?

Very sincerely,

To a CORRESPONDENT†

February 26, 1976

You were a love to bring me the poetry and it is very naughty of me to be wholly unable to get up any interest in the War of 1812.

And as for old New Orleans, I wouldn't touch it with a pole. There is far too much of that in the world. It has become charm-repertory and is corny as hell.

Everbest,

To WILLIAM PARKER‡

May 17, 1976

Dear Mr. Parker:

Three cheers for the Joy in Singing prize.
I hope I can hear your recital on October 21.
For an American work I naturally think of my Blake songs. They

---

★Raymond Leppard (b. 1927), British conductor and musicologist, who led the Santa Fe performances of *Mother*
†a personal friend and would-be librettist
‡American baritone (b. 1943), recipient of the prestigious Joy in Singing award, had proposed that Thomson compose a new work, perhaps based on *Billy Budd*.

have not been sung in New York for quite some time. They go fine with piano. If you are timid about our colored friends, simply omit "The Little Black Boy."

I am engaged on a long piece at this moment and do not feel confident about undertaking an important work for this recital.

In any case, it would have to be something other than *Billy Budd*. Benjamin Britten's opera seems to have exhausted that theme for the present.

Good wishes ever,

To Frederic James*

June 7, 1976

Dear Freddy,

Your picture has been importantly displayed in my flat for well over a month now, and the pleasure it gives me has augmented constantly.

It is monumental indeed, and very grand. I could not be happier owning it.

At this moment, I have been at the Roosevelt Hospital for a week and a half and shall remain for the rest of this week. There is nothing gravely wrong except a spinal disc pinching a nerve that controls a muscle in my right thigh. This gives pain when I walk. In hospital, however, I do not walk, so that I am really quite reasonably comfortable, even, with mild sedation, floating a bit.

The present plan is to send me home on Saturday, June 12 and keep me there while nature makes its own cure. This process will no doubt be slow, but I have a secretary (mornings) and a former cook and personal houseman (available at other times) to see that I want for nothing.

I shall not go to Europe now, as I had planned, but I may be able by mid-July to go to Aspen as planned (comp.-in-res. for four weeks) and in early August to Santa Fe for the production there of my opera *The Mother of Us All* (visuals by Robert Indiana).†

I am writing so that you and Diana will know where I am. Also to tell you how solidly memorable I am finding your portrait of the old Calvary Baptist Church.

Everbest,

---

*(1915–80), American artist from Kansas City. In his youth Thomson had played the organ at Calvary Baptist Church.
†Indiana (b. 1928), American painter and visual artist, designed sets and costumes for the Santa Fe production of *Mother of Us All;* the subject of a 1966 piano portrait by Thomson.

To Lou Harrison

June 14, 1976

Very dear Lou,

A delight was your letter received today. I have been for a little over two weeks now an inmate of Roosevelt Hospital, the diagnosis being sciatica, the improvement steady. I expect to go home at the end of this week, say 19 June.

George Balanchine is in the next room, same disease and same doctor. I am greatly enjoying my stay here—lots of visitors, very good cooking, and acres of crime fiction. I have even worked a little —nothing original, just some needed editorial supervision for G. Schirmer, Inc.

My good wishes...

To Mr. and Mrs. Eugene Ormandy

June 30, 1976

Dear Gene and Gretel:

For congratulating you on the new and very fine honor of a knighthood, I had hoped to address you as Sir Eugene and Lady Ormandy, but it seems that your American citizenship makes that inappropriate.

Anyhow, I am very happy for both of you and send you witness of my old and deep affection at this happy event.

My own news is not so happy. I have been in the hospital just over a month now with leg pain roughly known as sciatica but still in process of a more precise diagnosis before very much real treatment can be applied.

I am not unhappy in the hospital or radically uncomfortable. I read and write and communicate, as you can see from this letter, with the outside world. I shall not be able to be composer-in-residence during the month of July in Aspen, Colorado, as had been planned. I am hoping that I may be able to be in Santa Fe for the dress rehearsals and opening performances of my opera *The Mother of Us All,* which will take place there in early August. The work is also to be recorded complete as part of an American music recording program subsidized by the Rockefeller Foundation.

All that makes me happy, as does also your recent great honor.
I wish I could be there to see it take place.

All my affection ever to you both,

To ELIZABETH LUTYENS*

July 22, 1976

Darling Liz,

I go home day after tomorrow, Saturday the 24th, and shall stay
there for a few weeks.

In addition to normal convalescent loafing, I do special exercises
that involve lifting weights with my ankles.

The hospital has been quite fun, good food, a good room, and
charming nurses, many of them blacks from Africa or from divers
British Islands.

I presume that the York Festival and your term in residence at the
University are by now quite over. Do let me hear from you when
you have a moment to write.

L & K,

To RAYMOND LEPPARD

August 3, 1976

Dear Mr. Leppard:

The English-horn tune in the prelude to Act I, scene 4 is correct.
Leave it in.

A *pp* snare-drum roll before the "Cold Weather" intermezzo is no
invention of mine. Some conductor may have needed a bit of activity there to help fill up an empty spot. If you feel the same, don't
hesitate to use it. But unless its presence seems to you desirable,
there is no need for using it.

Band on stage at the beginning might well be fun.

Regarding the matter of enunciation, it seems obvious that the
répétiteur who prepared the opera did not cope with the problem.
Your only hope now, I should think, is to tell all the cast firmly that
no singer whose every word cannot be clearly heard will be allowed

---

*(1906–83), British twelve-tone composer, known for her stage works, film scores, and
chamber music

to take part in the recording. This may be just a bluff, unenforceable on your part, but it should scare hell out of everybody. You yourself can, of course, keep the orchestral volume low enough not to interfere with enunciation; but that kind of balancing, which you have no doubt already planned for, is of very little value unless a clear verbal projection is already present.

The following indication may be too late to be used. But I assure you that in Act I, scene 1, Gertrude S. and Virgil T. can balance better both verbally and vocally if they stand and move always close together and if they keep away from S.B. and Anne.

Thank you for your kindness in consulting me about all these matters. And good luck to us all.

Sincerely,

To a CORRESPONDENT

August 13, 1976

For the charming letter about *Mother of Us All* in Santa Fe I could not thank you more. My own messengers in many cases preferred Chicago's* musical production.

I do not know the director of the Santa Fe production but I gather that he is not accustomed to doing opera as opera. So many of the not-very-musical theater people do not *trust* music. They do not believe it capable of holding the attention. If it were not, of course, opera would not exist. But when this doubt exists, every opera production gets turned into an extravaganza of some other kind.

We shall see what is left of the Santa Fe musical performance when the recording comes out. It has been suggested that I may have a test pressing by Thanksgiving. It has never been suggested that I might be of any value in either the casting or the musical direction of this recording.

As for Bob Indiana's patriotic layouts, they are bound to be showy, quite pretty, and on the whole innocent.

My health is quite satisfactory and my progress in convalescence seems to please my medical men. I walk well; I do all sorts of things around the house; I do not go out very much, on account of the rather unpleasant hot weather, but I am perfectly capable of doing so.

Sincerely ever,

---

*a production by the Chicago Opera Studio

To Jere Abbott

September 9, 1976

Dear Jere,

I did not go to Santa Fe for *The Mother of Us All.* Nor to Aspen, where I was expected in July as comp.-in-res. Actually I spent most of the summer (pleasantly enough) in Roosevelt Hospital, where I ended by leaving behind me a part of a spinal disc which had got out of place and was causing me leg pains.

Now I have no more leg pains and I recuperate quite effectively, though the full comeback from major surgery may take six months or a year. But I can walk up to a mile, negotiate stairs, and lift weights with my formerly painful leg.

I knew Caresse Crosby quite well indeed, but only after Harry's* death. I did not know him ever, nor was I an active part of her benefaction program, since that involved only writers and painters, never musicians.

She was a nice woman, pretty, affectionate, amorous, and not stupid at all. Harry, of course, was more than a little crazy.

A very interesting book about the Crosbys and about everybody else who published English-language books in Paris between the two wars is called *Published in Paris,* by Hugh Ford (Macmillan, 1975). I wrote a piece about it in the *New York Review of Books* of February 19, 1976.

The Mother of Us All has had a number of productions this year. It has these every year, but Santa Fe was the first to involve, as *Four Saints* had done, my connections with modern art.

The work is absolutely foolproof and never fails no matter how it is performed, directed, or decorated. Actually I have no objection to this version by Robert Indiana, though I did not at all like the one he did five years ago in Minneapolis. This one is quite heavy, and all the colors are opaque, but it is an actual structure (both sets and costumes) built to copy literally the artist's maquettes. In this sense, it is the first production of anything in some years to follow the Diaghilev principle.

If there were a chance of seeing you in New York this winter, I should like that very much. Myself I shall be 80 on Thanksgiving Day.

Affection ever,

---

*Harry (1892–1929) and Caresse Crosby (1892–1970), a wealthy and eccentric couple, particularly close to Hart Crane. After Harry's suicide in New York, Caresse became an arts patron of some renown. Harry Crosby is the subject of a biography by Geoffrey Wolff, *Black Sun* (1976).

To Matthew Paris*

September 15, 1976

Dear Matthew:

I have enjoyed the Dorothy Sayers, which I had not read for many years. Myself I never could identify too well with Peter Wimsey. My dream of myself is much nearer to Nero Wolfe.

By all means let us broadcast the complete *Lord Byron* on WNYC.† I should be very happy to see you. Do phone and come to the Chelsea.

Everbest,

To Betty Stouffer‡

October 12, 1976

Dear Betty,

When mother moved from her house in Kansas City, Ruby and I divided the things we thought worth keeping.

She took the Victorian chairs and table, the Seth Thomas clock, the walnut bedroom furniture (which Roy made things out of), and our grandmother's mahogany dresser. What else I don't remember.

I took the gold china marked *T,* some glasses, and a batch of kitchen utensils.

We divided also the Victorian coin-silver spoons. There were table and teaspoons marked *FET,* some marked *Q and M,* and some un-marked. Later she received Aunt Lillie's§ teaspoons with an incised pattern.

It was understood (Ruby will remember) that when my house is broken up everything that came from our family will be yours. I am adding to that list all the china I have that was painted by her. There is also a large picture painted by our Grandma Betty Gaines, an American primitive of possible historical value, should you want it.

As I mentioned to you on the phone, keeping together the coin-silver spoons might be a good idea. And since I could actually use them now, and since they will be returned to you intact, perhaps you

---

*Paris (b. 1938), an American musician, broadcaster, and writer, had sent Thomson a gift of several detective novels, including his own *Mystery* (1973).

†New York's public radio station, which plays a considerable amount of contemporary music

‡née Margaret Elizabeth Gleason, Ruby's daughter (b. 1920)

§Lillie Gaines Eubanks Post (1868–1946)

might be willing to lend them to me pending their eventual return along with the gold china and my other pieces of Ruby's work.

I should be glad to have also any of Ruby's china that you do not want to keep. And whatever kitchen utensils may be left over.

The pictures will be stored till I can transport them. Also anything that might not fit a suitcase. The bedroom furniture will be a separate problem.

As documentary material for the library where my papers will be, I should appreciate having any and all letters from me that you come across. Also any photographs you are willing to part with of yourself, Ruby, Mother, Father, or me. The genealogical papers I already have in the form of copies. If you ever want to give the originals to a library (for tax deduction) I can give you Xerox copies to replace them.

There are a worn silver tea kettle belonging to me (unless one of the girls would like it) and a small framed watercolor of green cedar trees in a mist.

I suggest you check all of this with Ruby.

I am very happy that she is near you and do hope that a private phone will enable her to keep up with her friends.

Love,

To ANDREW RAEBURN*

November 16, 1976

Dear Mr. Raeburn:

I have played the tape, and much thanks.

The orchestra sounds fine and the musical direction is convincing throughout.

Miss Dunn is musically convincing too, and her sheer vocal presence is most impressive.

Some of this presence, however, may be due to over-miking, since whenever she sings the orchestra seems to fade.

Everybody else, in consequence, seems under-miked. The ever-so-characteristic solos of Jo the Loiterer, John Adams, Indiana Elliot, Constance Fletcher, and Daniel Webster, not to mention the briefer vocal entries of minor characters, are lacking in presence. In these I sometimes hear nothing *but* the orchestra, rarely much vocal life or dramatic characterization.

---

*(b. 1943), Director of Artists and Repertory for New World Records and producer of the recording of *Mother of Us All*

The recording ends up by suggesting a cast with little dramatic purpose beyond giving cues to Susan B.

Whether an improved acoustical mix could be made I do not know. But I do regret the absence of a broader human panorama expressed through vocal characterization, an equalized presence throughout the cast. One would not have needed to worry about protecting the prima donna's volume or star quality. She has those by nature, and by the sheer length of the role she dominates every scene she is in, and she is absent from the stage actually in only one short scene out of eight.

The work needs strong and varied character actors to support a protagonist so self-determined as Susan B. Carrying the performance all alone, she risks being monotonous, a situation not alleviated by the fact that much of the time Miss Dunn is working in a tessitura that is not entirely comfortable.

She wants, in consequence, some musical cushioning and lots of dramatic buildup. Treating the cast as chiefly acoustical background does not give much help. I should have preferred her surrounded by vocal sound rather than standing in front of it.

Anyway, these are my thoughts. I hope they are not unwelcome.

With my thanks and warm greetings,

Sincerely,

To Andrew Porter*

January 25, 1977

Dear Andrew,

As you may well imagine, your piece about *Lord Byron* was for me more than merely gratifying. To be treated as a serious composer of operas, just imagine! And not as the operator of some shell game, or as an amateur who had once met Gertrude Stein in Paris.

As for the shortened version, its purpose was the same as that behind the similarly smoothed-out final version of *4 Saints,* namely to assure in performance a trajectory without hesitations or digressions.

I am not sure that all this interior cutting has helped. In case of a really first-class production, a choice about it could be left to the conductor, since I still possess the 1972 score (3 copies of it), plenty of vocal scores, and a full set of parts. The publisher, of course, has

---

*(b. 1928), critic, musicologist, and translator, who wrote a favorable review of *Lord Byron* for *The New Yorker,* after a broadcast of the 1972 Juilliard production on WNYC

new scores and a materiel to go with them.

As you have noticed, this is neither an Italian nor a German opera, not even a French one, though it might be closer to that. Chief literary predecessor of the Stein operas may well be the English masque, and Larson's continuity a bit resembles hers, as viewed through his film experience perhaps.

My ideal of a staging would be one in which everybody except the two Italians acts very very English, directed by the sure hand of Freddy Ashton, who seems to understand as no one else does the stances and the choreographies of English life.

Certainly our view of Byron is far from the standard continental ones, all of which are derived more from his heroes than from him. After all, my opera deals with a poet still under thirty and, in spite of his (largely private) misbehaviors, surrounded by posh people. His wife was a relation of the Melbournes and the Lovelaces and Augusta was lady-in-waiting to the Queen. He himself was a sixth earl (Lizzie Lutyens insists "only a baron"), had been to Harrow and Cambridge, and certainly knew how to behave in graceful society, including a skiplike walk with cane that he had perfected for not appearing to limp.

All this might be for later, though I fancy not for England, where even at the Victoria and Albert Museum the special connection with his half-sister was not mentioned.

I did want you to know my awareness of the rare service your piece has done for my morale and to inform you about the two versions, both complete and available.

I wish we saw each other oftener.

Everbest,

To Yvar Mikhashoff*

February 9, 1977

Dear Mr. Mikhashoff:

I am ever so happy with your plans for playing my piano music.

Jean Ozenne, now deceased, was a French stage and film actor of considerable distinction. Having come to that profession rather late in life, he always played men of middle age or older. Before that he had been a dress designer employed by the house of Molyneux in Paris.

---

*(b. 1941), American pianist, specializing in twentieth-century music, who had inquired about the subjects of several of Thomson's portraits

Some subjects turn out in portraiture to be definitely of a pastoral nature. This happened to Aaron Copland, also to the poet Tristan Tzara. When it happens I am always a little surprised.

I do not have the original piano holograph of Aaron's portrait but I am sending you a Xerox copy of the piece as I used it in a film by John Houseman entitled *A Tuesday in November*. This was a 1945 documentary made in Hollywood for the United States government. It was translated into 46 languages and shown all over the world but never in America, since it was designed for exterior propaganda. It explains in two reels how we elect a president.

Very sincerely,

To a CORRESPONDENT

February 25, 1977

I am glad you like my music.

Unfortunately, I am not an expert on music's future. Its immediate past is hard enough to keep up with.

As for "civilization," I see no reason for supposing that it will not survive another 25 years. I imagine that nothing short of a worldwide atomic doomsday would interfere with that.

People always think "the country is going to the dogs," but it seems to survive. So do Europe and Asia. South America and Africa are in a mess, always have been. Australia seems to be booming.

Good wishes to you, and to the world in general.

Very sincerely,

To MARIO DI BONAVENTURA*

March 25, 1977

Dear Mario,

Five hundred bucks most welcome. When do I see them? Opera department unbelievably dilatory about paying up. I have not yet had anything from *The Mother* in Boston (February 1976), in Santa Fe (August 1976), or at Inverness Festival–San Anselmo, California (September 1976).

At least I find no notice of these productions among my royalty

---

*(b. 1924), an American conductor, then employed by G. Schirmer, which published *The Mother of Us All*

sheets. Nor of the Queens College performances that took place in December 1975. I hope I am in error.

My "thoughts," which you so kindly ask regarding the New World Records, are that authors should not be asked to give away their rights even to libraries, especially to libraries, which are a sizeable source of profit for books and music. If New World had asked me to relinquish my royalties I would have refused. So I am happy that you have secured some payment for me on the 7,000 giveaways. (I do not complain about customary services to the blind, the armed forces, or WNYC.)

I do think, however, that a decision needs to be made regarding broadcasts. If these are to be generally permitted, then the opera should be listed with ASCAP as a "small right," hence available to their subscribers. On this matter I shall respect your preferences.

Everbest,

To a CORRESPONDENT*

May 6, 1977

After I wrote to you yesterday I happened to be dining with John Huszar,† who showed me some of the rushes from the film (excellent from every point of view) and also his film about Robert Indiana, which I had not seen.

I am writing again to assure you that I found the Indiana film distinguished, imaginative, informative, and quite without vulgarity. It is accompanied very tastefully by music of mine played on the piano by Robert Helps, an excellent composer and one of the best piano soloists in America.

I have no reserve now about Huszar's treatment of me as subject matter, and I am collaborating not only by my presence in the film but also by lending him a very large number of still photographs from past times. The use of still photographs from *Louisiana Story,* accompanied by music or not, seems inappropriate, and I should be wretchedly unhappy if this highly important work of both Flaherty and myself should have to be omitted from John Huszar's film.

I do hope that you can persuade the Flaherty Foundation trustees to permit the usage of some section from this wonderful film.

From the musical point of view the soundtrack is remarkable,

---

*representing the estate of Robert Flaherty

†Huszar (b. 1941) produced and directed *Virgil Thomson: Composer,* a film for public television which was revised in 1986 for Thomson's 90th birthday and rebroadcast as *Virgil Thomson at 90.* Permission to use the Flaherty footage was denied.

made by the Philadelphia Orchestra with Eugene Ormandy, and it is the only film score ever to receive a Pulitzer Prize.

The film itself being now thirty years old, perhaps the time has come for helping out its distribution by quotations from it in other cinematographic work. The whole question seems to reside in a reserve on the part of one of the trustees, who has seen Huszar's Indiana film. Myself, I assure you, I have no such reserve and seriously hope that something can be done to influence your board toward a favorable decision.

Very sincerely yours,

To Ruby Gleason

Paris
Saturday, June 18, 1977

D.R.:

Yesterday a film crew was in my flat all day taking it and me and me talking. This is part of a documentary film about me that has already been mostly taken in N.Y. But the director wanted some of my Paris background. Earlier I had done an interview for French TV in the new museum called Centre Beaubourg. Last weekend I went to visit friends in Amsterdam and saw acres of Dutch pictures in museums. Tomorrow night I go to London on a train that gets put on a ship and then taken off without waking people up. I am thinking of selling the Paris flat. I don't really need it and it seems to be quite valuable.

L & K,
V

To Betty Allen*

July 15, 1977

Dear Betty,

Answering your question of June 27:
1. A music student's priorities are learning his art and performing. Study of science and the humanities will be good for him provided it

---

*(b. 1930), American mezzo-soprano, who first came to public attention as St. Teresa II in the American National Theater production of *Four Saints;* executive director of the Harlem School of the Arts

does not gravely take time away from practicing and performing.

2. Solfège, ear training, and sight singing must be a part of his training. All such skills acquired before going to college are an advantage. If he does not have them by the time he goes to college he must quickly acquire them. This will be done usually off-hours and at his own expense.

I also favor the adding of private lessons to conservatory and college curricula. They speed up everything.

Everbest,

To Jere Abbott

September 12, 1977

Dear Jere,

I sympathize with your altered hearing as regards pitches. My own pitches are so completely falsified by now that I cannot listen to music under any circumstance and get a believable report of it from my ears. I write music, but only at the table. I cannot even proofread at the piano, much less try out anything.

After fifty years of residing at 17 *bis,* quai Voltaire I have sold my flat for a very good price and shall be going over in October to clean it out. Maurice will join me there for a final fling of seeing old friends. I shall not regret the flat. Paris is no longer a place that tempts me for any length of time.

I am in splendid health and hope you are. I long ago observed in my long-living family that the eighties can be quite pleasant. I don't think the nineties look like lots of fun, though my sister, now ninety-two, is having a quite pleasant life, in full possession of her mind and spirits. But as Lili de Clermont-Tonnerre remarked when she got to be old, "Il y a tout de même le drame de la chair."*

Affection and everbest,

To a Correspondent†

September 20, 1977

The list of your literary and theatrical activities is most impressive. Naturally I have no reserve about your abilities.

On the other hand, I am not inclined to do anything about your

---

*"All the same there is that drama with the body."
†a poet who had sent Thomson a libretto

libretto, since I have never composed an opera to a libretto already in existence. My way of getting involved is to share with the poet from the very beginning the choice of theme and subject.

I do not necessarily interfere with my librettists during their writing periods, but I do rather need to be involved with the subject itself. It has to be something close enough to my own preoccupations to make it seem likely that my devotion to it will be sufficient to inspire me through the labors of composition. Any other approach would be like decorating somebody else's house.

I am grateful that you should have thought of me in connection with your work and sorry that at my advanced age I do not find it likely that we might collaborate on a stage work.

Very sincerely,

To a Correspondent*

November 11, 1977

At 17 I knew I was a "modern." At 28 I was ceasing to be a neo-classical, neo-medieval, neo-baroque modern and beginning in my own way to be what I still think of as a highly independent composer. I follow no leader, lead no followers. As for being "American," I learned 50 years ago that all you had to do for that is to write music. National qualities follow. Similarly, of course, for being "modern." Once your apprentice years are over, only the discipline of spontaneity has value. And that, please realize, is the toughest of all the disciplines.

Everbest,

To Ruby Gleason

December 14, 1977

Dear Ruby,

The white fruitcakes arrived and I am very happy to have them. They will make dessert for unexpected occasions well into the spring.

The Flenders† came on Monday for dinner and brought the chil-

---

*who had asked Thomson about his relationship to American musical modernism
†Richard Flender (b. 1929), a banker and vice-president of Morgan Guaranty Trust, and his wife Norma Flender, a pianist

dren, who also brought a cedar wreath for my door with angels on it and a small-to-middle-size Christmas tree for which they had made decorations themselves, including pieces of cardboard cut out to look like notes of music.

They also brought a dozen quails shot in Florida and frozen there. I roasted them and cooked vegetables and things to go with them. We were eight for dinner, including Maurice and some friends who arrived from California. The next day I made broth out of the bones.

I am having Christmas Eve dinner for American friends from Paris, a man, wife, and child. I will give them wild turkey and wild rice, some other things, and plum pudding.

L & K,

To Donald Sutherland

January 30, 1978

Dear Donald,

Our day together was a delight to me, especially in view of your improved condition.*

I know the doubts and mental dramas that you are going through with regard to Max Jacob. His outrageousness in all respects has always been hard to take, as his charm, warmth, and brilliant fellowship were impossible to reject.

Eric de Haulleville, who could not bear him, or whose poetry had possibly been rejected by Max, insisted that he was "un faux juif, un faux catholique, un faux Breton, un faux Français, un faux peintre, un faux poète, et un faux ami." Henri Sauguet, on the other hand, who lived in daily contact with him at the Hôtel Nollet for something like ten years, found his friendship a privilege and rewarding.

I have been finding his letters to Cocteau to be Max at his hardest to take. The children's book, however elegantly written, seems to me a pot-boiler. Let us go on with the subject when next we meet, which I still think will be toward the end of April.

I found on arrival many copies of Parnassus, and I hope you have received one by this time. Your piece on me is a delight, the Rimbaud essay plain marvelous, I think the most penetrating I have ever read and certainly the least dizzy.

Affection ever,

---

*Sutherland was suffering from lung cancer; he died later that year.

To Lou Harrison

February 15, 1978

Dear Lou,

Your beautiful letter of recent vintage,* though a little large for framing, has been filed with the rest of your correspondence as a precious document.

My hunch about a possible rapprochement between the popular and the intellectual tradition is so far only a vague smell. I have no tangible evidence beyond the fact that John Rockwell reviews both kinds of music in *The New York Times* with understanding and that their differences do not seem to impress him.†

My love to you both,

To Jack Beeson

March 6, 1978

Dear Jack,

The reason for giving a course‡ would be to find more examples (in both old and new English-language music) and to give answers to all sorts of questions that bright students might raise.

A half-course would be enough, and I think it should be a composition seminar limited to, say, 10 students, 2 hours once a week.

I wonder if, being busy yourself, you might know somebody prepared to take it on with me. Alone I fear the library work and my lack of teaching routines. The main lecture is already typed out, but I think of a book as containing lots more material—how to project the meaningful syllables for instance, how to distort for passionate statement, to go into and out of patter, to syncopate the line for avoiding methods that fit German or French or Italian *but not English*.

It's not really a job to take on casually.

Everbest,

---

*actually a fine piece of calligraphy as Thomson described it
†Rockwell (b. 1940) would later help assemble *A Virgil Thomson Reader* (1981) and write its introduction.
‡a projected course at Columbia University on music and language

To Maurice Grosser

May 19, 1978

D.M.,

The NYU speech that you asked about was a University Lecture. I wrote a new one, very good I am told, and the fee was good.

I got my Columbia degree two days ago. Along with it came an elaborate silk robe in gray-blue and a black velvet mortarboard without the board, a square tam-o'-shanter with gold tassel.

Next week I give a graduation speech at Peabody in Baltimore, where they are doing at that time a production of *The Mother of Us All* with a fine black Susan, Veronica Tyler. I also pick up from there a degree from Johns Hopkins along with a gold robe.

All the big-time colleges are now moving out of black and into fancy dress. The *Parson Weems* ballet is fine in its new version, everything repaired, and some quite entertaining masklike headdresses.

For tonight's dinner I am making fried chicken and strawberry shortcake.

L & K

To Maurice Grosser

June 8, 1978

D.M.:

I am glad of the big pictures. Ça change. Otherwise your summer seems to have been a series of mild disasters. For that I am sorry.

My academic gowns can be worn in academic parades or as bathrobes. One is powder blue with pink velvet bands, the other gold with black bands.

My NYU speech is hard to repeat in 15 words, but it is about history—the constant factors vs. the changing ones.

It turned out that my graduation speech at Peabody in Baltimore was the same I gave there in 1952. I didn't tell them and nobody recognized it. It was a huge success. I gave it again at the Mannes School and it was also a success.

I had dinner at Buffie's.* A quite grand loft building. She owns it and rents out part. A girl carpenter has done spectacular things. The new paintings are huge, all flower forms out of O'Keeffe and as was

---

*Buffie Johnson (b. 1912), American painter

said of a de Mille ballet "wildly gynecological." OK I guess for decorative panels in a ladies' bath house and really quite pretty. And dinner was good.

L. & K.

V.

To Irving Kolodin*

June 28, 1978

Dear Irving,

Your letter gave me a deep pleasure. Praise from Sir Hubert and all that.

I too regret that we do not meet up. Since my hearing has become both faint and false I avoid musical events.

I learn by asking around that many of my contemporaries suffer from both volume loss and pitch distortion, but few of them have as exaggerated a wrong-note experience as I do. What I hear is quite far from what is played. Even at the piano, the sound has no dependable relation to what my fingers do.

I write music still, because I remember sounds, but I have no way of verifying what I write. This phenomenon, not unknown among musicians, is more inconvenient for listening than for composing. In neither case is it an ideal situation.

My very good wishes,

Everbest,

To Donald Sutherland

June 30, 1978

Dear Donald,

Thanks many times for the Debussy book, especially since it contains such wonderful photos of my beloved Mary Garden.†

I am undecided whether to worry about you intensely. Not lest you should die; you are too strong to be doing anything like that right off. But I do get preoccupied by the possibility of your being in pain and other discomforts.

---

*(b. 1908), American music critic and author, long associated with *Saturday Review*
†Thomson no longer recalls which book this was; it is not one of Sutherland's own.

So I send along intensified vibes. They can't hurt and they often help.

Everbest,

To His Colleagues*

September 25, 1978

Dear ——,

There is a question of reissuing the record of my Five Songs from William Blake.

One of these poems is the well-known "The Little Black Boy."

Once or twice there have been objections on the part of the black community to this being performed.

I would love to know your view of the matter. The verses go as follows:

My mother bore me in the southern wild,
And I am black, but O! my soul is white;
White as an angel is the English child,
But I am black as if bereav'd of light.

My mother taught me underneath a tree,
And sitting down before the heat of day,
She took me on her lap and kissèd me,
And pointing to the east, began to say:

"Look on the rising sun: there God does live,
And gives his light, and gives his heat away;
And flowers and trees and beasts and men receive
Comfort in morning, joy in the noonday.

"And we are put on earth a little space,
That we may learn to bear the beams of love;
And these black bodies and this sun-burnt face
Is but a cloud, and like a shady grove.

"For when our souls have learn'd the heat to bear,
The cloud will vanish; we shall hear His voice,
Saying: 'Come out from the grove, My love & care,
And round My golden tent like lambs rejoice.'"

---

*Thomson sent this letter to several people in the musical community. The record was reissued without "The Little Black Boy."

Thus did my mother say, and kissèd me;
And thus I say to little English boy.
When I from black and he from white cloud free,
And round the tent of God like lambs we joy,

I'll shade him from the heat, till he can bear
To lean in joy upon our father's knee;
And then I'll stand and stroke his silver hair,
And be like him, and he will then love me.

To Ruby Gleason

December 12, 1978

D.R.,

Can you remember how Mother used to make chicken cro-
quettes? All my cookbooks describe the kind that are made with
white sauce, in a cylindrical shape, and deep-fried.

I remember them as being mostly chicken in the shape of small
patties, rather like hamburger. They were sauteed in butter on two
sides. But there must have been something holding them together.
What do you suggest that I use? Egg would help, also possibly a bit
of bread crumb soaked in milk.

Your chocolates arrived and I thank you.

My painting has been over for a week, but my floors are still
drying. They will be given another coat tomorrow night.

Love and kisses,

To Jere Abbott

January 15, 1979

Dear Jere,

Philip J[ohnson] is full of commissions and glories. I find all the
buildings pretty German, some of them shockingly so. The interior
of the NYU library looks like a jail courtyard. So does the prome-
nade lobby of the [New York] State Theater. The latter adds further
disregard by being lit only to show the architecture, leaving the
public in semi-darkness. It was not reported in the papers, but the
Glass House in Canaan exploded recently and two sides of it blew
out.

My old friend Avery Claflin died and there was a funeral in

Greenwich. His wife had died exactly a year before. When you are as old as we are, your friends tend to die off in batches.

Maurice is about to have a retrospective show at Fischbach Galleries and another in Washington.

Good luck with the photos. Since the prices have gone so silly on painted pictures photos seem to be the only thing anyone can afford, and they are on the way up.

My *Four Saints* is about to be given in Swedish at Stockholm. I have a concert date mid-February in San Antonio, a city I love, and the time of year is right.

Everbest,

To a FRIEND

January 17, 1979

When your birthday present arrived last November I opened it with joy. Both my secretary, Victor Cardell, and I remember that fact distinctly. But neither of us can remember what the gift was. Neither can I identify it with any of the small objects visible around my house.

Please remind me what it was, excuse me for not thanking you promptly, as I should have done, and allow me to enjoy it all over again when I can lay my hands on it knowingly.

Throughout the month of November and mostly through Christmas my flat was in disorder due to the whole place having been freshly painted, the floors scraped and shined, certain ones carpeted, and an acre or two of upholstery done on chairs. During this time Mr. Cardell and I tried to keep up the correspondence, but some letters did get mislaid and some packages went unacknowledged.

Do send me a note or postcard telling me what the lovely object was. I remember well the size of the box but for the life of me cannot recall what came out of that box.

My opera *Four Saints,* now translated into Swedish, is opening in Stockholm on May 2. Being invited, I shall go over.

Affection ever,

To a Correspondent*

March 19, 1979

Artists when young do tend to idealize older artists and to imitate them.

After a while, when they grow up, they are more influenced by the artists that they *don't* like.

In my case the chief dislikes of my maturity have been Tchaikovsky, Sibelius, and Brahms—exactly the composers that teenagers tend to go for.

Good wishes sincerely,

To Maurice Grosser

May 16, 1979

Dear Maurice:

I received your letter in Cambridge. All that to-do went off fine, including a session with Ivan Tcherepnin's† composition class and a concert of my choral works in Boston. I did not do the Harvard Glee Club banquet speech, being kept in New York that night by a grippe-cold that involved a complete *extinction de voix*. The *extinction* left rapidly. I suspect it was acquired in order to avoid making the speech. Anyway I didn't make it.

I sent you a program from Stockholm. The *Four Saints* in Swedish was charming and even rather brilliant. The people who put it on were a young group, early to middle thirties, just like we all were when we put it on in Hartford. The singing, as always with Swedes, was wonderful, also the orchestra, and the scenery was imaginative and quite fun. Some of the stage direction was a little silly but most operatic stage direction right now is silly anyhow. The Swedish reviews, which I cannot read, are said to be super-favorable. The translation, I am told by Americans, is wholly satisfactory, and every word of it can be heard in performance.

Ben Weber died of huge complications following a ten-years-ago crisis of liver disease.

Ruby seems to be fading a bit.

L & K,

---

*who had asked Thomson to enumerate his influences
†(b. 1943), American composer, youngest son of Alexander Tcherepnin

June 5, 1979

Dear Matthew,

Thanks for the very touching letter about Ben [Weber]. I loved him also and shall miss him, as long as you will, and Willie [Masselos] too of course.

The death, long due, was painful and his patience about it was grand. Not wishing to be a part of it, and quite unable to help him or to hold it off, I avoided witnessing the spectacle. I now remember him during our thirty-five-year (at least) friendship as looking a great deal better than he must have at the end.

I knew about a piece dedicated to me. He had mentioned it. But not what happened to it.

Everbest,

To J. Lewis Blackburn★

June 19, 1979

Dear Lewis,

It was nice of you to write about Ruby. As you know, we were very close and I keep thinking about her. At nearly 94 she was certainly entitled to die, and I am happy that she did not suffer. She merely faded away, largely stopped eating, then one night she didn't breathe anymore.

My affection to you all forever,

To Maurice Grosser

Montecatini Terme
July 27, 1979

Dear Family:

I arrived here for lunch and I am glad to be alone after visiting. Saw the doctor right away, and he found (as I knew from N.Y.) that my liver is a bit enlarged (French of me, n'est-ce pas?). Nothing to be done about it but not drink, which is part of the diet anyway. I

★(b. 1913), a consulting engineer and the son of Lela Garnett, one of Thomson's first cousins; Ruby had died on June 5.

also have two kinds of massage every day, the regular one and the underwater one, which is vastly entertaining. My room has the usual abundance of linen sheets and towelings (even for stepping out of bed) also an icebox full of wines & liquors which I don't use, and a *bidet à jet montant* which is as joyful a toy as can be imagined.

The Villa d'Este at Como was a proper luxury hotel with a view, good sheets, and right food (wonderful fresh pesto, also wild mushrooms) but I like it better here, am relaxed and quite at home. Nothing to complain about at all.

L & K

To WYE JAMISON ALLANBROOK

August 22, 1979

Dear Wye,

The *Don Giovanni* analysis is thoroughly interesting, though for me not as thrilling a revelation as the exposé of dance-meters in your *Figaro* treatment.

Just a suggestion regarding the "seductions." Whatever was the Don's earlier behavior with Elvira and all those catalogued others, the only affairs that occur as part of *this* play (those involving Zerlina and Anna) are attempts at rape. The Don, as we are shown him, was an "activist."

Everbest to you both,

To MAURICE GROSSER

[Aptos, California]
Tuesday, August 28, 1979

D.F.:*

The Cabrillo festival goes on casually and not very good because the conductor is not very good but Dennis [Russell] Davies† who *is* good takes over today and it will be better. Yesterday at an 18th-century mission church a new str. q'tet by Lou [Harrison] got a big applause so I guess it was good and Lou said it was. He also is rehearsing a gamelan concert for Sunday.

---

*"Dear Family"
†(b. 1944), American conductor with a particular expertise in twentieth-century music

Lou & Bill are camping in their new house (very pretty) while I live alone next door in the old one. Mostly during the day I am alone reading thrillers I bought one day in Berkeley. Thursday & Friday of this week [Jack] Larson will be here, also Betty Freeman* & her sculptor. They will hear my *Chiesa*, Violin Sonata, some piano pieces, *Seine at Night* and *Sea Piece w. Birds*. Al Frankenstein may come too, if his sciatica allows. He is in lots of pain. Lou & Bill work all the time and are cheerful. Charles Shere,† who has your G. Stein film script, still thinks he may find money to put it on. He has written an opera about Marcel Duchamp and it will be produced next year. Frankenstein has left the *Chronicle* and is now curator of American art in all the S.F. museums. I saw in Berkeley a lovely exhibit of Arp drawings, collages, tears, and cutouts. The King Tut show is on in S.F. but tickets sold out way ahead and huge crowds. Anyway I think I will not be going to S.F. except on Tuesday 4th to airport for N.Y.

Weather has been wonderful—sunny, cool nights, flowers everywhere, and sea or mountains or both in every view. Costumes incredibly sloppy except that the topless-barefoot young are pretty to look at. Food is OK, but nothing remarkable. We have just outside the door quantities of rosemary, chives, mint, comfrey, and similar herbs, bay of course too. Not much basil right here. One hostess had chicken liver pâté with a touch of curry in it—a help. On Friday after the concert Lou is having 75–100 people for me in the new house with cold buffet. He has 2 gamelans (home-made) and they have a rich sound. You once painted a California landscape with the gold-colored hills and dark live-oak trees. I wonder where it is.

P.L.M.

Lots of solar heating around. It is believed to work. Lou's is not yet connected, but looks pretty in the front yard and preferable to nonfunctional sculpture.

*(b. 1921), Southern California patron of the arts, especially of modern music
†(b. 1935), composer and critic, *Oakland Tribune*

To Stephen Holden★

September 17, 1979

Dear Steve,

Your book arrived in June as I was leaving town. I put it away, forgot I owned it, found it on Saturday by accident, spent all Sunday reading it straight through.

I could not put it down. I love it. It is the kind of thriller that I usually have to depend on English writers to provide. My favorites there are Len Deighton and Desmond Bageley. All these are thrillers offering detailed acquaintance with a milieu.

Your picture of Rockbiz is utterly convincing and your porn is the most distinguished I have yet encountered. The whole book, in fact, I find to be a distinguished product, and I only hope its elegance of structure and phraseology will not hinder circulation. Anyway I love it and am cherishing it against Maurice's return from Africa. We pass books back and forth, this one will be further valued, being signed by your father.

Warm greetings everbest,

To Craig Rutenberg†

November 2, 1979

Dear Craig,

Happy the music arrived.

The Piano Sonata No. 3 is dedicated to Gertrude Stein. My inscription that it was for her to "improvise on the pianoforte" came from her habit of playing on the white keys only, since she "did not like" the black keys and could not read music anyway. Having no musical "ear," she was obliged to improvise if she played at all since there was not enough musical memory for her to play anything "by ear." Obviously, she was not going to either read or learn to play my Sonata No. 3, though it is composed entirely for the white keys, just in case such a miracle occurred. My whole idea was fanciful and, if you like, absurd. It did, however, allow me to offer her the manu-

---

★(b. 1941), American poet and music critic, son of Alan Holden (1904–85), a crystallographer and a Harvard friend of Thomson's. The book referred to is a novel, *Triple Platinum*.

†(b. 1952), pianist and opera *répétiteur*, who wrote Thomson for background information on his piano sonatas.

script as a present. Alice, of course, could read it either with or without a piano. Anyway, the only piano that was ever available domestically was a small antique instrument belonging to the manor house the ladies had hired.

Weather here is wonderful. I am going to Pittsburgh for Thanksgiving and my 83rd birthday.

Affection ever,

To PAUL BOWLES

December 23, 1979

D.P.:

Very happy with good reviews of your story book.* I am well. Ditto Maurice. People visit constantly for writing books about us all. This month it's mostly Nadia Boulanger. But there is lots of George Antheil too coming up. So far I am more a source than a subject.

Everything ever everbest
V.T.

To JOAN KRIST†

March 10, 1980

Dear Joan,

My acquaintance with Joyce ran from 1925, when I met him through an American composer friend, George Antheil, also through Sylvia Beach.

I knew Sylvia from my first days in France, which began in 1921, and I had subscribed for a copy of the first edition of *Ulysses* when she published it in 1922.

Later I saw Joyce with some frequency, but always in some connection with Antheil or Sylvia or her French friend who lived in the same block, Adrienne Monnier. He used to come to my concerts because he liked my music.

I did not see him after about 1928 or 1929 for several years. His

---

*Bowles had recently edited and translated *Five Eyes* by Abdeslam Boulaich.
†one of Thomson's cousins (b. 1947) and an allergist associated with the University of Washington; Krist had asked him about his association with Joyce.

eyes were in a bad state and he did not go out much. Then in 1936, I think it was, occurred the incident recounted in my book [*Virgil Thomson*] of his asking me to come to see him and proposing that I write a ballet on the Children's Games chapter of *Finnegans Wake*. This would have been for the Paris Opéra and I declined on the grounds that ballets don't have words. Actually, in view of the rivalry between Joyce and Gertrude Stein, I did not wish to play one against the other.

After that I did not see him again. During the war he went to live in Switzerland and I think he died there in 1941.

Very happy to hear from you and wish you everything nice.

Everbest,

To LINDSEY MERRILL*

March 31, 1980

My dear Dean Merrill,

Nothing would make me happier than a V.T. festival, as occasion my 85th year, which will begin on November 25.

I am delighted that you have a new hall where operas can be given. Mine, as you probably know, are three: *Four Saints in Three Acts, The Mother of Us All,* and *Lord Byron.*

Of these, *The Mother of Us All* is the easiest to produce and the most assured of success. *Four Saints,* being pretty obscure as to text, gives less guidance for staging, though an imaginative director-cum-choreographer can do wonders with it.

Lord Byron (text by Jack Larson) is the one closest to my heart, because it is the most recent. I suggest, if you do not know it well, that you get yourself sent a perusal copy from Southern Music Publishers.

The orchestra for *Four Saints* and *The Mother* can be effective with as few as 25 or 26 players. *Lord Byron,* using wind instruments in pairs, four horns, and three trombones plus percussion, would sound better with more strings than the others need.

I had it on my mind for some time to send you some manuscripts or scores, and I am sure that I can manage to do so in spite of the departure of all of my pencil holographs (some 10,000 pages) for the Yale Music Library.

Sometime this spring or summer I shall go through the remains

---

*(b. 1925), then dean of the Conservatory of Music at the University of Missouri–Kansas City

and find some nice things for you. It would be absurd if my own hometown had nothing at all.

An hour-length film about me has just been completed. That would be appropriate to show at a festival. I shall also have another book coming out next year, a sort of memorial volume called *A Virgil Thomson Reader*.

Maybe one of our local artists, Frederic James perhaps, could be mobilized for designing scenery and costumes.

Naturally I would be present for such a festival, before, during, and after.

Everbest,

To James D. Brasch*

June 4, 1980

My dear Brasch:

I never knew of Ernest Hemingway having any especial interest in contemporary music other than that of George Antheil, who was after all a protectorate of the rue de l'Odéon, and a literary man's idea of a musical genius.

Not that Antheil was not a perfectly good musician and an interesting composer, but surely Hemingway would have encountered his work far more easily in literary than in musical circles. Myself, I don't remember ever seeing Hemingway at a musical event.

His own memoirs speak frequently about pictures and painting, a taste for which he might very well have acquired through Gertrude Stein.

I am sure that if Hemingway had had a notable interest in music itself, rather than merely reading about it, that fact would be known still to persons acquainted with him in Paris, Spain, Africa, New York, or Havana. Many of these people are still alive and could possibly help you.

Very sincerely,

---

*(b. 1929), Hemingway scholar; member of the English department, McMaster College, Hamilton, Ontario

To Howard Hanson

October 28, 1980

Dear Howard,

Warm greetings at 85. I am 84 myself in November. I rather like being old, so long as I feel well.

I hope you are writing music. I am, though it comes more slowly than it used to.

And I hope you are conducting. Nobody else understands so well what each American piece should sound like.

We are all grateful to you and admire you sincerely for your achievements in all the musical ways.

Ever warmly,

To a Correspondent*

November 17, 1980

I am glad you like my ever-so-Protestant *Symphony on a Hymn Tune*.

I am enclosing also the piano-vocal score of my Requiem Mass, which though no longer ecumenical I like to think of as ever-so-Catholic (though I am not).

Very cordially,

To a Correspondent†

February 18, 1981

The course in music reviewing that you refer to took place during the academic year 1941–42.

It was a graduate seminar at New York University taught by all four music reviewers of the *New York Herald Tribune*. These were, besides myself, Francis Perkins, Jerome D. Bohm, and Robert Lawrence. It met once a week and was limited to ten students.

Perkins taught them newspaper routines, how to check information, also how to analyze an orchestral score. Bohm showed them how to review records and how to listen to anything. Lawrence

---

*a Catholic priest
†who asked about Thomson's classes in music criticism

explained the opera and went through with them quite a lot of opera repertory. Myself, I treated the seminar as a course in English composition.

My standard for a passing mark was that the students should be capable of writing reviews and special articles well enough to be published in the *Herald Tribune,* and many of their papers were so published. I provided through management sources tickets for every kind of musical event. The students did, as I remember, remarkably good work.

At many other times and places I have later given courses in music reviewing. I always treat these as if I were teaching English, because I practically always find that the students are better prepared in music than they are in writing. Music criticism, of course, is primarily writing; music is the subject. If they are ignorant on the subject they should not be reviewing music. But if they are not accomplished as writers they are hopeless for reviewing anything, or even for taking examinations in their music courses.

Yours truly,

To David Ostwald★

March 6, 1981

Dear Mr. Ostwald,

Mr. Locklair's† remark to you that I had "enjoyed" last year's production of *The Mother of Us All* was true but insufficient.

I found the musical production on the whole excellent when not interfered with by what I considered overbusy staging. I actually do not think that your concept of the "3-ring circus" was a good idea for that opera, which involves a number of extended solos in which the meaning of the words needs to be understood.

It seemed to me that no sooner would any soloist begin an aria than activities in other parts of the stage would start up. This kind of run-around staging can sometimes be of service in situations overtly comic. I did not find it helpful in this case. It added a dimension to the spectacle which seemed to me inappropriate, and all too casual to my taste, for a work so essentially serious.

I would not have bothered you with my thoughts on the matter if

---

★(b. 1943), theatrical director, staged *The Mother of Us All* at The Juilliard School in 1980
†Wriston Locklair (1925–84), public relations director at Juilliard

you had not written me. But the truth of the matter is that I found your staging of this particular work somewhat less than a pleasure.

Good luck with your next opera.

Very sincerely,

To JOHN OBETZ*

March 9, 1981

Dear John,

Indeed I did play on the organ at the old Grace (Episcopal) Church. I practiced there every day, had my lessons there from Clarence Sears, assisted him at Sunday services, and occasionally played a postlude. I was thirteen at the time.

If you want to play something of mine on the new organ, I suggest the Passacaglia or the *Pange Lingua*. My favorite is the latter but the former is possibly more "accessible" to organ lovers. Both are at G. Schirmer. Neither would be a first performance except in Kansas City.

The *Pange Lingua* was composed for inaugurating the then-new organ at Philharmonic Hall and was played on that occasion by E. Power Biggs.† I wrote it in full possession of the specifications for that instrument.

I am glad the new organ is to be at the back of the church, also that the choir will not have to pretend it is paying attention during the sermon. A small choir and chancel organ might be useful for responses.

I shall probably be in Kansas City at some time next September and would love to be shown the new instrument.

Greetings everbest,

---

*(b. 1933), American organist based in Missouri
†(1906–77), English-born American organist

To Richard Burgin*

March 16, 1981

Dear Mr. Burgin:

Among the various addresses listed on your masthead the one I am using seems most probable for editorial purposes.

Anyway, my sincere compliments to both you and Dominique Nabokov† on the interview, which I find first-class.

I am mad for the photograph also. It makes me look almost human.

I am sending a copy of this letter to Dominique's New York address. She will be back from Paris, I understand, in a week.

Do you think it might be possible, for the second installment of this admirable interview, to ask of the typesetters that they omit the "p" in my name?

Very cordially, very warmly, and

Gratefully,

To a Correspondent‡

March 20, 1981

I did not know Charles Martin Loeffler, but of course I used to hear his music in Boston. My piano teacher Heinrich Gebhard§ often played in the *Pagan Poem*.

His music, French Impressionism, cleanly composed and elegantly orchestrated, seems not to have had much influence, though it is possible that Bostonian composers of similar tendency—Edward Burlingame Hill, for instance—may have been inspired by it. I must say that Hill, who was my own teacher and whom I assisted for several years in his Harvard classes, never mentioned it to me.

I'm sorry that I cannot tell you any more than this about Mr. Loeffler or his music. I'm not aware of any influence it may have had on mine or, to be exact, on anybody else's.

Very sincerely yours,

---

*(b. 1946), American literary critic and author, then editor of *New York Arts Journal*; son of longtime Boston Symphony concertmaster of the same name

†photographer, fifth wife and widow of Nicolas Nabokov

‡for whose dissertation Thomson was asked to relate memories of Loeffler (1861–1935) and to assess his importance

§(1878–1963), pianist and composer, who taught in Boston for many years; Leonard Bernstein was another of his pupils.

May 25, 1981

D.M.:

I went to see Saint Teresa* in her nursing home. She seems to be well off there and intending to stay. She is taken out of bed every day, has her lunch in the wheelchair, and stays running around on wheels for about four hours. Amelioration of her injury from the stroke is delayed by a progressive and quite painful arthritis, for which she is having therapy. Her expenses seem to be taken care of by Medicare and Medicaid, and she has a little money in reserve for burial expenses. She is very cheerful, can have visitors and can read. She is planning to give up her flat and be moved out of it on the first of July. Her furniture will be put in storage at somebody else's expense. Your picture is locked up carefully in somebody's house. She thinks it would be a good idea if your dealer could sell it. That would give her some extra money. It is my idea that possibly some purchaser might be willing to give it tax-free to Virginia State College, where she had planned to give it herself. Anyway, that can be looked into when you come home. To move from her flat on July 1, she will have to pay three months' rent, which amounts to $600. I am sending her that now so that she can make her arrangements well ahead of time. If you feel like sharing this with me, just send me a check made out to my Foundation. There is no obligation about this, but you can, of course, deduct it from your taxable income.

I also went to see Sylvia [Marlowe], who is also back in hospital and will be kept there for some time. She is very nervous and fidgety. I suspect that some of this inability to relax may be due to all that oxygen she is breathing. In the Hindu exercises, deep breathing is known to produce visions and ecstasies. In her case, breathing too deeply has already caused her to crack a rib.

L & K,

---

*Beatrice Wayne Godfrey, the original Saint Teresa I in *Four Saints*

To Maurice Grosser:

[Corfu]
August 26, 1981

D.M.

The visit has been thoroughly successful, which is surprising for so long a one—already 4 weeks & 1 more to go. The other guests go to beach every morning. I stay home & work, don't like sun or sea water. Sometimes they stay out for lunch but mostly home by 1:30. If not I make scrambled eggs. Lots of fruit & salad veg. around & good cheese. Sometime we go out for dinner at a restaurant, mostly in the last week or so. I have written an orch. piece called *Thoughts for Strings*, a *Hymn to Venus* for choir & piano (Elizabethan, Fletcher, fine text), and 3 portraits. Also revised for publication my lecture called *Music Does Not Flow*.

I feel good and look good; have loved the Mediterranean climate and the island mountain air. Have kept my Montecatini waist & even lost a bit more. Enjoyed the Greek food & wine, especially the red; also we get a very good retsina and quite wonderful feta cheese not hard or salty. Shrimps and fishes fine, lots of squid & small calamari, good ham, spit-roasted chickens & lamb (bought that way), incredible peaches, white figs and ripe tomatoes, also especially good bread and olive oil. Have met some nice residents Greek & Italian. No complaints at all but I shall be glad to get home, which happens via Athens & Rome on Wed. 2 Sept. Do come along when you've had enough Maroc. I'm sorry we didn't get our visit. Friends die, Anita Loos & Alfred Barr. Greek mail service 5–6 days from N.Y. English-language paper from Athens *very* good. We get also from Paris *Times* of London even *NY Times* only 2 days late. I like the place, good roads, lots of everything. I wouldn't mind coming back, but not alone. You might like it. I'm sure Paul [Bowles] would. Beaches everywhere, cars available, also buses. Prices quite modest. People pleasant.

L. & K.

To Robin Holloway*

September 21, 1981

Dear Robin,

I am grateful for the *Debussy and Wagner* book and reading it made me very happy. Actually it is a remarkable piece of musical analysis.

There must be somebody just real bright about music in the Cambridge landscape. Your book and the Gowers on Satie† are far out of the ordinary.

Regarding Kundry,‡ Mary Garden, who was the perfect Mélisande, always wanted to sing the role, but opera houses wouldn't let her do it. She had a special interpretation in view, which was to make the character *irréelle,* which does not mean that she could not have produced a rather grand breakthrough for the "kiss."

Regarding the tower scene with hair, in France we always supposed that Pelléas had an orgasm then and there. The music, which contains, I think, the only *ff* in the opera, seems to illustrate something like that. If this is true, then that is the point where everybody's future is determined, because he now knows his own mind.

Garden used to say that "the secret of Mélisande" is that she always lies. Even on her deathbed she avoids a clear statement. Apparently she has been so deeply hurt that though she will do *anything* to be loved, she trusts no one. Actually her unwillingness to be trustful is the source of the whole tragedy, since it brings hopeless discord into the life of a French family previously quite well organized for mutual understanding.

Regarding the second act of *Tristan,* one had been taught in former times that the lovers ejaculate simultaneously seven times and that these moments are clearly marked in the music. I wonder if I am right in reading your account to think that you credit them with only one such moment, and that something close to *coitus interruptus.*

In any case, Isolde's female orgasm is the first ever to be admitted in classical myth or fiction. As such, it seems to have deeply impressed the well-to-do classes, at least the women. I doubt whether the popularity of this opera ever touched the lower-middle classes in Germany as obviously as the *Ring* operas and *Die Meistersinger.*

---

*(b. 1943), British composer and Cambridge don
†Patrick Gowers's *Erik Satie: His Studies, Notebooks and Critics* (1966)
‡the penitent seductress in Wagner's *Parsifal*

Enough of all this. I am delighted with the book and deeply grateful to you for having written it.

All my thanks,

Everbest,

To RUSSELL FRASER*

September 21, 1981

Dear Russell,

I have your bound proofs of the Blackmur book and I have read it and find it quite wonderful.

As you are aware, I knew him in his early Cambridge [Massachusetts] days, also a little bit in his Princeton time. Always he was a prick, and your book shows that aplenty.

It also says he was first-class as a critic of poetry and English lit. Since several bright people agree with you, I guess I must. I would anyway. It so happens that I have never read any of his major pieces.

Your book quotes mostly just the poetry, which was nothing special. Anyway it's a fine book and I am very happy to have read it.

Warm greetings,

Everbest,

To SIDNEY COWELL†

September 29, 1981

Dear Sidney,

To cook pears evenly throughout, simply do it slowly and stop when they are a little underdone. For all stewed fruits, it is best to add the sugar only when they are cooked and you are taking them off the stove.

For rhubarb cut the French way in long pieces, you add sugar before cooking and do the whole thing in a rather high oven in a covered glass dish. As soon as bubbles begin to appear, take it out of the oven. The long pieces of rhubarb will be whole and the juice

---

*professor of English at the University of Michigan (b. 1927), and biographer of American poet and critic R. P. Blackmur (1904–65)

†(b. 1903), photographer, folk-song scholar, and widow of Henry Cowell; assembling a book of recipes by musicians.

clear. I sometimes add to this before cooking chunks of unpeeled orange and pieces of vanilla bean. Strawberries also go well with rhubarb.

Everbest,

To BETTY FREEMAN

November 23, 1981

Dear Betty,

I am happy you could come to my *4 Saints* evening* and happy that, though far from perfect, it came off so well.

Actually the recording, which took place beginning the following Monday night, the 16th, in four-hour sessions, seems to have corrected practically all the inefficiencies. I went to one session; Maurice and Chuck Turner† went to two of them. The words had all become clear, even I could tell that. The others found the vocal and instrumental ensemble harmonious and rich. Turner, who is a composer and a violinist, a real musician, said it gave him goose pimples, which is the sign of a good sound.

The engineer, whom I liked very much, seemed to understand the work and to be in complete agreement with me about positioning the microphones. Anyway, Nonesuch is a first-class recording firm, and I am looking forward to their issue of the complete *4 Saints,* which they expect to bring out next August. I have agreed to write liner notes for the jacket.

I am extremely grateful, as you may imagine, for your help given to [Joel] Thome's orchestra toward this achievement, which has been for them quite costly. I understand the concert alone ran to sixty thousand dollars. As a present to Joel to reward his devotion and persistence, I am arranging that Maurice paint a small portrait of him.

The other birthday celebrations have gone off quite well and this week there are still a publication party for my new book and a rather grand dinner at Chanterelle. Then comes a concert in Alice Tully Hall and a dinner, concert, and music-criticism round table at the Maison Française. Then I go to Montreal and Cambridge, back in

---

*Joel Thome had led a concert version of *Four Saints*, featuring Betty Allen, at Carnegie Hall earlier in the month, as part of an 85th birthday tribute to Thomson; the performance later became the basis for the first complete recording of the opera.
†(b. 1921), American composer

New York for Christmas Eve dinner. As you can see I am having fun being made a fuss over.

An interviewer from Norfolk, Virginia is here, the latest in a long line of them, including every kind of media, from the big nationals to a local broadcast company in Canada. I'll have to go meet him.

Affection and

Everbest,

To FLORENCE BUCHANAN*

December 14, 1981

Dear Florence:

I am very happy to hear from you.

At this moment I am in a hospital myself, the Roosevelt, having a very small pneumonia. There was far too much activity of concerts and ceremonials regarding my 85th birthday. They went on daily for two months, then when they were over I took to my bed.

I am rather enjoying the hospital, having a room to myself with a view of the Hudson, lots of fruit and flowers and visits.

Maurice comes every day and so does my secretary.

Maurice will be very happy to know that I have heard from you and he would be sure to ask me to send you his warm affection, which I am doing.

Along with it comes my own devoted love permanently,

Ever yours,

To CHARLES AMIRKHANIAN†

January 6, 1982

Dear Charles,

I am glad to hear about the new Armenian from Uruguay.

There are always composers in South America, charming when young, but mostly they do not ripen well.

Brazil and Argentina have done best, with a moment in Mexico when Chávez and Revueltas‡ shone out. Let's hope the Armenian

---

*widow of Briggs Buchanan, by then confined to a hospital

†(b. 1945), composer, critic, and broadcaster, who had written Thomson praising a young composer and decrying the state of music criticism in San Francisco

‡Silvestre Revueltas (1899–1940), whose music Thomson had admired: "it reminds one of Erik Satie's and of Emmanuel Chabrier's. It is both racy and distinguished" (*Virgil Thomson*).

strength of character (plus a Greek wife) can keep your new man growing. The artistic life of Spanish America is not a hearty weed. Brazil, being Portuguese and highly Negroid, is far more lively.

As for mus. crit. in S.F., at least it can still make waves. And the repetitive composers, being around fifty by now, are fully successful everywhere else, not rich yet, but played and known.

In my day the New York and Paris press behaved just like in San Francisco now, but when we got into our early forties, reviewers began to be respectful. Thank God for a little war somewhere.

Everbest,

To Brent Williams*

February 24, 1982

My dear Williams,

The case I telephoned you about involves Mrs. Beatrice Wayne Godfrey.

She sang the dramatic soprano leading role in the first production of my opera *Four Saints in Three Acts*. Also in many broadcasts of that work, including the New York Philharmonic. And in the RCA Victor recording of 1947, since reissued several times.

She also had a long and successful career as a vocal teacher and choir director, which was ended only in the last year or so by a paralytic stroke.

She was a fine musician and a distinguished singer.

Since she has been in the nursing home I have helped her several times and I shall probably do so again.

If the Musicians Fund can be mobilized in her favor, that would be a great help to both of us. I have told her that she may receive inquiries from you. She will answer these promptly, being perfectly able to write and to speak, and in full possession of her mental faculties.

I should be most grateful if you would write or telephone me again when you have investigated the case. I am very grateful for your interest.

Greetings everbest,

---

*(b. 1918), president of the Bohemians

To Harry Haskell[*]

April 14, 1982

Dear Harry,

I am sorry I didn't see you at the opening occasion.

The reporter who reviewed me beforehand was utterly charming. I am sure the city editor was right to send him.

My favorite newspaper story is about the reporter on tour in Brazil. Being fired by telegram, he answered in telegraphese, at company expense, "Upstick asswards."

Everbest,

To Léonie Rosenstiel[†]

May 14, 1982

Dear Miss Rosenstiel,

I enjoyed your book, I like it, and I thank you for sending it.

Actually it is the opening wedge of a research that will probably go much farther when all the materials still reserved by the estate become available, an enterprise that might be called the "debunking" of a legend.

Two items: one is the exclusion of Ernest Boulanger[‡] from the memorial masses at La Trinité. I don't find any clear reason for that in your book. The other is your idea that I was disappointed with Nadia's failure to introduce or recommend me in 1925 or -6 to the Princesse de Polignac. I had actually met her in 1921; I knew at least a half-dozen other friends of the lady who could have been mobilized as further connection; and only a very little later I actually declined when Jean Cocteau proposed writing her in my behalf. I was not interested in pursuing that particular career line; nor did the question of doing so ever arise in my long friendship with Nadia.

But I did greatly enjoy your book, especially for its information regarding Nadia's life before I first knew her. At that time she was 34 and I was 25, and our man-to-woman understanding was considerable, as indeed it was also between her and Roy Harris in the years 1926–30. After that the female mafia grew stronger and eventually

---

[*]long associated with the *Kansas City Star* and *Times*
[†]American musicologist, author of *Nadia Boulanger: A Life in Music*
[‡]Nadia's father

390

replaced the earlier dominance of Raissa.* Nadia bullied women, but she served men.

About the Catholic matter, a Dominican priest who had been her pupil told me only recently that on one occasion when she asked him to confess her, he was astonished by the simplicity, almost simple-mindedness of her faith, "like a peasant's," he said.

Greetings and good wishes,

Sincerely,

To Noah Creshevsky†

September 29, 1982

Dear Noah,

By all means use me for Guggenheim.

A deaf man recommending a composer is a strange idea, but maybe it will work.

Everbest,

To Lester Trimble‡

October 8, 1982

Dear Lester,

I should think Elliott Carter would obviously be next in line for the MacDowell Medal.

Leonard Bernstein is a handy celebrity to have around and a wonderful conductor, but he is not an interesting enough composer, in my opinion, for this honor.

Yours everbest,

---

*Nadia's mother
†(b. 1945), American composer, a student of Thomson's
‡American composer Trimble (1923–86), who once had written for the *Herald Tribune* under Thomson, was on the selection board for the Edward MacDowell Medal, awarded annually since 1960 by the MacDowell Colony to a distinguished composer, writer, or artist.

To Charles Shere

December 8, 1982

My dear Charles,

It doesn't make any difference how big your leg of lamb is. The cooking will still, at 550°F, take only eight-and-a-half minutes per pound (oven weight, stripped of all fat).

Nor does it make too much difference if your guests are late in coming to table, or if there is a first course to delay matters. The roast will keep warm on a hot-tray without cooking any more.

If you have no hot-tray, then the guests must come to table when it is done. There is a five-minute leeway here for carving. But roast lamb, short of a hot-tray, is like a soufflé; it will not wait.

Lord Byron will be given in Sacramento, spring of '84. To you both,

Devotion everbest,

To Anthony Tommasini★

April 20, 1983

Dear Tony:

I have never been able to make much out of my portrait by GS.

Have been looking at it lately with some intensity. So has Maurice. Neither of us can get very far.

It is quite grand, but terribly dense.

Do let me know what you make of it.

Everbest,

★(b. 1948), pianist, musical scholar, and teacher, then writing a study entitled *Virgil Thomson's Musical Portraits* (Pendragon Press). He had asked about the word-portrait Stein had written of Thomson in the late 1920s, which began: "Yes ally. As ally. Yes ally yes as ally. A very easy failure takes place. Yes ally. As ally. As ally yes a very easy failure takes place. Very Good. Very easy failure takes place. Yes very easy failure takes place." And so forth, for another forty-odd lines.

To a Correspondent*

June 20, 1983

I read it, all of it.

I could have put it down but I didn't.

I didn't like it except for a few moments of let-down-the-hair by people being interviewed, and a few maybe funny stories.

I didn't believe much of it either—the remarks are too pat, wise-cracks from repertory, observations about life and art, work and sex, far too familiar. You see, public characters talking about themselves always talk tommyrot, and nobody, literally nobody, remembers right. Rambling recollections undocumented make neither history nor literature.

The phoniest handout of all was Mae West's. Her only "number" was that of a drag queen. Even Tallulah, also a female impersonator, could act a bit (best in comedy). Carl Van Vechten, a devoted celebrity-hound, told me West's male friends tended to be heavy political types who helped her to invest in Brooklyn real estate. The muscle boys appeared with her after she was eighty, and right on stage. I'm sure they were part of the makeup.

Film celebrities, who are only images, are very different from actors and opera stars who work in public "live." Gertrude Stein, thirsting always for the kind of celebrity her close friend Picasso had achieved so early, described film people as "publicity saints," and she would have loved to be one, not just charismatically but through her work. But had she achieved that she might have become as worried and monotonous an old moneymaker as Picasso turned into.

Your "publicity saints," though miracle workers all, are pretty monotonous too (and no end garrulous). They all say the same things, declare the same faith (in work and sex), and are constantly quoting other celebrities. They all belong to the same club and never mention outsiders. They lack scale, some perfectly nice neighbors to measure their interestingness against.

If you can use any of the above, please do so. Maybe one of the first two sentences.

Everbest,

---

*who had asked Thomson to contribute a jacket blurb for a friend's forthcoming book

To Jay Rozen*

September 19, 1983

Dear Jay,

I am meditating a tuba piece.

I have no fixed prices, but like any doctor or lawyer I charge what the traffic will bear.

You might meditate on that.

Warm greetings,

Everbest,

To William Parker

September 26, 1983

My dear Parker,

Like all your other admirers, I am pleased that the City Opera has finally taken notice. If they ever produce my *Four Saints in Three Acts*, you would make a fine St. Ignatius. They won't, of course.

Beverly† had a beautiful voice and, when young, beautiful hair; but she has not shown much executive skill beyond money raising.

I heard the Massenet *Cendrillon* many years ago in Chicago, about 1912, I should think, with Maggie Teyte‡ as Cinderella and Mary Garden as the Prince. Mary had good legs and liked men's roles; her most successful being *Le Jongleur de Notre-Dame*.

About October 7, midnight parties are not a specialty of people in my age bracket. All the same, maybe. I shall not be going to the performance, because my ears now hear music wildly off-pitch.

Lots of success to you. Forty is young for baritones; I'm sure you are good for two more decades at least.

Everbest,

---

*(b. 1955), American tuba player and archivist at Yale University, who commissioned a portrait by Thomson

†soprano Beverly Sills (b. 1929), general director of the New York City Opera, which was reviving *Cendrillon* with Parker as Cinderella's father

‡(1888–1976), English soprano, who specialized in French music; much admired by Thomson

To Joseph Horowitz*

September 26, 1983

Dear Mr. Horowitz:

A discourteous treatment by attendants at the NBC broadcasts in Studio 8-H and earlier rudenesses at the concerts taking place in the Museum of Modern Art were mentioned by me in my newspaper column. Roy Harris referred to the guilty ushers and doormen as "the watchdogs of capital."

Radio music commentators varied hugely. I always found Ben Grauer both intelligent and intelligible. Similarly for Deems Taylor. Some were more patronizing, and others showed a lack of professional (or "inside") acquaintance with music.

The musical instruction of laymen, commonly called "music appreciation," was rife in the 20s, 30s, and 40s. Research on the subject covering both books and broadcasts would surely entertain you.

The ideal explainer of music, both classical and modern, has always been Leonard Bernstein. I suggest you look into his books for model treatments of the subject.

Warm greetings,

Very sincerely,

To a Correspondent†

November 15, 1983

I have never considered that being an arbiter of musical taste was a legitimate aim for a music reviewer. He would do much better to aim at setting standards of good English writing and clear musical analysis, particularly regarding contemporary works.

My former colleague Olin Downes was not a musician of much French background. He had the usual German pedagogical upbringing, later becoming fond of cold-climate composers, like Sibelius and the Soviet Russians.

There is no accurate way, to my knowledge, of measuring any writer's influence, or any composer's either for that matter. I am sure, however, that aspiring to have influence is a form of vanity

---

*(b. 1948), American music critic, at this time preparing *Understanding Toscanini: How He Became an American Culture-God and Helped Create a New Audience for Old Music* (Knopf), a study of the music business in the United States
†who had asked Thomson about the critic's role as arbiter

which can only be injurious in the practice of anything. The best idea is to make your work clear intrinsically, not to count heads.

Very sincerely yours,

To Nicolas Slonimsky*

April 23, 1984

Dear Nicolas,

Warm greetings.
I shall be joining your club in about two years.
Wait for me.

Affection everbest,

To Joelle Amar†

May 16, 1984

My dear Joelle,

The good information is that the Dinosaur Annex‡ wants you to play my new portrait piece at their concert of January 20, 1985. I think that that is the date, and I do hope you can accept. They have no doubt written you.

The less good item is your unhappiness with the piece itself. If this is merely an artistic disappointment, it may change as you play the work more.

Regarding its length, I am somewhat confused. Certainly it is shorter than we had counted on. That can no doubt be adjusted, not by lengthening the work but by simply chopping off a bit of the fee. I should not like for you to feel you have been shortchanged. May I leave this to your judgment?

As I continue to re-examine the trio I cannot find that it would benefit by either additions or stretching out. It is so tightly organized in itself, so unified, compact, and self-contained that I can only see tampering with it as probably injurious.

For playing it in public or recording, of course, length is no matter. A five-minute piece works just as well as a ten-minute one.

*(b. 1894), composer, critic, conductor, lexicographer, and *bon vivant* of Russian birth, then celebrating his ninetieth birthday
†(b. 1954), bassoonist. Thomson had composed a portrait of her and her husband.
‡a Boston new-music concert series

Actually, several of my most successful chamber works—the Flute Sonata, for instance, and the *Stabat Mater* for soprano and string quartet—last only five minutes, as does also one for large orchestra called *Sea Piece with Birds*.

And since any contrapuntal music, unless it follows a dance-meter, can be played at any speed, the exact length of my trio is not yet fixed in my mind. I might enjoy better the tonal beauty of both oboe and bassoon if the three movements were to last, say, by slow playing, nearer seven minutes than five.

The actual speeds and the run-through timing will certainly settle themselves in rehearsal and after a performance or two. Meanwhile I remain available with regard to phrasings and for making the breathing easy, especially for the oboe.

Do let me know what you would like me to do, short of a general overhaul. It is after all a portrait and must keep its spontaneity. Also, it has been carefully checked both before delivery and after. It has no major flaw, I assure you, and should run O.K. Just let it flow as it wants to, and you may come to feel better about it. I hope so.

Do let me hear whether you can play the Dinosaur date.

Sincerely everbest,

To Bernice Cohen*

May 18, 1984

Dear Mrs. Cohen,

This is to apply, as it has been requested that I do, for a continuation of the awards that I have been receiving for several years now.

In spite of my advanced age, I am still an active composer, having published in the last year and a half the following original works:

Nineteen Portraits for Piano (Boosey & Hawkes, Inc.)

Sixteen Portraits for Piano (in the process of publication by G. Schirmer, Inc.)

Stabat Mater, revised version (Boosey & Hawkes, Inc.)

"The Cat," duet for soprano and baritone with piano accompaniment (G. Schirmer, Inc.)

---

*manager of the Awards Program, and director of musical theater activities, American Society of Composers, Authors, and Publishers

A Prayer to Venus, for mixed chorus with piano accompaniment (G. Schirmer, Inc.)

Cantantes Eamus, for men's chorus with piano accompaniment (G. Schirmer, Inc.)

Fanfare for Peace, for mixed chorus and piano (Southern Music Publishing Co.)

Southern Hymns, for mixed chorus and piano (Southern Music Publishing Co.)

Bell Piece (in the process of publication by G. Schirmer, Inc.)

Five Ladies, for violin and piano (G. Schirmer, Inc.)

A Portrait of Two, for oboe, bassoon, and piano (in the process of publication by G. Schirmer, Inc.)

Eleven Portraits for Orchestra (in the process of publication by Boosey & Hawkes, Inc.)

Parson Weems and the Cherry Tree (ballet) (Boosey & Hawkes, Inc.)

Works of mine released on commercial recordings during this period include:

String Quartet No. 1 (19 minutes; one side of album by the New Music String Quartet; produced by ASCAP)

Thoughts for Strings (4 minutes; part of record by the Missouri All-State Orchestra)

Various piano works (2 sides of an album by pianist Yvar Mikhashoff, Spectrum Records)

Tres Estampas de Niñez (6 minutes; part of a record by mezzo-soprano Reyna Rivas; privately recorded)

Eleven Portraits for orchestra (and Acadian Songs and Dances from *Louisiana Story*) (2 sides of album, Oshkosh Symphony Orchestra)

Various piano works (2 sides of an album by pianist Nigel Coxe; Musical Heritage Recordings)

Party Pieces (with Cage, Cowell, and Harrison) (15 minutes; part of a recording by the Brooklyn Philharmonic; Gramavision Recordings, Inc.)

Two Sentimental Tangos and Two Portraits (7 minutes altogether; part of a recording by pianist Bennett Lerner; Etcetera Records)

Sonata for Flute Alone (10 minutes, part of a recording by flutist Angela Koregelos; Carleton Records)

The Plough That Broke the Plains (original motion picture sound-track) and *A Tuesday in November* (original motion picture sound-track) (2 sides of a recording; American Entertainment Industries Records)

I hope this list is sufficient to justify my continuing to receive an annual award.

Very sincerely yours,

To a CORRESPONDENT*

July 11, 1984

The best thing for an aspiring composer still only 15 years old is to take lots of lessons (good ones) in harmony, counterpoint, fugue, orchestration, all the musical elements.

Playing the viola with orchestras and in chamber music ensembles will also be valuable.

It is lucky you are a string player. Most composers nowadays are merely pianists. The orchestra is, after all, predominantly a string combo.

Good wishes,

Warmly,

To BETTY STOUFFER

August 28, 1984

Dear Betty,

I came back from Montecatini and Paris a week ago, then went off to the Catskills for three concerts.

While in Europe, my New York flat was robbed. Since that time, detectives from the Major Crime Unit of the Police Department, six of them, have been in and out of the place every day. They seem to have figured out how the burglars got in (through the bathroom window giving on an airshaft) but have not yet found the guilty parties or any of the loot.

---

*a young composer who had written Thomson for advice

The looting was systematic: no pictures or clothes or high-fi equipment were taken, but all the good silver was (nothing plated). This includes the teaspoons and tablespoons from my grandmother and my parents, also the incised ones from Aunt Lillie. These all belonged eventually to you. Unless they turn up, which flat silver seldom does, they are probably lost for good.

Also taken were my jewelry (chiefly cufflinks, some quite valuable) and three Vuitton suitcases (two others were travelling with me) and about three cases of wine.

Leaving the Chelsea in the middle of the night with all of this no doubt presented complications, though it is not certain yet whether the stuff or some of it may not still be in the hotel.

There was a very good set of plated silver, French, about 1910, which the Stettheimers had given me when I set up housekeeping here. That is still here, as are my mother's silver coffee pot and sugar bowl, and two plated-silver trays.

Anyway I can eat and have company for meals and close my shirtsleeves with borrowed links. My own are all gone because I took only short-sleeved shirts to Europe.

Everybody I know has at some point been robbed, jewelry and flat silver being the items most easily disposed of.

I am sorry about the FET spoons, the Q and Ms, also the Lillies, which were a rare kind of work known as "cut silver."

I hope all of you are well.

My book with addresses and telephone numbers was also taken, but this list is being reconstituted from old correspondence, which is how I have your address.

Love to all,

Ever,

To Charles Shere

August 29, 1984

Dear Charles,

Marcel [Duchamp] ate frugally, enjoyed his food, but did not drink much.

For an unusual meat, why don't you serve guinea? The big ones are best, if not too old. Not the baby broilers either. Farm guineas are dark meat and should be so treated; they can even be hung.

The following is a good French way of treating them: Brown the outside, then pot-roast them with small bits of lean salt pork (cooked), chestnuts, and salsify (also browned in the pork fat and maybe cooked a little bit in broth). A mixture of chicken and beef broth (which can later be thickened) is good for the cooking. So are a bit of coarse-cut shallots and a little very good wine, red or white.

Here is another suggestion. Very small young turkeys, stuffed with foie gras, chestnuts, and blood sausage. This is a regular roast, not a pot dish. Add to the pan gravy dry sherry or madeira.

Since you have in California such fine vegetables, why not serve a course of several after the roast?

Let me know as soon as possible how I can contribute to your enterprise★ in some tax-exempt fashion.

Also send me advance notices about the production.

Everbest ever,

To Anthony Tommasini

October 12, 1984

Dear Tony,

I do not know what the wooden pasta fork is called either in English or in Italian. I am not even sure that it *is* Italian.

I shall be delighted to write recommendations to both the Rockefellers and the Mellons. If you want to put in your applications that I am willing and eager to write, by all means do so. You can also say that my help and documents are completely available to you for your project.

Lord Byron has been postponed till June. I have no further word about it.

John Houseman sent me a photograph which I shall give you when I see you. I wrote him that I did not like it. It was more like a press photo than a portrait, slightly simpering. He and his wife are at this moment on a tour of Greece and Egypt but should be back around Thanksgiving. I imagine that my letter of protest is still waiting for him in Los Angeles because he sent me a postcard that did not mention it.

I too am a Ferraro† fan. Of Cuomo‡ too.

Affection everbest,

★of producing Shere's opera about Duchamp
†Geraldine Ferraro (b. 1935), New York congresswoman, Democratic Vice-Presidential candidate in 1984
‡Mario Cuomo (b. 1932), elected Governor of New York in 1982

October 29, 1984

Dear Margery,

The estimates submitted by the public relations firm for concerts at Alice Tully and Merkin [halls] seem to me a bit high. Also, they make no mention of a manager for the concert. In my experience a professional manager for such an occasion is far more important than a public relations firm.

As for possible cuts in the projected costs, newspaper advertising may be dispensable and so may sixty-second spots on WQXR and WNCN.

A good manager can frequently do better through the known musical mailing lists, all of which should be available to him.

One guest artist, like last time, might be helpful in assuring newspaper coverage. More than one, in view of your known excellence, seems to me unneeded.

If the tickets do not seem to be selling, one usually, at the last minute, starts papering the house through free tickets to the music schools.

Making a concert a benefit for some well-known New York charity is also a device that could be discussed with your manager. With such an arrangement, concert costs or a part of them could still be deducted.

A concert such as you are planning to give is not easy to organize from a distance. The matter needs some reflection and a bit of advice from colleagues with New York experience.

Myself, I am resistant to all public relations firms except the very few of them who specialize in music. (Certainly your people were not very effective about filling up the house.)

Of the two houses proposed, Merkin and Tully, the former seems to me by far the more practical.

Everything everbest,

---

*(b. 1937), California soprano, then planning a New York recital

To Robert Lewis*

November 26, 1984

Dear Bobby,

You are a love to write me.

I think of you often, but come seldom to your neighborhood. I hope you are having fun and making money.

Our Truman died, as you know, and had a memorial service in a theater, just like Arnold Weissberger.†

I am 88 and in perfectly good health, making no plans at all for my funeral.

Everbest,

To Betty Johnston‡

November 30, 1984

Dear Betty,

Thanks for greeting.

I had a quiet birthday, except for a lunch party, a sort of brunch, which I was supposed to attend in a neighbor's flat. Then a fire in the hotel drenched that flat with water. So the party was moved up to mine. After that I had a nap and later went to bed early.

Maurice and Paul were here. They had been to other friends on Thanksgiving.

All quiet.

Everbest,

---

*(b. 1909), director, teacher, and a founder of the Actors Studio, who had worked with Thomson on Truman Capote's *The Grass Harp*. In his memoirs, *Slings and Arrows: Theater in My Life* (1984), Lewis wrote: "I cannot leave *The Grass Harp* without remarking on the high professionalism of Virgil Thomson. No fancy talk from him. What a pleasure it was to be able to say, 'Virgil, I need a bit of music here to cover this change.' 'How many bars?' he'd ask. 'Oh, about sixteen,' I'd say. 'Fast or slow?' 'Fast,' I'd reply, certain that he would know from that that the music should presage the next action rather than conclude the bit before. No need for a lot of palaver. And every bar he wrote was not only beautiful, it was apt."
†prominent lawyer (1907–81), who worked for many distinguished artists
‡sister of Maurice Grosser

To Mrs. John Stephen Heggie*

July 17, 1985

Very dear Johana:

Please don't be a promoting or a pushing wife. That would be a nuisance. Let him make his own way.

For your info and his:

1. Music publishers hate string quartets. They are hard to handle and bring no profit. Mine were published at my expense, and so, I think, was Roy's early chamber music.
2. He should concentrate on performances, scrounging to pay himself for getting parts copied.
3. Publishers also resist songs.
4. They tolerate piano music and sometimes viola or cello pieces.
5. Save copies of all reviews, favorable or not. They will come in handy.
6. Many composers find it useful to circulate in music circles; be seen at concerts and in conductors' green rooms.
7. Make friends among composers. Be a good colleague.
8. It helps to teach a little; pupils make good fans.
9. Writing about music is also valuable.
10. Any form of public appearance does him good.

There is no easy way to make a career composing. It is long, painful, and expensive. Friends and colleagues are of the utmost value. Wives, too, but chiefly as colleagues. Never let him, or anyone else, suspect he is not doing it all himself.

Love ever,

---

*(b. 1913), pianist, formerly Johana Harris, widow of Roy Harris, now married to the young composer John Stephen Heggie

INDEX

About the Author:

A native of Kansas City, Missouri, Virgil Thomson was educated there and at Harvard. His books include *The State of Music, American Music Since 1910,* and his autobiography, *Virgil Thomson.* Over the last sixty-five years he has written music in practically every genre. His many awards include membership in both the American Academy of Arts and Sciences and the American Academy of Arts and Letters; the Pulitzer Prize, which he was awarded in 1949 for his score to the film *Louisiana Story;* and the gold medal for music of the American Institute of Arts and Letters (1966). He is a member of the Academia Argentina, a correspondent member of the French Académie Nationale des Beaux-Arts, and an Officer in the Légion d'Honneur.

About the Editors:

Tim Page and Vanessa Weeks Page met when they were students at the Mannes College of Music in New York. Tim was a music critic for *The New York Times* from 1982 to 1987 and is currently the chief music critic for *Newsday.* He is the host of a program devoted to new and unusual music on WNYC-FM and teaches at the Juilliard School and the Manhattan School of Music. Vanessa is a freelance writer and editor. The Pages live in New York and Hartford with their son, William Dean.